We Have Tired of Violence

WE HAVE TIRED OF VIOLENCE

A True Story of Murder, Memory, and the Fight for Justice in Indonesia

MATT EASTON

NEW YORK
LONDON

Requests for permission to reproduce selections from this book should be made through our website: https://thenewpress.com/contact.

"Pulanglah" Words and Music by Virgiawan Listanto. Copyright © 2007 PT. MUSICA PUBLISER INDONESIA. All Rights in the United States Administered by UNIVERSAL—POLYGRAM INTERNATIONAL PUBLISHING, INC. All Rights Reserved.
Used by Permission. Reprinted by permission of Hal Leonard LLC.
"Di Udara" Words and Music by Cholil Mahmud. Copyright © 2007. All Rights Reserved.
Used by Permission.

Published in the United States by The New Press, New York, 2022
Distributed by Two Rivers Distribution

ISBN 978-1-62097-381-3 (hardcover)
ISBN 978-1-62097-382-0 (ebook)
CIP data is available.

The New Press publishes books that promote and enrich public discussion and understanding of the issues vital to our democracy and to a more equitable world. These books are made possible by the enthusiasm of our readers; the support of a committed group of donors, large and small; the collaboration of our many partners in the independent media and the not-for-profit sector; booksellers, who often hand-sell New Press books; librarians; and above all by our authors.

www.thenewpress.com

Book design and composition by Bookbright Media
This book was set in Janson Text

Printed in the United States of America

2 4 6 8 10 9 7 5 3 1

For Alif & Diva, Sjahrazad & Alchemisha, and Loreley & Willa

Contents

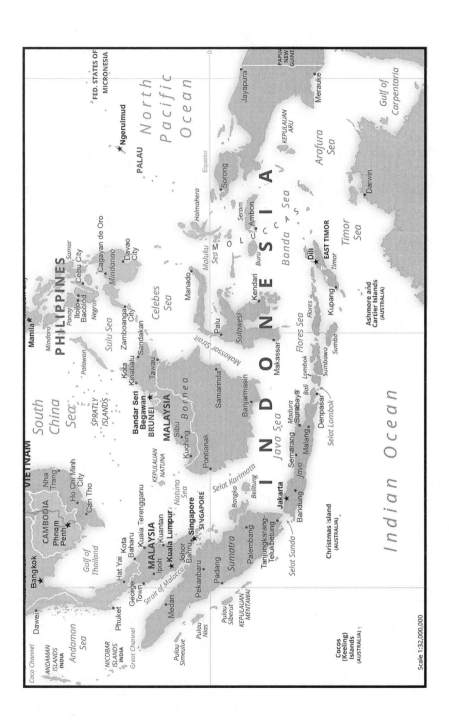

Scale 1:32,000,000

People

Abdurrahman Wahid (Gus Dur): Former Suharto critic and Muslim leader who became president in 1999, only to be impeached in 2001.

Adnan Buyung Nasution (Buyung): A founder of the Legal Aid Foundation (LBH) and the broader human rights movement in Indonesia.

Anton Charlian: Police investigator who worked on the case for the first several years.

As'ad Said Ali: Deputy Director of BIN at the time of Munir's murder.

Asmara Nababan: Senior figure in the human rights community and vice-chair of the Munir fact-finding team.

B. J. Habibie: Named vice-president in March 1998, he became president upon Suharto's resignation in May.

Bambang Hendarso Danuri (Hendarso): Director of the Criminal Investigation Division during the most effective phase of the police investigation.

Bambang Irawan: Medical doctor and BIN agent rumored to have been on Munir's flight, and with Pollycarpus in Aceh under martial law.

Bijah Subiakto: BIN Deputy VII for Information, Communications, and Technology, he spoke to Suci several times after Munir's death.

Bimo Petrus (Bimpet): Courier for the underground pro-democracy organization PRD, he disappeared in 1998.

Brahmanie Hastawati: Purser on Munir's flight from Jakarta to Singapore.

Dr. Budi Sampurna: Forensics expert who worked with Munir on exhumation of bodies in West Timor and later provided expert testimony in the Munir case.

Budi Santoso: BIN agent who provided significant testimony to police.

Chairawan Nusyirwan: Army colonel and head of Group 4 of the Special Forces (Kopassus), tasked with covert operations. He was brought before the military honor board in August 1998, alongside Gen. Prabowo and Gen. Muchdi.

Cyrus Sinaga: Prosecutor in the trial of Muchdi Purwopranjono.

Dr. Hakim Tarmizi: Prominent doctor who was a passenger on Munir's flight and treated him on board.

Hendardi: Former LBH colleague of Munir who served on the fact-finding team and testified at trial.

A.M. Hendropriyono: Retired general who directed BIN at the time of Munir's murder.

Indra Listiantara: Former KontraS staffer who took part in investigations by Kasum and the TPF.

Indra Setiawan: Director of Garuda Indonesia in 2004.

J. J. Raymond Latuihamallo (Ongen): Christian singer who became a pivotal witness to events in Singapore Changi Airport.

Karmel Sembiring: Chief of Pilots, Pollycarpus's direct supervisor.

Maria Catarina Sumarsih (Sumarsih): Mother of Wawan, a victim of the Semanggi I shootings. Sumarsih was a cofounder of the weekly protests known as *kamisan*.

Marsinah: Young worker who was abducted and murdered after helping to win a salary increase at her watch factory in 1993.

Marsudhi Hanafi: Police general and chair of the TPF, and later head of the police investigation until his abrupt removal from the case.

Megawati Sukarnoputri: President of Indonesia from 2001 to 2004, leader of PDI-P, and daughter of President Soekarno.

Muchdi Purwopranjono: BIN Deputy V at the time of Munir's death, and Kopassus commander in the last days of Suharto's rule.

Nezar Patria: PRD activist abducted and tortured in March 1998, roommates with Mugi, Aan, and the missing Bimo Petrus.

Nurhadi Djazuli: BIN principal secretary at the time of Munir's death.

Poengky Indarti: Long-time friend and colleague of Munir at LBH Surabaya and Imparsial.

Pollycarpus Budihari Priyanto (Polly): Co-pilot for Garuda Indonesia.

Prabowo Subianto: Commander of Kopassus and Kostrad under his father-in-law Suharto, candidate for president, and minister of defense in Jokowi's cabinet.

Rachland Nashidik: Friend and colleague of Munir, and member of the TPF.

Ramelgia Anwar (Ramel): Vice-President for Corporate Security at Garuda Indonesia.

Rohainil Aini: Secretary to the Chief of Pilots.

Soekarno: First president of Indonesia, Soekarno was removed from power by General Suharto in stages beginning in late 1965.

Suharto: President of Indonesia from 1967 until 1998.

Susilo Bambang Yudhoyono (SBY): First directly elected president in Indonesia's history, SBY created the fact-finding team in the Munir case and was president from 2004 to 2014.

Tuti Koto: Mother of Yani Afri, a young bus driver and Megawati supporter abducted in 1997. Tuti Koto was one of the first family members to turn to Munir for help, leading to the founding of KontraS.

Ucok: Nickname of Muhammad Patma Anwar, who claimed to police that he was a BIN agent tasked with killing Munir.

Wiji Thukul: Radical poet and PRD activist, he disappeared in 1998, not long before Suharto's resignation.

Wiranto: Commander of the armed forces when Suharto resigned and during the early *reformasi* period. He later ran for vice-president and president, before serving in President Jokowi's cabinet.

Terms and Acronyms

Badan Intelijen Negara (BIN): State Intelligence Agency.

dalang: The puppeteer of the *wayang* shadow plays performed on Java and Bali, in which the Hindu epics are performed behind a backlit screen. The term also refers to a person secretly in control of a plot or conspiracy.

dukun: A practitioner of various forms of magic or divination.

dwi fungsi: Dual function, a doctrine used to justify a military role in social and political affairs.

kampung: The term can mean either village or poorer urban neighbor-hood. The English term compound, for a collection of buildings, derives from *kampung*, by way of Dutch and Portuguese.

Komando Pasukan Khusus (Kopassus): Special Forces branch of the army.

Komisi untuk Orang Hilang dan Korban Tindak Kekerasan (KontraS): The Commission for the Disappeared and Victims of Violence, an organization founded by Munir and others in 1998 to address a wave of politically-motivated disappearances.

Komite Aksi Solidaritas Untuk Munir (Kasum): Solidarity Action Committee for Munir, formed in 2004 by friends and colleagues to carry out investigation and advocacy for the case.

Kostrad (Komando Cadangan Strategis Angkatan Darat): The Army Strategic Reserve Command.

Lembaga Bantuan Hukum (LBH): Legal Aid Foundation, a network of offices across Indonesia that is the country's oldest and largest human rights organization.

Majelis Permusyawaratan Rakyat (MPR): People's Consultative Assembly, an elected body that meets every five years to set broad policy and, until 2004, to select the president.

Nahdlatul Ulama (NU): The largest Muslim organization in Indonesia, with a base in the more traditional religious boarding schools.

Negara Kesatuan Republik Indonesia (NKRI): Unitary State of the Republic of Indonesia, a term that emerged during *reformasi*, appealing to fears of disintegration and disunity due to rampant democracy and foreign intervention.

Netherlands Forensic Institute (NFI): A research institute and forensics lab that is an agency of the Ministry of Security and Justice of the Netherlands.

NGO: Non-governmental organization.

Pancasila: An official state philosophy of five principles: belief in one God, just and civilized humanity, the unity of Indonesia, democracy, and social justice.

Partai Demokrasi Indonesia Perjuangan (PDI-P): Indonesian Democratic Party of Struggle, Megawati Sukarnoputri's faction that split from the nationalist semi-opposition party of the Suharto years.

Partai Persatuan Pembangunan (PPP): United Development Party, the Muslim-oriented semi-opposition party also allowed to operate under strict restraints before 1998.

Partai Rakyat Demokratik (PRD): People's Democratic Party, pro-democracy party that emerged from student activist circles and was forced underground in 1996.

preman: From the Dutch for "free man," *preman* refers to criminal gangs operating partly in service of the state, and sometimes to soldiers in civilian dress.

Team Mawar: The Rose Team was an eleven-man unit of Kopassus that was behind the abductions of activists in 1997 and 1998.

Tentara Nasional Indonesia (TNI): Indonesian National Military, which replaced the older name ABRI following the fall of Suharto and the separation of the police into a separate civilian force.

Tim Pencarian Fakta Kasus Meninggalnya Munir (TPF): Fact-Finding Team on the Case of Munir's Death.

Note on Sources and Translation

Dialogue from trials and other public events were recreated from monitoring reports, witness transcripts, videotapes, and news articles. Direct quotes from private meetings are from interviews with one or more people present and have been confirmed as much as possible. In most cases, this manner of sourcing is indicated in the text by noting that someone remembers or recalls a conversation.

Where sources gave diverging accounts of an event, the text describes that version most supported by documentary evidence or contemporary news accounts, with the alternative sometimes described in the endnotes. Cited embassy cables are from the Wikileaks release, unless it is otherwise specified that they have been declassified.

Some sources requested anonymity for their own security. As an indication of their concern, several sources referred to the State Intelligence Agency, or BIN, only as "three letters" and avoided mentioning key actors by name.

Indonesians often use one name, and also may refer to public figures and others by first names. The text generally uses the name a person is most commonly known by. The current spelling conventions are used except where proper names (such as Poengky or Soekarno) more commonly use the older orthography.

Some pronunciation is indicated, but otherwise Indonesian is very consistent and easy to pronounce. The letter *c* is pronounced *ch*, and most words emphasize the second to last syllable. For example, Suciwati is pronounced Soo-chee-WAH-tee, though friends call her Suci (SOO-chee).

We Have Tired of Violence

Prologue

A Red and Clouded Sky

2004

On the evening of September 6, 2004, their final family dinner came to an end, and it was time for Munir to say good-bye. Knowing an airport parting would be too hard for their two young children, he and his wife, Suciwati, pulled Alif and Diva into a tight hug. Munir told them softly, "I have found my heaven." Leaving their son and daughter in the care of a young niece, the couple drove through Jakarta's outskirts. The gathering dusk had begun to hide the posters of the candidates, plastered everywhere ahead of Indonesia's first direct presidential elections in its eventful half century as a nation.

The couple arrived at Soekarno-Hatta International Airport with enough time to order some milk and hot chocolate at a Dunkin' Donuts stand. To Munir's surprise, a minivan of friends arrived, not content with a week of good-bye parties held over Munir's protests. "The thing I've always been most afraid of is the farewell party," he'd said after being lured to one he believed would be an enjoyable discussion about politics and law.

In the lofty departure terminal, its design inspired by the teak roof beams of Java's villages and the sculpted stone temples of Bali, the group gathered around the pink seats of the donut stand. Just before 8:00, Munir went to check in while his old friend and colleague Poengky ordered a box of donut holes for everyone. When Munir returned, Poengky handed him a stack of checks to sign to keep their human rights group running while he spent the year studying in the Netherlands. She made him promise to send his critique of a draft law to reform the army as soon as he got to Utrecht. Seated next to her husband, Suci finished his hot chocolate, gently tapping the cup with a swizzle stick between her fingers. Her arm rested on one of the two suitcases she'd carefully packed with clothes, gifts for Dutch friends, and some *kayu putih* oil for stomach aches or sore muscles.

Munir told a story. A few months before, an immigration officer had stopped him as he was trying to depart for Geneva. The man told him he was banned from leaving Indonesia. Unsure if the officer was following a genuine order or fishing for a bribe, Munir took out his phone. He called General Hendropriyono, the head of the State Intelligence Agency. Munir had recently asked a court to bar Hendropriyono from that job due to his role in a massacre years before. The effort had only succeeded in angering the general, but he answered when Munir called and assured him he was free to leave the country. As Munir described handing his phone to the wide-eyed immigration officer to hear for himself, the group burst out laughing around the box of donut holes. Suci smiled as her husband drained a threat of power, and made it, somehow, seem funny.

Munir's former driver realized he had no pictures with his old boss after all their years together. Sugiarto had been with Munir during some fraught moments, once driving him and Suci through the dark streets of

Munir sits with Suciwati and his former driver Sugiarto at Jakarta's airport shortly before his departure. (Poengky Indarti)

Jakarta until the sun came up to avoid a rumored abduction. Munir didn't like posing for pictures, but he readily stood up for a photo with Sugiarto, which Poengky took with her first digital camera.

Munir took a picture with Poengky, her fingers held up in a V. After that with a staffer who had just had his long hair straightened ("You're prettier than I am now," joked Suci). Munir and Suci took a last photo together. He draped his left arm over her shoulders, as her hand reached up to hold his fingers. Munir grinned broadly under his mustache, while Suci managed a closed-mouth smile. The group left the couple alone to say good-bye. He held her tight, and seemed to waver. Then he said, "*Bismillah*, I'm sure I can do it," as if trying to reassure them both. "I can do it." It was one of the only times she'd ever seen him cry. With luck and funding, the family would reunite in time to spend a damp Dutch winter together.

As the car carried Suci away swiftly along the airport road in the dark, Munir texted to say he'd passed through immigration. He passed through a final security checkpoint around 9:00 and proceeded down one of the airy corridors arrayed like spokes within the terminal's arc, to Gate E7.

Poengky had already begun to worry about Munir. He had given Poengky her first job a decade before, back home in East Java. She'd witnessed Munir's courage many times under President Suharto and in the turbulent six years since his fall, but Poengky's impulse to protect "our Munir" never faded. Just a few days ago, she'd asked a friend to meet Munir at the airport in Amsterdam, saying, "I'm entrusting Munir to you, okay?" Munir had said he just needed a map and an airline ticket and he'd find his way. "I already asked her to pick you up," Poengky had told him. "There's no point discussing it."[1]

Worried Munir might already be lonely, Poengky called him around 9:20 and passed the phone around the Toyota Kijang for a final good-bye from everyone except Sugiarto, who preferred to keep his hands on the wheel. When they hung up, Munir called his mother in the hill town of Batu, in keeping with the Javanese tradition of asking permission before leaving. She promised to pray for his safety. Around 9:30, Munir boarded the aging 747, its tail emblazoned with the airline's mythic namesake, Garuda—Vishnu's mount, king of birds, devourer of snakes, and protector against their poison.

After a 9:55 departure, Flight 974 gained altitude over the red-roofed villages of West Java. It passed over Pulau Seribu, hundreds of tiny islands sprayed like shotgun pellets from Jakarta Bay out into the Java Sea. The plane flew in darkness across the Sunda Strait and over the dwindling mangrove forests that fringed the Sumatran coast. It descended over the Riau Islands and crossed the ten-mile expanse of the Singapore Strait at the edge of the Indonesian archipelago. After an hour and fifty minutes in the air, the plane landed in Singapore. The passengers spent under an hour in the quiet midnight corridors of Changi Airport before returning to the plane for the long flight to Amsterdam.

Soon after midday prayers the next day, Suci answered her home phone. It was Usman Hamid, Munir's friend and successor at the human rights group KontraS.[2]

"Suci, where are you now?" he asked.

"I'm at home. Don't you know you called my home?" Her voice rose: "What is it, Usman?"

"Suci, have you heard the news about Munir?" Usman stammered. His voice was shaky and hoarse.

She hadn't, and Munir really should have texted or called her by now from Amsterdam.

Usman told her, simply, "Munir has died."

Suci felt as if she'd fallen from high up in the clouds onto hard earth. A darkness choked her, and her legs felt weak. Suci struggled to think. She needed to know what happened. She needed to prove it wasn't true. Decades of censorship and lies, followed by years of political turmoil, had created an environment ripe for rumors in a village of 10 million like Jakarta. Many arose spontaneously, sometimes compared to mushrooms in the rainy season. More often, rumors were crafted to threaten and frighten.

Suci would not believe Munir was dead until she saw his body herself or spoke to someone who had. Her disbelief came not just from years of rumor and threat. She could not accept that someone she felt to be a part of her soul could be gone in an instant. Her suspicion and denial grew as Suci called the airports, the airline, and friends in the Netherlands. No one would confirm the rumor. No one would tell her anything at all. On her fourth call to Amsterdam, she erupted at a Garuda employee, "I have a right to information about my husband!"

There was a long pause, before the man whispered, "Yes. Yes, he's dead."

Had he seen the body, seen it with his own eyes? He had.

"Please," he said. "Don't tell anyone I told you."[3]

1

Suciwati

1990s

The small city of Malang lies on a cool plateau among mountains at the eastern end of Java, four hundred miles from Jakarta as the crow flies. Such a trajectory would run almost parallel to the equator and to the island's central spine of forty volcanos, one segment of the Ring of Fire that encircles the Pacific. Among the thousands of islands in the Indonesian archipelago, Java is the most populous. With 150 million people, more people live here than on any other island on Earth.

On the southern edge of Malang lies Mergosono, a tangle of lanes just wide enough for motorbikes and food carts. Like many poorer urban neighborhoods, Mergosono is like a village. In fact, the term *kampung* is used to describe both.

In 1968, when Suci was born, Mergosono's one-story homes still mingled with rice paddies that reflected the slanting afternoon sun. Tiny shops, sometimes just a house's front window, sold necessities in portions even a bicycle trishaw driver could afford: a packet of instant noodles, a single cigarette rolled at nearby factories, a sachet of laundry soap. Mergosono was the type of *kampung* known equally for producing street toughs and Islamic scholars, though most residents worked at the small factories within its boundaries.

Suci's parents, however, were fruit and vegetable vendors. Once or twice a week, they bought fresh coconuts from a village to the south, halfway to the coast of Java and the Indian Ocean. They sold them ten or a hundred at a time at the morning market in Malang. Neither parent could write, though her father could read enough to know his ID card was not accurate. Indonesians had to choose from five faiths: Muslim, Protestant, Catholic, Hindu, or Buddhist. Suci's father's card said he was the Muslim he once had been, even though he'd become a follower of *kejawen*, a combination of Javanese mysticism, Hindu-Buddhist practices, and Islam, the parade of faiths carried to the islands by traders from China, India, and the Middle East.

Suci usually went to a Protestant church with her mother. In grade school, Suci could have skipped the religion class required for Muslims, but she loved the teacher's stories about the prophets and his answers to any question put to him. When she was ten, she asked her teacher to lead her in the profession of faith in his home nearby, and she became a Muslim. Her mother was surprised, but very tolerant, even waking Suci for optional prayers after midnight. Her father, however, grew upset when he saw her going to pray. Suci didn't understand why, until at last he explained. He had no problem with Muslim beliefs, but couldn't separate the religion from the terrible events of 1965 and 1966. He'd watched friends being taken away, never to be seen again. He'd seen people killed before his eyes.

The people of East Java had been many things before they were Indonesians. The ruins of palaces and temples testified to the great Hindu–Buddhist empires that once stretched for thousands of miles. (The name Mergosono was perhaps a kingly relic, deriving from the Old Javanese for deer park or game reserve.) After the fall of the Majapahit Empire in the 1500s, Mergosono's inhabitants became subjects of smaller kingdoms and sultanates, which brought Islam inland from the coastal ports. In 1619 the Dutch East India Company, a precursor to the modern publicly-traded corporation, used military force to establish a beachhead on Java at Jayakarta, which they renamed Batavia. The enterprise was dissolved in 1799, making the Netherlands East Indies a vast and lucrative colony of the Dutch state.

An independence movement was well under way when the Japanese invaded in World War II. The occupiers were often brutal, but they had defeated the colonial power and then, for their own ends, supported a common Indonesian language, local defense forces, and other boons to the independence struggle. Upon the defeat of the Japanese in 1945, the charismatic figure of Soekarno and a band of founding revolutionaries declared independence. After four years of intermittent fighting against a colonial power weakened by the war in Europe, Indonesia was recognized as an independent nation in 1949.

Indonesia's first leader was the revolutionary hero Soekarno. Famous for his oratory and charisma, Soekarno embodied the anticolonial spirit of a young nation at a time of global decolonization. He positioned Indonesia as a leader of a Non-Aligned Movement trying to thread the needle between the United States and the Soviet Union. Indonesia spent most of its first decade as a boisterous parliamentary democracy. That period ended in 1957, when Soekarno announced that a form of governance called Guided Democracy would replace a Western model driven by strong parties and regular elections. Instead, a national council would reach consensus decisions under the leadership of a strong president acting much like a village elder.

For Soekarno, the next few years were like riding a tiger, as he played off the three main power blocs of the military, Islamic organizations, and the Communist Party, one against another. The Partai Komunis Indonesia, or PKI, was the world's largest communist party outside of China and the Soviet Union. With more than 3 million members, and 23 million more in affiliated organizations for farmers, workers, artists, women, and other groups, the party might have won elections in 1959 if Soekarno hadn't canceled them. The military was also a potent force. After defeating CIA-backed regional rebellions, the army began benefiting from a new American strategy. The United States showered the army with training and aid to position it as a counterweight to Soekarno's embrace of the left and to his increasingly anti-American rhetoric. Attacks on the West filled much of Sukarno's three-hour Independence Day Speech in 1964, a year he dubbed the Year of Living Dangerously.

The end of Soekarno's perilous ride began in the early hours of October 1, 1965. A small group of leftist soldiers, led by a member of the presidential guard, abducted six senior generals and a lieutenant. Claiming to be saving Soekarno from a coup by right-wing generals, the group seized the airwaves to proclaim a new revolutionary government. They killed their seven captives and threw their bodies into an abandoned well named Lubang Buaya, or Crocodile Hole.

The origins of the coup attempt remain cloaked in mystery and controversy. Some observers believe it was a communist plot, while others insist it was staged to justify a right-wing counter-coup. Most likely, the plan arose from political schisms within the military, though a few communist leaders may have known it was coming. A young one-star general named Suharto may have known in advance as well.[1] At the very least, he was prepared to put down the coup and then to seize an opportunity to blame the communists. The army distributed photos of the dead generals, claiming that communist women had sexually mutilated them. Military leaders called for the annihilation of the communists, down "to their roots."

Killings spread across Central and East Java, Bali, and Sumatra, followed by outbreaks on other islands. Declassified documents confirm that the CIA cheered and supported the killings with communications equipment, propaganda, and lists of targets. In many areas, the army rounded up PKI cadres, members of leftist groups, and others caught up due to mistaken identity or local rivalries. The army directly executed some, but more often it detained them in temporary prisons before handing over a few truckloads each night to armed civilian groups.[2] The captives were taken to forests, plantations, or riverbanks to be killed with knives, bamboo spears, clubs, and garrotes.[3] Those bodies not left on display disappeared into mass graves, caves, rivers, and oceans. While estimates hover at around half a million deaths, scholars believe it might be half or twice that number.[4]

Many of the killers were members of Muslim groups, in particular the youth wing of Nahdlatul Ulama (NU), an organization with deep roots in rural Java. But secular gangs and Catholic youths also took part, and some of the worst bloodletting took place on the largely Hindu island of Bali. East Java was a stronghold for both NU and the Communist Party, and the violence there was intense.[5] Corpses floated down the Brantas River, which flows through East Java in a great spiral from Mount Arjuno to the north coast.[6]

The worst of the killing was over by March 1966. That month Soekarno, outmaneuvered and deprived of the support of the decimated leftist parties, formally handed over power to Suharto.[7] The general's Orde Baru, or New Order, steered Indonesia away from revolutionary anticolonialism and toward Western investment and alliances.

Many accused leftists who were not killed were subjected to torture, deprivation, and sexual violence while imprisoned for months, years, or decades. Even after their release, a stamp on their ID cards barred them from certain jobs, education, and government services, restrictions that were passed on to their children and grandchildren like a grave hereditary disease.

Suharto took control of history and memory as well. He opened a memorial at Crocodile Hole, where the kidnapped generals had been disposed of. Dioramas and murals were added to showcase the horror of alleged Communist atrocities. Orwell wrote in *Nineteen Eighty-Four*, "Who controls the past controls the future: who controls the present controls the past." It was fitting that in 1984, Indonesia's state-owned film company released *The Treachery of the 30 September Movement*. For over four hours, the movie dramatized the murder of the generals with vivid torture, wild dancing, eye-gouging, genital mutilation, and killing. All schoolchildren were required to watch it in theaters; later it was shown in schools and broadcast on each anniversary. As the years passed, these simulacra justified the government's constant vigilance and repression against an imagined threat.[8]

This myth was only one part of Suharto's effort to suppress opposition. From 1971 on, elections took place every five years under conditions of intimidation, massive patronage, and bureaucratic control that ensured Suharto definitive victory overlaid with a thin veneer of democracy. Between elections, Suharto deftly managed factions within his two main bases of power, the military and the ruling Golkar party. He allowed no rivals or political heirs to emerge, and co-opted or repressed challenges from religious groups, politicians, students, workers, or farmers.

Suharto's skills as a tactician were buttressed by the recent memories of mass brutality. People knew where the mass graves of 1965 lay, under the fields and plantations of Java and Bali and North Sumatra. Warnings about the "latent threat of communism" could silence demands for fair wages or political reform. If this threat failed, authorities might arrest or prosecute critics or other troublemakers, with violence by the security forces or their proxies a final option.

Sometimes, the government decided a new dose of violence was required. Suci was fifteen when suspected criminal gang members started turning up dead in the street. Over two years, the bodies of more than five thousand gang members were left in the streets as a warning. The mysterious killings (*penembakan misterius,* or *Petrus* for short) were planned and executed as tightly as a military operation, which it surely was. Soon after the operation began in Yogyakarta, the commanding officer there promised, as if to reassure the public, "No one will be shot by mistake." Suharto explained in the first edition of his autobiography, "Some of the corpses were left just like that. This was for the purpose of shock therapy." This display was needed so that people "understand that there was still someone capable of taking action." The shock therapy was intended for the general public, not the criminal underworld.[9]

The events of 1965 traumatized Suci's father in ways she recognized only later, when she came to know many victims of state violence. He was a strict man, often old-fashioned, but as long as Suci didn't stay out too late, her parents' long days at the market gave her the freedom to play in the alleys of Mergosono.

Her father was untraditional in some ways. He wanted his daughters educated to become independent, confident thinkers who could secure their own livelihoods. In a deeply gendered society, he was an egalitarian man who cooked and did housework and expected his son and four daughters to do so equally. Suci was an intelligent child, with the discipline she learned from her parents. The combination put Suci at the top of her class, one of few in her *kampung* to attend a government school instead of a lower-quality private or religious school. But with money tight, Suci's father convinced her, despite her great promise, to forego general high school for a vocational program that would provide short, practical training as a teacher followed by a reliable job.

Suci graduated and found a teaching job, but she also kept up her studies in Indonesian language and literature at a good teacher's college. For a national language, the new nation had selected a version of Malay, a *lingua franca* for trade in maritime Southeast Asia. The language was tasked with knitting together into one nation the Javanese, Balinese, Moluccans, Bataks, Torajans, Dayaks, ethnic Chinese, Indians, and Arabs, and hundreds of other peoples scattered across an archipelago of seventeen thousand islands that stretched from Malaysia to New Guinea.

One of Suci's first jobs was at a school known for smart, unruly students. She was a young teacher with a similar rebellious intelligence, and she enjoyed teaching them, but she quit before a year was up.

Mergosono had come to feel less like a village. Families had grown, even under the strict Two Children Are Enough policy.[10] Migrants had moved in, many of them fleeing ethnic violence after being moved to Borneo from the little island of Madura off Java's north coast.[11] A new roadway running north to Surabaya now sliced through the neighborhood. On the far side lay a small industrial zone of low-slung factories and warehouses.

By the 1990s, many rural Indonesians were leaving their small farms to find jobs in factories, services, and construction. A major brand like Nike might contract with a Korean firm to open factories in Indonesia. Suharto dangled the promise of low wages and a docile workforce before these foreign operators. Independent labor unions were banned, and the army was authorized to prevent organizing and strikes and to oversee negotiations.[12] Employers could increase their leverage over workers further by putting soldiers on the security payroll or the board of directors.

Factory jobs paid less than a dollar a day, and they were in high demand. Many of Suci's friends from grade school lived at home and worked at nearby factories. In Mergosono, people stayed put. Thirty years after high school, Suci could visit her sister in the house they grew up in and bring her daughter next door for a haircut in an old classmate's living-room barber shop. She could even look out his front window and see a familiar cart pass by, its glass case stacked with *kue putu*. Suci remembered not just the soft little cakes—palm sugar wrapped in pandanus and rice flour, steamed in bamboo, and dusted with coconut—but even the vendor himself, now middle-aged and sinewy from pushing his cart up and down these alleys for three decades.

On an afternoon in 1990, that *kue putu* man might have passed right by Suci sitting with her friends. Tired out by ill-behaved students, she joined them on benchlike cement walls jutting from their houses. Songbirds chirped in wooden cages dangling from zinc roof overhangs among a cat's cradle of phone and power lines.

Her friends worked at a cigarette plant, churning out clove-scented *kreteks* and Pall Malls for the huge domestic market, and at a garment factory next door. Suci's experience was limited to teaching and helping her parents in the morning market, where they were their own bosses. Suci knew about the low pay in factories, but she was shocked to hear about beatings if you were caught talking, and the constant sexual harassment, including comments, pinches, kisses, and assaults. The idea that such things happened, day in and day out, infuriated Suci. She felt naive for believing the government's rosy version of economic development for all.

Even worse, Suci felt a growing prickle of hypocrisy for feeding that propaganda to her students. Since 1978, all students, and many adults, were required to study the state philosophy of Pancasila. The term was Sanskrit for Five Principles, which were: belief in one God, just and civilized humanity, the unity of Indonesia, democracy, and social justice. Indonesia's first president, Soekarno, drew from a mix of religious and cultural traditions, hoping to create a philosophy to unite a new and wildly diverse nation. It was scarcely more than a set of aspirations, and Suharto further stripped the principles of meaning and bent them to his use. He required every organization to accept Pancasila as its sole basis, rather than any political, social, or, most controversially, religious belief. Suharto wielded Pancasila flexibly against ideological threats from left or right, whether alleged communist remnants or evolving strains of political and radical Islam.[13]

Suci tried to reconcile the stories of factory life with the lessons and slogans she'd learned and now taught.[14] In October 1990, after weeks of wrestling with these contradictions, Suci quit her teaching job and got a job on a factory floor. She began stitching red-and-white leather jackets for export.[15] Suci also began forming a branch of the only union allowed, known as SPSI, the All-Indonesian Workers Union.[16] Forming a factory-

Suciwati on a camping trip in the
early 1990s. (personal photo, Suciwati)

level unit of this toothless body was not especially radical, but it wasn't easy either. Suci gathered signatures and organized a brief strike. Management offered a few concessions, then fired Suci when they identified her as the source of the trouble.[17]

She found a job at another garment plant and again she started to organize. She kept talking to friends at nearby factories, becoming an expert on the labor map of greater Malang. She knew by heart the salaries, policies, and the state of organizing at each factory. She helped workers win a raise at one, and a few days off at another.

Suci was working overtime at the garment factory, and then secretly organizing workers after hours. It was hard, dangerous work, and Suci did it without training or support. A friend urged her to make time to visit the Legal Aid Foundation, saying, "Just show your face." Founded early in the New Order, Lembaga Bantuan Hukum, or LBH, took on individual cases but also pushed for legal reforms and educated people about their rights.[18] By the 1990s, LBH was just the oldest of a fast-growing field of non-governmental organizations, or NGOs, working on labor, the environment, and human rights. With tight controls on unions, student groups, and political parties, NGOs were one of the few vehicles for

people to organize and pursue their rights. They were also open to the
children of former political prisoners, who were often barred from aca-
demics or government work. NGOs were too numerous and dispersed to
co-opt, with foreign support that made it hard to shut them all down. In
fact, Suharto welcomed them up to a point. Having consolidated power
and stabilized a growing economy in the 1980s, Suharto started the 1990s
with a new policy of *keterbukaan,* or political openness. He wanted Indonesia to be seen as a democracy with a functioning civil society, and that
meant NGOs, and even a National Human Rights Commission.[19]

LBH had recently opened a small post in Malang, a sub-office of the
Surabaya branch, and Suci stopped by on her lunch break. Tucked behind
a house on Jalan Commander Sudirman, LBH Pos Malang wasn't much
bigger than a one-car garage, perhaps the structure's original purpose.
The director invited Suci to use the office for discussions, and introduced
her to his three staff members, each assigned to a legal flash point: labor,
land, and the environment. The labor director, a skinny young lawyer
with unusual reddish hair, was on the way out the door, but he told Suci,
"Hey, stop by on Sunday, okay?" Like Suci and many other Indonesians,
he used only one name, Munir. It was Arabic for shining or luminous.

2

Munir

1990s

Suci told co-workers they should join her at LBH on Sunday, their one day off. They'd been looking for a safer spot to meet, though no place was totally secure. The authorities could raid any meeting they considered political if held without a permit. Suci explained that LBH offered more than they'd hoped for. It had space to meet in private, with lawyers to train them and to help if they got arrested. It was like a ripe durian falling from the tree and coming to rest right at your feet.

Before long, Munir asked Suci for help at the office, and then with a research project on Malang's northern fringe.[1] She liked being part of the research team, until she heard that Munir was telling people she was interested in him. Suci confronted Munir, telling him that she took her work seriously and didn't want it mixed up with emotions. She had no choice but to resign. As she walked out the door, some visitors arrived, and Munir could only watch her go. He came to her house that evening to apologize, but she wasn't there. He returned the next day, and she accepted his apology, but did not return to the research team or the office work. She liked to be with the workers where the action was, and in June she took another factory job, though she kept volunteering at LBH as well.

In fact, Suci was finding herself drawn to Munir. She liked his passion for his work and the way he combined this serious commitment with humor. Once, he took her to a political discussion at his old campus. Afterward, she revealed her fear that his bold words there would get him shot by an *intel* agent concealed in the crowd. At the sound of his warm laughter, her fear evaporated. In fact, outside of conflict zones, overt state violence was rare. For many Indonesians who were not especially political, the late New Order was a time of increasing prosperity and religious tolerance. By the 1990s, Suharto could assert control mostly through a vast bureaucracy governing all organizations, discussions, and publications. If an especially bold or outspoken group defied those controls, their actions could then be prosecuted through both new and colonial-era laws on subversion or "spreading hatred" against the government.[2] If criminal charges failed to reassert control, violence remained an option.

Besides his humor, Suci was struck by Munir's approach to women, not unlike her father's and very rare in Indonesia. Munir could still be traditional at times, or just naive about women and relationships, but she always felt he wanted to learn and understand more. She found this openness surprising in someone from a religious, Arab-Indonesian family. Six generations earlier, a poor man from northern Yemen's Hadramaut region had followed the monsoon winds across the Indian Ocean, easier than crossing the mountains to southern Yemen. Like other Arabs, as well as Chinese, Indian, and other migrants of the time, he came alone and married a local woman. They tried to marry within the Arab community, but each generation mixed with the local population more. Munir spoke Javanese at home, and some Arabic when he helped out in his father's shop, especially when discussing prices without a customer's knowledge.

The Arab community in Indonesia was known for its traditional patriarchal values, but Suci saw that Munir's strong mother had inspired a more egalitarian impulse. In 1976, when Munir was eleven, his father was returning from a wedding to the family home in Batu, in the hills above Malang, when the car collided with an oxcart in the dark. He died after a week in the hospital.

Munir's mother, whom the family called Umi, had six children, no job, and not enough schooling to read and write. The oldest kids left school, helping their mother squeeze a living out of a series of small ventures, or traveling to other islands to find work when needed. Umi tried making and selling clothes, then opened a market stall to sell shoes. Munir walked there each day to bring his older brothers and sisters lunch, and in junior high he and his little brother Jamal manned the stall after school until ten at night, occasionally falling asleep in class the next day as a result. Raised in the independent world of small traders, Munir learned to talk to people of every type and class.

Suci learned that Munir was always the smallest in his class. He was self-conscious of his reddish hair, demanding to see the school doctor to learn why his hair wasn't black like everyone else's.[3] He never hung back from a fight, especially if he saw weaker or poorer classmates ganged up on.[4] He fought his way through junior high and high school.

Apart from his childhood sympathy for the underdog, however, Munir's commitment to social justice was something new. Born the same year as the New Order and raised under it, Munir never questioned that the government was right. His family wasn't political, and he really didn't know much about Suharto or the conflicts brewing in places like Aceh, Papua, and East Timor.

Just a few years before he met Suci, Munir had come down the slopes of Mount Arjuno to enroll at Brawijaya University in Malang. He'd joined the state-sanctioned Muslim Students' Association (Himpunan Mahasiswa Islam, or HMI). HMI had recently split, and Munir joined the more pro-Suharto faction.[5] He was not just a supporter of the president, but a militant one, often clashing with street activists demanding democracy or human rights. They generally fought through public debates, wherein Munir earned a fearsome reputation, and student government races, but the competition grew tense. Munir considered himself a soldier in a religious war, and by his own account carried a knife in his bag in these years, ready to fight.[6] Munir might have developed into a lifelong pro-Suharto ideologue or a religious hard-liner.

But not long after arriving at college, friends, books, teachers, and his own curious mind began challenging his constricted views. He enjoyed taking the pro-government side when arguing with the radical street activists, but some of their arguments were persuasive. Munir also began excavating the history of HMI. He was surprised to discover its founding documents were almost radical in their challenge to state authority and capitalism. Drafted in 1960 by an influential and progressive Muslim intellectual named Nurcholish Majid, they used the Quran and the Hadiths to argue that Muslims should side with the oppressed.

One of Munir's professors was a religious Arab-Indonesian like him named Abdul Malik Fadjar. He asked Munir how his inquiry into the documents was faring. Munir was already wondering if his extremism had caused him to lose sight of the purpose of religion. Was religion created for God, or for building a better society? His professor pushed him to see that Islam didn't side with itself, but with the oppressed. Fadjar chided him, "I never met a young person as dumb as you, running around carrying an impulse to fight with tools of religion, to control other people." Munir felt himself begin to sweat, not just from the challenge to his beliefs, but because he'd encountered something inspiring.

Deciding that God had no need for bodyguards, Munir left behind fighting and extremism. His way of thinking and talking changed so dramatically that other Muslim students leveled the serious accusation of leftism at him. A pro-democracy student activist from Yogyakarta was shocked to learn that the same hardliner whose debating skills had given her such a hard time had become an ally.[7]

Munir took any spending money he had to the book vendors on Jalan Majapahit. He scanned the used books and bound photocopies stacked high or laid out on the sidewalk like patchwork quilts, searching for hard-to-find books. He came across *The Democratic Path to Socialism: Chile's Experience under Allende*, an Indonesian sociologist's Harvard dissertation. The author, Arief Budiman, was drawn to the subject in part because the violent end of Allende's Chile has a grim link to Indonesia. In advance of General Pinochet's 1973 coup against President Salvador Allende, the phrase JAKARTA IS COMING had been spray-painted on walls, invoking the anticommunist killings of a few years before. The term Operation Jakarta was used in several countries in Latin America to describe programs for the violent destruction of the left.[8] Budiman noted, "the Indonesian coup seems to have been consciously emulated in Chile."

The book opens with the words of the poet Pablo Neruda, imagining a meeting with South American liberator Simón Bolívar. The poem ends, "And he said, looking at the barracks on the mountain / I awake each one hundred years when the people wake up." Munir was fascinated with the analysis of Allende's use of mass movements, and the example of a non-violent leader advancing the rights of workers. The book also considers the role of the military in radical social change, whether peaceful or violent, and notes Allende's concern for the well-being of soldiers, especially the lower ranks. Allende's support for workers, as well as Budiman's lucid political analysis, almost certainly served as a model for Munir, just as the Chilean generals emulated the Indonesians. The book ends with Allende's final speech, made the day he died, either by murder or suicide, as Pinochet's coup unfolded around him. Allende said, "I am ready to resist by any means, even at the cost of my own life, so this will serve as a lesson in the ignominious history of those who have strength but not reason."[9]

Inspired by the book and looking for ways to channel his new sense of the purpose of religion into something specific, Munir became interested in the workers of East Java. On many days off from school, he went up to Batu to see Umi and help with the business, walking twelve uphill miles if he'd spent all his pocket money on books. But on other days, he lingered at the cheap food stalls, or *warung*s, that clustered outside factory gates.

He made cigarette factory workers the subject of his thesis, research that led him to the threshold of a new world. He focused on the Bentoel cigarette factory in Mergosono, a large, neat complex of white one-story buildings, next to the grittier leatherworks, where Suci worked on red-and-white jackets. For six months, he talked to workers in the *warung*s and dormitories. He rented a room nearby so he could stay up late doing interviews, get some sleep, and start writing in the morning.

One day some workers he knew asked for advice on a strike they were planning. Munir had never even seen a strike, but he agreed to meet them to go over their plans.[10] When the short strike led to many arrests, Munir began to grasp the reality of Suharto's Indonesia. He became interested in what forces made workers so helpless and how they could be countered.[11] He'd always had an impulse toward justice, but it was limited to what he could see with his own eyes: a schoolyard bully or a policeman harassing vendors in the market. His sense of justice began to widen, taking on the vocabulary of worker rights and human rights.

Munir spent so much time with workers and engaged in campus politics that his grades suffered. Classmates warned that hanging out with workers wasn't a job. He didn't care, knowing he'd never seek a job at a law firm or in business. He took a volunteer position at the new LBH post in Malang in 1989, selling and installing TV antennas on the side to earn money.[12] That year LBH identified the lack of independent unions as a structural problem underlying many cases, and the legal aid organization began organizing workers in East Java.

Munir was given a staff position as director of labor rights, and he quickly impressed one of LBH's founders, a legendary lawyer named Adnan Buyung Nasution. On a visit to Malang, Buyung turned to ask a colleague, "Who's the skinny kid with the cheap clothes and the red hair? His questions are sharp."

Munir was soon in charge of the Malang office, and then was promoted to direct the labor and civil rights work at the East Java branch headquarters in Surabaya in 1992.[13] The city takes its name from a twelfth-century king's psychic vision of a battle between two great white predators, a shark (*sura*) and a crocodile (*buaya*). Surabaya has been a major port ever since, a waypoint for ships traversing the Java Sea from the Spice Islands to the Straits of Malacca, and on to South Asia and the Middle East. Surabaya once rivaled Hong Kong, and is still Indonesia's second largest city.

In Surabaya, LBH operated out of one in a row of little red-roofed houses between the intersecting lines of a canal, train tracks, and the Surabaya River. Just inside the front door sat Munir's desk, cluttered with cardboard binders, a helmet, and empty glasses of tea. All day a parade of workers sat in the folding chair across from Munir, seeking help after being fired without cause, cheated out of wages, or threatened by soldiers. Munir helped them file complaints with the Ministry of Manpower or the courts.

The LBH strategy was to use specific labor cases as an entry point for education and organizing. Munir would duly help file the complaints, but the real work began in the evening after production lines came to a halt. He'd hop on his Honda motorbike and head to the industrial areas to hold discussions that often ran until eleven at night. Factories and worker dormitories were side by side in the industrial zones, allowing Munir to efficiently meet many workers after hours. Sometimes, if a strike was planned for the next day, or if workers just wanted to keep discussing labor and politics, they would move the conversation to LBH and go all night. Then Munir would sleep for an hour or two on one of the desks until the sun rose. He usually chose one under a ceiling fan to keep mosquitoes away, pulling on a sweater and socks with his plaid sarong.

Munir went back down to Malang often, and his connection to Suci deepened with each visit. He was struck by what an unusual woman had walked into his life that day. She was strong-willed and independent, characteristics he associated with men.[14] Men and women had few chances to be alone together, but Suci and Munir managed long, roving conversations that started in the office, continued on foot to a *warung* and over a frugal dinner, and then back to the office again.

Munir in front of the LBH Surabaya office in the early 1990s.

One day in November 1992, they were walking along Jalan Pattimura when Munir posed a slow and thoughtful question.

"Suci, do you believe in love at first sight?"

"Why?'

"Just answer."

"No, I don't believe in that. For me, love needs a process. You don't just see someone and fall in love. And, it's like, our eyes can deceive us. Maybe it exists for other people, but for me, I don't think so. Why? Who fell in love at first sight?"

Munir evaded a direct answer but picked up the conversation a few days later.

"If a woman is invited out to the movies, to eat meals together, would you consider that *pacaran*?" he asked her. *Pacar* means boyfriend or girlfriend, and adding *-an* to the end gave it a sense of an ongoing activity, something like dating.

"No, that might just be considered a sister, or a best friend. You have to have the feelings. *And* you have to express them. If you like someone, tell them. If they reject you, well, deal with that later. If she feels the same way, okay, *then* it's *pacaran*. You need to be in agreement."

"Huh!" He exhaled thoughtfully.

She suspected he was sounding out her feelings. She also knew many young female activists and volunteers became taken with Munir, and he might just have been asking for relationship advice. A week later he invited her out to eat. Over catfish, a favorite food of his, they returned to their favorite topics: workers, strikes, and salaries.

It was only on the way home that Munir told Suci that he loved her. She started to respond, but he stopped her. He'd be back in Malang in a week. Please, let's just think it over.

The following Saturday she waited at home as agreed. She planned to let him down gently, to explain how important their work together was. She didn't want to complicate it, or have a fight and mess it all up. When his usual arrival time of six p.m. slipped past, Suci headed out to a friend's house. She ran into Munir, who asked, "Where are you going?"

They walked and talked again, and he said again that he'd fallen in love with her. There had once been a girl who wanted to marry him, but he hadn't been sure about her. He was sure about Suci. Suci said nothing. She'd planned to turn him down. Until the very last minute she'd planned to tell him no.

Somehow, it came out as yes. She had to be honest. She had feelings for him too. She agreed to give it a try, but only if they kept it a secret for now. It was nobody's business but theirs.

In 1992 Munir visited Malang for a "barefoot lawyer" training to arm workers with knowledge of labor law and rights. A young new colleague named Poengky came with him from Surabaya. At her job interview, Munir had asked no questions, smiling to himself as others asked about her skills and training. He could see she was committed to helping workers. The rest she could learn.

Poengky did learn quickly, surprised by the gulf between the idealized depictions in her labor law books and the reality of workers' lives. As a sheltered young woman from a religious family, she was also shocked at how free the workers seemed. Young men and women mixed freely, earning their dollar a day far from their watchful villages and *kampungs*.

Leading the training from the front of the single room at the Malang Post of LBH, Munir wrote on the dwindling empty space of a whiteboard. Suci sat on the floor with the workers. "The owners benefit, the workers lose out," he said. "The rich get richer, the owners get richer, and your suffering mounts."[15] The analysis was simple but effective, and to Poengky it seemed very risky. She was right.

The authorities quickly picked up three of the new barefoot lawyers. When they were released after three days, it was clear that they'd been beaten and the two women sexually harassed or even assaulted, but even backed by LBH, none of them dared lodge a complaint.[16]

The lesson was starker, and the stakes higher, in Munir's first major case in Surabaya. Marsinah was a twenty-four-year-old factory worker, known in her family as very quiet and very brave. There are few photos of her, and in all of them she has the same serious expression, eyebrows slightly raised over her dark eyes in a pretty, oval face. An avid reader who couldn't afford to study past high school, Marsinah joined the tide of young rural people looking for work in Surabaya, three hours by bus from her village. She found a job at a watch factory in the city, only to be transferred to Porong, on the outskirts, after taking part in labor organizing. In May 1993, she helped lead a strike there, seeking better conditions and a raise of 25 cents per day as required by law.[17] They negotiated with management in the presence of representatives from the Ministry of Manpower, as well as police officers and soldiers. Despite this united front of business, government, and the military, the workers secured the raise and most other demands, including protection from retaliation.

Immediately afterward, however, the other strike leaders were summoned to the Sidoarjo District army post. They were accused of being communists, a deadly serious charge, and forced to sign letters of resignation on the spot. Two features distinguished the Indonesian military from most modern, professional defense forces. First, the doctrine of *dwi fungsi*, or dual function, gave the military a formal role in politics and society, well beyond national defense. Second, the territorial command structure posted troops at regional, provincial, district, and subdistrict levels within Indonesia. Both of these features demonstrated that the military's primary focus was not foreign threats, but internal control. Their proximity to civilians and involvement in their economic and political lives made violence and other human rights violations common. The military was given an explicit role in resolving labor disputes.[18]

When Marsinah learned of the arrests, she went straight to the army post to ask about her fellow workers, before going home to plan next steps with others. They headed out again around ten, parting ways under a mango tree. Marsinah went to get food at a *warung* along the main road.

Three days later, some children found her body in a seated position under a shelter, among the bright green rice fields and teak forests close to her village, three hours to the west. There were wounds on her neck and wrists, a crushed pelvis, and injuries consistent with the insertion of a sharp object in her vagina.

For two weeks there was no press coverage. Then local army officials announced that Marsinah's death was unrelated to the strike. Authorities blamed an inheritance dispute, or a love triangle, or a threat by Marsinah to expose counterfeiting by the watch factory.

Munir helped form KSUM, the Support Committee for Marsinah. Made up of twenty NGOs, the group pushed for justice for Marsinah. LBH tried to look for bigger issues behind a court case, and in the Marsinah effort, that meant trying to end the military role in labor disputes. Munir represented Marsinah's co-workers in a legal action against the factory, the government, and the local military post. The court threw it out, but the suit embarrassed the army and educated the public about the tight alliance of soldiers, businesses, and government. The Marsinah case eventually became one of the country's best-known labor cases of the 1990s, and her name was raised in trade talks with the United States and at United Nations meetings in Geneva. In Indonesia, Marsinah became a symbol of struggle and resistance for workers, challenging the myth of the docile Indonesian workforce.[19] The case was also a focal point, alongside the Kedung Ombo Dam in Central Java, for a new generation of student activists to find common cause with workers and farmers as they challenged the excesses of economic development.

Seeing that the fiction that Marsinah's death was not connected to the strike could not withstand public scrutiny, the army tried a new tack. After months without progress in the case, the army suddenly detained the factory owner and eight employees without a warrant and held them incommunicado for two weeks. They were then handed over to police and charged, along with one low-ranking soldier accused of not reporting the crime to his superiors.

When the trial began, thousands of workers surrounded the courthouse. Concerned for the safety of the defendants, court security knocked out part of a back wall for a secret exit. The trial began with two factory employees admitting to planning to kill Marsinah, abducting her, torturing her at the factory owner's house, beating her to death with an iron bar, and disposing of her body. But partway through the trial, one began asserting that none of this was true. He told the court that he was tortured with beatings and electrocution until he signed the false record of interrogation. "The scar on my left shoulder is still there today," he said taking off his shirt to show the judges. Other defendants spoke up that they had their teeth knocked out, were forced to drink urine, or were forced to clean the floor with their tongues. After these revelations, security increased and instead of workers, the courtroom was filled with police and military in plainclothes. Other defendants later reported being threatened during the trial that they would be returned to the hands of their torturers, or released to the mobs of workers outside, if they too recanted their forced confessions.

Despite these revelations, all the defendants were convicted, the owner getting a seventeen-year sentence. They were later acquitted on appeal. Some may have been involved in the crime, but their trial was clearly invalidated by rampant torture. Others who bore responsibility, most likely soldiers of the Sidoarjo District Military Command and their commanding officers, were never prosecuted. The Marsinah case was unusual, in that most repression of workers' rights did not end in murder, and most trials were not so blatantly engineered to shift blame to civilians. Yet even with those extremes, and with the eyes of the world on the case, there was no justice.

Munir realized the limits of trying to advance human rights through the courts. The alternative approaches, such as press conferences on the courthouse steps, lobbying in the United States and Geneva, and the mobilization of thousands of workers to show their solidarity with Marsinah at the trial, had had only limited effect. Munir learned that when state agents commit a crime, political obstruction usually means it will remain forever unresolved.[20]

In LBH's analysis, the case also revealed the link between violence, law enforcement, and power. Police and prosecutors were servants to power and routinely used violence, including the torture of suspects, not just to secure confessions and convictions, but to protect the state and support its ideologies of development and stability.[21]

A co-worker described Surabaya as Munir's Candradimuka crater. In the *wayang* (shadow puppet) stories, a blunt-spoken hero is thrown into a sacred crater, only to emerge from the lava with muscles like wire and bones as strong as steel.[22]

On his visits to Malang, Munir and Suci left the office separately at the end of the day. They met up again where nobody knew them and they could stroll and talk freely. *Pacaran* for them was little more than that, some dinner, and the walk to Mergosono, but Suci loved it that way. She wanted to keep what they had to themselves.

They joked about getting married, but she wasn't sure Munir would end up as her husband. More than once, they broke up. Walking her home one evening as rain bucketed down, no closer to marriage and under pressure from his family as he neared thirty, Munir made a pronouncement. "I'm freeing you," he said, "so someone else can be with you."

Suci was amused, but not impressed. "Fine," she said. Munir might be a progressive activist, but the patriarchy seemed bred in the bone. The main road out of the *kampung* was flooded, so she walked him out the back way. They climbed the railway embankment and crossed the tracks, walking closely as they both held her umbrella. When he slid his hand over hers on the handle, she brushed it away. They descended to the road on the far side of the tracks, with minivans hurtling back and forth picking up passengers. One swerved to a stop, and Munir climbed in. Suci walked back over the railbed, picking her way through the flooded alleyways.

Their work kept them in contact, though, and soon he tried again. This time he proposed directly, and this time she said yes, but with one condition. She wanted the freedom to remain responsible for herself, not cared for like a bird in a gilded cage. "Yes," he said. "Of course." Her independence was one of the things he loved about her.

Neither family was happy with the match. She knew that she was far from what his family had hoped for, not being from the Arab community nor wearing a headscarf.[23] For his part, Suci's father held firm to his suspicion of religion, and Arab-Indonesians were especially observant. Suci convinced him that it was *her* life, and Munir's, and had nothing to do with ethnicity or religion. Munir, in particular, was nothing like the men who'd taken away her father's friends. The families consented, and Suci and Munir married in June 1996. The wedding ceremonies lasted for several days and many costume changes, as the couple went from a slightly oversize gray suit and white wedding dress to brightly colored silken Arab dress, to Javanese outfits of batik.

Munir continued his rise in LBH with a promotion to Jakarta, after some brief seasoning as branch director in Semarang on the north coast of Java.

It was time to bring Munir's skills to the national stage, and beyond a focus on workers.

It was a pivotal moment in the fight for human rights and democracy. Political, economic, and social changes were creating small cracks in state control and in the unity of the security forces. Suharto chose this time to shower ever more wealth on family members and business cronies. His six sons and daughters owned hundreds of companies, most of them based on monopolies or other forms of favoritism. Even the poorest *kretek* smoker helped put money in Tommy Suharto's pockets through a clove monopoly he created. Poor clove farmers in the outer islands were forced to sell to Tommy at low prices, even as the scion bought not just a Lamborghini but the whole company, among other extravagant purchases. Wealthier Jakartans contributed to the $184,000 a day his sister Tutut collected through her network of toll roads.[24] First Lady Tien Suharto was known as Madam Tien Percent, a play on the Dutch word for ten, her rumored percentage of major new investments in Indonesia. Many in the military had already begun to feel sidelined, and rising corruption only widened schisms between the president and the civilian and military elite.

At the international level, it had become clear that authoritarian regimes could not compete and prosper over the long run. The end of the Cold War had also made Indonesia less indispensable, and the United States and Europe began linking aid and trade to the treatment of workers and respect for human rights. The murder of Marsinah, the controversial Kedung Ombo Dam project in Central Java, and other cases had brought together students and activists working on human rights, labor, and the environment and given them experience taking their case to the wider world. Students, journalists, political parties, and activists tried to use the growing fissures among elites to push for democratic reform through the press, the courts, and, eventually, in the streets.[25]

A month after their wedding, Suci joined Munir in Jakarta. They settled into a room attached to a house for visiting LBH staff in East Jakarta. She had not been there more than a few days when Munir did not come home one night. He'd been caught up in a spasm of state violence that changed the political calculus in the country.

As usual, the background to the violence was Suharto's sense of a threat to his hold on power. Communism had been obliterated, and political Islam was largely neutralized for the time being. However, the populist nationalism embodied by President Soekarno remained a potent force. In 1973, Suharto had grouped all the old nationalist parties into a single, manageable Partai Demokrat Indonesia, or PDI. Due to the ruling party Golkar's monopoly on power and patronage, as well as tight curbs on campaigning, PDI usually won less than 10 percent of the vote. With its compliant leadership, PDI was more a prop in a piece of democracy theater than a true opposition party.

However, after Soekarno's daughter, Megawati Sukarnoputri, joined PDI, the party gained seats in parliament. In 1993, the party selected Mega as chair with the approval of some military officers who were unhappy with Golkar's dominance and had begun pondering life after Suharto. One of them was General A. M. Hendropriyono, commander of the troops in Jakarta.

In 1996, Suharto tried to regain control of the situation by installing a puppet to head the party. Mega's supporters refused to yield party headquarters, instead filling the street in front with rallies and speeches. After a month of this unruly rebellion against the accepted rules of New Order politics, the pro-government faction of the party, along with army-backed thugs and riot police, moved in on July 27, 1996.

The LBH office was just down Jalan Diponegoro from the party headquarters. When Munir saw soldiers kicking an old man in the street, he jumped over a fence to help. A soldier stomped on Munir's hand, breaking the index finger. Munir managed to get himself and the old man over the fence to safety. His hand needed care, but there was word that the authorities were sweeping Central Jakarta's hospitals looking for PDI supporters, and taking them away. In the end, five deaths and twenty-three disappearances were confirmed.[26]

A colleague patched Munir up, and in the morning they went to a doctor they trusted. The doctor sutured the wound, but couldn't perform surgery to fix the broken bone. It never healed properly, and Munir typed without using that finger thereafter.

Under pressure to investigate the violence, the government instead prosecuted the victims. They also accused a new leftist pro-democracy group called the Democratic People's Party, or PRD, of plotting to over-throw the government.[27] They arrested the chairman, and began hunting for its members.

When the government felt threatened, all critics faced a spike in scrutiny and threats. Munir had been visible in Malang, and more so in Surabaya after the Marsinah case. Jakarta at this time would be a new level of danger. Suci knew some women might make a new husband adopt a lower profile or even change jobs, but she felt that Munir's life was in God's hands, and that being unable to do the work he needed to would kill him slowly. She wanted him to do that work. She chose him because she loved him, but also because she knew she could help him transform their country.

3

But Don't You Wait

1998

For over three decades, Suharto skillfully co-opted opponents, played rivals against each other, and deployed show trials and violence as needed. He also delivered economic growth as Bapak Pembangunan, the Father of Development, further contributing to his hold on power. But inequality and rampant corruption were already spurring discontent when the Thai baht collapsed in July 1997. By October the monetary contagion had spread to Indonesia. Banks and businesses collapsed, savings evaporated, and unemployment soared. The crash wiped out years of economic progress.

There is never a good time for a *krismon* (short for *krisis moneter*, sometimes called with grim humor *kristal*, for *krisis total*), but this one came at a particularly bad time for Suharto. Parliamentary elections had taken place in May 1997 as a prelude to the reselection of the president. Every five years, Suharto's electoral machine, Golkar, garnered about two-thirds of the vote, providing the illusion of democracy without risk of defeat. The remaining votes went to the only two legal parties, the nationalist PDI and the Muslim-oriented PPP. Rather than true opposition parties, they were forced amalgams of a once fractious array of smaller parties. Their leadership, candidate lists, funding, and campaigns were strictly controlled.[1]

In May 1997, Golkar won 74 percent of the vote, ensuring domination of the People's Consultative Assembly session scheduled for March 1998. The Majelis Permusyawaratan Rakyat, or MPR, was a kind of super-parliament of a thousand delegates. It was made up of all members of the House of Representatives, or DPR, joined by hundreds of other functionaries, including military representatives. The People's Consultative Assembly set broad policy for the five-year term and selected the president. The body had chosen Suharto six terms so far, and there was little doubt of the outcome this time. Indonesians joked that anyone could become president, as long as they met age and citizenship requirements and had previous experience *as* president.

However, before the assembly could meet, the financial crisis exacerbated those cracks already spreading across the edifice of the New Order. Suharto was old enough to make talk of succession unavoidable, while his family's corruption had mushroomed to a level that caused grumbling even within the military and civilian elite. When the currency fell, subsidies had to be cut, and demonstrations broke out over the cost of fuel and food. Cell phones and the internet allowed new and better forms of coordination, and in early 1998 the largest student protests in years began to spread throughout the country.

On the morning of January 18, 1998, an aging housing project in the Central Jakarta neighborhood of Tanah Tinggi was rocked by an explosion. The residents of the apartment in question fled, but one returned to retrieve his wallet and was arrested. He was a member of the pro-democracy group PRD, which had been operating underground since being blamed for the violence at Indonesian Democratic Party headquarters a year and half earlier. Inside the apartment, police found a stockpile of explosives and detonators.

Soon after, a young man with an injured leg came to LBH, which had become a bustling headquarters in the gathering fight for democracy. The man said he was a friend of Munir's and had hurt his leg in a traffic accident. When it became clear that he was a PRD member hurt in the explosion, some LBH leaders wanted to hand him over to the authorities. Munir didn't support violence and didn't want to put the organization at risk, nor could he justify delivering someone to torture or worse. After a fierce argument, LBH's leadership gave Munir three days to evacuate the injured man.

Munir hid him inside an office, where he lay on the floor. The steady

stream of clients, journalists, and activists didn't suspect there was a fugitive inside, nor did the soldiers from the army's special-forces branch,
Kopassus, hanging around outside. Munir finally called one of his most
trusted colleagues, the driver Sugiarto. He was on leave, but Sugiarto
quickly came and took the secret guest outside the city to be treated for a
spreading infection.[2]

Munir and Suci had just learned that she was pregnant, a source of joy
that also raised the stakes of his high-risk work. The explosion, meanwhile, set in motion a chain of events that made Munir a national figure
and an even greater target. Amid the shards of glass and chunks of ceiling
littering the Tanah Tinggi apartment was a laptop with incriminating
emails and documents. Using these documents, together with their own
suspicions and intelligence, the security forces compiled a target list of
PRD leadership and other government critics.[3] The economic crisis, the
spread of student protests, and the Tanah Tinggi blast were all making
Suharto and his allies nervous about the normally pro forma selection of
the president to another term.

On the afternoon of February 3, with the People's Consultative Assembly
a month away, a legal aid lawyer named Desmond Mahesa left his office.
He boarded a minibus and later changed to a kind of shared minivan taxi
called a *mikrolet*. A man sat down next to him, getting off when he did.
Once on the sidewalk, the man pointed a gun at Desmond and shouted,
"Don't move!" Several men roughly forced Desmond into a gray jeep,
which drove off with the music at full volume. The only trace left behind
was a pair of glasses lying in the street.

At a bus stop the next day, armed men seized Pius Lustrilanang, a
supporter of a speculative presidential ticket combining the two semi-
opposition politicians Megawati and Amien Rais. He too was cuffed,
blindfolded, and taken away. On February 12, armed men with military
haircuts and shoes came looking for the PRD member Suyat at his family's house in Central Java. Suyat was the one who had survived the Tanah
Tinggi blast, hidden in the secret sanctuary of LBH for days. He had
escaped Jakarta, only to be tracked down in his hometown. Suyat was not
there, so they took his older brother and tortured him until he agreed to

help look for his little brother. Suyat was found at a friend's house, and taken away before his older brother's eyes.[4]

On the evening of March 8, while the People's Consultative Assembly was under way, a Megawati supporter named Haryanto Taslam exited the toll road in a light rain, followed by a blue Toyota Kijang and a brown one. One of the vehicles, headlights off, overtook him and tried to run him off the road. The chase ended in a crash near Taman Mini, a theme park that was a pet project of the president's wife. At the gates of this costly replica of Indonesia in miniature, Haryanto was blindfolded and bound, pushed into the Toyota, and driven off.

The People's Consultative Assembly wrapped up on March 11, having granted the president another five-year term—with enhanced powers, no less. Each term Suharto chose a different vice-president to prevent rivals or clear political heirs from emerging. This time he selected a close ally, a German-trained engineer and Muslim intellectual named B. J. Habibie. The new cabinet included a number of Suharto cronies and even his daughter Tutut, the toll road entrepreneur.

The next day, three PRD activists took part in an event at LBH to reject these results.[5] Immediately afterward, men in plainclothes chased two of them into a hospital, where they hid in a bathroom. They were found and taken away. The third activist was abducted nearby.

The following evening, March 13, Nezar Patria had just arrived at the apartment he shared with three other activists. He and a roommate, Aan, had just turned on the lights and started to make some warm fresh orange juice to ward off a cold in the waning days of Jakarta's rainy season. He froze at the sound of a rough knock on his door.

Aan opened the door to find four men, some in ski masks, led by a man in jeans, a black jacket, and a military haircut. The man pulled Aan toward him, passed him back to another member of the team, and entered the room to face Nezar, frozen in the act of cutting oranges. Seeing the small knife in Nezar's hand, the man stepped forward to press a gun against his stomach.

"Don't ask questions. Come with me."

Nezar lived on the second floor of Klender Flats, a cheap apartment block in East Jakarta. He, Aan, and their roommates Mugi and Bimo

Petrus were among the leaders of one of the student groups that had given rise to the PRD.[6] Nezar had left his home province of Aceh, where a long insurgency had been met with a series of major military operations, with plans to become a journalist. But in the student city of Yogyakarta, Nezar decided his plans made no sense in a country with no press freedom. Amid the political ferment of campus life in the early 1990s, he helped found a student organization that boldly rejected the usual government restrictions.

Like many PRD members, Nezar went underground after the group was blamed for the July 1996 unrest at the Indonesian Democratic Party headquarters. The four roommates organized secret political discussions, while scraping together livings as journalists and translators. Hoping to stay one step ahead of *intel*, Nezar used five ID cards and kept changing his look. He chopped off his thick long hair, grew a mustache, and later shaved it off. They used an intricate system of pagers, memorized phone numbers, and code words to arrange clandestine meetings at bus stops, train stations, and other public spaces. The strategy worked, until it didn't. The four had hoped to blend into the large, crowded housing project, but were discovered a week after moving in.

The men cuffed the two roommates together, blindfolded them tightly, and hustled them down the stairs and into a car. They drove off, windows shut tight and a cassette of house music turned all the way up. Mugi returned home to the empty apartment soon after. Within minutes he was taken as well. Their fourth roommate was Bimo Petrus. He was from Malang and, like Munir, he'd been called up from East Java to Jakarta, though as part of an underground movement rather than a legal-aid office. He had the high-risk job of running PRD's couriers, bringing information and instructions from leadership to members, and helping to rescue those in danger. He was cheerfully certain democracy would prevail, and serious about the work. If you arrived at the rendezvous spot ten minutes late, as Indonesians often to do, Bimo Petrus would be gone. He seems to have evaded capture for two more weeks, as he called his parents on March 28.

On March 27, the head of Nezar's student group, Andi Arief, was tracked down and abducted from his brother's house in South Sumatra.

A blue Kijang and a red one carried him off, traveling by ferry across the Sunda Strait to Java and back to Jakarta.

The mother of one of the men seized while hiding in the hospital came to LBH for help. So did Tuti Koto, a thin older woman with a delicate, lined face framed by a patterned headscarf. Her son Yani Afri was a young bus driver who supported Megawati, and had been missing for almost a year. The women were afraid to go to the police and unsure whom else to turn to. They asked Munir who was handling missing people, and he had no answer. He contacted friends and colleagues, and then talked over an idea with Suci.

Suci and Munir were still staying at the LBH property in the East Jakarta neighborhood of Jatinegara. It was really just a bedroom, in front of which they had built a small room to receive guests, an essential part any Javanese home. Sitting together in the formal front room, Munir asked Suci what she thought of him founding an organization to investigate missing activists, victims of a human rights violation known as enforced disappearance.[7] It would be more confrontational and proactive than either LBH's litigation approach or the more passive documentation and analysis of other groups.

Indonesians use a rich lexicon of terms to avoid naming perpetrators. The person behind a crime is a *dalang*, the puppeteer of the *wayang kulit* shadow plays, who controls heroes and villains behind the screen. The term is nearly synonymous with *aktor intelektual* (intellectual actors, from a Dutch legal concept) and *otak pelaku* (the brains of the operation). There were even vaguer terms to obscure the guilt and identity of perpetrators even when known. *Aparat*, literally meaning "apparatus," referred to unspecified members of the police or military. An *oknum* is a person acting in a certain capacity, with negative connotations, such as a member of the security forces committing a crime. *Orang-orang tertentu* simply means "certain people." Munir had seen enough of these obscuring terms. It was time to name the perpetrators, even if they were generals or other powerful figures with an arsenal of methods to silence or punish accusers. Munir needed to know Suci was on board.

She asked him, "Well, what's the greatest risk of being alive?"

"That you will die."

"And you can die while eating, while sleeping, while doing anything. If you can help people, and be of use, you should do it," she said. "I don't like it. But you should do it."

The new organization, KontraS, was formed on March 20, 1998. Members of top human rights organizations and student groups came together to analyze failed cases like the murder of Marsinah, to devise new forms of advocacy and investigation. They agreed to keep a tight focus on disappearances and to adopt the confrontational approach Munir wanted. The name KontraS was an acronym for the organization's full name, but it also signaled that they were *kontra Suharto*. Munir expected this fight to be a long one, during which they would face violence, perhaps even be disappeared themselves.[8]

The request for help from the mothers of the missing had spurred Munir to action, but he'd already been thinking about new approaches to address grave crimes.[9] Like other Indonesian activists, he read intensively about the path to democracy in Latin America. These transitions from military governments were a better model for Indonesia than post-apartheid South Africa or post-communist Eastern Europe. Activists passed around translations of a series called Transitions from Authoritarian Rule, and especially one volume covering Latin America's remarkable transformation.[10] Once, the threat "Jakarta is coming!" had been used in Argentina, Brazil, and Chile to promise the mass murder of leftists. Now those countries, and the victims of these atrocities, might show Indonesia the way to democracy and justice.

After its transition, Argentina created an official commission on disappearances that was a likely inspiration for the full name of KontraS: the Commission for the Disappeared and Victims of Violence (Komisi untuk Orang Hilang dan Korban Tindak Kekerasan). But a movement that emerged earlier, during Argentina's dark days, was an even greater influence. Las Madres de la Plaza de Mayo was a group of mothers who began gathering weekly in 1977, demanding to know the fate of their missing sons and daughters. The power of KontraS would not lie in legal skills or advocacy strategies, but in the moral force wielded by victims and survivors.

There was another factor at play in Munir's decision to put victims at the center. In East Java he'd directly organized workers, spending time with them over meals and in their homes. He told a family member that the move to Jakarta made him feel "cut from the roots." Helping families to become central actors in the struggle for human rights was more like the organizing he'd loved and found to be effective in Malang and Surabaya. KontraS used newspaper ads to find more families searching for missing relatives.[11]

Munir held daily press conferences, sometimes inviting parents to speak about their lost children. He put up billboards with the faces of the missing. Due in part to these efforts, some of the missing began to turn up. On April 3 the legal aid lawyer Desmond Mahesa was transported in a blindfold to the airport. Desmond was ordered not to talk about his ordeal and given a ticket home to South Kalimantan on the island of Borneo, along with some money to replace his lost eyeglasses. Pius Lustrilanang, the political activist seized next at a bus stop, enjoyed a similar escort to the airport before he was sent home to South Sumatra. Two weeks later, and forty days after being abducted at the gates of Taman Mini, Haryanto Taslam was bundled back into a car. His captors drove him to a spot near the Bandung airport, removed his cuffs and blindfold, and gave him a plane ticket and travel money. If he opened his mouth, they would poison his son after a week, a month, a year, or any time at all. Then he was allowed to walk away, squinting in sudden sunlight. The two PRD members cornered in the hospital were released after a month and half, given new clothes, sent east across Java to their hometowns.

Pius Lustrilanang was the first to risk going public with his story. On April 27, he returned to Jakarta and gave a public statement to the National Human Rights Commission. Dozens of journalists crowded in to record his words. "I am saying this at the risk of being killed," he told them. The slender thirty-year old with short-cropped curly hair halted his testimony twice to hold back tears. He softly asked for a glass of water and pushed on, describing his abduction, torture, and confinement into the microphones with as much clarity and detail as the blindfolds and trauma allowed. He urged others to come forward. He asked for protection for his family.[12]

When the event ended, staff from the American embassy drove him straight to a flight to the Netherlands. In the rush he left his bag in the car, and flew to Europe with only the clothes he was wearing. He spoke to journalists, parliamentarians, and human rights groups. He traveled on to Washington, DC, where he testified before Congress and sat for a *New York Times* interview.[13] Before Congress, he recounted the words of his captors: "There are no laws here and no human rights. You simply have to answer all our questions. And remember, some people leave this place alive and some as corpses."

The next victims to be released were not sent home with travel money and a threat, but handed over to the police and charged with the capital crime of subversion. The roommates Nezar, Mugi and Aan were among these, as was the head of their group, Andi Arief. When Munir found them in police detention, their stories of abduction and torture were strikingly similar, from being tossed into a back seat with bound hands and blindfolds to torture with electricity, beatings, and blocks of ice. Many were asked about PRD's links to opposition figures and other challenges to Suharto's rule. It looked like the abductions were part of a coordinated campaign, perhaps even a state policy.

Nezar's detention had been typically brutal, if shorter than most. The car had pulled away from the apartment block in Klender, windows rolled tight and house music blaring. Nezar heard the cassette turn over once, and guessed the ride took close to an hour. He prayed for a miracle, that before the men killed him Suharto would collapse and die. He considered leaping from the speeding car, thinking he would die whether he jumped or stayed. He performed *dhikr*, a prayer of rhythmic repetition. At last they stopped, and a man said into a walkie-talkie, "*Merpati. Merpati.*" At this code word, meaning "dove," a gate opened for them to proceed. When the car stopped again, Nezar was hustled into a cold room, stripped to his underwear, and tied to a folding chair.

The questions came fast: "What are your aliases? Where's your leader? Who funds you?" They asked about the explosion in Tanah Tinggi.

The first time Nezar said, "I don't know," a foot smashed into his jaw and the folding chair collapsed. He lay on the floor, lips warm and salty with blood, trying to catch his breath, while the men found another chair. That one was smashed to pieces soon enough too.

They moved him to a cot, and his left hand was handcuffed and his feet tied. When he answered another question with "I don't know" he tensed up, ready for a blow that never came. After a pause, someone barked, "Get the generator." Nezar heard a sound like the crack of a whip, as the device charged. Someone roughly attached electrodes to his calves and to his thighs, and a moment later electricity coursed through his body in waves. He was sure his bones would break, and he heard his own voice cry out in unbearable pain, "Allahu Akbar!"

"Do you want to overthrow Suharto?" asked the voice fiercely. The shocks came again and again for three hours, no matter what answer he gave. Finally, they electrocuted his chest until the whole bed vibrated. Just before he passed out, he heard a voice, perhaps a doctor, warning his tormentors not to shock his chest again.

When he wasn't being tortured, Nezar was locked in a cell. It was about two by three yards, with walls and ceilings made of the type of iron mesh used for reinforcing concrete, with doors of iron bars. Each cell had a *mandi* for bathing, a toilet, and a wooden bed. Raffia twine bit into Nezar's wrists and he shivered in his underwear on a cot. He couldn't tell day from night through his blindfold. There was an occasional ear-splitting siren to disorient and frighten the captives. Whenever he was not being questioned himself, he could hear Aan's screams, a sound worse than torture.

Soon he recognized another voice screaming in pain, and realized their roommate Mugi was there as well.

Mugi had come home with a bag of Japanese fast food from an Australian activist, a meaningful gift for the cash-strapped roommates. He'd even called ahead to tell Nezar the good news. But now when he knocked on their door, there was no answer. He knocked again, and a neighbor emerged to tell him, "Your friends are out. They said they'd be right back." Believing the lie, Mugi searched for his key and went in.

He entered to find the apartment ransacked. On the table, next to a bag of oranges, there was a glass of water, still warm from when Nezar had poured it from the kettle.

Mugi kept calling Nezar's phone, up until the moment he looked out the window to the street below. Seeing men surrounding the building, he whispered, to no one, "I'm dead." Mugi killed the lights and sank to the floor. Then he stood and turned the lights on. There was no point in hiding now. Within moments came the banging on the door, and a shout, "Open the door! Open the door!" Ten men, two of them in uniform, took him away. Mugi was sure he would be killed.

But something confusing happened instead. It seems that two competing abduction squads crossed paths. After Nezar and Aan were taken, a member of that team had remained outside, waiting for the two remaining roommates. Around eight p.m., he headed inside, only to be detained along with Mugi by soldiers from a local army post. They were both taken to the Duren Sawit Subdistrict Military Command, and then the district military command, Kodim 0505.[14] The first abduction team eventually came to extract both their colleague and Mugi, but by that time many people had seen Mugi in custody.

The mix-up may have saved Mugi's life. Or he might have Munir's press conferences or billboards to thank. Whatever the cause, the torture stopped after three days, and the three friends were handed over to a local police station. Police questioned Nezar again, made him sign a detention order for the capital crime of subversion, and put him in a cell two doors down from Mugi. Aan was on his other side, a little farther down.

One day, a guard told Nezar he had a visitor. He recognized Munir immediately. He was getting famous and was also known as a friend to PRD after hiding the fugitive from the Tanah Tinggi explosion. Munir told Nezar that he'd been searching for the roommates, gathering any clues to the whereabouts of those still missing. In low tones, Nezar told him that between torture sessions he'd been brought to the bathroom. He'd been blindfolded, but heard the sound of drilling and marching, and sometimes voices from the yard yelling, "*Hidup* Kopassus!" Long live the Special Forces! Munir asked Nezar to be ready to go public with his story once he was free. His visit put Nezar in good spirits, confident that if he was patient and kept fighting, the law would function in the end.

Munir was closing in on the detention site. Nezar had a sense of how far they'd been driven. Others reported the sound of soldiers training and aircraft landing. Pius believed the site was near an airport and not far from the Jakarta–Bogor toll road. Another detainee later said he'd heard radio stations from both Bogor and Jakarta.

In two months of captivity, Pius never saw the face of his captors. They wore ski masks during the rare moments he wasn't blindfolded. Focusing on the eyes of the people who delivered food, Pius counted at least a dozen different people. The questions they asked him indicated the kidnappers were intent on safeguarding Suharto's reelection in March. He couldn't say with certainty they were soldiers, but the abduction and detention seemed far too professional for civilians, and every afternoon he heard a trumpet sounding for roll call. On the morning Pius was released, one captor revealed he was a graduate of the armed forces academy, before delivering a final electric shock as "a token of remembrance."[15] When Desmond Mahesa was ready to go public, he stood and spoke into a dozen mikes at a packed press conference at LBH. He said that although the blindfold and the lost glasses made it hard to identify his captors, he could see that one carried an FN pistol, the army's sidearm of choice.[16]

Taken together, this information led to a possible location: the sprawling headquarters of the army's Special Forces in Cijantung, East Jakarta. Until recently the red berets of Komando Pasukan Khusus, or Kopassus, were under the command of General Prabowo Subianto, the president's son-in-law. Suharto had just given Prabowo command of Kostrad, the Strategic Reserve.

Prabowo had then interceded with his father-in-law to overrule the army commander and name as his replacement a close friend and ally, General Muchdi Purwopranjono. Muchdi was a few years ahead of Prabowo at the academy but had only two stars to Prabowo's three. He'd drafted behind Prabowo's rapid rise through the ranks, and he was known as a loyal follower. Muchdi became Kopassus commander on March 28, right in the middle of the abductions.

As important as pinpointing the captors was identifying victims who had not yet surfaced. Detainees had come and gone from the two rows of three cells, earlier victims overlapping briefly with new arrivals. Desmond, the first detainee of 1998, joined two young bus drivers, supporters of Megawati, who had been missing for almost a year. One was Yani Afri, Tuti Koto's son, the other was his friend Sonny. When Pius arrived the next day, he was put into Sonny's suddenly empty cell. When the torture stopped, often past midnight, and if there was a break in the Mustang FM hit radio or the house music cassette playing full volume, and if the detainees could gather the courage, they began to whisper through the rebar grids that separated the cells. They learned who was there and who had been there recently. They memorized phone numbers, promising to call parents if they were ever released. Yani Afri made jokes that had Pius laughing in the dark.[17] He also told the others of seeing three missing supporters of the semi-opposition United Development Party (PPP), back in May 1997.

By the time Nezar and his roommates arrived on March 13, Yani Afri was gone from the cells. When Pius was released in April, he called Yani Afri's home as he had promised to do. When he asked Tuti Koto if she was the mother of Rian, a name only his family used, she knew that Pius had seen her son alive. And when Pius learned the young man had not returned home, he knew he was dead. His captor had told him, "Some people leave this place alive and some as corpses."

In the cells, Pius also spoke to Herman Hendrawan. He told Pius he was abducted after the press conference at LBH on March 12, near the hospital where his two colleagues were cornered in a bathroom. Those two, Raharja Waluyo Jati and Faisol Riza, never spoke to Herman during their captivity, but they were sure they heard him singing two love songs, "Widuri" and "Camelia." One interrogator showed them a polaroid of Herman, further proof he'd been there. Pius thought Herman spent a day and a night in the cells. He was never seen again.

Another missing figure was never seen there, but his name was heard. Several of those freed had been questioned about the whereabouts of Wiji Thukul, a radical working-class poet who headed the PRD artists' organization in Solo. He'd been underground since 1996, like Nezar working to advance the organization's daring agenda of regime change in and around Jakarta. A poem he wrote on the run includes the lines:

I will surely come home
maybe in middle of the night

maybe at dawn
surely
and maybe
but don't
you wait[18]

Wiji Thukul spoke to his wife for the last time in December 1997. It appears the authorities were still searching for him in April, and must have found him soon after.

There had been previous disappearances in Indonesia. Countless were missing from the violence of 1965, as well as the running conflicts of Papua, Aceh, and East Timor, and smaller acts of violence, such as the attack on the PDI headquarters in 1996 or the Petrus killings of alleged criminals in the 1980s. These disappearances were a by-product of mass murder, as bodies were disposed of in mass graves or the sea.

It was not until 1997 and 1998 that disappearances were used in Indonesia as a systematic tactic to destroy opposition and instill fear, as they had been in Argentina and Chile. The targets were clearly political, whether party loyalists or pro-democracy activists. The interrogations of survivors focused on threats to the selection of Suharto for another term. The similarity of the victims' stories indicated that abductions had become a policy of the state.

By early May, KontraS had decided to publicly accuse the army of carrying out the kidnappings. Munir and his young crew of volunteers agreed not to back down, no matter what.

4

Usman

May 1998

The pressure on Suharto was building to unprecedented levels. His broad promises of future reforms were failing to tamp down the student protests. Prices continued to surge, sparking unrest beyond the campuses. The decisive moment arrived at Trisakti University, a small campus tucked into a curve of the Jakarta Inner Ring Road. Trisakti students were not known for being politically engaged or outspoken. Classes were filled with the relatively affluent children of civil servants, businessmen, and military officers. The joke went that instead of protesting against Suharto, the students could just go home and convince their parents he had to go.

But on the afternoon of May 12, 1998, Usman Hamid joined classmates to watch the lowering of the red and white bars of the Indonesian flag to half-staff in protest of the Suharto government. They broke into the national anthem:

Indonesia, my homeland
Land where my blood is spilled

Usman's pride in the protest was undercut by a rising fear. He wondered if this protest would lead to a better country or just to more violence.

Until now, Usman's mode of rebellion had been musical. When he was twelve, his brother gave him a cassette of *Imagine*, and later an acoustic guitar. He started playing John Lennon songs in a grade school band, before turning to the Sex Pistols in search of more edge. He practiced whenever his father was at his building supply shop or at the mosque. He wanted Usman to become a religious scholar, not a musician, though he did acknowledge the role of music in spreading Islam across Java five hundred years before.[1] When Usman was fourteen, his father fell very sick. One December night, his father tried to get out of bed to pray with Usman as they usually did, but he couldn't manage. After midnight, Usman woke up to the sounds of his father being taken to the hospital. He died just before dawn.

While two of Usman's brothers studied at a respected Islamic boarding school, three others were *jagos*. Literally meaning fighting cocks, the centuries-old term referred to village or neighborhood enforcers with a love of street-fighting and perhaps a hand in protection rackets.[2] Usman's father had founded a well-known martial arts group, and all the brothers studied kung fu and tae kwan do, while their little sister studied karate. All the siblings learned some *tenaga dalam*, or inner power, a mix of magic, martial arts, and dangerous tricks, like chewing razor blades or pressing a *keris* (dagger) into the chest to prove their invincibility. Those who mastered the art were said to be able to become invisible or knock down foes from a distance. Usman fought a little in junior high, but by high school, he was more interested in religion, girls, and above all, music.

Usman's broad, open face easily betrayed his emotions, with a tendency to grimace while puzzling through a problem before erupting in easy laughter with the answer. He kept his shaggy hair parted in the middle like a teen idol. In college, Usman pursued both music and religious studies. By his third year at Trisakti, Usman's band was taking off, even recording an album at a villa in the Puncak hills. He felt like the Rolling Stones recording in a French chateau. They shot footage for a video near Jakarta's old harbor, strutting around the collapsing godowns that once stored Moluccan spices and Sumatran tobacco for the Dutch East India Company. But Usman was unsure if he wanted a career in music. He was studying law, and was drawn to both religion and politics.

He lived at home, where his older brother bought an array of newspapers each morning. Usman read about the economic crisis at the breakfast table, and the brothers discussed it worriedly with their mother. She was an Islamic teacher whose followers, many of them poor, met in a hall in the back of Usman's house. Usman occasionally worked with other students to purchase sugar, salt, coffee, and instant noodles in bulk to make holiday care packages for the poor. But as 1998 began, Usman saw a much broader swath of society lining up, desperate for the basics of living.

This desperation brought demonstrators to the streets in numbers not seen for decades. Student groups had once mounted protests against Soekarno in 1964–65, contributing to his downfall and Suharto's rise. But students were also among the first to challenge the New Order, taking to the streets in 1974 to demand lower prices and an end to corruption. When violent riots broke out, most likely instigated by Suharto's intelligence apparatus, the authorities cracked down, arresting hundreds of people. Three years later, when students dared to protest around the elections, Suharto began reining in campus activism. By 1980, a Law on Campus Life Normalization had eliminated the independence of student councils and similar bodies.

After 1989, consistent with the policy of *keterbukaan*, or openness, the government eased its grip on demonstrations and free expression on campus, though organizers never knew if they would end up on trial for subversion. Activists formed underground discussion groups, and organized to support the victims of economic development, like the labor activist Marsinah or farmers displaced by a dam.

The economic crisis arrived in late 1997, and by March of the following year, there were thirty or forty protests *each day* at universities throughout the country. As long as they remained peaceful and on campus, the army tolerated them, so much so that some observers wondered if the military sympathized with their positions.[3] Through these protests, students helped crystalize broad anger about corruption and the economy into clear political demands: an end to the military's role in politics, repeal of repressive laws, and a transition to democracy.[4] By April, their demand was even more pointed: Suharto must step down. By the end of that month, students started marching out the campus gates, risking direct confrontation with the army. In Bandung, Bali, and Semarang, there were clashes with security forces. In the country's third largest city, Medan, students escalated to hurling stones and Molotov cocktails, while security forces moved from batons and rattan canes to tear gas and rubber bullets.[5]

Tensions were already rising throughout Indonesia as the protests reached Trisakti. The campus's first big demonstration, on May 8, pulled in more than five thousand students. The next demonstration was planned for May 12, including a high-risk march on the parliament building. That morning Usman went to his property law class. Partway through a lecture on condominiums, he got word that heavily armed troops were moving toward campus. He informed the lecturer that the students had to prepare themselves for the march, and she ended the class immediately, one of several acts of support from the faculty.

That afternoon, Usman watched the crowd swell around him, first a hundred people, then a thousand, then three thousand. A chant began, *"Turunkan harga! Turunkan harga!"* It was literally a call to bring down prices but was also shorthand for TURUNKAN SuHARto dan keluar-GA, or "bring down Suharto and his family!"

Even in code, the bold statement was thrilling. A few feet away from Usman a protestor set fire to a large poster of Suharto. Usman watched as the flames licked at the face adorning every government office and classroom, the ex-general in a suit, graying hair poking out from the formal black *peci* perched on his head. Usman watched the president's impassive face crinkle and blacken. The smell of burning paper mixed with the sweet smoke of clove cigarettes, the faint ozone smell of a coming storm, and the exhaust settling from the overpasses that cradled the little campus. Seeing the portrait burn was exhilarating, but frightening too. Provocateurs often infiltrated protests, finding clever ways to give the military an excuse to move in.

The loud chanting eased and a new phrase threaded its way through the crowd, less a cheer than a rumor of war. *Turun ke jalan.* "Into the streets." Their target was the parliament building, a straight shot down the General S. Parman toll road. Student leaders led the way out through the campus gates, a human fence on each side to protect the march from violence or infiltration by provocateurs. They quickly found the roadway blocked by a phalanx of riot police, their shields raised, face guards down, batons in hand.

Usman saw his friends Wanda and Nadya passing out roses, even tucking them into the scuffed helmets of the riot police. They were trying to counter the propaganda that leaving campus was a prelude to rioting and violence. A line of motorcycles revved behind the riot cops, as trucks brought in more police and then, to Usman's alarm, soldiers. The air crackled with a sense of imminent violence until, at the last minute, a deal was reached. If the students returned to campus, the police would let them protest there. And so they all marched back in through the gates, deflated but relieved that state violence had been averted.

A little before five o'clock, Usman Hamid left his classmates milling about in light drizzle. With the rain coming down and no sign of further action, Usman crossed the road and climbed into a blue, three-wheeled shared taxi, a *bemo*. A half-dozen cramped passengers could sit knee to knee just inches off the slick pavement. He rode the *bemo* and two more buses past jammed intersections, over fetid canals, passing shacks and food stalls, and farther away, great glass malls and luxury towers. The skyline was also pocked with the fast-rusting skeletons of projects gone bust.

Usman clambered out and walked past the tree he used to quickly scale for an armful of mangos if he heard his mother giving them all to a passing street vendor. Beneath the tree were slides and swings for the kindergarten his mother ran, and a cement bench. On the back of the bench, Usman had stenciled the round-lettered logo of the Doors.

The second floor of the L-shaped home was Usman's, with a bedroom and a small music studio. An exterior staircase led to his own entrance, but Usman stopped in downstairs to see his mother. He'd just reached his room and put in a cassette, most likely Guns N' Roses, when his mother yelled up that he had a phone call. He picked up the receiver to hear a friend choke out, "Something happened, Usman, and four people are dead. We're picking up the bullets. We need you here."

Realizing that he should never have left campus, Usman started to head back out until his mother stopped him, begging him to stay home. He agreed, relying on a steady series of calls and footage of the violence on TV to piece together what had happened. Minutes after Usman had left, an argument broke out between students and a man claiming to be an alumnus. He was run off campus, fleeing toward the police. At 5:10, the police surged forward, wielding shields and truncheons, and kicking and stomping those who fell. Students ran down the carless highway ramp or ducked down side streets. Tear gas and rubber bullets sent them diving behind the wooden carts of noodle vendors, or burying their faces in the curb to avoid the blows of the batons, or huddling in the sooty brush that lined the road. A foreign journalist saw two policemen firing rifles indiscriminately as a third walked behind them, collecting the shells.[6]

Camouflage-clad soldiers issued commands from the side of the road, one even kicking a hesitating policeman from behind. No longer in neat rows, the police moved past a student lying awkwardly on his backpack, his face to the falling drizzle. One cop leaned down to punch him, another casually landed a kick to the head without slowing. The boy moved slightly, one of many crumpled figures on the asphalt lying among rocks and lost sandals.

Water cannons opened up from the truck-tops. Helicopters hovered low. A squad of motorcycles chased after the fleeing students, a few of the drivers breaking off to roar up the Grogol flyover. They dismounted, took aim, and opened fire on the campus below. At street level, other armed men fired bullets of some kind through the campus fence.

Hafidin Royan, a civil engineering student with a boyish face and big eyes, was shot in the parking lot, not far from where an architecture student named Elang Mulia Lesmana fell. An IT student named Heri Hartanto went down near a flagpole in the center of campus, and Hendriawan Sie, an economics student, died on a balcony.

In cell nine at police headquarters, Nezar heard singing. It was the song *"Gugur Bunga,"* or "The Fallen Flower," often played for dead heroes. "One falls," it went, "a thousand arise." A cell filled with demonstrators had begun to sing, joined by Mugi and Aan from their cells. Nezar knew the song meant that students must be lying dead somewhere in Jakarta's streets, even before word was passed down to him about Trisakti. Nezar felt this must be the last straw, the end of Suharto.

Early the next morning, Usman performed his dawn prayers and returned to campus. He gazed at the bloodstained ground, marked off with rebar and yellow tape. He exchanged updates on the wounded with his friends, as around him students hugged each other and cried. They hadn't been prepared for anything like this. Trisakti students usually kept their heads down and avoided politics. They didn't really understand the forces that had swept them up. They were, for the most part, having fun, not planning a revolution, and were surprised to have mobilized thousands, then shocked when it turned bloody. Telegrams came in from around the country, one reading:

> The accounting staff of the Holiday Inn
> offers our condolences
> for the fallen heroes of Indonesian reform.
> Forward!
> Never retreat!

Four coffins draped in Indonesian flags were lifted from the wooden tables they rested on and carried out through the campus gates to the cemetery. Thousands of students from various schools walked alongside. But Usman stayed close to campus, sitting in the grass under a tree. He wrote in his diary, "This is what I feared would happen."

A crowd gathered outside the gates, and by midday it became restless, urging the students to leave campus. Usman saw men dressed like civilians but with army haircuts, and thought the soldiers were hoping to provoke the students again, seeking an opportunity for more violence. Usman patrolled the inside of the fence. Instead of the anti-Suharto slogans of the previous day, the people he saw yelled anti-Chinese slurs.

When he got to the corner of campus nearest Glodok, Jakarta's Chinatown, he saw a garbage truck with no driver rolling below the flyover. The crowd set it on fire, and when the truck exploded, they moved on to a gas station and burned that too. The riots spread into Glodok and across the city. Groups of ten or so men were seen arriving at various locations by motorbike, armed with clubs, accelerants, and walkie-talkies. They lobbed stones and Molotov cocktails and called on the crowd to join in the looting and arson.[7] Small units of marines and police tried to control the situation in some areas, but the army did little. There was widespread speculation that factions of the military had encouraged violence to discredit protestors or justify martial law.

Arson consumed a thousand homes and forty shopping malls, where many of the more than 1,200 victims died, trapped in the flames. They had to be buried in mass graves, their bodies burned beyond recognition.

As in other times of economic and political unrest, ethnic Chinese Indonesians were targeted. In his desperation to shift blame for the economic crisis, Suharto had been encouraging propaganda targeting Christians and Chinese Indonesians for months. The widespread arson and looting of Chinese businesses, as well as reports of Chinese women being targeted for sexual assault, sparked an exodus of that community.

On the afternoon of May 13, knowing his mother was scared for him and for her Chinese neighbors, Usman returned home to his neighborhood of Jelambar Baru for a few days. He took pride in his *kampung*, despite the drugs and occasional violence. Residents of the unusually diverse neighborhood celebrated each other's Muslim, Christian, or Buddhist holidays.

When the riots broke out, Usman's brothers and their *jago* friends barricaded the streets leading into the neighborhood. They armed themselves with machetes and a scimitar inscribed with Arabic that had belonged to Usman's father, pulled off a wall in their house where it had always been displayed.

In Cairo for a conference, Suharto watched the riots unfold on TV. He returned to Jakarta early in the morning of May 15, promising elections "as soon as possible" and pledging that he himself would not be a candidate. It sounded like a delaying tactic, and the students demanded nothing less than his immediate resignation or dismissal.[8]

Every morning Nezar shouted from his cell, "Mugi, Aan, how are you?" to keep his friends' spirits up. It was easy to lose hope in the dim cells at police headquarters, between meals of dry old rice with a bit of tempeh or vegetables, facing unfair trials on grave charges. Some prisoners showed the political detainees respect and even kindness. A man accused of stabbing a soldier to death gave Nezar a packet of fresh food from a visitor. It was rice with *jengkol*, a bitter, pungent tree nut Nezar was not accustomed to, but he was grateful for the best thing he'd eaten in a long time.[9]

Nezar ached for news and occasionally got his hands on a scrap of newspaper. What he read gave him hope. One morning he shouted to Mugi, "Don't worry, we'll be free soon!"

"Why, Nez?"

"Students have started demonstrating, all over the city!" cried Nezar.

Then one of the trusties who brought the awful food told Nezar quietly, "Outside of this hell, the students are in the streets. The police are very busy. Every other minute, they grab their equipment and guns, and run to the parliament building and to the campuses."

"How many students?"

"A hundred thousand students. My brother told me he couldn't get through to visit me, that every street was blocked!"

Protestors, looters, and criminals were brought into the cells, all of them mixed together and bringing news of the demonstrations and the riots. Nezar felt a thrill, tempered with an unshakable sadness. He'd risked so much, dreaming of this moment. He was supposed to be out there.

Seven days after the Trisakti shootings, thousands of students marched on the parliament building. Built in 1964 to showcase President Soekarno's leadership of the developing world, the building was to be the site of his boldly named Conference of New Emerging Forces. The event was never held, and throughout the Suharto years the great round structure, with a green roof that sloped skyward in two halves, housed the rubber-stamp parliament.

Demanding the resignation of Suharto, the students, to their surprise, quickly took control of the building without opposition from the army. They transformed it into a symbol of resistance, occupying the offices and clustering on the roof like insects on a great green leaf. More students arrived in buses from all over Java and the outer islands, and parallel protests broke out in every major city. Their exhilaration was mixed with the fear that they might be shot down the moment the army decided enough was enough. Trisakti was only the most recent instance of the security forces opening fire on a demonstration they no longer tolerated.

Suharto's last pillars of support began to collapse around him. Religious leaders abandoned him. The army appeared loyal, and yet the days passed, and they did not remove the occupying students.

There was a rumor that the leaders of LBH would be abducted from their homes. Word might have come through the founders' army contacts, or perhaps one of Munir's sources. The army was deployed throughout the city, the atmosphere was tense, and just a few days before, some men with army haircuts had been asking for Munir's house. The driver Sugiarto picked Munir and Suci up at the house in Jatinegara, as well as two more colleagues (another had decided to stay at home and face the threat).[10] They went first to a hotel near Kampong Melayu terminal, but it was crawling with soldiers, so they pushed on. It was too risky to stop anywhere, so they drove all night. They drove past the National Monument, Sukarno's obelisk topped with a sculpted golden flame, past the Dutch governor's mansion now serving as the presidential palace, past all these monuments to power. Suci, pregnant and unsure when the danger might end, felt fine. Munir was there, making jokes, and they were facing danger together. When the sun rose, Sugiarto dropped them off at home.

Usman, after a few days helping his brothers protect his neighborhood from rioters and agitators, wanted to see the action at the parliament building. On the morning of May 21, he took a bus to Central Jakarta. He walked through halls strewn with garbage after days of occupation, and climbed onto the soaring green roof. He scanned the smoking cityscape and looked down at the army units positioned just outside the grounds.

When Usman came in off the roof, a friend called out, "Usman! We did it!" They pressed in around a TV, everyone hushing to hear the president step to a mike and speak the five words they had all been risking their lives to hear: "I have decided to resign." Suharto was driven away from the palace in a stretch Mercedes with civilian plates, as his stunned vice-president of two months, B. J. Habibie, was sworn in as an interim president.

Usman's ears rang with songs and cheers from the halls and from outside the building. Thousands of students had come to parliament ready to die, and now they were singing, drumming, and dancing in the streets. Usman couldn't believe it. Suharto had already been president for a decade when Usman was born; his face was on the money, the stamps, the walls, year after year, decade after decade. Usman had gone from picking out "Revolution" on his guitar, deciphering lyrics from bootlegged punk cassettes, and other small acts of rebellion, to being part of a real revolution. On his way home, Usman joined with the other passengers to cheer out the bus windows. He breathed in the cooling night air, feeling like a hero in his blue Trisakti blazer.

In the cells at police headquarters, the food improved after Suharto fell, upgraded to takeout Padang food, and the police became nicer. One told Mugi, "Later, when you're an official, don't forget us, okay?"[11]

Nezar was released about two weeks later. Too traumatized to be alone in a hotel, he stayed with Munir. They stayed up late each night for political discussions laced with jokes. Munir confided that he was scared too, but they both had to be brave.[12] After a few days, Nezar was ready, typing out a statement on Munir's laptop and delivering it at a press conference before leaving on the next available flight to Australia. The fall of Suharto did not mean that accusing the military of serious crimes was a safe thing to do. But for Munir, it was essential for victims to find the courage to transform rumors into official reports, to announce them to society. "Without that," he warned, "they would remain rumors. Experience shows that rumors always contain a great danger: they will give birth to, or even consist of, terror itself."[13]

Nezar was among nine kidnapping victims eventually freed. Nobody ever saw the courier Bimo Petrus again, nor the driver Yani Afri, nor the poet Wiji Thukul, nor ten other abductees.

5

Reformasi!

1998–2001

Despite low expectations for the accidental presidency of Suharto's hand-picked vice-president, Habibie's first steps were promising. He lifted press curbs, announced elections, and proposed a vote on independence for East Timor. He released political prisoners, including the aging men convicted long-ago in show trials of communist supporters. He launched inquiries into human rights violations in Aceh and the May 1998 riots.[1]

But Munir held no illusion that Suharto's sudden absence would change everything. For more than three decades, he had hollowed out the core elements of a democracy, such as courts, legislatures, the press, and civilian control of the military. There would be a long fight ahead to build a working democracy, secure justice for past crimes, and end the politics of violence.[2]

The vast project of undoing Suharto's legacy was known by the term *reformasi*, meaning reform or reformation. The word encompassed an agenda that activists had pursued for years at great personal risk—repealing political restrictions, banishing the military from politics, and ending corruption, collusion, and nepotism.[3] The last three items were so familiar and pervasive that, to save time they were referred to collectively by the Indonesian acronym of KKN, for *korupsi*, *kolusi*, and *nepotisme*.

The question of past crimes by the state ran like a subterranean river beneath the fierce debates on *reformasi*.[4] There was a lot of history to reckon with. Suharto had gained power while overseeing one of the worst massacres of the terrible twentieth century. Many Indonesians had been witnesses, victims, or perpetrators. Younger Indonesians were raised on myths, propaganda, and fear of a communist menace. Killings, disappearances, torture, and political trials persisted throughout Suharto's rule, culminating in the shootings, riots, and disappearances of his final months.

Complicating the matter, some factions of the military had, in the end, refused to impose martial law and even encouraged Suharto's resignation. That restraint helped these generals, and the military as a whole, survive Suharto's downfall despite a deep, long connection to him and to atrocities under his rule.

After the police released Nezar, Aan, and Mugi in early June, only the head of Nezar's student organization, Andi Arief, was known to be alive and in police custody.[5] When he was released on July 21, he told of being abducted in South Sumatra by men with the documents and authority to order Military Police at the terminal to let them board the ferry across the Sunda Strait to Java. Once in Jakarta, his interrogators began by saying that, while only God decides if someone lives or dies, "sometimes God works through our hands."[6]

Survivors like Arief provided riveting, effective public testimony. But they were political activists focused on the democratic transition they'd risked their lives to bring about. The family members of the thirteen victims still missing, however, had an enduring commitment to resolving these cases, as well as moral authority and the attention of the public. Munir organized them to become effective advocates for justice.

The military commander, General Wiranto, remained in place, and had promised to protect the former president. The old faces of the New Order hoped to quickly turn the page for the country, or at least for themselves. But even a veneer of reform provided Munir with leverage to address the disappearances. Under pressure to act, on August 3, General Wiranto announced the creation of a body known as a military honor board to consider the continued military service of three officers: Suharto's son-in-law General Prabowo Subianto; his successor as Kopassus commander, General Muchdi Purwopranjono; and Colonel Chairawan, head of the covert operations unit of the Special Forces.[7]

Prabowo had been Kopassus commander for many of the abductions. His faction within the army was also suspected of playing a role in the May riots, presumably to discredit protestors or to force his father-in-law to put him in charge of restoring order.[8] The final straw came on Habibie's first full day in office, when Prabowo ordered his Kostrad troops to take up positions around the presidential palace and the new president's residence, without informing the armed forces chief, Wiranto. Habibie ordered Prabowo removed from his command "before sundown."[9] Muchdi was transferred from Kopassus to a noncombat post. As the army tried to reposition itself in a new Indonesia, Prabowo and his ally Muchdi were left out in the cold.

The honor board hearings took place behind closed doors over several days in August. There was no public decision, but it was reported at the time that the board recommended that Wiranto dismiss Prabowo from military service, and that he did so. Prabowo's offense had been misinterpreting orders, leading to the nine abductions of those released alive. Prabowo left for a comfortable self-exile in Jordan, where his friend King Abdullah, a special forces commander himself, had recently ascended to the throne.

The board also reportedly recommended that General Muchdi and Colonel Chairawan be relieved of their commands. Muchdi had already been transferred to a noncombat role, and he was never given another command. His military career was effectively over, and in 2001 he moved to the newly empowered State Intelligence Agency.

Munir believed that Prabowo's discharge was due more to his defeat by his rival Wiranto than to his role in the abductions.[10] What's more, the abduction operation also clearly relied on cooperation from military intelligence, the Jakarta military command, and the national chief of police.[11] The honor board assigned blame as if the policies and practices of the New Order were just the business of a few rogue officers, rather than a broader, high-level effort to keep Suharto in power. The victims' families deserved justice and truth, but Prabowo and these senior officers also deserved their day in court.[12] Otherwise, the accusations might continue to dog them, and the young democracy as well.[13]

———————

Munir was born the year that Suharto began his seizure of power. Thirty-three years later, in September 1998, Munir's first child was born alongside the new era of *reformasi*. He and Suci decided their son would go by Alif, the first letter of the Arabic alphabet, as a nod to his heritage and birth order. The rest of his name also drew on an Arab tradition of naming children in a way that reflects one's prayers for them. Munir's parents had hoped he would be a source of light to the world and so named him the Arabic for bright or shining. Munir and Suci wanted a just and peaceful leader and gave him a first name of Soultan. The baby's full name was Soultan Alif Allende, in honor of the martyred president whose example inspired Munir to fight for workers' rights.

Alif was only a few weeks old when it became clear that state violence was not a problem of the past. In November 1999, the one thousand members of the People's Consultative Assembly held a special session to schedule elections and decide other reform issues. The super-parliament's membership was the same as it had been seven months before when it returned Suharto to the presidency with greater powers.

Impatient for change, tens of thousands of students and workers returned to the streets. They demanded a transition that did not depend on the compromised leadership and tattered constitution of the Suharto era. They called for Habibie's resignation and the immediate expulsion of the military from politics. On November 9, a march started at the LBH office, choosing routes to draw in residents of poor *kampungs* along the way to swell the ranks beyond the usual student protests. The column faced off against the army, the police, and thousands of members of *pam swakarsa*, civil defense forces organized and trained by the army. These young men from the urban poor communities and villages were armed with bamboo spears, simple arms with symbolic meaning as the onetime weapons of the fight for independence.

After days of protests and clashes, on November 13, Usman entered the same parliament building he'd climbed atop the day Suharto resigned. Recently elected to lead his student senate, he and other student leaders moved through the halls to lobby for reform. They weren't allowed in the main auditorium, where General Wiranto was making a presentation on the role of the military in the new Indonesia.

Munir and Suci with Alif, 1999 (personal photo, Suciwati)

Usman could hear the loud singing and chanting of the protestors out-side. Then came another sound, a long volley of gunfire. Around him, people took off at a run. Usman wanted to stay with the protestors, but was persuaded that Trisakti students had shed enough blood, and he was evacuated. When the smoke cleared and crowds had fled, 17 protestors lay dead and 400 more injured. The incident became known as Semanggi, a kind of water clover that had given its name to a nearby highway cloverleaf.

A year later, another round of violence near the same location became known as Semanggi II. On the night of September 23, 1999, security forces confronted great crowds of protestors opposed to a bill to expand military powers during emergencies. For twenty-four hours, the police and soldiers deployed tear gas, rubber bullets, and beatings, and suffered injuries themselves from Molotov cocktails and other projectiles. On the evening of September 24, Yun Hap was eating some bread near Jakar-ta Hospital before returning to campus. He'd spent the day protesting, despite his mother's warning that the year of the snake was a bad time to take such a risk. Army trucks sped by, with soldiers shooting in a manner described as *babi buta*, like blind pigs. One bullet lodged in Yun Hap's jaw and killed him.[14] He was one of six fatalities, alongside more than a hun-dred injuries, over two days.[15]

Usman was leading the effort see the Trisakti shooters identified and punished. It seemed natural for him to take on that role for Semanggi I and
II as well. He met with lawmakers, the attorney general, and even General Wiranto, commander of the armed forces. Receiving only denials and
delays for his efforts, Usman felt his limitations. He was a twenty-two-
year-old student of agrarian law who liked to play music. He felt guided
more by a desire for justice than by knowledge of human rights, international law, or investigations. He needed someone to teach him to swim in
this new ocean.

Usman had first heard of Munir just before Suharto's fall. He hadn't
really followed the abductions at the time, but after the Trisakti shootings, he carefully followed Munir's words and tactics.

Usman met Munir near LBH headquarters. KontraS was moving out
of its single room there to its own office nearby, and the two found a quiet
place to talk nearby in the welcome shade of a spreading tree. The air
felt fresh and warm to Usman, the surroundings surprisingly green for
Jakarta. He explained to Munir that the police and the army were blaming
each other for the Trisakti shootings. Ballistics tests failed to prove who
fired the live ammunition. The police invited Usman to go to Canada for
more tests, but he wasn't sure he should go.

Munir shrugged. "Usman, go to Canada if you want the experience. But
you can't lose sight of the big picture."

He told Usman about his work on the case of the young factory worker
Marsinah, who went out to buy dinner one night and was never seen alive
again. Munir warned Usman, "Don't be too preoccupied with the bullets.
I was just like you, following the lead of the army and police during the
investigation. We were focused on the blood in the car, in the military
post, or in the police station. Was it Marsinah's blood? We went abroad to
different labs, and at the end of the day, it wasn't anybody's blood. Whose
blood was it, then? A chicken's?" Munir asked Usman, his voice rising in
anger. "I experienced this before, Usman. And I got tricked."

Munir first worked on the Marsinah case just after her death, but he was
telling Usman about something more recent. Authorities in East Java had
reopened the investigation into Marsinah's death, questioning more than

a dozen witnesses and suspects again. Evidence was again collected from the factory owner's house, the district military command, a vehicle, and other possible crime scenes. There were preliminary reports of a positive match to Marsinah, but in the end the investigation went nowhere, and no new charges were brought.[16]

Munir continued, "If you wait for the ballistics results, you won't get anything. It's too technical, Usman. You don't understand. We don't understand. In the Marsinah case, I got trapped, and it wasn't the right direction to go in. Don't fight with them in their own boxing ring, Usman. Take them outside the ring, and fight them there."

"How do I do that?"

"It's simple, Usman. The soldiers were deployed to counter the students, to block them from moving off campus. There are rosters of the low-ranking military and police in the field at Trisakti. If the army wanted to take responsibility, they could start with these guys and go up the chain of command to hold commanders responsible. Usman, those low-ranking soldiers and police didn't have the *autonomy* to decide to shoot students! The one with authority is the head of the armed forces. General Wiranto."

"But he was so far removed from the shootings! And the demonstration had already ended. It didn't look planned."

"He wasn't so far removed. Look at his statements in the days before the shooting: 'Students, don't leave campus, or something will happen.'[17] The military was ready to do anything to stop the students. Now connect this to what happened on the ground."

Munir urged Usman to look at the timeline of the Trisakti shootings. There were plans for a huge action a week later, modeled on the People Power demonstrations that toppled President Ferdinand Marcos in the Philippines in 1986. Trisakti was an opportunity to "precondition" students to stay home, not an accident or the "excesses" of a few low-ranking soldiers. While some observers pinned the shootings on the more extreme Prabowo faction, Munir saw them as fully consistent with even the more cautious Wiranto, part of an effort to protect the Suharto government.

Usman began to reject the official investigation as a whitewash. He also began spending almost every day at KontraS. When the head of the

Military Police rebuked him, "What's wrong with you? You're like Munir now!" Usman took it very much as a compliment.

The honor board was not the last word on the abductions. A military police investigation had begun even before the fall of Suharto. By the end of June 1998, the armed forces commander Wiranto revealed that the military had identified those responsible for the kidnappings.[18] They were members of a Kopassus task force called Tim Mawar, the Rose Team. All eleven members were arrested in July 1998, and in December a court martial convened in East Jakarta.

Eleven young men in uniform, red berets tucked into their epaulets above Kopassus patches, sat on benches, a few biting their nails or jiggling their legs. The only survivor to testify was Nezar, who described his capture at the Klender apartment and his torture and interrogation that followed. Unlike the honor board, the court martial was open to the public. Yani Afri's mother, Tuti Koto, knew about the trial only from Munir. She'd never been informed that it would take place, but Tuti Koto sat there for every minute of the three months of hearings. She listened as the leader of Team Mawar, Major Bambang Kristiono, claimed that the idea to form a team and kidnap people spontaneously arose from his concerns about radical activists disrupting national stability.[19]

Kristiono stated, "Because we were compelled by the voice of conscience, we took safeguarding actions towards them." That euphemism, safeguarding, or *pengamanan*, is expansive. Munir noted that the Indonesian military has always constructed a logic, even a mythology, to justify human rights violations as not just tolerable, but heroic. Munir described the soldier's statement not as a fantasy, but as an absurd reality. For the soldier and to some extent to the rest of the country it was indeed a reality, no matter how absurd or wrong-headed.[20]

One day, in the driveway outside the courthouse, Tuti Koto brushed off the cautions of her companions and approached a laughing member of Team Mawar. Walking alongside, she tried to engage him.

"May I have a word with you? My son was kidnapped."

The smile faded from the soldier's face.

"Can you help me?"

He looked straight ahead.

"He hasn't come back."

The young soldier did not respond.

In April 1999, the eleven soldiers stood for their sentence. All were found guilty of deprivation of liberty, with prison terms of twelve to twenty-two months. Five were also sentenced to be discharged from the army. They marched out in cadence, arms swinging, as fellow soldiers cheered, "Commando!"

Munir found the trial no more satisfying than the honor board. The soldiers were charged only with abducting the nine who were freed. There was no mention of the thirteen missing, some of whom were abducted in the same manner and held at the same site. The systematic use of torture was not raised at the trial. Team Mawar operations must have been supported by senior military, intelligence, and police officials and institutions, but there was no investigation into command responsibility or testimony by superior officers.

What's more, some abductions predated the formation of the team, and nine took place after Prabowo handed over the Kopassus command to Muchdi. The range of time and leadership, as well as the facilities and coordination required, convinced Munir that the disappearances were a political policy of the Suharto government to preserve its power. The targets in each of three phases were those who most threatened the president's power at that moment: first, supporters of his political rivals around the parliamentary elections of 1997; then, activists who might disrupt his rubber-stamped reappointment in March 1998; and finally, participants in the street protests that ultimately brought him down. Interrogators asked many questions about Suharto's political opponents. The abductions were not the rogue actions of soldiers motivated by individual patriotism. In Munir's view, the honor board and the court martial were not so much legal processes as attempts to accommodate public pressure without ever going beyond the comfort zone of the military.[21]

A stark demonstration of the lack of civilian control over the military came in September 1999 in East Timor. Once a Portuguese colonial backwater set obstinately among the Dutch East Indies, East Timor shares an island with Indonesia's West Timor. In 1974, Portugal abruptly dismantled a dictatorship at home and a decaying five-hundred-year-old empire abroad. Citing fears of communism on its border, Indonesia promptly invaded East Timor, with the approval of President Gerald Ford and Henry Kissinger, just months after the fall of Saigon. Indonesia was responsible for widespread killings and mass starvation, and decades of torture, detention, and attacks on civilians, as the military tried to wipe out a small band of guerrillas in the mountains and a clandestine resistance in the towns. As Indonesia poured funds into its newest province, East Timor became a cash cow for the army, while deployment there became a means to promotion.

Early in his presidency, Habibie offered East Timor a chance to vote on whether to stay within Indonesia. The United Nations would administer the voting on August 30, 1999, although Indonesia would remain in charge of security. President Habibie's decision to remove "the pebble in the shoe" of Indonesia's foreign affairs dismayed many elements within the armed forces.

As in other conflict areas, in East Timor the military had begun creating armed civilian groups soon after the 1975 invasion. Prabowo, after serving in East Timor in the 1970s and 80s, played a key role in counterinsurgency strategy in the mid-1990s as Kopassus commander.[22] He is believed to have set up a paramilitary group called *Gadapaksi* in 1995 to infiltrate and destroy the clandestine resistance movement. Dressed in black and armed with knives, *Gadapaksi* combined elements of death squads with features of *preman*, gangsters involved in smuggling, gambling, and protection rackets. Once the referendum was announced, *Gadapaksi* and older civil guard units quickly transformed into militias, joined by new groups to ensure a presence in every district. The army supplied these pro-Indonesia militias with weapons, equipment, training, and, in some cases, active duty soldiers.[23]

Munir followed these events as they unfolded through the work of the local KontraS office. In Covalima District, KontraS documented a January 24, 1999, attack by the Mahidi militia. The name stood for the slogan *Mati hidup dengan Indonesia*, or Live and die with Indonesia. The name was also an homage to an Indonesian general named Mahidin Simbolon, who helped create and support the militias. The Mahidi attack caused thousands of inhabitants from ten villages to flee to the district capital of Suai.[24] A tent camp grew up around an old parish church and a half-built cathedral nearby. Suai was by no means secure, as it was in the territory of both Mahidi and another of the new and unpredictable militias, Laksaur.

In April, just before UN staff arrived in the long-closed territory, the army backed the militias in mass killings in several districts. The violence continued even after international election staff and observers arrived. Their militia proxies allowed the army to claim to be upholding their neutral security role under the UN-brokered agreement.

The Sunday before the August 30 vote, three priests in Suai held a reconciliation mass in the old church. Militia leaders surrendered a bundle of handmade weapons, and Timorese from the pro-independence and pro-Indonesia groups embraced with great emotion.[25] Later the same day, militia leaders met with the district head, Colonel Herman Sedyono. He'd spent his army career subjugating East Timor, and was about to see his life's work put to a vote. Sedyono told the militias to be ready to burn the district to the ground and to force its inhabitants across the border if they chose independence. It would discredit the ballot results by showing that Timorese were voting with their feet.[26]

On August 30, after nearly 100 percent turnout nationwide, armored cars took the ballot boxes from Suai to the capital for the count. Many voters fled to guerrilla cantonments in the mountains or to the church compound, the indelible ink still on their fingers. On September 4 the results were announced, with 78 percent rejecting the option of staying within Indonesia.

That night the militias and soldiers began burning Suai down. The next day hundreds of people fled from the compound into the forests at the urging of the priests, leaving about 1,500 people, mostly women and children. On the afternoon of September 6, an armed Laksaur convoy headed to the church, backed by soldiers and the district head, Colonel Sedyono, armed with a rifle and clad in jungle-green fatigues. The soldiers lobbed grenades and fired guns into the compound, and the militia poured in with machetes, swords, and homemade guns. Militia members went to the priests' quarters, killing as they went. Witnesses saw a Laksaur leader shoot Father Hilario in the chest and step on his body. They saw Father Francisco stabbed and slashed to death and Father Dewanto killed in the old church.[27] Those who tried to escape the compound were shot by soldiers and police. The militias had threatened that if East Timor stayed within Indonesia, blood might drip, but that, if it left, the blood would flow.[28] They had kept their promise; a crimson rill flowed out of the church, across the compound, and into the street.[29]

The events in Suai were just one part of a coordinated campaign of murder, arson, rape, and forced removal of a third of the population over the border. According to communications captured by Australian intelligence, as well as testimony from a defecting militia leader, the forced expulsions received logistical support from the Minister of Transmigration, A. M. Hendropriyono. The retired general also helped channel funds to the militias before the vote.[30]

After weeks of extreme violence that took around a thousand lives, the Indonesian military withdrew under international pressure. Militias looted and killed freely until international peacekeepers arrived and began to assert control on September 20. The militias fled to West Timor, joining a hundred thousand hostages, as well as some pro-Indonesia families who came voluntarily.

While the rampage was under way, Munir sent the KontraS head of investigations, Indra Listiantara, to gather information in Atambua, just over the border in West Timor.[31] But Indra saw a chance to slip into East Timor by car with journalists. He crossed the border at Balibo under the guns of Indonesian soldiers perched on age-blackened Portuguese battlements. Indra drove along the high coastal cliffs, past razed villages and abandoned militia checkpoints, until he reached the ruined capital of Dili. Almost three quarters of the buildings in the territory had been burned down or smashed to pieces. Machete-wielding militiamen owned the streets, fueled by fear, fleeting power, and amphetamines.

When he called to check in, Munir asked, "How did you get to Dili? Atambua was enough!" Munir tasked him with checking on local KontraS staff, gathering testimony, and looking for evidence of military support for the militias. At night Indra slept in an abandoned police building by the harbor. Indra found an empty militia post littered with partially destroyed files that he carefully collected. Several times a day he called Munir, who took down his report, offered advice, and urged Indra not to be reckless. When it was time to leave, Indra talked his way onto an Indonesian military aircraft. He claimed to be a stranded Indonesian just trying to get home, which, in a sense, he was.

The violence in East Timor showed that the military was unreformed and beyond civilian control. The question now was whether free elections, new laws, and other reforms could hold the perpetrators to account for crimes against humanity. Justice for the Timorese was at stake, but so was the future of Indonesia.

In October Habibie ordered an inquiry as a first step. The Commission for Human Rights Violations in East Timor (KPP-HAM) was made up of five members of the National Human Rights Commission and four human rights activists, one of whom was Munir. Soon after, the United Nations launched an inquiry, intensifying pressure on Indonesia to make a credible effort or face a possible international tribunal.

In November, Munir traveled with a University of Indonesia forensics expert named Budi Sampurna and the head of the inquiry, a respected human rights figure named H. S. Dillon, to a village just across the serpentine border between East and West Timor. A witness had told them of soldiers and militia members burying bodies at the site on the morning of September 7. Guarded by thirty policemen, investigators began digging at seven a.m., just yards from the edge of the Timor Sea that separates Indonesia from Darwin, Australia. One grave held the bodies of the three priests murdered in Suai. As the day warmed and the sun began to beat down, two other graves gave up twenty-four more bodies from the Suai church killings. Schoolbooks were found among the belongings, and the youngest victim was a five-year-old who had bled to death from stab wounds to the chest. Other bodies showed gunshots to the head, or neck bones and spinal cords severed by sharp weapons. Helping to lift the remains out of three mass graves in the heat and the stench, Munir held in his hands the grim evidence that Suharto's fall did not mean an end to horrific state violence. Most of the bodies were handed over to the International Committee of the Red Cross to be buried in their home villages, but Munir and Dillon brought the priests' remains to Dili themselves.[32] In Suai, the team found more charred bones and clothes, burned in an attempt to conceal the massacre.

The team worked quickly, issuing their report on the last day of January 2000. They found evidence of systematic, wide-scale, and gross violations of human rights, including murder, torture, disappearances, violence against women and children, forced evacuation, and a scorched-earth campaign. Countering the propaganda in Indonesia, the report attributed these violations not to a spontaneous civil war among the Timorese, but to a systematic campaign by militias armed, trained, and funded by Indonesian military, police, and civilian authorities.[33] These acts amounted to crimes against humanity.

Remarkably, the report also identified the suspected perpetrators by name, something even the international commission did not do. They included the governor, five district heads (including Colonel Sedyono from Suai), six militia leaders, soldiers with ranks from private to general, and the head of the police in East Timor.[34] The report also noted, "General Wiranto as Armed Forces Commander is the party that must be asked to bear responsibility." By now Wiranto served in the cabinet as coordinating minister of politics and security.

The report requested that the government investigate the suspects and form a special court to try them. It also called for reform of both the armed forces and intelligence institutions. Munir's influence on the report was clear in the bold decision to name names, but also in the emphasis on rethinking the entire role of the military and intelligence in a democracy. Prosecuting the perpetrators would be essential, but Munir was not interested in just "getting" some generals. Munir wanted to transform a nation and a political culture based on violence.

The violence in Timor tested Indonesian reform just as a more democratic process was determining new leadership. In June 1999, Indonesia had held its first democratic elections since 1955. The unchanged constitution still specified indirect elections, with voters choosing representatives to the People's Consultative Assembly, who would then select a president in October. Instead of three quasi-parties under Suharto, forty-eight political parties took part. Six met the threshold to earn seats, led by Megawati's faction of PDI known as the Indonesian Democratic Party of Struggle, or PDI-P. With her party taking a third of the seats, she was presumed to be the next president, particularly once the Assembly rejected Habibie's "accountability report" and he withdrew from the running.

However, an opportunistic coalition of Islamic parties, the old ruling party Golkar, and the military came together to oppose Megawati. They chose instead a respected religious figure and liberal reformer named Abdurrahman Wahid. Known as Gus Dur, the blind, wily political veteran was the leader of Nahdlatul Ulama, or NU, a moderate grassroots Muslim organization with an estimated following of 30 million.[35] To placate Megawati's supporters, Wahid encouraged her to become his vice-president.

Munir was always looking to build the ranks of committed young activists. He was more interested in how people chose to live their lives than whether they had skills that could be learned on the job. He'd used this principle to hire Poengky for her first job in Surabaya. He once explained, "I don't need a thousand people who are smart but lack the values to put it into practice." Munir started bringing his new volunteer Usman to high-level meetings, and even sending him to speak in his place, over Usman's protests.

After a late-night discussion, Munir would say, "Okay, I want to sleep. Usman, write down what we talked about." At five a.m., Munir would emerge from a back room of the office in his plaid sarong to read Usman's summary. He always told Usman to rewrite it, with the same advice: "Don't try to cover too many issues. Choose the most important thing and go deep, find the root of the problem. And move beyond the law. You're too much of a lawyer. You have to think of the politics!" Munir gave Usman books on democracy and military reform and a dog-eared volume on the fall of the dictatorships of Latin America. If Usman admitted falling asleep before finishing them, Munir chided, "You're the worst! You don't have to sleep. You have to read!"

Usman's work with KontraS began to make his mother afraid for him. One night in early 1999, Usman came home after midnight to find his mother waiting up. She brought him a kettle of hot water, and went to make him a packet of instant noodles. Usman mixed the hot water with cold water from the tiled *mandi*, using the plastic dipper to slough off the soot and sweat of the day. He went to his room to pray. His mother found him there, beside the wall he'd painted a few years before. Large letters, each a different color, spelled out, "The Rolling Stones."

"Are you sure about joining KontraS, Usman? Aren't you worried you'll be kidnapped? Those students are still missing. You could be one of them. I don't want to lose you." She started to cry. She'd seen her older sons, the neighborhood *jagos*, get into fights, and one had once been arrested. He was known as Si Kancil, the name of a Javanese mouse deer that is also used to describe a clever person. Accused of attacking a nightclub that didn't pay protection money, the police had arrested and tortured him. Usman never had any interest in street-fighting and had always been busy in his recording studio or absorbed in studies. His mother wasn't used to fretting about him, but now she worried about him the most.

Usman took her hand and said, "Umi, the Quran says not to fear any-one but Allah."

Usman's mother, the religious teacher, said, "Yes, *I* know that. But don't you think . . . the reality is they can hire someone. They can kill you."

"I've lived a long time without my father. I'm strong. I can be brave."

She sighed, seeing it was no use. "Alright then," she said. "Go ahead."

Usman spent months as a general volunteer before Munir tasked him with building public support for their issues. Usman protested, "Why'd you put me in mobilization? I want to work in the legal department. I'm a law student!"

"The law isn't functioning, Usman. I don't need you to be a lawyer. I need you to be an activist. I don't need you in court. I need you to get people into the street."

Several official inquiries were now under way, and Munir wanted any human rights violations they identified to be prosecuted. The dated crimi-nal code and corrupt, inefficient courts were not up to the task, and it was clear new laws were needed. Even filled with New Order politicians and military representatives, parliament passed a law in 1999 that strengthened the National Human Rights Commission and provided for special human rights courts within four years.

But the international pressure around the mayhem in East Timor allowed activists to push for this new judicial option much sooner than that, and not just for Timor. Munir joined the team drafting a law on human rights courts, hoping to introduce features of international law, like command responsibility and crimes against humanity. He also wanted to ensure that new laws could be used to prosecute past cases. The law addressed this thorny problem of retrospective prosecution by establishing two kinds of human rights courts: permanent courts for violations occurring after the passage of the law, and temporary or ad hoc courts for older cases.[36]

The families kept pushing for justice. Tuti Koto, mother of the missing young bus driver Yani Afri, learned to speak to powerful men with whatever volume and directness the situation demanded. In 1999, after waiting for three hours to see the military commander, she spoke to a more junior officer, as Munir observed silently, his arms crossed.

"We want to know if they are no longer alive," she said. "Just be honest, so that we know the fate of our children. So that we don't have to spend our days searching."

The soldier said, "I feel the same but we can't make statements without proof. That wouldn't be right. In the meantime we should pray. Hopefully . . ."

Tuti Koto interrupted, "We've never stopped praying!"[37]

6

Reformasi Stalls

2001–2004

Wahid's presidency was short and tumultuous. The stricken economy lurched along. Conflicts between ethnic and religious groups that broke out under Habibie matured into festering wars. Muslim and Christian communities in the Moluccas and Central Sulawesi waged battles with machetes, homemade firearms, and weapons procured from the army and police. An armed Muslim militia called Laskar Jihad was allowed, despite President Wahid's orders to stop them, to cross Java and travel by ship to join the fray. While local economic and political competition often set the stage for such conflict, Munir and others believed hardline elements in the military encouraged the violence to undermine the civilian leadership and pressure for reform.[1]

President Wahid's efforts to curb the military's role in politics, and his more conciliatory policies toward separatist movements, earned him enemies in uniform. He moved Wiranto out of the chain of command by making him a cabinet minister and then dismissed him from that position soon after. Alongside his reform agenda, Wahid sometimes behaved erratically, with autocratic and ethically questionable tendencies. Such actions provided openings for his political foes, who included his own vice-president, Megawati.

On July 23, 2001, a special session of the People's Consultative Assembly impeached Wahid on a controversial corruption charge, and Megawati Sukarnoputri became president.[2] Like Wahid, she had once been a popular critic of Suharto as well as a member of an elite that had learned to compromise and prosper within the New Order. She seemed even less prepared than Wahid to take on the potent forces that had outlasted the regime.

Despite her populism and opposition credentials, Megawati was a fairly conservative politician who embraced her father's nationalism. She relied on serving and retired generals for advice and support, and one longtime advisor in particular. General A. M. Hendropriyono was a controversial figure, having once commanded soldiers who opened fire and burned down buildings occupied by members of an Islamist community during a siege in Talangsari, on the island of Sumatra, in 1989. More than a hundred people died and dozens were detained and tortured.

He had spent twenty years in the Special Forces, and had seen extensive combat after Indonesia's invasion of East Timor. But he also had strong political skills, several advanced degrees, and a reputation as a shrewd survivor. He'd lost favor with Suharto in the 1990s after his role in approving Megawati's ascendance to party chair. He worked his way back into Suharto's cabinet as transmigration minister in time to support the militias and the forced population transfers of the Timorese in September 1999.

Megawati and Hendropriyono had remained close.[3] Once president, she made him head of the State Intelligence Agency (Badan Intelijen Negara, or BIN), elevating that post to cabinet rank. He accompanied Megawati to Washington in September 2001, where she was the first head of state to meet with President Bush after the World Trade Center attacks, while Hendropriyono had meetings at CIA headquarters. The surging American interest in counterterrorism cooperation provided the Indonesian military and intelligence with new opportunities to push back against a reform agenda.[4]

KontraS and the victims' families kept up their pressure for accountability for past crimes, but the roadblocks remained formidable. The Law on Human Rights Courts that Munir helped draft had provided for ad hoc courts to handle the disappearances, shootings, and other major cases, once certain conditions were met. First, the National Human Rights Commission would carry out a preliminary inquiry, usually after persistent lobbying by victims and their advocates. The attorney general's office would then fully investigate and prosecute the crime in a court set up on the recommendation of parliament and by decree of the president.

But in case after case, after the Human Rights Commission did its work, the attorney general's office sent cases back because parliament had not recommended, or the president had not decreed, creation of an ad hoc court. The complex and circular process provided many opportunities for obstruction, intimidation, and delay, and perpetrators made full use of them.[5]

Sometimes the president failed to act, but other times parliament was the obstacle. When a special parliamentary committee was formed on the Semanggi student shootings, it was a major step forward. But as the government had lurched toward the impeachment crisis of July 2001, the panel voted along party lines to declare that the shootings weren't gross human rights violations. Military courts could handle the matter, if they chose to.[6]

A small, white-haired, neatly dressed woman lobbed three eggs at the panel. Sumarsih's son Wawan had been at the Semanggi protest in 1998 as a member of a humanitarian team. He was helping an injured protestor when a single bullet pierced his chest, killing him. Sumarsih, a civil servant at the parliament building and a loyal member of Suharto's old ruling party, Golkar, didn't leave her room for months. She found her son's notebooks, containing poems she read over and over.

Just as Usman and Tuti Koto had, Sumarsih found her way to Munir. With his support when she was feeling hopeless, she too became a highly effective activist. The eggs were not Sumarsih's last word on the subject. KontraS, Sumarsih, and other families persuaded the National Human Rights Commission to mount an inquiry into the student shootings, a possible precursor to a trial. Similar to the East Timor inquiry, this time it was Usman who was named to the team.

In March 2002, the team wanted to question Wiranto, armed forces commander at the time of the shootings, but he refused to recognize their authority. Sumarsih and other family members of those killed went to Wiranto's house with flowers. They explained that they wanted to remind him of the summons, and offer him a ride to the commission.

The next day a group of men visited KontraS to tell them to leave

Wiranto alone. The day after that more than twenty cars and minibuses pulled up outside the office. They disgorged a larger group of hired thugs who smashed furniture, computers, and windows, sending shards of glass sliding across the white floor tiles. They injured staffers and carried off research files. Attacked in his office by four or five men, Munir took up a position in a bathroom, armed with a mop, a rare resort to force since he'd given up the scrapping of his student days. He fought off one attacker before being grabbed by three others. They forced him to read out their demands, which included leaving Wiranto alone and dropping the Trisakti and Semanggi cases. In all the chaos, Munir was moved to see his old driver pull up. Sugiarto still worked at LBH, not far from KontraS, and when he heard the commotion, he came to help. Sumarsih heard the news on the radio and went to KontraS. She saw Munir was injured, and burst into tears. "Don't cry," he consoled her. "It's just computers. Don't be sad."

Police arrested some attackers, who swore they had no *bekking*, or backing, from any generals. The term needed no explanation in the press. It described a common relationship between someone with power and those who doled out violence and threats on their behalf, in exchange for money or leeway to carry out criminal activities. But the attackers claimed their assault was just a spontaneous act of violence sparked by frustration that KontraS wouldn't defend the rights of militia members in another case. Munir was sure the attack was linked to the student shootings inquiry and the East Timor trials. When he'd offered to hear the attackers out about the case they supposedly wanted his help with, they'd said, "No, we just want you to stop investigating the student deaths."[7]

Munir was proud of his young staff for neither fighting nor running. After the arrests, the attackers wanted to meet with KontraS to get several members released from jail. Munir was ready to meet, figuring the hired thugs were not the real enemy, but his staff refused on principle, saying, "So what if we're attacked again?"[8]

Suci was not in Jakarta at this time. Alif had been diagnosed as being on the autism spectrum, and Suci took him back to Malang, where there was good therapy, clean air, and family support. When she heard about the attack, she wanted to return to Jakarta, but Munir told her not to take the risk. She was pregnant, and he also needed to concentrate on work. As a solution, he joined her in East Java for a while, bringing staff along for a work retreat.

Munir's lens had expanded over the years from workers' rights to the role of the military to the violence that permeated politics and society. The threats against people's lives, including his own, showed how much work there was to do. The Indonesian word *teror* differs from the direct translation. *Teror* can refer to politically motivated violence, as in English, but more often it means spreading fear, often through text messages or calls from agents of the state. Munir thought much of the fear came from oneself. "If we perceive what someone says as terrifying, then he's truly terrorizing us," he said. "But if we see it only as a joke, then it becomes a joke." He believed he had a moral responsibility to be unafraid, if he was asking victims to take the risk of speaking out. And besides, "What is fear but an act of *teror* against yourself?"[9]

The assault on KontraS took place on the day of one of the Human Rights Court's hearings on East Timor. Hoping to prevent an international tribunal, the Indonesian government created the court, bringing eighteen defendants to trial over the course of a year. Wiranto and other top generals were not among them, and no one was ever charged with planning or ordering the violence. One of the three generals who were charged was Major General Adam Damiri, who had led the regional command that included East Timor. He was charged with failing to control his subordinates as they took part in five mass killings, including the Suai massacre. Evidence included a forensics report describing the bodies Munir helped exhume.[10]

Damiri missed four sessions of his trial because he was overseeing combat operations in Aceh. He was present on June 5, 2003, when something very unusual occurred. The prosecutor tried to convince the judges that Damiri was *not* guilty of crimes against humanity. He noted Damiri's medal (for service in East Timor, the location of the alleged crimes) and his politeness in court, and requested an acquittal. The prosecutor insisted that the reversal was his decision alone, but Munir thought he may have come under enormous pressure in such a political case. Munir had seen documents signed by Damiri authorizing violence in East Timor and believed he deserved twenty years or more in prison.[11]

There had already been serious problems at every stage of the trial process. Indictments and prosecutions never demonstrated the widespread and systematic nature of the violence, essential elements of a conviction for crimes against humanity. The prosecution and judges, as well as the public, seemed to agree with defense arguments that the violence arose spontaneously from armed Timorese groups, with no role played by the Indonesian army. This view had been disproven by the international inquiry, UN prosecutors in East Timor, and the Indonesian inquiry Munir took part in, which concluded that the violence was financed, orchestrated, and encouraged by the military at the highest levels.[12]

Surprisingly, the judges ignored the prosecutor's request and found Damiri guilty of crimes against humanity and sentenced him to three years in prison, far short of Munir's hope of twenty. Damiri's verdict was the last issued by the ad hoc court, one of six guilty verdicts. Some of the six were given nominal sentences and all remained free while the verdicts were under appeal. Damiri used his freedom to continue supervising military operations in Aceh.

Suci stayed in Malang in 2001 and 2002, with Munir visiting once or twice a month. In Jakarta, Munir stayed in a room upstairs from the offices of a radio station. Realizing lawyers alone could never transform society the way he hoped, Munir helped found Voice of Human Rights Radio to foster respect for rights more widely. The first floor of the rented house was filled with desks, with a sofa and a small kitchen in the back. Most nights, journalists and activists gathered to loudly debate the role of the media, the army, and human rights. One typical night, the radio journalists were working late when they heard Munir's motorbike clatter down the alley. After changing into a T-shirt and his brown plaid sarong, he asked, "Have you eaten?" Munir sent someone to a street stall for *pecel lele* a favorite dish from East Java consisting of fried catfish and vegetables with sambal.

A reporter remembered: "After dinner, as usual, 'casual university' began, as the cigarette smoke curled between the furrowed brows of our serious faces. We listened intently to every sentence." Munir laced his speech with Javanese, English, and Jakarta slang, all overlaid with the East Javanese accent he hung on to. He spoke so rapidly, it could be hard to catch it all, as conversation turned to the role of the media. Munir described how TV and radio could "enter the houses of farmers without knocking on the door, enter the dormitory rooms of workers, escort the boats of fisherman at sea, even reach beneath bridges to rag pickers and the homeless." After midnight, Munir asked, "Sleepy yet?" "No, Cak! Go on!" the young journalists shouted. Munir explained how media could reconstruct a society torn apart by violence, but only if it could rise above propaganda and find truth.[13]

One late night at the radio office only Munir and Usman were left. Munir was worried that Usman's rising profile in the inquiry into the student shootings was putting him at risk. It was not just a general concern; he had heard something specific.

"You have to be believe me. This is valid," Munir said. "Do you want to know?"

Munir's network of contacts within the army and police was not so unusual in the human rights community, but his skill in securing information and assistance was unmatched. Munir explained to mystified colleagues that not all soldiers were vicious; you just had to find friends inside the ranks. For their part, some senior officers found that a human rights activist could be a useful ally in efforts to professionalize the military, and sometimes in their internal rivalries as well. Military contacts might send word if threats became more dangerous than usual, as they had the night Munir and Suci were warned of imminent abduction, and drove through the night in Suharto's final days.

That night at the radio station, Munir told Usman of a meeting he'd been warned about. Senior generals had become very upset over Usman's demand that they answer questions about the student killings. It was the same sensitive nerve that most likely led to the attack on the KontraS office. According to Munir's sources, a general at the meeting complained, "After Munir, there's another one." Due to his lack of respect for them, they said Usman was like a child who betrayed his parents, comparing him to the folk tale Malin Kundang. In this legend, a son betrays his mother and is turned to stone, still visible as a rock formation on the coast of West Sumatra. The generals couldn't turn Usman into stone, but they discussed silencing him in other ways, such as kidnapping or shooting him. One general had objected but others wanted to carry out the plan.

Munir grew quiet, then climbed the stairs to his room and returned with a heavy black jacket. It took Usman a few moments to realize what it was.

Munir said, "This is the bulletproof vest I got when I did the investigation in East Timor. You need it. You need to wear it."

"I don't want that, Cak. Because I trust . . ." Usman pointed skywards.

Nodding, Munir said, "I'm like that too. But don't be killed for stupid reasons. I've been in some really critical situations, and I wouldn't hesitate to wear this. We have to protect ourselves, prevent things from happening."

The words hung in the air a long moment. Then Munir laughed, and added, "Actually . . . the vest belongs to the UN. Don't tell anyone!" He had failed to return it after his work in East Timor.

Usman wore the jacket twice when threats got particularly serious. Munir kept worrying, especially after the student shootings inquiry issued its report and their press conference was attacked by hired thugs. Munir ordered Usman to leave for a month of lobbying in Europe, hanging out with other homesick exiles in Geneva and then in a canal house in Amsterdam that served as an unofficial embassy and dormitory for Indonesian activists.

The night of the vest was eye-opening for Usman. It had always seemed that Munir relied solely on his deep reserve of courage, mixed with humor, rather than taking special steps to protect himself. But Munir knew exactly what he was doing. He was always the first person in the office, his desk blanketed with four or five newspapers he read carefully before anyone arrived. He analyzed dangers and openings in the political landscape, paying special attention to how officials responded to his public statements. Munir seemed ready for every situation.

Munir told friends he didn't want KontraS to belong to him, or even to the victims and their families. He wanted it to belong to all Indonesians, he said, "So I have to slowly remove myself from here." He did just that, though he stayed on the board and stopped by often to give advice and support.

Four years into *reformasi*, Indonesia was still drafting and passing a raft of laws on human rights, the military, police, terrorism, and intelligence. While KontraS mainly provided legal support and advocacy for victims, Munir had an idea for a new organization, Imparsial, to analyze and improve laws and policies. With Munir as the first executive director and staff that included Munir's old friends Poengky and Rachland Nashidik, Imparsial began operations in June 2002. One of its first campaigns, as the so-called Global War on Terror got under way, focused on counterterrorism and human rights. Munir had already tried and failed to block the appointment of General Hendropriyono to lead the State Intelligence Agency, BIN. He'd argued without success to a court that the general's role in the 1989 Talangsari massacre in southern Sumatra disqualified him for the job.

Hendropriyono may have attracted Munir's attention by making it into the transition period with his reputation mostly intact. Prabowo had been forced abroad. Wiranto had persevered in the world of politics but not without damage to his reputation over the mayhem in East Timor. But Hendropriyono's political survival skills and close relationship with Megawati and her party had protected him so far, which made him a target for advocates of accountability like Munir. It also gave him more to lose than generals already mired in allegations.

Counterterrorism took on new urgency when Jemaah Islamiyah, a Southeast Asian affiliate of Al Qaeda, bombed two nightclubs on Bali in 2002, killing 202 people. They struck again at the Jakarta Marriott in August 2003. These attacks were followed by antiterrorism decrees that Munir feared would curb civil liberties.[14] Then Munir obtained a leaked draft of an intelligence law written by BIN. If it passed, BIN agents would be armed with weapons and arrest powers, with a presence down to the local level. Munir argued that BIN should be restricted to collecting and analyzing information. He spearheaded a wave of criticism, comparing the proposed powers to the East German Stasi. The bill never went to a vote.

In January 2003, Suci returned to greater Jakarta with Alif and his new baby sister, Diva Suukyi Larasati (named in part for Burma's Aung San Suu Kyi). In a little house in Bekasi, the whole family would stay in the big bed in the morning, laughing at their jokes for an hour before Munir got up to bathe the children and give them breakfast. Suci was well aware of how rare these actions were.

Munir often gave Suci his writing to read and edit while he got the kids ready. She enjoyed editing his work, and pushed him to make his style more literary, drawing on her education in Indonesian language and literature. Eventually, Munir would say good-bye to Suci and put on a motorcycle helmet, outsize on his thin frame, and a brown leather jacket to protect against the wind. He'd climb onto his Honda to ride an hour into Central Jakarta.

The motorbike was of a type known in the industry as an underbone, with the fuel tank under the seat rather than in front of it. The step-through shape appeals to women in conservative societies, but it's the price that drives its popularity throughout the developing world, especially Asia. It's a commuter's ride, a motorcycle taxi, a way for a rural child to reach her school. Indonesians call it a *bebek*, meaning duck. (It must be something about their cute but ungainly profile, because Greeks call them ducks as well.) Even in the middle class, the motorbike is often the family car, and it's not unusual to see a whole family balanced on one. When Munir took Alif to preschool, the boy often insisted that Diva come too, and so all four of them would climb on.

Munir loved his old bike, often faster than a car in Jakarta's extreme traffic. It allowed better interactions with people, with poor people in particular.

Munir's *bebek* was stolen once, but when the theft was reported in the press, the thief realized whom he'd robbed and immediately returned it. (Munir made the young thief get the broken lock fixed before he accepted its return). That bike was stolen again a few months later outside KontraS, and never seen again. "I guess this thief was poorer than the last one," Munir said. That bike was part of his reputation as a seemingly ordinary, even humble, man who was able to accomplish extraordinary things.

Munir had his small salary deposited directly into a bank account under

Suci's control. She would put a modest 100,000 rupiah in his wallet, about
$10, and then he'd take 80,000 back out, and she'd sneak it back in when
he wasn't looking. He asked Suci, what did he need money for? Breakfast
and dinner were at home, and the office provided lunch. He just needed a
little money for gas, and a *bebek* didn't need much. Once he got a flat and,
lacking the small amount of cash to get it patched at a roadside stand, had
to walk the bike several miles home.[15]

Six years after Suharto was driven away from the palace in a stretch Mercedes, the transition dragged on. Indonesia had moved from authoritari-
anism to electoral democracy, while reforming its laws and constitution.
Political parties and a free press had returned after decades in eclipse. The
military had by now lost its automatic seats in the assembly, and the police
had been separated from the military to become a civilian force.

However, many of the new laws produced change on paper only. Imple-
mentation of reforms fell to the same corrupt and beholden officials.[16]
Active and retired generals still wielded influence in areas of politics and
the economy with no connection to national defense. After protests broke
out over rising fuel and electricity prices at the start of 2003, Megawati
had turned even more to the generals. She'd brought military reform to a
virtual halt and authorized renewed military operations in Aceh in May
2003. While it was true the insurgency had been stepping up operations
and recruitment, the declaration of martial law there was a setback for
Munir's efforts to get the army's policies, budgets, and operations into the
open and under democratic control.

By 2004 momentum for transitional justice was fading fast. In the first
few years, human rights inquiries and a couple of ad hoc courts became
possible when reformers like Munir found allies in politicians and generals hoping to distance themselves from the past and regain public confidence. But there had been no political commitment to see these difficult
processes through. The new laws and special courts were shot through
with weaknesses to exploit as soon as public pressure faded.[17] The international community had moved on as well, and American pressure to reform
withered quickly after the September 11 attacks made Indonesia a valued
counterterrorism ally.

The East Timor trials in Jakarta succeeded in what they were intended to do, which was to prevent Indonesians from being brought before an international tribunal. After final appeals, every defendant was acquitted, a crisis almost as great for Indonesia as for the new nation of East Timor, now known as Timor-Leste. The perpetrators and architects of crimes against humanity remained not only free, but major figures in the Indonesian political landscape. Munir viewed the acquittals as a serious threat. The East Timor verdicts had only reinforced the belief that state violence against civilians was legitimate in defending the unity of Indonesia and the authority of its government. They gave the state free rein to violate human rights.[18] As for the student shootings, despite Usman's investigative team finding evidence pointing to senior officials, there were never more than a few secretive military trials of low-ranking soldiers.

The first direct elections for president were scheduled for July 5, 2004, If no candidate received a majority, a run-off would take place on September 20. Megawati was campaigning for reelection, and also running were Wiranto and another retired general, Susilo Bambang Yudhoyono. (Yet another retired general was the vice-presidential candidate on another ticket.) For the first time, Munir endorsed a candidate. Amien Rais was another former critic of Suharto and a leader in a major Muslim organization, Muhammadiyah. Munir's endorsement caused controversy in the usually nonpartisan human rights community, but he believed supporting Rais was the best chance to elect a president who was neither a former general nor close to the military, like Megawati.

Munir's candidate didn't make it past the first round, but he maintained his ardent opposition to an unchecked military throughout the campaign season. One day in August 2004, Munir spoke from the steps of the Supreme Court. A megaphone dangled at his hip from a strap across his chest like a bandolier. Behind him police officers were arrayed in a line, hands behind their backs. Most stared ahead but a few glanced sidelong at Munir. The Supreme Court emblem looked down from the building above, a flaming wheel, jasmine garlands, and an invocation of justice and truth in Old Javanese.

Two young activists held up a second megaphone and a corded mike, as Munir spoke quickly, with tightly controlled anger.

"They've seized power, they carry guns. They kill people and hide behind those in power. Should we let these cowards keep acting tough?"

"*No!*" the crowd roared. They held up signs demanding justice for those killed, tortured, and disappeared.

Munir continued. "No! They are only tough in uniform. But deep down there is something shameful, something irresponsible, and they will pay, *wherever they go!*"

In a few weeks, Munir was to leave for the Netherlands, to take a break and build his knowledge. "I have to go to school now. I'm thirty-eight this year," he told Poengky, "It's now or never."[19] Suciwati had encouraged Munir to go. She wanted him to open up options beyond legal aid and advocacy, or at least to take a break from the journalists, victims' families, and officials who contacted him from dawn prayers until late at night.

He'd tried to study abroad once before, and he'd been ready to be the first civilian to study under an American program originally designed for the Indonesian military. But then he'd criticized the U.S. invasion of Iraq, and the opportunity evaporated.[20]

In mid-2003, Munir had ridden his motorbike to South Jakarta to meet an American academic he knew well, Jeffrey Winters. On the quiet veranda of a guest house, they discussed the idea of studying at Northwestern University in Chicago. Munir explained he wanted to deepen his understanding of the politics of human rights violations, to take what he had learned in practice to another analytical level. He had a second motive to leave the country for a while. The threats to him and his family seemed to be escalating, whether explosives left outside his home or attacks on the office.

Munir explained to Winters that during the New Order, activists knew the dance. They knew what lines not to cross, how to dial their criticism up or down depending on the government's predictable response pattern of warnings, phone calls, and threats, and their own tolerance for risk. But since 1998, the perpetrators had begun to feel less untouchable, while attacks on activists had become more unpredictable. If a group attacked you or your office, you could only guess at who sent them or how to make the *teror* stop even if you were willing to adjust your actions. To Munir, it felt even more dangerous than it had under Suharto.

Winters told him studying in Chicago could be arranged, but he would have to commit to getting a PhD. He would also have to focus on improving his English over the next year, an unusual use of time for a figure of his stature. Winters asked Munir to let him know, but did not hear back for a while. Some months later, he ran into Munir in Yogyakarta with the family. With Alif and Diva pulling on him, they did not talk long. Munir said he had decided to study at the University of Utrecht, where he had the option of returning home after a master's degree.[21]

A Protestant development organization had offered him a scholarship to study human rights. His proposal for a master's degree said he would trace the Indonesian government's practice of disappearing people, going back to the 1950s, through Suharto's first years of power, and into the present era of impunity. He wanted to understand and overcome obstacles to ending disappearances, and to ensure that perpetrators were held accountable, drawing on international mechanisms when Indonesia's couldn't deliver justice. He wanted to answer the puzzling question of why it was so hard to protect human rights even after a military-backed government had come to an end.

Munir looked forward to time to study and write. At one of the good-bye parties he'd been unable to avoid, he infused his rapid patter with a mock solemnity that drew laughter from the banquet tables.

"While I'm abroad, please don't contact me about difficult problems," he said. "If you come to Holland, I won't show you around. I only want to read books and go to libraries. It's been a while since I studied, and I was never good at school. I was always dumb. All I did was fight, from kindergarten until I finished college. But this time I'll be serious. This year I'll be serious."

7

The Red Thread

2004

After calling Suci with the news of Munir's death, Usman made his way to the little house she and Munir rented in Jakarta's outskirts, and he was not alone. The house filled with friends, and a glade of wreaths formed in the lane, sent by old friends and colleagues from all over the archipelago, as well as politicians Munir never thought much of. Holding tight to a child's cup, five-year-old Alif wandered among the metal stands, sounding out the words of condolence on each wreath: *Turut Berduka Cita*. We join in your sorrow. All this fuss made no sense to him. His father was just going to school. It was somewhere far away, but he promised to come home to visit in a few months.

In the evening, a call came from the Netherlands, from an officer of the Royal Dutch Marechaussee, a military branch responsible for securing airports and borders. They wanted Suci's permission to conduct an autopsy. He was told she was in no condition to come to the phone, but would arrive in Amsterdam in two days to bring Munir's body home. Poengky, Usman, and Munir's older brother Rasyid would go with her.

Arriving at Schiphol Airport before sunrise on Thursday, September 9, they were met by an airport chaplain and by members of the Marechaussee.[1] These investigators led them on a route that bypassed the Indonesian embassy officials waiting for them at immigration. Usman noticed other men in plainclothes keeping pace with them at staggered distances. He quietly said to Suci, "That's strange, isn't it? So much security. As if they're protecting us. What's going on?" Seeing alarm edge across Suci's face, he added, "I'm sure it's nothing."

The somber group was escorted to the airport mortuary, the only one of its kind. The facility handles two thousand bodies a year, mostly repatriation to and from the Netherlands of those who die abroad. An imam had ritually washed Munir's body and shrouded him in white, leaving hands, feet, and head visible. Seeing him on the stainless steel table, they all began to cry, silently at first, their sobs building until Usman began a slow prayer and the mood calmed. Suci asked everyone to leave the room. She looked down at Munir's face. Later, it was hard to remember what she felt. Sorrow for sure, but also hollowed out. She took his hand, and she remembered him. She remembered them both together. Something shifted within her, a sense that she must somehow accept that he was gone. Suci offered up a prayer: *Ya Allah*, give my husband a place of honor by Your side. Amen.[2]

Dutch investigators interviewed Poengky in a small room at an airport police post. She described the parting at the airport, and they asked for copies of the good-bye photos that she had on her laptop. Poengky told them Munir had been threatened with death before, was very critical of the government, and had tense relationships with certain generals.

Just after noontime, two men took Suci into the quiet room to ask about Munir's work and his health. She told them he had a minor liver condition that was being managed, and that a recent checkup had found no problems. They asked her to list everything her husband ate on the family's last day together: an early glass of tea at 6:30 a.m., a breakfast of rice and vegetables, a similar lunch. Mid-afternoon, out shopping for shoes for Alif, they'd stopped in to McDonalds as a treat and had French fries and fried chicken. Their early dinner before leaving the house for the airport was Chinese cabbage, onions, and chicken. And then she and her husband had shared a hot chocolate at the airport Dunkin' Donuts.

She described the death threats Munir received so often that they had become routine. However, one recent phone call did stand out as unusual. A few days before Munir's departure, a man claiming to be from Garuda called to ask when her husband would leave for the Netherlands. The investigators put all this in their notes.

There was a disagreement about how to bring Munir home. Among the wreaths and mourners at Suci and Munir's house, President Megawati's husband, Taufiq Kiemas, had pushed some open tickets on Usman. But he was notoriously corrupt and not someone to incur an obligation to, particularly two weeks before election day. Garuda had offered them free seats, but Suci said that was out of the question. It was an instinctive, angry reaction that she couldn't really justify. She only knew she would not fly on the airline, maybe even the same plane, Munir had just died on. They'd traveled here on the Dutch carrier KLM, and Suci insisted they return the same way.

But where should they bring the body? Some people wanted Munir buried in Kalibata Heroes Cemetery in Jakarta. Usman liked the idea of Munir buried as a national hero, but he knew Munir would have hated the pomp and militarism of the place. Suci knew Munir had always wanted to go back to East Java when his work was complete. Munir would go home to Batu. There, on the lower slopes of Mount Arjuno, a sleeping volcano named for a hero of the Hindu epics, Munir would be buried in a simple grave.

The Schiphol Airport mortuary sealed the pine box with a lozenge of red wax impressed with their stamp, before wrapping it in black cloth and plastic for the trip to Jakarta. From there the coffin was transferred to a plane chartered to take Munir home to East Java in the company of friends. The aircraft retraced his life's path in reverse, flying over Semarang and then Surabaya on the north coast, before turning south over the mountainous interior. The plane banked over a neat patchwork of rice paddies to descend steeply within the mountains that encircled Malang. In this small city, Munir and Suci had been students, organizers, friends, secret *pacars*, and bride and groom.

The plane landed at a small military airfield, the Indonesian flags around its perimeter resting at half-staff. The base commander came out to watch the coffin transferred to an ambulance waiting in the dark for the drive to Batu. The hill town had grown since Munir was small, attracting

ever more local tourists with hot springs and a cool climate. There were
new hotels, colorful statues of fruits and vegetables, and stalls selling rabbit satay to visitors. Batu's flags were lowered for a full week, and a great
red apple in front of city hall, a tribute to the fruit the town was known
for, had been swathed in black cloth.

A crowd waited at Munir's childhood home to help carry the coffin
inside and to pay respects to his mother. Five days earlier, Ibu Jamila had
learned of her son's death from a neighbor who ran over after seeing the
news on TV. Her mourning had been disrupted the next day by a taunting
anonymous letter that read, "Congratulations on the death of Munir. We
hope he isn't roughed up by the spirits of the nation's heroes."

Friends and activists from all over the archipelago gathered at the little
house. Mothers of the disappeared had traveled eighteen hours by bus
across Java. They came together in the eerie quiet that trails a sudden
death, where disbelief and raw grief mix and the everyday is put on hold.
Some of the mourners slept out on the sidewalk, but many did not sleep
at all, sitting up together in the mountain air thick with the clove-scented
smoke of *kretek*s. They sat on chairs lined up under a canopy in the middle
of Jalan Diponegoro, listening to prayers and eulogies.

Under the grim cast of a tube light, some of the mourners traded suspicions. Munir was only thirty-eight and had many enemies. These men
had killed before, mostly, but not only, in combat. But killing a critic,
especially one who was leaving the country, was not the usual pattern,
even under Suharto. Troublemakers could be intimidated, or prosecuted,
or forced out of the country where they would be cut off from their networks, perhaps coming back when they had learned their lesson. What's
more, Munir always pushed himself hard, sometimes even forgetting to
eat. A year earlier, he'd collapsed and spent several days at in the hospital,
where doctors diagnosed a liver condition and urged him to rest and watch
his diet. But he easily passed a physical before he left for Utrecht, and
everyone agreed he'd seemed healthy.

The sounds of a small town at dawn reached them—the muezzin's call,
buckets of water hitting tile floors as Muslims performed ablutions before
prayer, the crowing of pampered fighting cocks, and tinny radios sup-
plying music for calisthenics. Mourners streamed in until there was no

more room under the canopy, and some opened umbrellas against the flat mountain sun. Pallbearers eased the coffin through the front door and down the street. It was draped in green cloth decorated with gold piping and verses from the Quran. Walking a few feet in front of the coffin, friends took turns holding up a framed black-and-white photograph of Munir. He wore a serious expression, as light bounced off his tousled hair and cast his tired eyes in shadow.

The procession turned through a blue portico into the courtyard of a mosque undergoing renovation. Leaving drifts of sandals amid neat stacks of handmade bricks, mourners entered the carpeted mosque. After the tumult of the street, the sudden silence felt like a blow. One of Munir's brothers led the prayers, repeating them for a crowd so big it filled the great room twice over.

At the cemetery, boys and photographers climbed the old trees twisting up from among the white and blue headstones. An imam prayed through a megaphone as the pine box was set into the grave and slowly covered with the loose soil of the dry season. A small cement headstone was inscribed with the full name he rarely used: Munir Said Thalib. As mourners threaded their way out through the graves, the crowd thinned until only one figure remained at Munir's gravesite. It was Usman and he stayed until his wife of just a few months came and gently pulled him away.

Most Indonesians like crowds. The word for crowded, *ramai*, has positive connotations of liveliness and bustle. Its opposite, *sepi*, can mean quiet or lonely. Some Javanese believe too much quiet makes you vulnerable to malevolent spirits and other unseen dangers. In the first days after Munir's death, Suci only wanted to be left alone. But the crowd in Batu boosted her spirits, confirming that her family didn't grieve alone.

After the funeral, she felt alone again, with a sense of emptiness she couldn't shake. She felt she had nothing left, that her body wouldn't do what her mind wanted it to. After the death of her mother three years before, Suci thought she knew what sadness was. Now she felt she was just understanding what it meant. This was a pure sadness. One day, just to do something, she had a bicycle trishaw take her to the market for something to cook. But once there, she just walked aimlessly, crying. She wasn't sure for how long.

About a week after Munir died, Suci went into the hospital briefly for a procedure. The disruption helped her to break through the grief, just enough to fully realize she had to be present for Alif and Diva. Suci also found consolation in her faith, and in one thousand-year-old prayer in particular:

> I asked for strength, and God gave me difficulties to make me strong. I asked for wisdom, and God gave me problems to solve. I asked for well-being, and God gave me wisdom to think. I asked for courage, and God gave me danger to overcome. I received nothing I wanted; I received everything I needed.

The words were a comfort, but she did not take them to mean that Munir's death was simply a turn of fate she must accept. She felt entrusted with the task of finding out what had happened to him. She was also driven by a fear that not being by his side when he died would burden her for the rest of her life. Maybe, through a search for truth, she could still do something for Munir, and for his life's work.[3]

Munir's body had not yet been buried when the foreign affairs minister announced that the autopsy had revealed nothing unusual. Hours later, the claim was debunked; there were no results of any kind. Weeks passed, with most of the country focused on the presidential campaign, and then the victory on September 20 of Susilo Bambang Yudhoyono. Two days after that, a front page announced, MUNIR AUTOPSY TO BE RELEASED THIS WEEK. That week, too, came and went. A senior government official called Usman, but it was only to ask if *he* had a copy of the autopsy yet.

Suci had told the Dutch investigators about the odd phone call from an airline employee. It still nagged at her, like an unsettling dream half-remembered after waking. A few days before his departure, Munir had puttered off on his motorbike to a copy shop. When Suci heard the ring of his phone, left behind in the rush of his final days in Jakarta, she answered it. A man's voice said hello, and asked what day Munir would be traveling.

"Who is this?"

"Polly. Polly from Garuda," he said.

Suci told him her husband would fly on Monday.

"Great," he said, "we'll be traveling together!"

As soon as the call ended, Suci felt she'd done something foolish. Why had she given out his departure date, even to someone claiming to be from the airline? When Munir came home, she told him about the call.

Munir asked, "Polly *who?*"

"Polly from Garuda."

"Oh, him. He's an odd one, and *sok akrab.*" It meant acting like you were already close to someone, with a pretense of familiarity.

Munir assumed it was the same Polly who'd asked him for a favor before a trip to Geneva a few months earlier: "He's a stranger, but he suddenly wanted me to mail a letter for him from Switzerland." Munir had turned him down. Who knew what was in the envelope?

This story only made Suci more worried about revealing Munir's schedule. Her husband reassured her, "It's okay, don't give it another thought." She put the call out of her mind.

In Amsterdam, Suci had mentioned the call to Poengky. It made her feel uneasy too, and she promised to look into it. Poengky wrote a note to herself to request a meeting with Garuda's director. Suci reminded her a week after the funeral, and a meeting was arranged.

The Jakarta Hilton occupied prime real estate developed in the 1960s by General Ibnu Sutowo, the head of the state oil company, Pertamina. He used the company as a massive slush fund, nearly bankrupting the country despite surging oil prices. A corruption scandal and the $10 billion debt eventually cost Sutowo his job, but the immensely valuable hotel properties, including what was for a time the largest Hilton in the world, somehow remained in his family's possession.

On the last day of 2004, the general's son would wrap up his New Year's Eve at the hotel's Fluid Club and Lounge. When the waiter, a law student from the poor island of Flores, informed him that a credit card had been declined, the general's son shot him in the head, killing him instantly.

Two months before that killing, and six weeks after Munir's death, Suci sat down at Lotus, the hotel's Chinese restaurant, to break the day's

Ramadan fast. After weeks of excuses, airline director Indra Setiawan had at last invited Suci to meet him on October 22. Setiawan, his deputies and some of the crew from the Amsterdam flight took their seats beneath Chinese landscapes in gilded frames. Suci brought several of Munir's colleagues, including Poengky and Hendardi, a senior human rights lawyer.

Peering through rimless glasses below a receding hairline, Setiawan apologized for the delay. He'd been busy escorting the vice-president of Indonesia to Mecca. After introductions and condolences, Suci and her team unreeled their questions. What did Munir eat on board? What are the rules for sick passengers and emergency landings, and were they followed? Setiawan and his staff explained these protocols and the rules of food handling. They assured Suci that meal service took place under tight security, especially since the Bali bombings of 2002. A member of the cabin crew from the Singapore–Amsterdam flight shared that Munir asked for an antacid before the plane took off. After that, he had only tea with sugar.

The meeting started to wind down, and Setiawan began getting ready to leave. That's when Suci posed the question she'd been waiting to ask.

"Is there anyone named Polly at Garuda?"

Setiawan answered immediately, "Yes, there is. His name's Pollycarpus, and he's a co-pilot."

"You've memorized the names of all your employees?"

"Well, it's true we have seven hundred pilots, but the thing is, his name is special, unique." Referring to a more common name, he added, "If his name was Slamet, I'd have forgotten it."

"Does Pollycarpus fly to Europe?"

"No, he's only qualified to fly Airbus planes." They flew only within Asia and to Australia.

The meeting ended. They had not left the hotel yet when Hendardi pulled Suci aside. He asked her why she'd brought Polly up, and she told him about the phone call.

"I know him," Hendardi told her. "He called me many times."

Hendardi had worked with Munir at the head office of LBH in the 1990s. They'd ended up on opposite sides of a fierce conflict about the future of the organization, and Hendardi left to found his own human rights group, PBHI. Years later, Munir asked Hendardi to help him establish his new organization, Imparsial. Hendardi saw how hard Munir worked and how stubborn he was in pursuit of his goals, and the two came to enjoy working together.

A few months before Munir died, a man walked into Hendardi's office.[4] He wore a pilot's uniform and said his name was Pollycarpus Budihari Priyanto. Hendardi was out, so a secretary scheduled a meeting. When the pilot returned, in three days, he brought two men from Timor-Leste, explaining that he wanted to help the stranded Timorese go home to their new nation. Hendardi was used to people coming to his office out of the blue for help, from wealthy businessmen to motorcycle trishaw drivers, so a pilot wasn't that unusual. The Timorese said little, but Pollycarpus talked a great deal. He said he liked talking about politics, and started asking about PBHI. Where was the funding from? What was the bank account number, so he could make a contribution? Was there a branch in Papua?

"No, just a Papua desk in Jakarta. But I don't handle that."

"Hey, let me know if you're going, I can get you a free ticket!"

Travel costs to the distant provinces of Papua and West Papua ate up PBHI's budget. But Hendardi rarely went there himself, and, anyway, the offer was strange. He turned it down, but Polly kept calling, sometimes twice a week. Once he called from Japan, presumably after flying there for Garuda. He spoke a lot, but was all over the place, asking for Hendardi's opinion about something in the news, before returning to the same question: "Pak Hendardi, when are you going to Papua?" Polly said the offer applied only to Hendardi, not members of his staff. Polly kept on asking, adding, "If I'm on leave, I'll go with you!" He'd done missionary work in Papua, he said, and he knew it very well. This went on from March until May. Eventually Hendardi just stopped answering, and if a secretary answered Polly usually hung up. By June, the calls had tailed off. Exiting the dated opulence of the Hilton, Hendardi realized that not so long after Pollycarpus stopped pestering him, he'd called Munir.

Back at the large house Imparsial occupied as an office, Suci and the others took stock. She'd confirmed there was an airline employee, a pilot even, named Polly, short for Pollycarpus. From Hendardi, she'd learned his full name, and that he'd seemed to want to travel with this other famous human rights lawyer. She'd also confirmed that Munir was already feeling sick when he reboarded the plane in Singapore. She'd eaten everything Munir had before leaving, down to the hot chocolate in the Jakarta airport. If something he ate made him sick, it must have been after saying good-bye in Jakarta and before reboarding in Singapore. Suci needed to meet the crew of the flight from Jakarta to Singapore. They'd seen him in his last healthy hours, and served him his last meal.

The vast Medan Merdeka, or Independence Square, lies in an old part of Jakarta, in the direction of the harbor at the northern edge of the city. At its center is the national monument, Monas (short for Monumen Nasional), a four-hundred-foot obelisk topped by a gold-plated sculpted flame, towering over an expanse of dry grass and flowerbeds, T-shirt stands, food stalls with dishes from each province, and tiny children's rides sporting unsanctioned images of Mickey Mouse that look just a little off. The sides of the square are over half a mile long, and along each lie prominent buildings separated by close-cropped swards and mature trees, an unusual luxury of space in this densely packed city. The presidential palaces, a national museum, and other colonial structures are interspersed with newer buildings like the Ministry of Energy and the American embassy. Near the southwest corner of the Medan Merdeka, a boxy white tower was topped with an avian logo and the words GARUDA INDONESIA in blue.

Four stories up, Suci sat across a long table from the operations director and four crew members from the short flight from Jakarta to Singapore. Suci was again accompanied by Poengky and another lawyer from Imparsial. Eleven days had passed since the restaurant meeting. After some pleasantries, Suci asked for a list of everything Munir ate on the first leg. Yetty, a young flight attendant, said that after Munir took his seat, she'd offered him a hot towel and a welcome drink. From a tray of juices and champagne, Munir chose orange juice. They took off soon after, and Munir then ate a light dinner of fried noodles and fruit salad, and had a second glass of juice.

Poengky asked, "And that was the halal meal he'd requested?"

Yetty shook her head. She explained, "In business class, no halal meals were requested. Munir was sitting in business, and ate what we served in business."

"Why was he in business class?" Poengky asked. "Didn't he have an economy ticket?"

She'd arranged the ticket herself. Bought on short notice, it was already expensive, and Munir would never let his sponsor, a Dutch nonprofit, pay for business class. His only request had been to fly on Garuda. He liked to support Indonesia's economy when he could.

The cabin crew supervisor, or purser, was a veteran flight attendant named Brahmanie Hastawati. She explained that while greeting passengers in business class, she'd been excited to recognize Munir, as she considered herself a fan. Munir had taken a seat that was assigned to a co-pilot flying to Singapore for an assignment. Onboard upgrades were very unusual, but the co-pilot assured her it was fine. His name was Pollycarpus.

Suci and Poengky asked to meet with Pollycarpus.

A week later, Suci returned to the fourth-floor conference room. As before, two long tables ran in parallel, joined in the middle by a smaller one holding a vase of brightly colored plastic flowers. On one side of this elongated H sat Suci, Poengky, Usman, and a KontraS lawyer named Edwin Partogi. Across from them sat Garuda's operations director again, and two members of the cabin crew from the much longer Singapore–Amsterdam flight. They were joined by Pollycarpus. His large eyes dominated a rectangular face topped with a bushy head of hair. His mustache angled downward on either side, neatly trimmed, though slightly sparse in the middle.

The noon sun slashed though the vertical blinds filling one wall. Behind the airline staff hung framed posters with bland images of a woman sitting at a keyboard, a plane coming in for a landing. One poster urged in English, "Begin with the end in mind," a habit of highly effective people.

Suci, Usman, and Poengky began by asking about the flight from Singapore to Amsterdam. A flight attendant, her face framed by a fashionable yellow headscarf, confirmed that Munir asked for an antacid soon after takeoff, but that she had none and could only bring him tea for his stomach. The purser described how Munir became sicker despite a doctor's efforts. Suci knew some of these details from news reports and a meeting with the doctor, and they were hard to hear again.[5]

Pollycarpus rested his arms on the sides of his chair, his hands curled into loose fists. Given a chance to speak, he took hold of the conversation and didn't let go. Suci's side of the table fell silent, focusing all attention on the mysterious figure. Polly pointed out his roots in East Java, just like Suci and Munir, and told a story of his own mother dying on a plane. It seemed to Suci that he was trying to gain her trust.

Finally, Pollycarpus arrived at his encounter with Munir at the Jakarta airport. After recognizing Munir while waiting to board, Pollycarpus approached him and asked in Javanese, "Where are you going, Cak?"

Hearing Munir was going to Amsterdam and was sitting toward the back, he offered his seat in Business. Munir said he'd be embarrassed to take a more expensive seat than the one he'd paid for. Pollycarpus insisted, and at last Munir agreed.

Pollycarpus explained to Suci that he'd just wanted to make Munir comfortable. He often gave away his good seats to make friends. He pulled out a letter from a couple of tourists from New Zealand, thanking Pollycarpus for just such an upgrade. Again it seemed to Suci the co-pilot was trying hard, but she wasn't sure what he hoped to do, or why.

Asked again about meeting Munir, Pollycarpus's answer changed a little. This time, he said, it was Munir who spoke first, asking which plane out on the darkening tarmac was theirs. Pollycarpus pointed out their 747, and Munir confided that he had developed a fear of flying after a patch of bad weather near Ujung Pandang. *That's* when Pollycarpus had offered Munir his own seat in the front of the plane.

Usman wondered, *Why give different versions? Which one is true?* Suci took note of the changing story, too. She also knew that Munir feared very few things, and flying was not one of them.

She asked, "Did you know Munir? From where?"

"Well, your husband's memory was very good, because I'd met him just once, at the Hotel Indonesia traffic circle, and he still remembered me."

A couple of years before, Polly recalled, he'd been stuck in traffic at the roundabout in the heart of Jakarta. He'd had a short conversation with Munir there. In 2002, Munir had indeed joined a demonstration for

Women's Day. In a purple shirt and arm sash, he'd handed out flowers and pamphlets on women's rights.

"Did my husband know your name?"

Pollycarpus gave a long reply that wandered from one topic to another without ever quite reaching the status of an answer. Suci focused on the cadence of his voice, his Javanese accent, his effort to seem light-hearted and to ingratiate. She was sure it was a voice she'd heard before.

Pollycarpus ended his digressions, and Suci asked, "Did you ever phone Munir?"

"No."

She considered challenging his answer, but decided to move on.

"What were you doing on the flight?"

Polly said he was there as Aviation Security.

The phrase was unfamiliar to Suci's side of the table, and Edwin asked, casually, "Oh, like *intel*?"

"No!" Pollycarpus quickly replied. "No, no. Just monitoring pilots and passengers." He said something about dumping fuel that nobody understood, before explaining that employees with seniority could arrange security assignments to earn extra money.

Suci's suspicions began to coalesce, until a thought came to her, hard and sharp. *It's him. He did it*, she told herself. *Just keep him talking.* She kicked Usman's foot, and he nudged her back under the table, urging her to keep calm.

The meeting ended soon after. Downstairs, in the lobby of the Garuda Indonesia building, Suci couldn't keep it in any longer. She said, "Usman, he's the killer, isn't he?" Usman cautioned her to wait until they were somewhere safe.

The group gathered at KontraS, before moving to Imparsial and bringing in a few more trusted people. They went to work on a whiteboard, trying to figure out what they knew and what the next steps should be. At the very least, Pollycarpus was acting suspiciously. He was probably lying, and might be *intel*, despite, or because of, his strenuous protests. They split up the job of finding out as much as they could about him. Where was he really from? Whom did he spend time with?

They had no evidence that Pollycarpus—or anyone—had killed Munir. And anyway, how could he have done it? Did he inject him with something on the plane, or in the airport? They would have to be very careful. If someone of Munir's stature *had* been killed, by unknown actors with the ability to put the state airline to use, then no one was safe.[6]

8

King of Poisons

2004

Suci didn't like waiting at home for something to happen. At the Imparsial office, she could find old friends and activists like Poengky and Rachland. When Munir had been briefly hospitalized with the liver problem, it was Rachland who'd confiscated his laptop to make sure Munir followed the doctor's orders to rest. Munir had grumbled, "Great. Now I have *two* wives." Suci was at Imparsial on the evening of November 11, nine weeks after she'd prayed over Munir's body in the airport mortuary, and three days after she'd sat across from Pollycarpus.

Rachland sought Suci out in the rambling building, another large private home converted into an NGO office. He asked her, "Suci, have you heard?"

A journalist had called from Amsterdam. He was about to report that the Dutch government had handed over the autopsy report to the Indonesian embassy. Munir had died after ingesting a massive dose of arsenic. The reporter was calling to request a comment from Suci.

Along with the shock she felt, another feeling arose, a sense of betrayal that cut through Suci like a scythe. The report should have gone to her, not the Indonesian embassy or a Dutch journalist. And how long had the cause of death been known? She needed a copy of the report. She asked friends for contacts at the Ministry of Foreign Affairs but came up empty. She called a main number there, only to be transferred again and again. At last someone at the Ministry confirmed that the Dutch had given them the report. They had forwarded it to the Coordinating Minister of

Politics and Security, a powerful cabinet member who oversaw the police, the intelligence community, and other agencies. The minister had passed it to the national chief of police.

Suci fished Munir's cell phone out of her bag. When the Dutch investigators had returned it to her, she'd scoured the Nokia for clues about his last hours. It really just held text messages to her and friends, but she liked reading them, and began carrying the phone with her. All the numbers she needed were there, and anyone seeing a call from Munir's phone would surely answer. She called the security minister, the chief of police, and other powerful men, asking each, "Why haven't I been informed about the autopsy? What *happened* to him? What were the results?"

None of them would answer her questions.

"I swear by God . . ." one official started to say.

Suci cut him off. "Don't speak to me of God. Your business isn't with God. It's with me."

Around ten p.m., as Suci was in a car heading home, the security minister called back. He confirmed that the report was at national police headquarters, in the hands of the director of the Criminal Investigation Division. Suci called him, and he first demanded to know how she got his number. She replied only that she had a right to see the report, and he agreed to meet her at his office in the morning. Suci would be permitted take a look at the report there.

An article appeared that night in the Dutch newspaper *NRC Handelsblad*, with the headline INDONESIAN ACTIVIST POISONED. It began:

> The Indonesian human rights activist Munir appears to have been poisoned during his flight from Jakarta to Amsterdam.
>
> By the time he arrived in Schiphol on a Garuda Airlines flight after a stopover in Singapore, he was dead. He was thirty-eight years of age. During the autopsy conducted by the Netherlands Forensic Institute (NFI), a fatal dose of arsenic was discovered. This was disclosed by well-informed sources in the Indonesian Ministry of Foreign Affairs.
>
> Today the Ministry's Director-General for Europe and America received the NFI report from Dutch diplomats. The

diplomats also conveyed the request of The Hague to inform Munir's family as soon as possible. As of this afternoon, Munir's widow, Suciwati, had yet to be contacted.

The Dutch Foreign Office is of the opinion that a further criminal investigation is justified and conveyed this opinion to the government in Jakarta.[1]

The next morning, Suci, Usman, a friend and activist named Smita Notususanto, and two others arrived for their meeting at national police headquarters, a compound of modern glass buildings, close-cropped grass, and palm trees. In one corner a cracked and bare-chested statue of Gajah Mada, conquering prime minister of the Majapahit Empire, watched over a busy intersection.

The head of the Criminal Investigation Division, Suyitno Landung, invited the group into his office. He sat next to Suci at the large conference table and handed her a summary of the toxicology report. Suci's English was limited, and she passed the document to Smita to read out. Smita got as far as the first sentence, which stated that the cause of death was poisoning by arsenic. She heard Suci cry out and couldn't bear to read any more. She slid the document across the table to Usman, saying, "You read it." He read it out. The Netherland Forensics Institute had found enough arsenic—in Munir's stomach, the blood in his heart, and his urine—to kill him several times over.

The police helped Suci make a complaint and opened a criminal investigation into the premeditated murder of Munir. At Suci's request, the police agreed to involve a representative of the family in the investigation. She asked Usman to take on this role.

Once outside, Suci had to squeeze through a crowd of reporters shouting questions. She kept her head down and climbed into a waiting car as journalists yelled, "We just want information!" The reporters hooted with disappointment, as her friends begged the scrum to back off. An hour later, Suci was ready to talk to the press on her terms, at a press conference at KontraS. She demanded a copy of the report, a thorough police investigation, and an independent inquiry. Holding tight to her mike, she spoke in a measured tone: "The results of the toxicological analysis show an unnatural and fatal dose of arsenic. Don't ask me how I'm feeling. The important thing, more important than that, when I learned my husband had been killed . . ." Her voice broke for a moment. "I ask that it be investigated until it is solved."[2]

Nine days later, a postal worker delivered a small package to Suci's house. She began to open it but stopped, brought up short by the smell. She called the police, who unwrapped the package to reveal a white Styrofoam take-out container. Inside was the decaying, dismembered remains of a rooster. A piece of paper was taped inside the lid.

The fluids from the carcass had given the scrap an eerie translucence, but the bold capital letters were clear: "BEWARE!!!!! DO NOT INVOLVE THE ARMY IN THE DEATH OF MUNIR. DO YOU WANT TO END UP LIKE THIS?!"

A few days later, another package arrived at Imparsial, also addressed to Suci. Its contents were an exact copy of the first, a grisly death threat in duplicate.

The police kept their promise, inviting Usman to come with a team to Amsterdam to secure the full, authenticated forensic reports and to meet with the toxicology experts. Just a few years before, Munir had warned him about getting sidetracked by technical aspects of an investigation that hinged on power and politics. But there was no question in Usman's mind that he should go to the Netherlands to try to fill the vast gaps in knowledge about Munir's death.

He also didn't really trust the Indonesian officials to do the job right, and his fears proved well founded. The team, made up of forensics experts, police investigators, and diplomats, ran into a bureaucratic brick wall at their first meeting. The Dutch wouldn't share anything without a formal request from the Indonesian government. The team's letter from the attorney general didn't meet diplomatic requirements.[3]

The head of the Indonesian team was a policeman named Anton Charlian. He'd worked with Munir on the reopened Marsinah investigation a few years before, but they had been unable to secure new prosecutions. In Amsterdam he seemed to be doing his best, but he spoke little English, and Usman had to translate entire meetings. Usman wondered what would have happened if he wasn't there.

Usman turned down an expensive hotel room, not wanting to feel obligated to the police. He preferred to sleep at an advocacy office called Indonesia House, which served as the Indonesian human rights community's unofficial embassy and hostel. Usman had stayed there before, when Munir sent him abroad for his safety, after the night of the bulletproof vest. Overlooking a canal lined by houseboats, the house was familiar and pleasant, though it had no bath and he had to bathe at the house of a Moluccan neighbor.

Dutch activists arranged a press conference and meetings with parliamentarians for Usman, but there wasn't much else to do until the diplomatic roadblock was resolved. Usman shared the sleeping quarters with Alif Iman Nurlambang, a radio reporter from Jakarta. Over meals of fried rice that they took turns cooking, Usman told Alif Iman about their inquiries so far. When Alif mentioned Pollycarpus to his boss in a phone call to Jakarta, her reply surprised him. She thought she'd met him once. She'd been covering the imposition of martial law in Aceh in 2003, and a co-pilot was staying at the same hotel, chatting up journalists and claiming to be on vacation—in a war zone. That was something for Usman to follow up on in Jakarta.

It's a safe bet that an Indonesian human rights office will have a battered guitar somewhere. Usman passed the time by picking out a pop song, then in heavy rotation on Jakarta radio, called "What Is It with You? ("Ada Apa Denganmu"). It was a breakup song, but given all the obstacles blocking Usman from the evidence he needed, the chorus's words of pain and longing struck a chord.

As the days passed, Usman tried to quell a suspicion that even the Dutch were complicit in a coverup. Jakarta finally sent a senior diplomat who cut through enough red tape to access some of the autopsy documents. On November 25, Usman took a short train ride to The Hague to witness the handover of eight thick files in Dutch, including twenty-six autopsy photos, to the Indonesian embassy. It was now legal evidence. The experts on the Indonesian team had full confidence in the findings, not least because they themselves had studied under the head of the NFI team, Dr. Robert Visser.

Usman had witnessed the handover but still couldn't secure a copy of the reports for himself. The chaotic incompetence also confirmed what he'd learned from Trisakti and all the other cases: the police would never solve this crime on their own.

After meeting with Usman, members of Dutch parliament started asking questions that uncovered a mysterious delay in the investigation. The work had started swiftly, even before Munir's plane landed. At 7:29 a.m., the Royal Netherlands Marechaussee was informed that someone died on an incoming flight. When it landed, thirty-five minutes later, the officers went to the cockpit to question the pilot, and they spoke to the purser. The crew and passengers were cleared to disembark after about thirty minutes, though the doctor who treated Munir was held longer. He couldn't say with certainty that it was a natural death, telling the investigators, "I didn't expect him to die. I think it's strange that it happened so quickly." He recommended an autopsy.

At 9:10 a.m., investigators learned that someone was waiting to pick up Munir. Sri, whom Poengky had asked to meet Munir, told them that Munir was a well-known activist who had been targeted with bombs and other attempts on his life. At 9:24, after a brief forensics investigation on the plane, the body was transferred to the mortuary. About two hours later, the municipal coroner of Amsterdam made an initial inspection of Munir's body. Unable to determine a clear cause of death, he filed a report of "unnatural death" (*niet natuurlijke dood*). Early the next day, the body was transferred to the Netherlands Forensic Institute for a limited autopsy called a *sectie*, or section. Investigators watched the pathologists collect samples of blood, urine, stomach contents, hair, brain tissue, lung, liver, spleen and spinal fluid. Dutch investigators also examined the medical kit used to treat Munir, his luggage, and his phone.

It was the next phase that raised eyebrows. A provisional toxicology report wasn't filed for three more weeks, on October 1. This report found no alcohol or sign of anaphylactic shock but did find high concentrations of arsenic in the blood and stomach contents. It was not possible to estimate when the fatal dose was consumed or in what chemical form it was ingested. That brief report concluded, "Munir's death can be explained by arsenic poisoning."[4] A full postmortem report two weeks later noted not just the toxicology results but also the symptoms of nausea, vomiting, and diarrhea and the watery content of the gastrointestinal tract, a feature of acute arsenic poisoning known as rice-water diarrhea. An internal memo to the Dutch Foreign Minister from the director for Asia noted on October 13, "Traces of arsenic were found in the stomach of the deceased. This dose is so high that it appears to be a crime." The memo recommended that the ministry inform the Indonesian authorities and request that they transfer the results to Munir's family and open an investigation.[5]

The Dutch foreign minister then visited Jakarta on October 28. He raised the death of Munir with the president and, in more detail, with the Indonesian foreign minister. Explaining that the toxicological examination would be completed soon and would most likely indicate a high concentration of arsenic, he promised full cooperation and said he assumed that Indonesia would inform the family as soon as possible. The Indonesian foreign minister said his government would review the report and probably send an expert to meet with the NFI.

After further analysis, the NFI completed a more precise and definitive toxicology report on November 4, and it passed through the Justice and Foreign Affairs ministries before reaching the hands of the Indonesian government on November 11, the same day the news leaked to the Dutch reporter.[6]

A suspicion formed that the Dutch had slowed things down until after Yudhoyono's inauguration on October 20, due to friction with the Megawati administration. The Dutch foreign minister denied waiting for a friendlier government, insisting that the delay was purely bureaucratic.[7] Whatever the cause, the holdup had left Suciwati without information she'd been demanding since she'd collected her husband's remains. The delays had troubling implications for the investigation as well. What had the perpetrators done to cover their tracks during those nine weeks? Had evidence been lost, forgotten, or destroyed? Had phone records or security camera footage been deleted?

That delay hurt the investigation, and then an inadvertent leak tipped off the only suspect. On the sidelines of a press conference, a KontraS staffer described the suspicious co-pilot to a reporter, thinking it was off the record. The next day, November 19, an article appeared in the *Jakarta Post* that never mentioned Pollycarpus by name but included details about a suspicious Garuda employee, the switching of seats, the call to Munir's phone, and the theory that he was poisoned on the flight to Singapore.[8] Pollycarpus was soon identified, and from that day on reporters chased him wherever he went.

Polly's press exposure prompted memories of more past sightings. Another prominent activist remembered being pestered like Hendardi. Yeni Rosa Damayanti had been an unusually outspoken critic of Suharto on East Timor and other sensitive issues. Like Munir, in 2004 she campaigned for voters to reject the ex-military candidates in national elections. Pollycarpus had called her almost daily in the run-up to the first round of voting in July, even phoning from Sydney and Japan when flying these routes. He claimed a common hatred of the military and especially the former armed forces chief and presidential candidate Wiranto. Polly had claimed his late wife was Timorese, her family massacred by the army. He urged Yeni to invite him to meetings with her anti-military friends, and once again promised free plane tickets to anywhere in the country if it was for activities opposing Wiranto. Offering to introduce her to other pilots opposed to the army, he urged her to meet him at a restaurant in South Jakarta, and to come alone. Yeni declined the offers, suspecting Polly was a Wiranto supporter scouting out critics, especially after she determined that his wife was neither dead nor Timorese. Invoking a stereotype of tropical laziness, she commented, "That's Malay *intel* for you, easily found out."[9]

More journalists remembered seeing Pollycarpus in the Hotel Vina Vira in Aceh in May 2003, just as martial law was declared. In a hotel jammed with reporters, with laptops and ashtrays scattered around the lobby and maps taped to the wall, Pollycarpus had claimed to be on vacation. People remembered that he had his arm in a cast and asked a lot of questions about what people had seen, where the latest clashes were. During a period of fierce fighting near the town of Lhokseumawe, he offered to take a journalist to meet the guerrillas. Some people remembered another man with him, someone quieter who mostly stayed in their room.

The police began questioning witnesses, starting with the Garuda crews. By December 3, they'd interviewed forty people.[10] When they called in Pollycarpus as a witness, the co-pilot retained a former head of the military police as his lawyer. Suhardi Sumomulyono had defended Timorese militia leader Eurico Guterres in his trial for crimes against humanity in 1999, as well as militia members charged with hacking three UN workers to death near the refugee camps of West Timor a year after the referendum. Suhardi, who was rumored to have links to Indonesian intelligence, denied that Pollycarpus ever called Munir or did intelligence work, saying he'd done nothing more than briefly chat with a fellow passenger in a departure lounge and then offer him a seat in business class.

Polly's lawyer also felt the need to deny a rumor that Polly was involved in other mysterious deaths. In an interview with Dutch radio, Rachland had recently called for a review of the deaths of three reformers. In July 2001, Baharuddin Lopa had been attorney general for only a month, during which he pledged to make corruption cases against senior politicians, including former president Suharto. He died suddenly while making a pilgrimage to Mecca. A month later, came the sudden death of General Agus Wirahadikusumah, a supporter of President Wahid's efforts to remove the military from politics, who also uncovered a $12 million scandal at an army foundation. Then, in April 2004, Mohammad Yamin, a prosecutor known for his incorruptibility, died after suddenly falling sick at a conference in Bali. Polly's lawyer told the press he'd already asked his client about these cases and his answer had been short and in English: "Bullshit, impossible."[11]

Even before the autopsy results, Usman and a small group of activists and researchers had begun sifting through rumors and reports. They pooled their information, such as a report that Munir had been invited to meet with someone at BIN a month before his death but had turned it down as unsafe. They drew up timelines and diagrammed the malign constellations of Munir's enemies. The Garuda meetings had already convinced some of them that Munir was murdered, and the autopsy report let them discuss this view with a larger, more formal group. They chose a name inspired by the coalition Munir had pulled together in Surabaya to campaign for justice for Marsinah, the murdered young labor activist. That one was called the Komite Aksi Solidaritas untuk Marsinah, or Action Committee in Solidarity with Marsinah. The acronym would again be KASUM (though sometimes written Kasum), but this time the M stood for Munir.

A core member was Indra Listiantara. As head of investigations for KontraS, he was the researcher who surprised Munir with a call from deep inside East Timor. Another time, while secretly in Aceh with another KontraS researcher, soldiers stopped a bus they were on. They took Indra's colleague off the bus, forcing Indra to decide whether to stay quiet or to accompany his friend. He said nothing, and then called Munir at the first chance. Munir happened to be in the middle of a meeting with a general. He took down the details, told Indra it would take time to go down the chain of command, but that their colleague would be released, and he was. Indra had left KontraS in 2002, ready for something new. He often thought of Munir's support for his field work with pride. When Kasum came together, he didn't hesitate to join the investigation, which was something personal to him. Indra pulled his old team of investigators together, whether they were still at KontraS or not.

Indra thought that Kasum's unofficial status could work to their advantage. Witnesses afraid to work with the police might talk to Kasum first and later agree to formal questioning. Indra forged ties to the more professional members of the police, starting with Anton Charlian, Usman's traveling companion from the Netherlands trip. Eventually the police allowed Indra to read typed interrogation records, but not to make copies. Each day for weeks, Indra pulled the records of three interviews from the files and quietly read them into a microphone tucked into his shirt. They were typed up and shared so the team could develop a sense of who the police were interviewing, what they were asking, and what they weren't.

Kasum set up an office on the grounds of KontraS, in an old garage unevenly renovated with tiles, cement, and plywood. At a meeting on December 6, Usman sat with Asmara Nababan, the former head of the National Human Rights Commission and a good friend of Munir's. Asmara was a Batak, an ethnic group from North Sumatra known for a certain combativeness. He was tall for an Indonesian, with a thick, swooping head of gray hair and sonorous voice. At this meeting, he used that voice to warn with authority, "If we communicate by cell phone, let's keep it neutral. If it's sensitive—just don't do it. Including text messages. If you want to meet, that's fine, but if you want to talk about this business, about Pollycarpus and so on, don't use a cell phone. It's no use being naïve. These are criminals."[12]

Suci had first heard Polly's name and voice on the phone, and Munir's phone records were a logical starting point. She'd requested Munir's records from the phone company, with no luck. Anton warned Usman that an official request might lead to records being hidden or destroyed. Bribing a phone company employee might be more effective. Eventually, Usman got his hands on eight hundred pages of Munir's records. The electronic file was searchable, if they knew what to look for. Hendardi found two numbers in his phone for Pollycarpus under "pilot," a remnant of his incessant calling.

Searching Munir's records, they came up with a hit on September 2, confirming Suci's memory. But there were others they had not expected. Pollycarpus had made brief calls to Munir's phone twice on the night the two men left Jakarta. The time stamps were shortly before departure, at 8:43 and 9:05, with location data placing both phones at the airport. Pollycarpus hadn't mentioned these calls at the Garuda meeting, where he had denied ever calling Munir. If they could get their hands on Polly's phone records, they would reveal whom else he called that day.

Another Kasum member was Choirul Anam. Anam had been a member of HMI, the Muslim Student Association, and was at Brawijaya University when Munir made a controversial campus visit in the midst of the 1998 disappearances. The unsanctioned event had to be held in a hallway. Munir had recruited Anam, first to volunteer at his old LBH Malang post, and then to come to Jakarta. Seeing he had no family near, Munir invited Anam stay with him at the radio station, and Anam had come to think of Munir as an older brother.

A few days before Munir's departure, he'd told Anam that a month earlier he'd gotten an invitation to meet informally with a senior BIN official.[13] The request came just after Munir had become especially vocal in his opposition to the draft Law on Intelligence. It seemed dangerous to meet him, and Munir didn't follow up.

Anam decided to track down the person who extended the invitation. Bijah Subiakto, the spy agency's deputy VII, was responsible for Information, Communications, and Technology. He was willing to meet. Anam, Poengky, and Suci met Subiakto several times, never alone and always in public places like a satay restaurant in front of Hotel Formula 1 Menteng or a Mexican restaurant in the Intercontinental Hotel.

Anam asked Subiakto if he had invited Munir to meet. He said he had, to discuss democracy and politics "because Munir's an expert in those issues and he's a national asset." The group met again at Subiakto's invitation, long enough this time to ask some hard questions.

"Who killed Munir?" Anam asked.

Subiakto said he didn't know, but suggested examining what cases or causes Munir worked on in the past year, especially ones involving important people. Anam ticked them off, starting with the draft laws on the military and intelligence. He'd taken up the matter of Sidney Jones, an American expert on Indonesia's emerging terrorist networks, whom Hendropriyono had expelled from the country. Suciwati mentioned the elections. Subiakto said the question could be answered from those cases, but offered no further help. They asked again and always the answer was the same: look at Munir's recent activities, especially concerning important people.

By the third meeting, Subiakto seemed nervous, thinking their meetings had been found out. After that, he refused to meet. Subiakto was removed from his position as deputy VII soon after.[14]

9

Getting Garuda

2005

On December 8, 2004, Munir would have turned thirty-nine. His friends and colleagues and the victims' families he'd helped held a march to demand action on the case, before converging at KontraS to dedicate a bust of Munir.[1] There was a performance by Iwan Fals, a Bruce Springsteen–like figure who could fill stadiums singing about corruption. Munir's musical taste mostly ran to blues and classic rock and some '80s bands like Guns N' Roses, but he had also idolized Fals, and it turned out the respect was mutual. When the singer heard of Munir's death on the radio, he wrote a song for him. Playing an acoustic guitar, Fals performed "Pulanglah," or "Come on Home." The song urged Munir to rest in the knowledge that his work would go on:

The paddy turns yellow, ready for harvest
Clear water from the mountain
Some are dry from drought
A breeze of change
A red and clouded sky
Let's come home, to the valley of rice fields

Good-bye, my hero
A generous fighter
You left when needed . . . when needed

You can go . . .

You can go cheerfully, because you are not wasted
You can go, wise fighter
One is lost, thousands rise
One is gone, others grow

The song's closing lines are "Accept these flowers / and prayers / true and sacred / true and sacred." The final words hung in the air. The Indonesian term for sacred, or holy, is *suci*.

For Usman, Munir's birthday of December 8 was already freighted with meaning. It was the anniversary of the death of his father and of the murder of his first idol, John Lennon. It was an emotional moment, but the event was also a form of advocacy to capture public attention and push the new president to act.

Three weeks after taking office on October 20, President Susilo Bambang Yudhoyono, or SBY, had met Suci and promised her an independent inquiry. SBY had limited combat experience, and some people called him a palace general, or an air-conditioning general. It was an insult, but one that reflected some distance between SBY and the army's worst abuses. He projected an air of professionalism after the lackluster, backsliding Megawati administration. Munir had been opposed to any retired general as president and wasn't convinced of SBY's democratic credentials, telling an Australian publication, "He is a user of democracy rather than a believer in it."[2] But SBY professed to have admired Munir. Learning of Munir's death, SBY had interrupted a campaign speech to praise Munir's critique of the military.

SBY kept his pledge to Suci by creating the Fact-Finding Team on the Case of Munir's Death (Tim Pencarian Fakta Kasus Meninggalnya Munir, or TPF) on December 24. However, the team's mandate was weaker than in the draft activists had hammered out with police just a few days earlier. It would merely assist the police, without clear authority to question witnesses, propose lines of investigation, or evaluate police performance. The decree also omitted senior religious and human rights leaders from the membership, including former president Gus Dur.

The team had three months to work, with a possible extension. A one-star police general named Marsudhi Hanafi would chair the TPF, with the senior human rights figure Asmara Nababan as vice-chair. The remaining twelve included Munir's old colleagues Rachland and Hendardi, as well as Munarman, another former LBH colleague. As secretary, Usman was responsible for day-to-day operations and scheduling. Other members came from the ranks of the police, prosecutors, and foreign service, with a forensics expert rounding out the team.

Hendardi thought the presidential decree provided enough political backing to give the TPF a try. Several others refused to join a process they felt was planned to fail.[3] Usman wondered if he should do the same, and not just due to the weaker mandate. He worried that the government officials who made up nearly half the team would impede its work or even spy on it. He talked it over with Asmara, who'd spent years battling the obstruction of human rights inquiries as secretary general of the National Human Rights Commission. Usman often turned to Asmara, especially once Munir was gone, for his experience and political sense. Together, Usman and Asmara decided the TPF was the best option they had to find the truth.

They would do the best they could, and if the obstacles were too great, they would walk away. As insurance, they would also keep the independent mechanism of Kasum running in parallel.

Three days after the president signed the decree, Indonesia experienced its biggest natural disaster since the eruption of Krakatoa in 1883. On the morning of December 26, 2004, an earthquake measuring 9.1 on the Richter scale heaved the floor of the Indian Ocean upward along a thousand miles of fault, unleashing a massive tsunami. The great swell of water slammed into South and Southeast Asia carrying vast rafts of debris.

Indonesia's Aceh province was closest to the fault and hardest hit, with an estimated 167,000 dead. The tsunami demolished huge swathes of the provincial capital and wiped away fishing villages along the western coast, leaving only a few cement foundations.[4] Hundreds of thousands were suddenly homeless in a province already torn apart by thirty years of anti-insurgency operations. Instead of their usual perilous work investigating violence by the army and guerrillas, KontraS staff in Aceh worked alongside Indonesian Marines and Malaysian soldiers to excavate bodies from the debris. Each night they laid out rubber boots and gloves in long lines and disinfected them with bleach, ready to start again in the morning. Aid workers and funding flooded a region long under tight military control and closed to the outside world just days before. The response brought a new opportunity for peace and reconstruction, but it also took attention away from other urgent matters, including the Munir case.

One Sunday early in the new year Police Brigadier General Marsudhi Hanafi was asked to come to the president's personal residence in Cikeas for a brief audience. There SBY asked if he had any questions about leading the TPF. Marsudhi asked, "Are we serious about handling this case?" It was an impertinent question, and on hearing it the president's face changed, but he solemnly said, "Of course we are serious," even raising his hand as if to swear. Marsudhi said he was ready to start.

Marsudhi was seconded three assistants from police headquarters and a room at the Criminal Investigation Division, outfitted with phones and computers. He made a sign and hung it on the door: MUNIR CASE COMMAND POST. Marsudhi was worried about the time that had passed between the crime and the start of the investigation. He was unimpressed with the police delegation to Amsterdam, which included no Indonesian members of Interpol and failed to get their hands on crime scene investigation reports or the full autopsy report. He was unhappy that the Dutch investigators had boarded the Indonesian territory of Flight 974, and unhappier still that they had cleared the plane to leave after a rudimentary review of the crime scene. Important evidence had likely been lost forever. Despite all this, he was confident that there was no crime that could not be solved.

For most of January, however, little happened. He wasn't sure if it was due to the tsunami or the activists' reluctance to put their faith in him. He spoke to prosecutors a few times. He timed how long it took him to walk from immigration to the waiting room at the airport. He waited at his command post.

Usman was also trying to make use of the TPF's brief window of opportunity. The three-month mandate gave them until March 23. He brought in two former KontraS investigators. Abu was a lawyer who'd served as Munir's security chief at KontraS. After the attacks on the office, he helped Munir build a secret escape route through the fence around the overgrown backyard. Abu was a big man, but mainly used persuasion and close observation to keep Munir and his staff safe. It helped too that he was from a royal lineage in the eastern islands, and could bring that influence to bear if a threat involved people from home. Usman tasked him with talking to sources and getting access to police documents.

Indra, already a core part of Kasum, became Usman's assistant on the TPF. The policeman Anton Charlian remained a useful contact for Abu and Indra, sharing advice and leads, and hinting at or describing evidence the police couldn't officially share. Once Anton had to step away for a moment, and Usman stood guard by the door while Indra photographed the papers on his desk. The TPF might not be able to cite these materials, but they could inform their interviews and document requests.

Usman, Hendardi, and Rachland went to visit Marsudhi at police headquarters. The police general knew that Usman and others had protested his appointment over fears that he would obstruct the investigation. And even if he had the best of intentions, there would be doubts that a one-star general would challenge the top police officials if needed. Marsudhi showed them the command post he'd set up as a sign of his seriousness, and they cautiously started to work together.

If the TPF was slow to start, the police weren't doing much better. The investigation seemed stalled in a preliminary stage, still far from naming suspects or making an arrest. At the TPF's first meeting with the police, on January 13, the national police chief clicked through slides touting the eighty-seven people questioned and summarizing data about toxicology and other technical matters. It all seemed pro forma to Usman. There were no preliminary findings or theories and certainly no mention of any state institutions playing a role in the crime. The police did share two basic airline documents that might prove useful in finding witnesses, or even perpetrators: Flight 974's general declaration, listing all airline staff on board, and the passenger manifest.[5]

To Marsudhi, the police seemed unfocused, distracted by other cases, and oblivious to the importance of this case. Marsudhi saw his job as piecing together a mosaic, but he had little power to collect the essential pieces of the picture. The TPF couldn't compel witnesses to appear or conduct searches. They could only share information with the police and make suggestions, hoping the police would follow up.

The TPF gave the police a list of questions for every stage of Munir's journey, from pre-departure until his last breath.[6] The name Pollycarpus ran through the list like a leitmotif. The TPF had already concluded that he was no ordinary pilot. But what was he, exactly?

One night Usman was working late at KontraS when he received a series of three text messages. He read them with amazement. Forwarded around Jakarta, their source was unknown, but their details about the inner workings of BIN, the State Intelligence Agency, were convincing:

> Garuda pilot Pollycarpus: In the month 02-2002 was recruited by Deputy V of BIN Muchdi PR as a state intelligence principal agent, appointed through BIN Director Decree No. 113/2/2002. He was given a pistol, signed off on by Sergeant Major Nurhadi and extended by Sergeant Major Suparto (SPT).
>
> The day after the case [and] Polly's name appeared in the media, said person was requested to return the pistol, and that day also all documents on Polly were removed or eliminated. The orders came from Muchdi PR, SPT and As'ad, Deputy Director of BIN. This Gang of 3 are the ones actually in control of BIN. Polly often came to BIN to meet Muchdi PR to plan the murder of Munir because they were afraid that outside the country Munir would again expose the case of the 1997 disappearances of activists at the end of the New Order.
>
> Police investigators and the new BIN director (Syamsir Siregar) are suspected of knowing of the involvement of these three BIN officials in the killing of Munir. But they do not dare to reveal it.[7]

The most senior name in the texts was As'ad Said Ali, a civilian and a career intelligence official with long counterterrorism experience in the Middle East. Muchdi PR, the co-pilot's alleged handler, was Major General (retired) Muchdi Purwopranjono. He was deputy V, the roman numeral denoting one of seven divisions at BIN. His name was familiar to Usman from the case that spurred the birth of KontraS. Muchdi was commander of the Special Forces branch Kopassus in Suharto's last days. He'd been called before the honor board over the abductions and had never been given a command again. Apparently, he had moved to BIN.[8]

Under Suharto, Indonesian intelligence was primarily a tool for monitoring perceived internal threats to the stability of his government. A year after Suharto's fall, one observer described both the military intelligence agency BAIS and its less powerful, nominally civilian counterpart BAKIN, as "completely incompetent, politically manipulated and full of old system people with nationalist blinders over their eyes."[9] In early 2001, President Wahid had renamed BAKIN as BIN, with an expanded remit and funding to coordinate all intelligence activities. When Megawati named Hendropriyono to lead the organization, she'd made it a cabinet level post. Hendropriyono sought to expand BIN's authority to deal with terrorism, often at the expense of the police, though Munir and others had curbed some of these ambitions. BIN remained largely staffed by active and retired military officers, and with much of the old focus on domestic threats like separatism and even communism. More worryingly, it remained largely unaccountable to the president or parliament with regard to its priorities, staffing, and covert actions.

Six hundred closed-circuit cameras were dispersed through Soekarno-Hatta International Airport, perched on struts and beams, on walls and kiosks. When the TPF met with airport authorities on February 11, they learned that this system was badly out of date. Rather than digitally recording the whole airport, the security staff could only operate a single VHS camera at a time.[10] There were no tapes of Gate E7 from the night Munir left.

There was another way to gather information at the airport. Indonesian police often have a suspect reenact a crime to evaluate witness statements or test theories.[11] Usman wanted this reconstruction done as soon as possible, and the police agreed that the exercise could help pinpoint when

Munir was poisoned.[12] The airline, however, claimed scheduling conflicts and the busy hajj season prevented it from securing the presence of a 747 and the crews on duty the night of Munir's death. At last the airline agreed to hold the exercise on February 22, 2005. A hangar was reserved for the night, the time of the events they were reenacting, and Usman confirmed that the police were ready to go. At the last minute, Garuda said the plane and crew weren't available after all.

Garuda's foot-dragging appeared even more suspicious after taking into account three internal documents that surfaced, each strange in its own way. When the police first questioned Pollycarpus about the reason for his travel to Singapore, he'd cited two documents. In the first, dated August 11, 2004, the airline director assigned Pollycarpus "to recommend solutions to problems at Garuda Indonesia, especially in matters connected to Aviation and Internal Security." The second document was a September 4 memo from the head of corporate security, Ramelgia Anwar, asking the chief of pilots to let Pollycarpus fly as non-active crew from Jakarta to Surabaya, Denpasar, or Singapore, "at the first opportunity." A third document was a notice of change signed by the secretary to the chief of pilots on September 6, allowing Pollycarpus to be added to Munir's flight at the last minute. The police obtained copies of all three by December 10, 2004.

Hoping to learn more about Pollycarpus's assignment to security and his task in Singapore, Marsudhi led a TPF team to Garuda headquarters to meet with the airline director, Indra Setiawan, on February 4. Setiawan explained that the August 11 letter authorized Pollycarpus to continue work he was already doing unofficially, serving as a kind of informant by reporting actions by crew that violate procedures. The Singapore trip was his first task for this official assignment.

Setiawan seemed defensive, as though trying to cover something up. The airline had never conducted an internal investigation as required by law.[13] On top of that, the documents were suspicious. The August 11 letter was remarkably open-ended. It was also unusual for the airline director to bypass three levels of hierarchy and issue a letter directly to a co-pilot.[14] Then there was the security director's memo issued on September 4, a Saturday. A stamp in the top corner had a different date: September 15.

After the meeting, the TPF recommended that the police investigate airline management, starting by questioning them about Pollycarpus's assignment.[15]

Marsudhi asked police officers to go to the Garuda office for the original of the September 4 memo from the security director, as well as the office logbook. Police confiscated a logbook and a version of the memo that had two crucial differences. This one was dated September 15 and stamped with a serial number showing it had been properly logged and filed.

There is a term in Indonesian, *aspal*, that stands for *asli tapi palsu*. It means "real but false" and refers to items like a passport printed by the right office, but handed out through the back door in exchange for a bribe, or an unauthorized run of designer shirts cranked out on the night shift and sold locally. An *aspal* document is not exactly counterfeit, but not quite valid either. A letter written by a security chief, backdated and missing filing stamps, might fit that category.

The TPF brought their new evidence to the next meeting with Garuda management, held at police headquarters on February 28. Journalists were allowed to take photos before being shooed from the room, where the two teams sat behind long parallel tables. Setiawan insisted his assignment letter was appropriate and that the memo was written on September 4. The TPF kept up their questioning, raising the fact that September 4 was a Saturday. Finally, Setiawan admitted that the memo was backdated. Marsudhi thought this manipulated letter was a key to the mystery and would have arrested Setiawan quickly if the TPF had had the authority to do so.[16]

After two hours, the doors reopened for a press conference. Asmara, peering over his glasses, leveled a charge against the airline in his steady baritone, "Okay, we have two options. The first possibility is that shoddy, unprofessional management by Garuda allowed someone to be murdered"—Asmara punctuated the word with an index finger in the air—"on a plane. Or, the second possibility . . ." He paused. "Garuda is covering up information about a serious crime."

A few days later, on the morning of March 3, Marsudhi led a large TPF delegation to the presidential palace. They were shown to a large room hung with portraits and took their seats on ornately carved chairs. Marsudhi gave President Yudhoyono an interim report of their activities: reviewing Munir's phone records, analyzing police interviews, and talking to Garuda and airport management. The evidence so far pointed to a conspiratorial crime, rather than the act of one man with a personal motive. They recommended that the police name as suspects Pollycarpus and the three Garuda staff who signed his documents—the director, security chief, and secretary to the chief of pilots.[17]

The president listened carefully, then asked the question that hung heavy in the air.

"What about BIN?"

The TPF had indications of the spy agency's involvement, but they needed more time. The team's three-month mandate would expire in just three weeks.

"Alright then, if that's the case, it's extended." The president agreed to a three-month extension, until June 23, and promised to help them get access to the intelligence agency.[18]

Hours after the report to the president, the airline director sat before a parliamentary commission on the Munir case. Clipped to an ID badge hanging from his neck was a pin with the stylized bird logo and the English words "Smile 'n care." Over five hours, Setiawan and his colleagues struggled to explain that discrepancies in the documents were just minor administrative mistakes made after Munir's death. Pollycarpus watched from the back row.

After the closed-door hearing, Setiawan stayed to repeat his denials to dozens of TV cameras and digital recorders for an hour, until 11:30 p.m. The airline's security director, Ramelgia Anwar, sat smoking, off to one side of the hearing room. An Australian journalist, David O'Shea, approached him to ask, "What was Pollycarpus's job in Singapore?"

Ramelgia inhaled slowly, his *kretek* glowing and then fading. He looked at his hands, smiled weakly, and gestured with the cigarette at Setiawan at the front of the room.

"No, sir, I'm asking *you*. *You* signed the letter. Why did Pollycarpus go to Singapore?"

Ramelgia shook his head and smiled as smoke wafted upwards. His eyes almost closed, he murmured, "I've . . . I've answered."

"You know. So why can't you tell me?"

"I've answered the investigators . . . because the investigation is still in process."

After a pause, O'Shea asked, "Who killed Munir?"

Ramelgia woke from his torpor. His eyes went wide and his mouth formed an O of surprise. "Whoooo, I don't know," he said, shaking his head with a nervous smile that almost became a laugh, but never did. "No comment, no comment."[19]

A few days later, it was Pollycarpus's turn to face the parliamentary commission. He brought his attorney and four Garuda lawyers. Pollycarpus wore a short-sleeved shirt and tie, and the usual reading glasses hung around his neck. He placed a model Garuda plane on the desk in front of him. Looking tired, with red-rimmed eyes, he said he was just back from a visit to his parent's graves in Central Java.

As in the previous hearing, the public was asked to leave, "including our journalist friends." This time reporters snuck into the upper gallery, from where they could hear and see Pollycarpus being asked when he heard about Munir's death. He claimed it was three days later, out with his wife, when he heard on the radio "that a person had died on a Garuda flight, something like that." Perhaps realizing this was an improbably long time to be unaware of front page news, he announced, "I just remembered!" He'd actually been told by a colleague at the Jakarta airport. He was not sure what her name was, because "there are so many flight attendants."[20]

He claimed to have forgotten almost everything about his trip to Singapore, even where he stayed. He said that his assignment in Singapore was to investigate the dumping of fuel by a plane in August. He'd fulfilled this task in a ten-minute conversation with the crew, with no record of the conversation or visit to the 747 that dumped its fuel.[21] Several lawmakers later used the same phrase to describe his answers: *berbelit-belit*, or convoluted. One told the press that Pollycarpus appeared to lie—a lot—and to be protecting "certain people."

Members of parliament recommended that the police detain Pollycarpus, mostly for his own protection, especially after the accident he'd described. A few nights before, a vehicle grazed him, knocking his motorbike down near his home. A hospital treated him for a mild head injury and released him that night. One lawmaker noted, "He says it was an accident, but we suspect that this accident was part of an attempted murder." But who would try to kill him? "Well, the actors who may be behind all of this."[22]

Usman's fears that the government officials on the TPF might obstruct its work had begun to seem unfounded. Asmara brought people together and made them feel part of something important. He had an even temperament and experience summoning generals for questioning at the National Human Rights Commission. Indonesians take pride in their habit of *jam karet*, or rubber time. Munir was rarely on time for meetings, and KontraS press conferences always started late. But if you had a meeting with Asmara, you'd better be on time.[23]

Usman was especially pleased with Marsudhi. He seemed committed to solving the case, although content to let Usman and others do much of the legwork. As a police general, Marsudhi wasn't afraid to argue with police investigators and even pound the table or raise his voice in a way other TPF members could not. Once he became furious at the police for delays in requesting security footage from Singapore, something the TPF had no legal standing to do itself. A senior policeman claimed the footage had already been deleted but refused to provide a paper trail. Marsudhi rose to his feet, and Usman wondered if the two police generals might come to blows, until Asmara convinced them to take their seats and talk it through.

Marsudhi also criticized the police for their gentle questioning of Pollycarpus, allowing him to expound on airplanes and technical matters rather than answering hard questions. Marsudhi had shouted, "That was not an interrogation. Bring us an interrogation!" Moments like this made Usman glad to have Marsudhi on the team.[24]

Despite pressure from the TPF, as March began the police still considered Pollycarpus a key witness rather than a suspect. They wouldn't name a suspect until they knew who put the poison where, and when, and who witnessed it.[25] On March 4, the TPF proposed six suspects to the police. Asmara came away from the meeting with some optimism, telling Usman, "They're serious. Give them time."

The policeman Anton Charlian announced that Pollycarpus would be called in for another interview on Thursday, March 10. Psychologists and a lie detector would be brought in because his explanations to parliament were so convoluted and inconsistent with other witnesses.[26] The night before the interview, however, a fax machine at the Criminal Investigation Division (or CID) ejected a sheet of paper with no date or official stamp, signed by an airline doctor. The letter excused Pollycarpus from pilot duty for three days, though without giving a medical reason or referencing the police summons. The doctor later admitted he'd never examined Pollycarpus.

Marsudhi urged the police to move. "Just arrest Pollycarpus," he told a journalist, "The proof is already there, right? Don't let him get rid of the evidence." If police didn't act, he threatened to make TPF findings public, including evidence pointing to the co-pilot *and* to "certain groups" behind him.

The police didn't arrest Polly, but they sent a team of doctors to his home. He agreed to go to a police hospital, later claiming the police had pressured him to feign illness in order to evade journalists. Polly finally came to the CID building on Monday morning for a physical and a psychological exam. In the afternoon, he was escorted to a lab next door for the lie detector test, using an indirect route to avoid journalists waiting out front.[27] Pollycarpus was connected to the machine, and police asked questions about his contact with Munir and the backdated letter in a variety of ways for the rest of the afternoon. After a thirteen-hour day, Polly was taken out a back door to the police hospital to sleep.[28]

Early the next morning, police hooked him back up to the machine and asked about his actions on the plane and in Singapore.[29] In mid-afternoon, the investigators disconnected the lie detector, the results of which are not admissible in court. Polly spent the next few days formally answering questions and sleeping at police headquarters each night. After almost a week, the police named Pollycarpus a suspect and moved him to a cell.[30]

Suci was not confident that Polly's arrest would lead to a trial and conviction. He was only an operational actor, anyway, not the brains of the
conspiracy.[31] Suci traveled to Europe with the message that the arrest of
Pollycarpus must be only the beginning of a criminal inquiry. She spoke
before the United Nations Human Rights Council and met members
of the Dutch parliament and the Council of Europe.[32] Back home she
was accused of airing Indonesia's dirty laundry abroad. The Minister of
Foreign Affairs publicly discouraged her from seeking support abroad,
cautioning, "Sometimes we have too high hopes for uncertain things."[33]
After her return, Suci received two handwritten letters warning her that,
if she continued to pry into Munir's death, she would be kidnapped and
blinded.[34]

Meanwhile, without a Mutual Legal Assistance agreement, police had no
access to evidence and witnesses in the Netherlands. On top of bureaucratic hurdles, the Dutch refused to hand over evidence that might lead to
the use of the death penalty.[35] The Indonesian attorney general promised
not to seek a capital sentence but couldn't guarantee that a judge would
agree. After months of letters, the Dutch minister of justice agreed, even
without an agreement, to share interview records, crime-scene investigation reports, and blood and tissue samples.[36]

However, an agreement was still needed to question two residents of the
Netherlands, one a Dutch citizen. The police had shown interest for some
time in a couple, both natives of Indonesia. On the flight to Singapore,
Yvonne Lie Lay sat in premium class, next to Pollycarpus. Her husband,
Lie Khie Ngian, sat next to Munir in business class. Lie was a chemist.
The Dutch eventually agreed to allow the Indonesians to interview the
two on a voluntary basis and not under oath.[37]

At the start of March, the TPF had told the president that four Garuda
employees should be considered suspects: Pollycarpus, Director Indra
Setiawan, security director Ramelgia Anwar, and the secretary to the
chief of pilots, Rohainil Aini. With Pollycarpus in custody and new leadership at the airline, Usman hoped the police would question Garuda staff
members intensively.

The police were indeed showing signs of interest in them.[38] Aini was secretly brought in while Pollycarpus was undergoing questioning. Police described her answers as convoluted at first (*berbelit-belit* again), before becoming more cooperative.[39] On March 29, journalists hanging around the parking area spotted Indra Setiawan leaving with two prominent attorneys. In the gray safari suit favored by civil servants, Setiawan had just wrapped up a full day of questioning. He directed all questions to his lawyers, who emphasized that Setiawan's only link to Pollycarpus was the August 11 assignment letter and that he knew nothing about Singapore or any events after that.[40]

To resolve conflicting testimony, on April 1 police held a "confrontation" between the suspect and his supervisor, Chief of Pilots Karmel Sembiring, as well as Polly's apparent supervisor in his security role, Ramelgia Anwar. Pollycarpus backed away from some of his earlier statements to police.[41] Most significantly, faced with Ramel in person, Polly admitted that the trip to Singapore was his own idea, not the security chief's. Still, he claimed that the idea was based on earlier guidance from Ramel about his security duties. Ramelgia, or Ramel, had supposedly been fired for "administrative carelessness" related to the backdating.

On April 5, the police named two Garuda employees as suspects, but neither were senior staff. They were two members of the cabin crew to Singapore: Oedi Irianto, who worked in the pantry, and Yeti Susmiarti, who served the food and drinks.

When police searched Polly's house on April 25, they confiscated a cell phone and a white memo pad. The pad contained a sketch of Flight 974's seating, with Munir and Polly's seats circled, and a timeline of Munir's flights. It also had the phone number of an army officer, Colonel Ketut, described as someone able to counter the Dutch forensics report, and a man named Umar.[42] Usman believed that when he and Suci retrieved Munir's body in Amsterdam, Ketut and Umar had been at Schiphol Airport, tasked with maintaining control of the body and the forensics investigation. Police also confiscated a bundle of newspaper clippings and a red phonebook, but some items they sought may have been destroyed. The police believed that Polly had phoned his wife and sister a month earlier with instructions to destroy a blue phone directory and a cell phone. When they asked him if he had done so, he claimed he could not remember.[43]

Once again, the media spotlight helped excavate suspicious activity from Polly's past. Former student activists recalled that during the May 1998 protests, a pilot had appeared one day at a logistics post they'd set up near Garuda housing. Pollycarpus offered them the use of his car to move supplies. They were hesitant at first, but needed the help.

Pollycarpus helped ferry food to the occupied DPR building and campuses, or wherever it was needed. He bragged about close ties to the army and police, his collection of vintage jeeps, and his gun. They were skeptical until he flashed a small pistol tucked inside his clothes, saying he had a permit. Once he ran a red light in Central Jakarta—intentionally, it seemed—and the police pulled him over. Pollycarpus hopped down and spoke to them briefly, and soon he was free to go without even the customary bribe. The students didn't know what to make of him. If he was *intel*, why boast like that? After a few days, he stopped coming by, and the next time they saw him was on TV, when he was arrested six years later.[44]

The TPF made note of such reports, but they were particularly interested in sightings of Pollycarpus in conflict areas, a sign of his links to intelligence. An Australian newspaper reported that Pollycarpus was spotted in East Timor during the 1999 violence, meeting with notorious militia leader Eurico Guterres, with whom he now shared a lawyer. Munir's friends kept digging into the enigma of Pollycarpus. They secured Garuda's manifest showing that Polly's trip to Aceh was May 14 to May 25, 2003, just when martial law was declared.

The question of Papua was even more interesting. At that first meeting at Garuda, Pollycarpus had told Suci he once flew for Associated Mission Aviation, or AMA. The organization hopscotches Cessnas and other small planes across one of the most rugged terrains on earth, bringing missionaries and supplies. Poengky thought there might be more to this story, but wasn't sure how to check it out. Then a neighbor of Imparsial's said she knew Pollycarpus and that his old boss at AMA was a relative of hers. In May 2005, Poengky flew eighteen hundred miles east to Jayapura, where she located the AMA office inside the little airport.

Polly was not from Papua, but from Central Java. He was named after Saint Polycarp on the suggestion of a Dutch nurse who assisted with his difficult birth.[45] His father was a senior noncommissioned officer, a sergeant major, as well as a *dalang*, a puppet master for the shadow plays. His parents divorced, and Polly followed a sister to Papua and stayed there, living in dormitories as he completed high school. Some vocational education led to an offer of a job and training as a pilot with AMA, where he worked from 1985 to 1988. His old boss and co-workers told Poengky they'd been surprised to see him offered a spot to train with Garuda. For an AMA pilot to move to a small airline would be impressive, but the national flag carrier was beyond all expectations. Stranger still was that Pollycarpus wasn't AMA's most reliable pilot. There'd been complaints about his habit of flying home before the job was done. They told Poengky there was "something wrong" with his promotion to Garuda. Polly was also said to be close enough to military officers there to join them for target practice. According to some reports, one of the soldiers he'd been close to in the late 1980s was the head of the Jayapura Military District Command, Muchdi Purwopranjono.

Chasing down these strands only raised more questions about the pilot, his motivations, and his connections. They all came back to a question Rachland posed after Pollycarpus's arrest: "Garuda doesn't have any reason to murder Munir. The question is, who has the power to use Garuda for their own benefit?"

10

Chasing BIN

2005

The police had Pollycarpus in custody and were questioning Garuda officials. It was a good start, but Usman knew that this first ring of suspects was the easiest. The TPF needed more evidence if they were going to push the police to overcome any intimidation or interference that might stop them moving up to the next ring.

BIN had been on Suci and Usman's radar since they first laid eyes on Pollycarpus at Garuda headquarters. When the co-pilot mentioned aviation security and had been asked, "Oh, like *intel*?" his denial was suspiciously abrupt. Then came the anonymous text messages. And when a reporter had asked the airline director if he'd allow an intelligence agent to work at Garuda. Setiawan had not ruled it out, saying, "The country owns the shares, so if they need to place a person there, then we're management. We're not the owner."[1]

In early March, Marsudhi would say only that the TPF was searching for whoever had given the orders in the criminal conspiracy. He added that they were looking outside the airline, since the "core business of Garuda is not to kill people." It was becoming clear by now where they were looking.[2] Usman stated publicly that the TPF already had preliminary, second-hand evidence of a BIN role, although the team still needed to carry out its own fact-finding.[3]

Syamsir Siregar had been BIN's director since December 8, the day Iwan Fals sang for Munir's birthday. Siregar was a military intelligence veteran who had retired from the army during the New Order. He was respected within the military and was an ally of SBY. Without a personal stake in BIN's actions before his tenure, he might be willing to conduct a credible internal investigation or make some files available to investigators. But his recent arrival might also make him unwilling to shake things up or antagonize his agents. Siregar's statements were mixed but leaned toward the second option. He made a broad pledge to cooperate with the fact-finding team, but only if he was shown evidence of his agency's involvement. He challenged journalists to either come up with proof or stop making accusations. After a meeting at the presidential offices, a reporter caught up with Siregar at the foot of a staircase. Asked if he was prepared for BIN to be investigated, he shouted back, "And who will investigate?" The reporter suggested the TPF, and Siregar paused before hurrying up the stairs.[4] Soon after, however, Siregar said he wanted to meet with the TPF before his agency's name was tarnished further.[5] The parties met April 6 and agreed to create a protocol for cooperation.

The TPF made a list of current and former BIN staff to talk to. Their first target, just below the top leadership, was former principal secretary Nurhadi Djazuli. The anonymous text messages had claimed that he signed Polly's gun permit. Nurhadi had recently been named ambassador to Nigeria but was still in Jakarta. Three summonses from the TPF led only to a press release from Nurhadi denying he ever met Pollycarpus and claiming the TPF had no legal basis.

Nurhadi's refusal showed the need for the proposed cooperation protocol. In early May, the two parties finally signed a two-page agreement pledging that BIN would look for information and documents, the TPF would report any findings to the president alone, and both would respect each other's authority and protect state secrets.[6] Securing these promises had consumed a precious month of the TPF's extension until June 23. What's more, even with the agreement, Nurhadi did not agree to meet until lawmakers threatened to revisit his ambassadorship.

On the afternoon of May 9, Usman, Marsudhi, Rachland, and several other team members met Nurhadi on the neutral ground of a Foreign Affairs Ministry building. Nurhadi explained BIN's compartmentalized structure, in which each of the seven deputies reported to the director and were unaware of each other's activities or networks. He explained that there were two categories of agent. "Organic" agents are permanent, salaried government employees, while "non-organic" agents are recruited by a deputy for an indeterminate period and paid intermittently. According to Nurhadi, there were no recruitment guidelines or employment records for non-organic agents. Only their handlers, and perhaps others in the same unit, knew they were BIN agents.

The TPF probed the rumors that BIN had issued Polly a gun. Nurhadi confirmed that he had been the person who signed gun permits. Indonesian gun laws are strict. To obtain a firearm, even a spy must demonstrate a clear need, shooting skills, and psychological fitness. If these requirements are met, even a non-organic agent could get a gun, most likely under an alias. Overall, Nurhadi offered little that was new or specific, though even on general topics, he was just evasive enough to further convince Usman of BIN's role in the murder.[7]

A second meeting with Nurhadi a week later was slightly more revealing. He said that if a state-owned enterprise had a problem, BIN might recruit someone from within it or place an agent there. It had done something of the kind with the state oil company Pertamina. This recruit might be given a gun permit with the BIN director's approval. Nurhadi acknowledged that the personnel office kept a dossier of agents and aliases, but denied ever hearing the name Pollycarpus.

The next day they met Nurhadi's successor as principal secretary, Suparto, also mentioned in the texts. Suparto contradicted Nurhadi, claiming he'd never heard the term non-organic at BIN, didn't know anything about a list of agents and aliases, and would allow only permanent BIN staff to obtain an ID card or a gun.[8] More concerning, Suparto said the director had ordered him not to share any written materials with the TPF, as they were protected state documents.[9] In the end, the only document BIN ever provided was a list of agents and their firearms. Pollycarpus wasn't on it, but it listed only organic agents and was dated just after the autopsy leaked. Usman suspected it had been cleaned up.

The TPF also visited BIN's arms storeroom, hoping to confirm whether Pollycarpus was issued a weapon. Asmara was skeptical of the visit's value and skipped it. But Usman wanted to see the registry of weapons and talk to the manager. On arrival, agents searched the TPF team and confiscated their cell phones. Usman felt watched through the mirrors, as in a movie. But Asmara's instincts were right: the storehouse manager answered every question with "I don't remember" or "I don't know." They learned nothing from the visit.

With or without BIN's cooperation, evidence continued to emerge. The police had seized Pollycarpus's phone, and two numbers in the call history stood out. One was a cell phone registered to Yohannes Hardian Widjona-rko, director of a timber conglomerate named Barito Pacific, at one time the largest company on the Jakarta Stock Exchange. When investigators got approval from above to question a man of his stature, Widjonarko told them that he just paid the bill each month. The phone was used by someone else: Muchdi Purwopranjono.

The second unusual number was a landline, 79179374. The number did not appear in the registry of the phone company, Telkom. When an investigator tried calling the number, someone answered but quickly hung up. On May 25, after learning from the police about the mystery number, Asmara wrote to the head of the phone company. He gave the letter to Rachland and two other team members, who raced to the Telkom office. They were told the director was talking with shareholders and couldn't meet on short notice. Telkom had been privatized for a decade, but the government still held a majority share, so Rachland contacted the minister of communications and information. It wasn't long before the Telkom director left his meeting and came down to the lobby. He said he'd check with his experts and have the answer in ten minutes, but when he returned he seemed mystified. He said he'd have to talk to colleagues at headquarters in Bandung.[10]

A Telkom official called late that night, asking, "Rachland, where did you get that number?" Speaking in a low voice, he said the company had traced the number to the South Jakarta neighborhood of Kalibata, home to BIN headquarters. It seemed that BIN used a system called Direct Inward Dialing, listing as many as six hundred lines under a single number. If you knew the number of the line you wanted, you could call it, but it would appear in the billing records as the main number.

Telkom's experts eventually traced the number to a specific office at BIN. It, too, belonged to Muchdi Purwopranjono. As deputy V, Muchdi was in charge of *penggalangan*, an Indonesian intelligence term derived from the word for girder or beam. It can mean support, but is often translated as mobilization or conditioning. *Penggalangan* includes covert operations to persuade, intimidate, lobby, or otherwise secure the support or compliance of various groups in society. These were central activities for intelligence bodies under Suharto, and they had not faded away. Muchdi described his job as creating "an advantageous situation for the state" in the areas of ideology, politics, economy, society, culture, defense and security.[11] The department covered a lot of ground.

The TPF identified more than three dozen calls between Polly's home and cell phones and Muchdi's office and cell phones. The first known call was on August 25, around the time Munir's travel was reported in the press. There were calls on the critical days of September 6 and 7, and then a long gap before they started again with eighteen calls or texts on a single day, November 17, a few days after the autopsy results became public. There were more calls in late November, after Polly made the papers.

Usman was tasked with trying to reach Muchdi by phone.

"*Assalamu'alaikum.*"

"*Wa'alaikumsalam.*"

"Who is this?"

"Usman Hamid from the fact-finding team on Munir's murder."

"Who?"

Usman identified himself again, and then a third time when asked, getting louder each time. Finally the voice at the other end said, "Wrong number."

Usman called back but nobody picked up, so he left a message: "It couldn't be the wrong number, because I got it from the police. This must be Muchdi, and I am extending the Munir TPF's invitation to you."[12]

The investigation hung on the ability to crack open the black box of BIN. The head of BIN at the time of Munir's death was a lieutenant general, A. M. Hendropriyono. He had a history with Munir, who represented the survivors of the 1989 massacre in Talangsari by troops under Hendropriyono's command. Munir also challenged his appointment to BIN in court, citing those killings. When that effort failed, Munir largely defeated Hendropriyono's efforts to dramatically expand BIN's powers. Munir also challenged his actions at BIN, such as banning American researcher Sidney Jones and drawing up a list of NGOs he said were a threat to elections.[13]

When the TPF tried to question Hendro, as he was known, the general pushed back. He published editorials denying BIN's role in the murder and attacked the TPF on television. At dusk on May 29, he filed a defamation complaint against Usman and Rachland for saying that, if necessary, they would hunt him down on one of his frequent visits to the United States. Hendro bristled at the term, saying, "Hunted! This sentence pierces the heart."[14] He said he'd assumed the TPF would be professional, but

Memo from Garuda's security director, dated September 4, asking Pollycarpus's supervisor to allow him to travel to Singapore at the first opportunity.

their statements were upsetting his life. Friends canceled plans, and foreign colleagues joked that he might put arsenic in their drinks.

Hendro insisted he'd never heard the name Pollycarpus. The co-pilot couldn't be an agent, he explained, because "I know my men." As for the phone calls, "Intelligence is collecting information, right?" and anyone was allowed to call BIN. He denied that Munir was ever on BIN's radar and claimed that killing him offered no political benefit. He denied any personal or professional conflict with Munir.

The police acted quickly on the defamation complaint, questioning journalists, naming Usman and Rachland as suspects, and calling them in for questioning. The TPF stuck to their guns and on May 30, the day after the complaint, they sent summonses to Hendropriyono as well as Muchdi.

Hendropriyono was asked to come for an interview on the morning of June 6. In preparation, the TPF developed six lines of inquiry, assigning lead questioners for each. They would ask about any intelligence operations, by any of the deputies, against people believed to be endangering the state or the security of elections. They would ask if Munir was considered a threat to security and whether any measures were taken against him. What was his opinion of Munir's work on the rendition of a terrorist suspect to the United States, or on the massacre by Hendro's soldiers at Talangsari? They would ask him about the evidence they had of extensive phone contact between Muchdi and Polly. They were well prepared, but Hendropriyono didn't show up to that meeting or two others requested by the team.[15]

Each time, his lawyers claimed Hendro was out of town or that the summons violated the protocol. Sometimes no reason was given. Once, the team waiting for Hendro was surprised to see a different retired general enter with a coterie of lawyers. Syamsul Djalal, the former head of the military police, was Hendro's new lawyer. Marsudhi, merely a *police* general, muttered to Usman and Asmara, "I'm not the one to lead this." Usman looked at Asmara, the most senior member of the team. Asmara usually just opened the meetings, and then let Usman or another younger TPF investigator handle questioning with his support, but he was ready to take on the challenge.

Asmara began with the normal pleasantries, and then he leaned forward to face Usman, two seats away.

"Usman?"

"Ya, Bang." The term meant big brother, a term of respect in Asmara's native North Sumatra.

"You know the summons letter? Do you remember it?"

"Of course."

"What's the name on it? Priyono . . .

"Abdullah Mahmud Hendropriyono."

"Say it again, Priy . . . What?"

"Abdullah Mahmud Hendropriyono, Bang."

"That's it! That is it." Asmara turned to face the lawyers. "Who are you guys? *Who* are you? What's your name? What. Is. Your. Name?"

"Syamsul Djalal."

"Usman, is that in the summons?"

"No."

"In that case, we have no business with you." And then, without even looking at them, he said, "Get out of here now!" As they collected their things, Marsudhi broke into a broad smile.

When the team asked the president for help, he expressed disappointment but took no action. Hendro responded through the press, saying he didn't believe the president could really be disappointed in someone who was once senior to him in the military.

Muchdi was sent four summonses, ignoring all of them.[16] The TPF also wanted to talk to a BIN agent named Bambang Irawan. A retired Kopassus colonel and military intelligence veteran with training as a doctor, Irawan had worked in Aceh for many years. Irawan was thought to be Pollycarpus's taciturn roommate at the hotel filled with reporters at the start of martial law in 2003. His name was not on the manifest for Flight 974, but some thought he might have been traveling under an alias. Kasum investigators found him on the manifest of a return flight from Singapore on September 10. Other rumors had him joining shooting practice with Pollycarpus or possessing expertise in chemistry that might be useful in a poisoning. Irawan agreed to meet with the TPF, but then refused at the last minute, giving a surprising reason. He'd already been questioned by police.

It turned out that the police had also interviewed Muchdi and Hendro-priyono.[17] Hendro was reportedly not interviewed at police headquarters, which would be beneath an army general, but in his hotel suite. While it could not be confirmed, one policeman told a TPF member that he turned down a large cash bribe from Hendro at that meeting.

Usman was surprised and not a little angry to learn about these interviews after the fact, and not directly from the police.[18] The police provided the TPF with only eighteen records of interrogation out of about a hundred, and they never shared those of Hendropriyono, Muchdi, and Irawan.[19]

Multiple summonses to Hendropriyono, Muchdi, and Irawan and weeks of negotiations for a protocol had yielded interviews with six low-ranking officials.[20] They netted only information on BIN's procedures and structure, which illuminated how BIN might recruit a non-organic agent in a state-owned enterprise, like Polly at Garuda. However, they yielded no concrete evidence that he was an agent or that the plot to kill Munir originated within BIN.

Signs of BIN's role in planning the murder did emerge. Marsudhi called Usman early one morning in June, around five thirty a.m. "Usman, let's meet," he said, "I have a lot of documents." They were too sensitive to discuss by phone, or even at his office in police headquarters. Usman met him two hours later at an office the TPF maintained at the Women's Commission.

Usman was stunned. Marsudhi would not reveal his source, but he had gotten his hands on a remarkable set of memos. They appeared to have been drafted after Munir's death, based on an investigation by military or police intelligence, or possibly a senior official's personal network. They described a series of meetings within BIN prior to the murder. At one meeting, a document stated, Hendropriyono said he wanted Munir killed before the presidential elections of September 20, 2004. The memos laid out four strategies to kill Munir: in a car crash, through black magic, inducing a member of Munir's staff to poison him, or poisoning Munir overseas, using arsenic. At one meeting described in a memo, Hendro,

Muchdi, and a military doctor agreed, "Munir should be finished off by poisoning his food or drink."

The appearance of a possible smoking gun sparked intense debate within the TPF. Were the documents real? Some on the staff thought the documents were *too* good, and that magic didn't really fit BIN's culture. The allegation about an office worker recruited to poison Munir caused tensions within the TPF after a journalist quoted Rachland about an *intel* agent in KontraS. An office boy came to Usman in tears, feeling he had been accused of trying to kill Munir. A fight nearly broke out between Usman and Rachland, until Asmara restored the peace.

While not all the elements could be confirmed, on June 15 the TPF announced that they had uncovered four scenarios within BIN to kill Munir.[21]

Meanwhile, the Dutch couple whom police wanted to interview in the Netherlands visited their native Indonesia. Police questioned Lie Khie Ngian in Surabaya but said they found no indication of a role in the murder. But Usman still wasn't sure. The fact that he sat next to Munir and his wife next to Pollycarpus was suspicious. There was also the fact that Lie was a chemist, helped the doctor look for medicine in the kit, and by one account gave Munir a bottle of water to drink after he fell sick.[22] Usman wondered if the couple were part of a team working to ensure the operation was successful.

In the final days of the team's mandate, Hendropriyono offered to meet the team before members of parliament. It wouldn't be a proper interview, and it felt like a stunt, so Asmara refused. Hendro arrived on July 21 at parliament with a large entourage and used his solo appearance to read a poem he'd written, titled "Save Your Nation." In a form he called "outpouring-of-the-heart poetry," he seemed to address the TPF with a show of humility: "Do not be arrogant by considering yourself as a hero and demeaning the old soldier who has served you, with all his shortcomings as an ordinary human." The poem went on in that vein before concluding with patriotic zeal, "God wants us to unite with total vigilance, to face the fierce enemies infiltrating the body of our nation with all means and powers of deception." His entourage erupted in applause.

On the last day of the mandate of the TPF, police finally held the reconstruction, using a Boeing 747 in Hangar 11 of the Garuda Maintenance Facility. Pollycarpus and the crew participated, with actors playing Munir, Suci, Poengky, and the Dutch-Indonesian couple as Munir's journey was traced from the Dunkin' Donuts to his death. There was particular focus on the in-flight meal, but there was also a reconstructed encounter between Polly and the Dutch-Indonesian Mr. Lie in front of the lavatory, a fact not reported elsewhere. The reconstruction was not shared with the TPF and received little mention in the legal processes that followed.[23]

The TPF's work was over. In six months, they had investigated Pollycarpus, before moving up the Garuda hierarchy to its highest officer. After months of efforts to secure documents and phone records, and to learn the jargon and procedures of telecommunications, airlines, and intelligence, they had demonstrated phone contacts between Pollycarpus and senior officials at BIN. They had obtained the scenarios memo. And they had secured pledges from police, legislators, and the president to follow the investigation wherever it led.

Usman was keenly aware that the work was unfinished. There were leads they had not been able to confirm or dismiss, such as the role of the Dutch couple and the presence of BIN agent Bambang Irawan on board. BIN had balked at handing over documents such as visitor logs or target-practice records, claiming they were missing or confidential. Efforts to get security footage from two airports had come to nothing. Most of April was wasted hashing out the protocol with BIN, only to send out summons after summons in May and June as BIN officials ran out the clock. They hadn't gotten Muchdi or Hendro to answer any questions at all.

The lack of support from the government was deeply disappointing. When the president created the TPF, his spokesman said, "The president will do whatever it takes to solve this case." The president had personally assured Marsudhi of his commitment at the outset, restating his support in later meetings. He'd seemed genuinely angry at the obstruction, and sometimes took action to move the investigation forward. However, the failure to get access to BIN officials and documents, and the delays in charging Garuda officials, indicated the limits of either the president's authority or his willingness to use it. The government also failed to provide funding for travel to Singapore, the Netherlands, Timor-Leste, or Aceh, making it harder for the team to investigate Munir's last hours and Pollycarpus's ties to BIN.[24]

The president's staff let it be known that he'd consider another extension, and the team talked it over. Marsudhi and Asmara believed they'd chased down every lead they had, right up to the locked doors of BIN. It was time to hand the president a final report. Extending the term would be pointless without a stronger mandate. They decided to recommend a new team with more power to summon witnesses and suspects.

The report ran to forty-nine pages, plus a summary and hundreds of pages of annexes. It found that Munir was murdered by a criminal conspiracy of field operators, accomplices, planners, and decision makers. The poison was carefully chosen to be undetectable except by autopsy. The location was chosen to ensure that medical help would not be available but that the crime would be committed while still in Indonesian jurisdiction to prevent prosecution by another country. The forensics and the onset of symptoms pointed to the arsenic being administered during the Jakarta–Singapore flight.

The report recommended that the president direct the police to further investigate the airline's former director and security chief, as well as three intelligence officials: Hendropriyono, Muchdi, and Bambang Irawan. The report concluded that the police were unwilling or unable to investigate the case effectively and recommended an audit of their performance.[25] The police hadn't followed up on TPF requests or cooperated on key elements of the investigation. They would not share Hendro's interview notes or even provide an oral summary, and they held the reconstruction without even telling the TPF. The report also noted that unknown parties had made calls and sent texts to investigators, and even followed them, as forms of intimidation and *teror*.

The team decided not to include the leaked scenarios document in their final report. BIN's stonewalling made it too hard to interpret or confirm the contents. They were also confident that the president already had a copy of it.

President Yudhoyono conducted most of his business out of the presidential offices in a huge modernist structure built with the early 1970s oil money. For the handover ceremony, he invited the TPF instead to Istana Merdeka, the Freedom Palace. Istana Merdeka is within a huge complex that includes a second palace, the presidential offices, a mosque, a museum, a helipad, and tennis courts. The white neoclassical building was built as Koningsplein Palace in the nineteenth century for the governor general of the Dutch East Indies and his burgeoning colonial administration. It was renamed Freedom Palace for the day in 1949 that the Dutch flag came down and the broad stripes of red and white ascended the flagpole in its place. A presidential advisor explained that the location was a sign of appreciation and support: "Look, Usman, this is very special. An invitation to the Istana Merdeka means that the president is receiving the report not just as head of his government, but as head of state."

On June 24, 2005, the president welcomed the full TPF to a large, formal room. Several cabinet members were on hand, as well as the attorney general, national police chief, and the director of BIN.[26] The TPF presented six copies of the report, large bound volumes with green covers embossed in gold with a garuda.

The president exuded optimism that the case would be solved. Usman, too, found grounds for hope in the political situation. Early in his term as the first directly elected president, SBY shouldn't feel the need to protect Hendropriyono or anyone from the previous administration. The president was a retired general, but one who adopted the rhetoric of human rights and the rule of law. His own army background might lead him to view the power of military and intelligence bodies as a surmountable obstacle.

It felt as though the Munir case had truly become part of SBY's own agenda and political battles. He had sparred with Hendropriyono within Megawati's cabinet, and the rivalry escalated when SBY formed a new party to successfully challenge her reelection.[27] A participant at the handover recalls the president saying, "*Someone* has been unhappy with me from the very beginning of my election. *Someone* has been attacking me through the media, though the parliament, through the political parties. Now I think it's time for me to finish this agenda, although I know it's not going to be easy. But it is clear that this man, the one who always attacks me, is involved in the murder." He never said the man's name, and he didn't have to.

Copies of the report were given to the attorney general, the national chief of police, the BIN director, the commander of the armed forces, and the minister of justice. The TPF officially disbanded, and its files were not preserved or maintained. The team itself did not release the report, consistent with the words in the decree: "It is the government that will subsequently announce the results of the team's investigation to the public."

But the government did *not* make the results public. At first, the report was treated as a *pro justicia* document, a basis for investigation and prosecution, therefore not to be released. However, long after that justification made any sense, after all the pomp and optimism of the handover, despite distribution at the highest levels of law enforcement and national security, the report was not released.

11

The Pilot's Choice of Poison

2005

Six weeks after the handover ceremony, the trial of Pollycarpus opened at the Central Jakarta District Court. The unlovely civic building with its facade of green latticework, a nod to Islamic architecture, squats along one of Jakarta's oldest, widest thoroughfares. The double roadway is separated by a canal first dug in the 1640s for sampans of cargo from harborside warehouses. The sampans are gone, along with the Dutch department stores and Chinese mansions that lined the avenue, but the canal still provides a strip of overgrown green and some open sky to a neighborhood of gritty retailers and government buildings like the courthouse.

Suci and Usman never missed a day of the trial. Each Tuesday they passed through a metal detector and climbed the dingy stairs to one of the upper two levels. On each floor, a cluster of courtrooms was encircled by a wide open-air corridor that allowed in a steady symphony of Blue Bird taxis, three-wheelers, street vendors, muezzins, touts, street cats, and police vans banging their doors shut.

At an Indonesian criminal trial, prosecutors open with preliminary arguments, similar to an indictment. The defense argues to dismiss all charges, and then the judges typically decide to proceed to the evidence. On the first day of his trial, as Pollycarpus was escorted into court, shouts of "Murderer!" rang from the back of the packed room. Prosecutors read out charges of premeditated murder and forgery, for the document he used to retroactively authorize his trip to Singapore. They laid out a theory of the crime: Polly left his seat and headed for the pantry, where he poured a large quantity of arsenic into a glass of orange juice. A flight attendant then carried the juice to Munir on the front of a tray of beverages. Munir's seat-mate, the Dutch-Indonesian chemist, chose champagne due to his European habits. Munir, as a Muslim, selected the juice. According to this theory Munir, and only Munir, would have had to select the poisoned glass.

Witnesses did see Pollycarpus out of his seat for much of the flight, but no one saw him enter the pantry. Usman worried more about the alleged motive, crucial to conviction and further trials. The prosecution argued that the motive was political, but still largely personal. The pilot believed in the need to defend his nation, the so-called Unitary State of the Republic of Indonesia (with the acronym NKRI), from those who wanted to break it up. Seeing Munir's frequent criticism of the government, Polly's "beliefs and values pushed the suspect to feel the need to stop the activities of the victim."[1]

The indictment referred to "certain parties" with the same motive, but never mentioned a conspiracy or BIN. Polly's secondary charge of forgery never mentioned the murder. Instead it cited the cost of Polly's unauthorized travel, making Garuda less an accessory to murder than a victim of fraud.

Usman knew a man could commit murder alone, but to poison a famous activist on an international flight would take resources, planning, access, and coordination. He recognized a familiar strategy: at the court martial for the 1998 abductions, the low-ranking soldiers claimed to have acted spontaneously to defend the nation, rather than on orders from above. Munir had called that version of events an "absurd reality."

Indonesian prosecutors rely almost solely on the police dossier for evidence and even for which charges to bring. They can send back a dossier that appears incomplete, but they don't question witnesses or gather evidence. They had to work with the material they had, despite its gaps. According to one of the prosecutors, rather than trying to lay the groundwork for future trials, the team set a goal simply to prove the case against Pollycarpus.[2] But such a personalized, individual motive made little sense and was hard to prove, particularly if it was not accurate. These flaws might jeopardize even a case against Polly as a lone actor.

———————

A week later, Muhammed Assegaf led the defense's response. A small man with a collar one size too big and his remaining hair refusing to lie flat on his head, he had a long roster of unsympathetic clients he had represented ably: former President Suharto, army officers charged with crimes against humanity in East Timor, and the Bali bombers who killed over two hundred people in 2002. Just a few weeks earlier, he'd secured a surprisingly brief sentence for the playboy who had killed a waiter over a declined credit card at the bar of his family's Hilton. Despite this dark résumé, Assegaf had two things in common with Munir. He was an Arab-Indonesian and a former LBH lawyer.

Assegaf enjoyed bantering with the courthouse press, mocking prosecutors' arguments. He would pretend to be Pollycarpus irrationally calling his victim only days before murdering him, or a flight attendant preposterously gesturing with her chin for Munir to select the one poisoned drink.

In his response to the indictment, Assegaf seized on the failure of prosecutors to lay out a conspiracy or a clear motive.[3] With the investigation still open, how could Pollycarpus stand trial as sole perpetrator? Assegaf used a Malay proverb to cast his client as a scapegoat: "When there is no rattan, a root will do. When there is no killer, Polly will do."[4] He claimed Munir himself would have loudly protested this injustice carried out in his name. He called for sympathy for his client: "In this great court, with his wife at the hearing, the man Pollycarpus, having done no wrong, is yelled at! Pointed at! Insulted! As a murderer. It is truly sad, because if this case stops with Pollycarpus, the true murderer will go free, laughing at this justice."[5]

The judges ruled that the trial should proceed, and testimony began on September 6. At the courtroom doors, the defendant passed between two protestors, silent as caryatids, in paper masks of the man Pollycarpus was charged with murdering. His police escort dispersed throughout the room as he took a seat at the defense table.

The legal teams faced each other across the courtroom in black robes with white cambric ruffles down the front, like two lines of burghers painted by a Dutch master. Five judges looked down from the dais, their robes and ruffles topped by crimson satin panels described in a Ministry of Justice decree as the color of blood (in Indonesian) or of wine (in Dutch).[6] The green felt that covered the desktops gave rise to an idiom for facing trial—"going before the green table."

Holding a Quran above Suci's head, a clerk swore her in as the first witness. Under common law, like the American system, judges primarily enforce the rules while the parties argue the case to a jury. Under Indonesia's civil law system, judges take part in inquiring into the facts and questioning witnesses. The courtroom reflects this approach, with witnesses facing the judges while legal teams face each other across the room.

From the witness chair, Suci relived her last moments with her husband at the airport. She told of Usman informing her that Munir had died, and her panicked efforts to prove it a lie. She described the call from "Polly from Garuda" and recalled learning about his overtures to other activists and his war tourism. She spoke of the dangers of life with Munir and the nature of his work. Prosecutors held up the black-and-white shirt he wore when she saw him last, now a piece of evidence with traces of a poisoning. They displayed his phone and Poengky's photos of the airport good-bye for Suci to confirm as genuine. The pictures demonstrated that Munir appeared healthy in the moments before boarding.

Suci batted away the defense's efforts to sow doubt about the cause of death. Munir had been ill before but had recovered. There was no second autopsy in Indonesia because even the police agreed there was no need for one. And she was sure he was poisoned after leaving Jakarta because they had shared every meal before he left, right up to the hot chocolate at the airport.

Finally, Suci read out a letter to the judges. It stated her belief that Munir was assassinated for challenging those with power. Putting the trial in perspective, she said:

> Today, it has been exactly one year that Munir is no longer at
> my side and that of our children. For one year, this case has
> moved forward, and I only see one person charged with killing

Munir, and I'm sure he is only a field operator. Meanwhile, the intellectual actors stay hidden, far from reach. This reality makes my heart long for justice for my husband, Munir.

She described Munir's disappointment in that very courtroom as judges had dashed the hopes of victims of violence. They still sought justice.

No longer just for themselves, but also for Munir, a friend who accompanied them as long as he lived, in *duka* and in *suka*, in sorrow and in joy. And not just for Munir, but for our future as a nation. . . .

Honored judges, through this letter, I once again place my hopes on the green dais. But I will not only hope. I have pledged to fight for this hope. Because I will not stop, will never stop, until the case is solved and I can secure justice for myself and for our children, Alif and Diva, who hope too that such savagery will never be repeated.

Indra Setiawan was the first of four witness from Garuda to testify about the interlocking puzzle of Polly's vague security assignment, schedule changes, and backdated memos. The paper trail started with Setiawan's August 11 assignment letter recommending that Pollycarpus be given a security role.[7] Setiawan once told police that his security director Ramelgia Anwar suggested the co-pilot for this role. Now he admitted in court that Ramel had only asked for some help, and Setiawan himself chose Pollycarpus. (Soon after, Ramel denied asking for help.) Prosecutors noted Setiawan's inconsistencies, and judges warned him for his evasive answers, but neither pressed him as to *why* he picked Pollycarpus for the assignment.[8]

The next three witnesses testified over several days with some consistency about Polly's travel and the backdated letter. Rohainil Aini said he called her around three p.m. on September 6, saying the security director had given him a task in Singapore. Her boss was on a long trip and the office was about to close, so she went ahead and added him as extra crew on a flight that evening—Flight 974, as he had requested. Polly promised her that Ramel would follow up with her boss.

About a week later, Aini's boss, Captain Karmel Sembiring, reprimanded her for changing the schedule without his okay. She was authorized to change schedules of working pilots without his permission, but not those of extra crew. When Captain Karmel asked Pollycarpus for an explanation, he again promised that Ramel would call.

When Ramel returned to Jakarta, he did call Captain Karmel, who angrily asked, "Did you assign Polly!?" He didn't want to be responsible for Polly's extra pay and hotel bill. Ramel told the court that this call was the first he'd heard of the trip to Singapore, and that he lacked the authority to send Polly to Singapore or anywhere else.[9] And the fuel-dumping incident, Polly's justification for the trip, was a technical matter that didn't concern the security department.

Despite all this, Ramel faxed a memo to Captain Karmel agreeing to cover the costs.[10] The next day, Pollycarpus dropped off a trip report for Ramel, and he mentioned that Captain Karmel wanted the memo backdated to before the trip. Ramel changed the date and printed another copy.[11] (Captain Karmel denied ever asking for the memo to be backdated.)

There were a few other points of interest from these witnesses. Ramel described the director's August 11 assignment letter as very unusual. Besides leaping over three tiers of a rigid hierarchy, from director to co-pilot, the letter lacked important detail about dates, duties, and budgets.

Aini had told police that when Polly called her on September 6 to ask to be added to the flight to Singapore, she made the change based on the September 4 memo from Ramel. A prosecutor noted that this was impossible, because that memo was actually written two weeks later. The witness fell silent. When pressed, she said she didn't remember when she saw the memo. A judge warned her and took over questioning, but he never asked why she'd lied to the police or whether someone had told her to do so.[12]

Police guarded the courthouse grounds with motorcycle patrols, pistols, and long guns. Inside, a group calling itself the Eastern Indonesia Students Committee passed out pamphlets and a magazine attacking Munir and blaming his murder on a funding dispute among activists.[13] Outside, protestors in paper Munir masks held up banners reading, EXPOSE THE *DALANGS*: WE DON'T NEED A SCAPEGOAT. One day protestors marched on the courthouse wearing black and white, the hues of death and grief. Pallbearers hoisted a coffin inscribed with the words, THE CORPSE OF THE LAW, DEAD SINCE 1965.

For several weeks, the crowd dwindled as more Garuda employees testified about procedures. On October 11, the courtroom filled again for the first of several days of testimony by cabin crew members who might have witnessed the crime. Two had even been named as suspects. The judges began limiting the number of questioners and cutting short lines of inquiry, and the pace quickened.

Brahmanie had worked on Garuda planes since 1975, rising to cabin crew supervisor, or purser. When she ran into Polly soon after he boarded the plane, he asked her in Javanese, "Where's 40G? I switched with my friend."

"Who's your friend?" she asked.

Then she recognized Munir in the third row. Brahmanie went to shake his hand and welcome him aboard. At her suggestion, Polly found an empty seat in Premium Class while Brahmanie returned to the cabin door to welcome passengers. She noticed Polly climbing the stairs to the upper deck, and later saw him near the Premium Bar, a small stainless steel countertop with a magazine rack, but no drinks stocked on short trips.[14] The pantry, where food is prepared, is next to the bar, but Brahmanie never saw Polly enter it.

Two members of her crew had been named as suspects. One of them, Oedi, testified that he prepared ten glasses of orange juice, three of champagne, and three of apple juice for his colleague Yetty to serve to fourteen business class passengers. He expected few champagne drinkers, as most were extra crew, about to work the long flight to Amsterdam. Oedi used pliers to open a numbered seal on the box of juice. The meals were also sealed, and no one else entered the pantry.

Also named as a murder suspect, Yetty told the court that she started serving from the front of the plane and had eight or ten glasses left when she reached the third row. Munir pointed to a glass of orange juice and took it from the tray. Later she collected the empty glass. After takeoff, she wheeled the sealed meals down the aisle, and Munir chose *mie goreng*. She handed him the fried noodles and poured him more juice at his request. He finished that too. She saw Pollycarpus standing at the Premium Bar twice, writing something.

The courtroom was half empty again on October 21 as witnesses from the second leg testified. They might not know how Munir was poisoned, but they had seen the result. Taken together, their testimony could be used to reconstruct Munir's last hours alive. Tia Ambari was responsible for the section of Economy that included Munir's ticketed seat in row 38. Munir asked her for an antacid about ten minutes before leaving Singapore. Soon after takeoff, during the first meal service, she told him they had none. He turned down the meal and asked for tea with sugar. She noticed him go to the toilet for the first time about thirty minutes into the flight.

Madjib Nasution, purser for the second leg, said Munir approached him holding a business card for a doctor. He said, "I have a stomachache. I already went to the toilet six times and vomited. Please help me. I have a friend who's a doctor—please find him." Madjib went to find Dr. Tarmizi in Business but soon returned and said he hadn't been able to wake him, adding, "Let's wake him up together. I'll take you."

Not long before, in the waiting area at Changi Airport, Dr. Tarmizi had recognized Munir, "because everybody knew who Munir was." He approached him and they chatted while walking to the jetway and waiting to board.

> I asked why he was going to Holland. He said he wanted to recharge his batteries for a year, in Utrecht. I said, "It's a loss for Indonesia. You're an important person." He said that he needed to do it for himself. I asked, "Who are you voting for?" He replied, "Ah, it doesn't make any difference, Doc."

Before they parted at the diverging jetways to Business and Economy, the doctor had given Munir his card. Once aboard, Tarmizi fell asleep quickly. He didn't remember who woke him, but once he was awake, Munir told him about his terrible stomach pain, vomiting, and diarrhea. Dr. Tarmizi asked Munir what he'd eaten.

"Nothing in particular, Doctor."

A flight attendant said, "Pak Munir drank the wrong thing. He has a gastric ulcer and drank orange juice." Dr. Tarmizi knew the symptoms didn't fit an ulcer. Stomach pain might have, but the diarrhea and vomiting made food poisoning more likely.

"Is anyone else sick?" No one was.

The doctor had Munir return to his seat to examine him. He ordered the crew to bring salted water and sweet tea. Dr. Tarmizi asked for the plane's medical kit. He saw no IV bag to rehydrate or effectively medicate a patient who couldn't keep anything down. Still thinking it must be food poisoning, he gave Munir an antidiarrheal, as well as an antacid from his own kit.

When Munir vomited up the medicine, Tarmizi searched the medical kit again. He selected a glass ampule and a needle, chose a site above the left biceps, and injected Primperan, a drug sometimes given to chemotherapy patients to quell vomiting. It can cause drowsiness, too, and Munir soon fell asleep in his seat. Even without the IV bag, Tarmizi wasn't too worried. Dehydration from even acute vomiting and diarrhea would take days to kill an adult. He decided an emergency landing in the nearest airport, Tehran, wasn't required, but asked the pilot to telex Amsterdam to have an ambulance waiting at the plane.

After about two hours, Munir awoke, and the crew helped him to the lavatory. Ten minutes later, the purser noticed the door slightly open. Inside, Munir leaned against the wall, too weak to return to his seat. The crew carried him forward to the emptier business class, and laid him across the fourth row. At the purser Majib's suggestion, Munir recited the Istighfar, repeating softly in Arabic, "I seek forgiveness in God."

The doctor gave him a shot of the sedative diazepam. Munir asked to lie down on the floor, and the crew brought blankets, one to lie on and two to cover him. Two flight attendants stayed with him, rubbing his back. Hearing his groans of pain, Majib felt tears coming to his own eyes. About two and a half hours before landing, the crew told Munir they had to perform dawn prayers and serve breakfast. He gave a weak thumbs-up.

When Majib returned to check on Munir soon after, he found his hand cold to the touch. His flashlight revealed a blue tinge to the skin. He went for Tarmizi, saying, "Doctor, please help Pak Munir." Tarmizi moved swiftly to the fourth row. He tapped Munir's shoulder, calling, "Munir, Munir, Munir!" He couldn't find a pulse, and noticed the blush of post-mortem bruising. "*Innalillahi wa inna ilaihi raji'un*," he said. "Verily we belong to Allah, and verily to Him do we return."

Then, turning to Majib, he wondered aloud, "How could this happen? He should have been able to make it."

They closed Munir's eyes. Dr. Tarmizi declared Munir dead at 4:05 a.m. Greenwich Mean Time and filled out a preliminary death certificate. The pilot sent a telex to headquarters asking them to inform the authorities in Amsterdam. In the predawn sky near the border of Ukraine and Romania, the doctor joined the crew to pray over Munir's still form, now wrapped in a thin blanket.[15]

Crew members also added to the catalog of Polly's suspicious behavior on the ground. In late 2004, soon after Polly's name appeared in the press, the purser Brahmanie was relaxing in the hills of Puncak on a day off when Polly called. It was hard to recall his precise words, as she'd been in the middle of something and he spoke very quickly in a mix of Indonesian and Javanese.

It was also hard to remember what he'd said on that call because, after that, he called again and again. She couldn't even guess how many times he'd called her home phone and her cell. He would ask about the Munir case, talk about how he was faring, and ask to meet. She grew tired of it. When a judge pressed her on what he actually said, she recalled Polly telling her, "Because someone died, anyone could be a suspect, and so we all have to meet to synchronize perspectives." She took that to mean the two of them plus Yetty and Oedi.

He'd fretted, "If the company doesn't give us a lawyer . . ."

She'd replied, "There's no need, if I didn't do anything."

In the end she lost all patience, telling him, "Enough, Pak Polly, just stay calm. We didn't *do* anything."

Polly called Yetty many times too, to complain about the press coverage, about reporters coming to his house, until she too had enough, saying, "What is it now? Enough. Don't bother contacting me again!" She'd never even given him her number.[16] Oedi got four calls, including one from Polly's wife.

During a break one day, Suci sat with supporters on the floor outside the courtroom, chatting and texting updates to friends. Some of the families Munir helped were there with small children, who played on the white floor tiles. A muezzin sounded in the distance.

As Pollycarpus passed with an escort, he neared a cameraman filming the day's events. Just as he was about to walk past, he leaned in close and said, "Once all this is settled, go with me to Papua, to Wamena. I'll pay." A free ticket to a remote town in the Papuan highlands, on the wild eastern edge of the archipelago where the army called the shots, could only be meant as a threat.

The cameraman was not the only one Polly approached. Late in the trial, Usman was walking along the terrace, talking to friends. He spotted Polly returning from the bathroom under guard and assumed the defendant would pass by with a glare at most. But Polly came right up to him, and spat out, "It's because of you that I'm here!"

Usman said nothing, but thought, *Okay, I'm still young. I can still fight you in ten or twenty years when you get out.* He was confident the co-pilot would go to prison, but was not so sure the top figures at BIN would join him. Usman anticipated Muchdi's coming testimony with hope and apprehension. The general's performance would be important for this trial, but also for those Usman hoped would come next: the trials of Muchdi, his men, and perhaps even Hendropriyono.

The judges wanted the trial over before the end of the year and accelerated from one to two or three hearings a week. On November 10, the courtroom was packed again, partly due to another case before the same chief judge. Two years before, the minister of religious affairs had been instructed in a dream to go to Batu Tulis, an archeology site in West Java named for a five-hundred-year-old inscription. He was told he would find a hoard of golden relics valuable enough to pay off the national debt of over $100 billion. Over the protests of archeologists, he supervised weeks of digging before giving up. He was in court accused of more prosaic looting, after $20 million disappeared from a religious activities fund.

Pollycarpus shook hands with his fellow celebrity defendant and took a seat for his own trial. Three forensics experts testified, including two from the police team that went to the Netherlands with Usman. They described how the Dutch team exposed a sample from Munir's stomach to X-rays, revealing dense matter suggesting the presence of metal ions. Further testing identified the substance as arsenic.

One expert explained the biochemistry of arsenic poisoning. All forms of life rely on a molecule called adenosine triphosphate to store and move energy at the cellular level. When energy is needed, a bond is broken, only to be reformed to store more energy. Arsenic interferes with the cycling of this essential energy currency, rapidly depleting the body's source of energy and causing organ failure.

The experts mostly relied on the work of the respected Netherlands Forensic Institute. The bureaucratic delays on the visit to Amsterdam had left only enough time for the NFI team to discuss the cause of death and concentrations in Munir's body. Left unresolved were the crucial questions of how much arsenic Munir consumed and in what form. These facts might point to the time, place, and method of poisoning. A police team had returned to the Netherlands in May 2005 to deepen the analysis and learn new findings.

Some questions could not be answered definitively, such as the exact physical characteristics of the poison before it reacted with Munir's body. Several compounds contain the element arsenic, but the toxicologists made a likely identification of arsenic trioxide, or As_2O_3, most likely in the form of a white powder resembling confectioner's sugar.

The quantity consumed could be estimated based on concentrations found in Munir's body. Because arsenic leaves the bloodstream in two to three hours, the high level found in Munir's blood indicated a massive dose, or perhaps repeated poisonings. Asked in court about Munir's total intake, the expert hesitated. It would take a long time to explain, he said, and you might never reach a conclusion. An estimate was possible based on the concentration in the stomach contents. The concentration indicated a figure of 110 milligrams of arsenic in Munir's stomach when he died. But that would be a low estimate of intake, since an unknown amount had been vomited up or absorbed by the body. Based on past testing with rats, Dutch scientists estimated an intake of 930 milligrams of arsenic, meaning 1.24 grams of arsenic trioxide, far exceeding the lethal dose for an average adult.

The question of timing was essential to the theory of the murder, but without knowing the amount or form of poison, one expert couldn't say how long it would take to work. He guessed ninety minutes, but four hours was possible. However, Dr. Budi Sampurna, a University of Indonesia professor who had once worked alongside Munir at the exhumations in West Timor, was more precise. Able to read the full reports in Dutch, he testified that the follow-up meetings with the NFI led to an estimate of *no more than* ninety minutes between intake and the onset of symptoms.

Solubility was a final important factor in figuring out how Munir was poisoned. Finding little research on the subject, the NFI ran experiments before the May meeting. They tried to dissolve a lethal dose of arsenic trioxide in a portion of orange juice. Five minutes of hard stirring left no solid residue, though some powder settled to the bottom after a while.[17]

For several weeks, witnesses were called but did not appear. Several lived abroad, such as the Dutch-Indonesian couple and Nurhadi, the former BIN official serving as ambassador to Nigeria. Another no-show was a woman named Hian Tian in Papua who had told police that Polly was like a son to her—a son with links to intelligence dating back to 1999 and a history of activities to defend the nation, and particularly the nationalist concept of NKRI, the Unitary State of the Republic of Indonesia, which the prosecution had cited as a motive.[18] The most anticipated witness summoned without results was Muchdi Purwopranjono. The judges warned prosecutors that they wanted a verdict by December 16 and time was running out.

On the morning of November 16, a legal expert testified about the definition of forgery.[19] The witness stepped down, and Muchdi's name was called again, with no response. Prosecutors promised to go to his house in person.

The next day, an antiterrorism unit named Detachment 88 took up positions outside the courthouse. Amid rumors of snipers and explosives, the rooftop was patrolled by another elite police unit trained in bomb disposal. The scuffed stairwells were cleared of the fixers and middlemen, the *makelars* and "bamboo lawyers" who could be hired to get a case postponed or dropped.

The courtroom was usually empty at the official 9:00 a.m. start time, but on this day Usman found there was nowhere left to sit. *Preman*, hired thugs, controlled every inch of linoleum and bench. Forced to testify at last, Muchdi was making a show of force. Usman insinuated his way down the aisle, settling into a kind of sitting position as if he'd located an invisible chair among the sea of *preman*. A huge Moluccan stood at the front of the room, blocking the view, but the judges said nothing.

In the alley alongside the courthouse, young activists and relatives of those killed in the May 1998 riots raised posters reading JUDGE THE DALANG, NOT THEIR PUPPET and calling for Muchdi and Hendropriyono to be prosecuted alongside Polly. About thirty young men advanced down the alley, members of the mysterious Eastern Indonesia Students Committee, ripping signs from the hands of women wearing Munir shirts and black *jilbabs*. The leader of the hostile phalanx of Muchdi supporters faced off against a protestor, whose torso was painted blood red save for one arm he had painted jet-black. The Munir supporter placed his bullhorn on the ground and paused, before pointing his black arm skyward and shouting, as he backed away:

"*Hidup!*"

The crowd responded, "*Hidup korban!*" Long live the victims![20]

The Muchdi supporter pointed sharply at the painted protestor, shouting and advancing. It looked like a fight, but others held them back. One Muchdi supporter seized a sign and ripped it over his knee. The attackers stomped on another poster—WHY WAS HE SILENCED?—and carried off an amplifier. When police at last intervened, it was to ask the Munir supporters for a protest permit, the first time they had done so since the trial began.[21]

Retired Major General Muchdi Purwopranjono had bags beneath his eyes but smiled broadly as he removed his black windbreaker. He was sworn in under the Quran and after some preliminaries began answering questions from the prosecutors.

"Do your duties include monitoring vocal critics of the state?"

"No . . . No such duties or activities. None."

Did he ever ask anyone to tell Munir to ease up on his criticism? Muchdi explained that he often met with figures like Adnan Buyung Nasution, a founder of LBH. Buyung was the one who, on a visit to the Malang branch of LBH, had seen promise in "the skinny kid with cheap clothes and sharp questions." Muchdi claimed he never told Buyung or anyone else to warn Munir off. *Maybe* informally, something like, "Would you please warn him?" He only meant that in difficult times people should build the country up.

The chief judge said, "The prosecutor asked you what was your statement to Adnan Buyung Nasution."

As far as he remembered, he'd asked Buyung, "Please warn Munir."[22]

"Warn Munir what?"

"Warn him not to be too vocal."

"Did you see Munir as someone who was too vocal?"

"Yes . . . I think so."

A judge asked about Buyung's response. Rubbing his ear thoughtfully, Muchdi said, "I don't remember, because it wasn't a serious matter."

"Yes, but now there's a death, a suspect, and a prosecution, and we're all trying to remember."

Muchdi rubbed his ear again, the large red stone of his ring moving back and forth. It was just an informal suggestion, he said, nothing memorable. His left foot bounced under his chair. Pollycarpus watched, his face rigid, the reading glasses around his neck rising and falling as he breathed.

The prosecutors moved on to the alleged plot. One leafed through phone records on his table, pen in hand, before asking, "Regarding the number 0811900978, under your control, and the number 081584304375, under the control of Pollycarpus, I want to ask you, have you ever directly communicated and spoken to that number?"

Muchdi turned left to face his questioner.

"Never."

"But do you acknowledge this printout?" It showed twenty-seven communications between the two phones.

"Yes, I acknowledge it."

There was a pause, and Muchdi looked expectantly at the prosecutors and then up at the judges. The prosecutor began to ask something, but Muchdi grabbed the mike to speak over him, "I acknowledge that the printout may indicate a relationship between *my* number and *that* number, but not between me and the defendant."

He kept the phone with him at night, but during the day he was very busy, and his security detail carried it. He let his driver, his adjutant, or anyone else use it, since a timber company paid the bill. Gesturing at the courtroom, he said, "If any of my friends in the back want to use it, go ahead! I've never refused anyone." He insisted he'd never heard the names Pollycarpus or Munir around BIN.

Muchdi's testimony concluded without major revelations, but Usman thought the prosecutors had a good day overall. They interrupted when Muchdi dissembled, telling him to listen to the question. The general, unused to being told what to do, had bristled. The general's presence in the courtroom showed he was not invincible and that he and BIN had some link to the question of Polly's guilt.

To Suci, Muchdi was something different altogether from Pollycarpus. The co-pilot was strange and slippery, but he didn't scare her. Muchdi was frightening. He was cold-blooded, with an air about him that killing someone was as easy as swatting a mosquito. He gave Suci goosebumps.[23]

Suci was not alone in this assessment. A history of the Indonesian military quotes a description of Muchdi as a "stupid, brutal officer." A leaked U.S. embassy cable cited descriptions of him as vindictive, unscrupulous, and crazy, with "a gigantic ego and no scruples" and an ability to commit human rights violations without it bothering him.

Muchdi stood and put on his windbreaker.

Suci texted Usman, "Come with me to stop Muchdi."

The general flicked up his collar and nodded to the judges. Smiling broadly, he shook hands with his front-row supporters, as his bodyguards kept photographers at bay. Usman found a position near the door of the courtroom. Watching the thugs and military men eddying past, he thought, *My God, Suci, we could be getting ourselves in trouble.* But there was no point in arguing with her. She would carry out her plan, and he would help. Usman placed a firm, almost gentle hand on the general's broad chest.

His heart racing, Usman said, "Just a moment, Pak. Someone wants to speak to you."

In the momentary stillness before Muchdi reacted, Suci said what she needed to: "You're a liar." Even with his sunglasses on, Muchdi tried to avoid looking at Suci or Usman. His bodyguards worked to extricate him as Suci raised her voice, until it rang across the courtroom, where they were calling the next witness.

"You are a liar!" she said. "You're the murderer, aren't you!?"

Muchdi pushed past them to descend the staircase. Journalists pressed in, leaping onto benches to catch the confrontation. They chased Suci downstairs, shouting questions. Usman retrieved his motorbike, pulling up at the entrance for Suci to slip onto the pillion. Face taut, he navigated the scrum, feet bouncing on the ground for balance, until they were free of the crowd.

One day later, even without Muchdi's supporters, the room was full when the defendant took the witness chair. Asked who authorized his Singapore trip, Polly cited the August 11 assignment letter from the director. It was flexible, he said, letting him take on security tasks anytime. Did Polly-carpus contact the secretary to the chief of pilots on September 6? Yes, he wanted Captain Karmel's permission, but he wasn't there. Pollycarpus had explained that he had a task from the security director and asked to be added to the next flight to Singapore.

A judge asked if Pollycarpus had ever met Munir before September 6. He said he had, near the Hotel Indonesia traffic circle, where Munir was giving out flowers on Women's Day. But he'd never *talked* to Munir until boarding. As for Munir's criticism of Indonesia, "I never paid any attention, and I wasn't interested." What business was it of his?

Pollycarpus now claimed that the seat change was just a misunderstanding. He hadn't really intended to offer his seat, but was just being nice to a public figure. "But, somehow Munir thought my suggestion was serious, and he then moved to Business. I couldn't stop him."[24] A skeptical judge warned him to tell the truth.

Pollycarpus said he stowed his bags before approaching the purser Brahmanie to ask about a seat for Munir. But then they saw Munir already sitting in Polly's seat. The chief judge cited Brahmanie's contradictory testimony that Polly had told her that he'd switched seats with a friend and asked how to find Munir's seat, 40G. Pollycarpus replied that was *after* he saw Munir take his own seat. The judge warned Pollycarpus again about his inconsistent testimony.[25]

Pollycarpus said he briefly sat in an open seat in Premium before visiting the cockpit to say hello. He was still there when welcome drinks were served because "pilots love cockpits." After sitting for takeoff, he got out of his seat and stood at the unused Premium Bar, reading a Dutch aviation magazine he found. He took his seat again briefly once, and then again ten minutes before landing. He sat so much when flying planes that he was "tired of sitting."[26]

Details of Pollycarpus's activities in Singapore emerged from his testimony. He explained that Corporate Security had asked him to find out about a costly incident on August 28, when a plane with wheel problems had to dump fuel and return to Singapore. There was no detailed assignment, just something like, "Please, look at the problem." Asked if he'd confirmed his presence in Singapore with anyone, he said he'd told one technical officer whose name he didn't remember.

And where did he meet the officer? Inside a plane. Which plane? A Boeing 737. The plane back to Jakarta? Yes. Did he have the information Pollycarpus needed? He didn't. Pollycarpus described his fact-finding efforts. He never examined the plane that dumped the fuel. Before boarding the flight home, he saw technical officers on the plane. He approached a mechanic and they spoke informally for about twenty minutes, Pollycarpus taking notes on small pieces of paper.

Weren't there mechanics in the airport? Yes, but his spontaneous "on the spot" interviewing was good for getting data directly, without all the bureaucracy and rules of going through the Garuda office. He never mentioned a mechanic in his trip report because such details might get someone in trouble. He hadn't even asked for the man's name.

The defense prompted Pollycarpus to state that he only learned Yetty and Oedi would be on the flight when he boarded, undermining the idea that the three conspired in advance to poison Munir. And would a pilot need to call a passenger to learn his schedule? No, he could just call the main office. Polly added, "I had access, but why? It's not my business."

A defense lawyer asked who had chosen the routes listed in the memo from security, Jakarta to Bali, Surabaya, or Australia. Polly launched into a story about a firecracker on a plane that was so long-winded, his lawyer interrupted, "Just answer the question. Who chose them?" He said Ramel, the security director, had.

Throughout it all, Pollycarpus maintained a smile, with occasional nervous moments as he paused to wipe sweat from his face. Most of his answers were indirect or irrelevant, and some clearly conflicted with those of other witnesses. Suci had testified he'd called Munir's phone. The security director swore he never tasked Polly to go to Singapore. The purser had said Pollycarpus told her he'd switched seats with a friend. The secretary had said he asked specifically for Flight 974, not the next flight to Singapore. There were also inconsistencies with his own prior statements on meeting Munir and the seat switch.

His testimony also revealed that his work in Singapore was no more than a brief conversation with a mechanic on his way home. This revelation supported a theory that the Singapore duty was a cover story. But for what, and on whose behalf? The only time BIN came up at all was when the defense raised the question, giving Pollycarpus an opportunity to deny any connection to the agency.

Pollycarpus's testimony capped the evidence phase. On December 1, prosecutors summarized their case and asked for a life sentence and, because the criminal code is not adjusted for inflation, a fine of twenty-five cents. Two weeks after that, Pollycarpus read out his emotional response. For forty-five minutes, he recounted how the media had ruined his name, upset his life, and traumatized his family. The police had ransacked his home and held him in protective custody under false pretenses. He said the prosecutors never proved a motive, adding, "What was Munir's importance to me? Not a friend, and also not an enemy." They accused him of murder simply because he offered someone his seat and then got up a few times. He asked the judges to release him from all charges. "I crave justice," he said. "If he was indeed killed, I condemn the killer."

That afternoon, his lawyers ascribed the demand for a life sentence to political pressure and worried about the failure to reveal the real murderer. Polly's claim to be on official business was supported by the airline documents, the fuel dumping, and the fact that a Garuda car picked him up. These facts were not really exculpatory, especially if the airline was complicit, but the defense was on stronger ground concerning gaps in evidence around the execution of the plot, since no one saw Pollycarpus enter the pantry or handle beverages. There was also little evidence of his supposed patriotic motive.[27]

The defense also raised a problem with the timeline. The welcome drink was served about fifteen minutes before takeoff on an hour-and-fifty-minute flight, while experts agreed that symptoms would appear in ten to ninety minutes. The first symptoms appeared soon after leaving Singapore, pointing to intake not on the first leg, but at Changi.

After one more round of repetitive filings, both sides rested their cases.

On December 20, Pollycarpus stood at the front of the packed courtroom displaying confidence, or perhaps bravado.[28] Usman was feeling optimistic too. Three overlapping investigations—by the TPF, Kasum, and the police—began by groping in the dark. They had started with only a welter of vague suspicions, and no idea where to find witnesses or how to prove that this co-pilot poisoned Munir. Usman had gained confidence in the TPF as members showed their commitment, homed in on a suspect, and saw him brought before a court. He felt sure of a conviction, waiting only to see how long the sentence was. The death penalty had been taken off the table to secure Dutch cooperation, but life in prison might encourage Polly or others to cooperate.

The crowd quieted as the chief judge read the verdict. He found the defendant guilty of both murder and forgery. The judge also used the opportunity to reject the claim that just anyone could use a senior intelligence official's cell phone. Then, referring to that phone, the judge noted, "The person speaking at telephone number 0811900978 was someone who wanted Munir to not be vocal in criticizing the government. So this aforementioned person had the motive to kill Munir." The content of the calls was still unknown, but Polly's travel and actions on board indicated that "there was an agreement between the defendant and the owner of number 0811900978 about how to carry out their desire to take Munir's life." Even without using Muchdi's name, these findings surpassed what prosecutors had dared argue. The judges also encouraged police and prosecutors to investigate further to identify "still other parties who wanted to take the life of Munir."[29]

In an unexpected turn, the judges came up with their own theory of the poisoning. Under rules passed from Napoléon to the Dutch to Indonesia's founders, judges were permitted to assert facts or theories not argued at trial. It was called a conviction *raisonnée*, proof based on a judge's logically reasoned belief. They surmised that once the cabin lights went down, Pollycarpus moved to the premium bar and pretended to read a magazine. The flight attendant Oedi brought two meal options for him to lace with poison. Oedi resealed them in the pantry, and then Yetty served Munir his choice, fried noodles, while Pollycarpus watched from the bar. This theory didn't require Pollycarpus to enter the pantry unseen, nor did Munir have to select the one poisoned beverage from a tray. But there was still no eyewitness corroboration.

On the charge of forgery, the judges found that the change notice signed by the secretary to the chief of pilots was a fraudulent document, because it was based on a nonexistent assignment in Singapore. The memo from the security director was then backdated to September 4 to cover up the lack of an assignment, causing losses to the airline. The judges again called for more investigation to identify anyone else with a role in the forgeries.

Usman was encouraged by the verdict's references to a broader conspiracy, but they helped Pollycarpus, too. Because he was one conspirator among others, the judges felt a life sentence was too severe. The chief judge intoned that the panel, "hereby states that Pollycarpus Budihari Priyanto is guilty as an accomplice to premeditated murder and sentences the defendant to . . ."

The judge picked up his pen to make a short note. Pollycarpus released his hands, which had been clasped before him like a schoolboy, and they came to rest stiffly against his legs.

". . . fourteen years imprisonment."

The gavel came down, and Polly was told to sit for his response. Gripping the wooden arms of the chair, his voice building to a shout, he said, "As for accusations and verdicts . . . *I reject them!*"

Both parties began the appeal process that same day, and the defense vowed to file a complaint against the judges for basing a verdict on facts not presented at trial.[30] Suci didn't care if Pollycarpus, merely a field operator, was sentenced to life or death. When a reporter asked her if she thought Muchdi was behind the murder, she replied, "It could be that behind Muchdi there's another *dalang*. Polly wasn't alone. This is a political conspiracy."[31]

12

I Will Not Only Hope

2006

The president never acted on the TPF recommendation to create a stronger fact-finding team, leaving the investigation solely in the hands of the police. Marsudhi was given command of the police investigation, however, leading a team that grew to thirty members from CID, the Jakarta police, Indonesian members of Interpol, the forensics lab, and other units.

Nevertheless, as the Pollycarpus trial had moved to a close in late 2005, the investigation had begun to lose steam. In December, a new national police chief, Police General Sutanto, transferred Marsudhi to a position on his staff with few responsibilities. Marsudhi never learned why he was moved to what he considered a "non-job," but suspected he was being punished for his work on the Munir case. Knowing that the risks of police work in Indonesia included not just criminal violence, but also the temptations of corruption, Marsudhi considered investigators to have one foot in prison and one foot in the grave. He hadn't anticipated a third possibility, of being sent into a professional limbo for doing his job.

A police spokesperson promised to act on any new evidence, but for now, "We are just waiting for developments in the trial." There were reports that the police had disbanded the investigation team altogether.[1]

This police inactivity was one reason it was so important that the Pollycarpus verdict pointed to senior Garuda and BIN figures. However, when Suci urged the attorney general to follow up on *all* the names cited in Polly's verdict, she was told the matter was in the hands of the police, who seemed to be doing little.[2] Muchdi, meanwhile, had hired prominent

Muslim lawyers, who took the unusual action of meeting with the judges from Polly's trial to question their call to investigate their client. They also threatened to sue anyone accusing him of murder.[3]

By July 2006, things looked grim. The U.S. embassy cabled to Washington that "all signs point to failure in the police investigation of the larger conspiracy behind Munir's murder." A priest who visited Pollycarpus in prison reported that he was badly bruised, and his wife filed a torture complaint against the police. Torture was common in police custody, sometimes leading to false statements. The abuse could be a sign that police didn't know how to persuade Polly to reveal whose orders he might have been following. It could also mean they were trying to force him to take all the blame.[4]

Kasum, the unofficial investigation and advocacy team formed by Munir's friends, was still operating. Suci had a complicated relationship with Kasum. Some members were frustrated when she would suddenly change the plan for an important meeting after they had already developed a strategy. For her, the group was a source of both support and frustration, and she often felt they weren't doing enough. Seeing her disappointment, Usman said he was ready to take a turn heading the group.

As the Munir case was pushed off the front page by natural disasters and terrorist plots, Suci and her allies stepped up efforts to build public pressure to charge the masterminds. Munir's face gazed from posters and stickers on campuses, food stalls, and street signs, along with the slogan, JUSTICE FOR MUNIR, JUSTICE FOR ALL.[5]

Suciwati and Usman went back to the Netherlands to ask the Dutch to release evidence that might point more precisely to the time Munir was poisoned, or shore up other elements the lower courts found weak. But concern about the death penalty, and about Indonesian police capacity to preserve tissue samples, made the Dutch reluctant to share all they had.

Not only was there no movement on the masterminds, but Polly's conviction itself was not secure. Both sides had begun appeals the day of the verdict.[6] After the verdict changed the vector of poisoning from orange juice to noodles, the defense argued that it would be impossible to defend oneself if a theory of how, when, and where a crime was committed could change during trial. Prosecutors argued that the substance of the murder charge was unaffected by these details. In March 2006, the High Court sided with the prosecution. A slim, 3–2 majority ruled that the trial proved Munir was given a fatal dose of arsenic, whatever the method of poisoning may have been.[7] Polly's lawyers appealed again.

On October 3, 2006, the Supreme Court issued a decision.[8] A three-judge panel found that the evidence did not support Polly's conviction. They found the trial judges had misapplied rules of evidence as they posited a murder plot unsupported by witnesses, documents, or confessions. They believed that prosecutors never proved Pollycarpus poisoned Munir, or even that Munir consumed poison on board the plane.[9] The Court upheld only the forgery conviction, cutting Polly's sentence to two years. With credit for time served, he'd be free by March.

A number of legal experts later found that although the lower court rulings had flaws, the higher court should have used its authority to address gaps and contradictions in evidence, rather than toss out the conviction.[10]

The decision shocked Suciwati and Usman to the core. Three days after the Supreme Court's verdict, they gave a press conference at KontraS. Speaking calmly and forcefully, Suci contrasted the police's skill in handling recent acts of terrorism with the lack of progress on the Munir case. But the police were not the problem. Suci still believed it was up to the president to produce results.

The press conference ended, and reporters began retrieving their microphones. Diva climbed into Suci's lap as a few more questions came. Asked if Munir could have been poisoned in Singapore, Usman said the TPF had found the poisoning might have been in Changi Airport, but he doubted it. The restaurants were closed and nobody saw Munir drink anything. The flight to Singapore still seemed the most likely crime scene.

As Usman stood up, a journalist asked if a protest was planned that day. None was, but Usman said, "What is certain is that sooner or later, we will protest again." Usman switched off the mike, tapping it once to be sure it was dead. He seemed deflated. On the wall behind him was a photo from 1998, of a jubilant protestor on the roof of the parliament building, on the verge of achieving the impossible.

The acquittal of Pollycarpus sparked scathing statements from governments and human rights groups around the world. Within Indonesia, the decision returned the case to the headlines. An editorial in the newspaper *Republika*, entitled "Did Munir Poison Himself?," stated, "We deserve to reflect. How human life in the land of Indonesia has no meaning. How the slogan that the Indonesian people are a civilized and dignified nation is just nonsense. The law and its officers are merely subordinate to power."[11] A *Jakarta Post* editorial noted that all the human rights trials followed the same dismal script. A few perpetrators are found guilty, then acquitted on appeal: "Their exoneration was only a matter of time."[12]

Facing a wave of criticism, the president issued an order to step up the investigation. The national police chief promised to "revitalize" the effort by interviewing new witnesses and reinvestigating possible crime scenes, including Singapore. A new team under police Brigadier General Suryadharma would report on progress every two weeks.

It all sounded good, except for the fact that Suryadharma had led the investigation before, in 2005. His failure to follow up on TPF leads was one reason the team called for an audit of police performance. There were also rumors that Suryadharma was close to Muchdi. What's more, the president never followed up his broad order with specific, written directives to the police. The "revitalized" investigation was old wine, in old bottles.

"We have to say no to this team," Usman told a journalist. He believed the police team was a farce, too afraid to expose powerful people. The police still hadn't taken such basic steps as seeking all records from the phone company for calls or messages between Pollycarpus and BIN.[13] Usman agreed with Suci that the fault did not lie with the police. He believed that if SBY had given his full support from the beginning, the perpetrators would be in jail. Instead, the field operator was about to go free and the masterminds hadn't even been investigated.

There was a way to revisit a Supreme Court verdict. Called case review, or *peninjauan kembali*, the mechanism required new and compelling evidence.[14] A Supreme Court panel might then deny the request or agree to review the case but uphold the earlier decision. But there was a chance the court would agree to the review and overturn the prior ruling, sending Pollycarpus back to jail for premeditated murder.

The effort was open to challenge, as the law could be read to say that only a defendant could request case review. There was a precedent for prosecutors to do so, but not a very just one. Suharto had used case review to send an acquitted labor activist back to jail. Moreover, the Supreme Court's decision on Polly had technically been final, and some human rights lawyers didn't want to undermine the independence of the judiciary.

After first throwing cold water on the idea, the attorney general announced he had instructed prosecutors to request a case review.[15] The chief judge of the Supreme Court was open to the idea even if the precedent was lacking, saying, "If there is a contradiction between law and justice, my guidance to all judges is to defend justice." He was preparing a panel to hear the case-review request.

Suci and Usman decided on a multi-pronged strategy. They would encourage the dormant parliamentary commission on the Munir case to reopen its inquiry. A civil suit against Garuda that Suci filed in September might unearth new evidence. Finally, Suci and Usman would head to the United States to generate pressure from abroad as well as headlines at home.[16]

Suci had been to the United States once before, to attend a human rights conference in Atlanta in June 2005. She met former president Jimmy Carter there and passed through Washington, DC, for meetings with officials. Soon after, sixty-eight members of the U.S. Congress had signed a letter calling for progress on the case. Covering the political spectrum from the socialist Bernie Sanders to future vice-president and arch-conservative Mike Pence, the signers strongly urged the Indonesian president to release the TPF report and act on its recommendations. That was the kind of international pressure Suci wanted to generate on this trip.

Two weeks after the Supreme Court's acquittal of Pollycarpus, Usman and Suci arrived in New York. The organization Human Rights First had invited Suci to accept an award honoring her and Munir.[17] On her first day in New York, she was greeted by an editorial by the *New York Times* that called for justice for Munir as the only antidote for "Indonesia's poisoned justice system." The visit was off to a promising start, but they headed to

Washington, DC, with apprehension, knowing that BIN had beaten them there.

Suci was stepping into the middle of a long battle over American military aid to Indonesia. Ever since the Americans eagerly welcomed Suharto as an anticommunist ally in the region, American military training and arms had flowed to Indonesia despite the invasion of East Timor in 1975 and other human rights abuses. The United States did impose some restrictions on training in 1991, after soldiers opened fire on Timorese protestors at a cemetery, killing at least 250. Congress then blocked some arms transfers in 1999 after the violence around the Timorese referendum. Each year since then Congress tinkered with the language in the law that appropriated funds, always linking the full resumption of military aid to progress on military reform and justice for past crimes.

Indonesia had met none of these conditions when the September 11, 2001, attacks changed the calculus. The Bush administration was eager to build ties with a moderate Muslim nation that might help fight terror networks in Southeast Asia. Against this headwind, activists in both countries had managed to keep the conditions tenuously in place. In fact, progress on the Munir case had recently been added to the conditions, alongside accountability for human rights abuses in East Timor and Papua.

About a month before their visit to Washington, Suci and Usman learned that BIN was playing a covert role in the effort to resume full military aid. Two investigative journalists, Andreas Harsono and Nathaniel Heller, had discovered that in 2003 wealthy backers of President Megawati, including her husband, had launched an effort to convince American lawmakers to resume aid.[18] Former senator Bob Dole's lobbying firm was retained for $200,000 per month, and Dole personally traveled to Jakarta twice.[19] Opposite Dole's signature on the contract was a familiar name, Yohannes Hardian Widjonarko, the timber baron who paid the bills for Muchdi's cell phone. Filings with the U.S. Department of Justice noted that while Widjonarko was paying for the work, it "may from time to time be directed by individuals within the government of Indonesia."[20]

That contract ended after SBY defeated Megawati, but lobbying continued. In May 2005, a team of American lobbyists arrived in Jakarta, ostensibly to meet with ousted president Abdurrahman Wahid's new foundation. Wahid had long been a friend to Munir and the human rights movement, even joining Suci the day after the first Pollycarpus verdict to demand that BIN be held accountable. Although his modest Gus Dur Foundation mainly supported orphanages, libraries, and schools, it signed a contract to pay $30,000 a month to American lobbyists to improve military ties with the United States.[21] The Richard L. Collins & Company's filings with the Department of Justice offered a clue to the mystery: "For the purposes of this contract, the Gus Dur Foundation are directed and funded by the Indonesian Bureau of National Investigation."

The name was mangled, but the document was referring to BIN. If there was any doubt, the contract listed as a contact BIN's deputy director, As'ad. His name was linked to the plot to kill Munir in both the leaked scenario memos and the anonymous text messages. The agency appeared to be using the Gus Dur Foundation to secretly fund a campaign to convince American lawmakers to resume full military aid.

On July 21, 2005, a month after the TPF report had recommended investigation of As'ad, he led a delegation to Washington, where he presented the American lobbyists with a traditional Indonesian knife before heading to congressional offices to discuss progress on human rights and the need for military aid. They covered the conflicts in Aceh and Papua, and, in at least one meeting, the Munir case.[22] Senator Patrick Leahy was the lawmaker with the most commitment and influence to restrict military aid; legislative restrictions on aid to military units that violate human rights are known as Leahy laws. Meeting with Leahy and his top aide just off the Senate floor, As'ad and the lobbyists covered various human rights issues. Leahy raised the subject of Munir, and As'ad insisted that BIN wasn't involved, had no interest in Munir, and was cooperating with investigators.[23] In October 2005, Collins signed a new contract directly with BIN for $30,000 a month to lobby members of Congress and staff. The Munir investigation was again one of the topics.[24]

With both governments pushing to restore military ties for counterterrorism purposes, the lobbyists had the wind at their backs. One target of Dole's lobbying had been Secretary of State Condoleezza Rice, and in January 2005 she'd lifted the training restrictions after determining the

Indonesian military had reformed enough. In November, the restrictions on arms transfers ended too.

In September 2006, after the lobbying was revealed, Wahid denied that he or his foundation ever made a deal with BIN or hired anyone to restore military aid. He said As'ad had asked for permission to use his name for the national interest and "Upon hearing the words 'for the sake of the nation,' I replied: 'Please do.'" But he said he had no idea his permission would be misused to lobby for an end to military restrictions. The man who'd signed the contract on behalf of the foundation had no formal role there and didn't speak English, the language of the contract. According to him, "BIN organized everything. I just signed the contract."[25]

Two months after the story broke, Suci was interviewed on a bench on the National Mall in Washington, DC, by reporters for Dan Rather's news show, which was investigating the business of lobbying. When the show aired soon after, Rather told the story of Munir's murder to an American audience, and explained its connection to the Dole contract.[26] The show also included footage of Suci at home in her garden, speaking of her children:

> When they miss him, I tell them that their father will remain with us because he loved us very much and we love him so much too. . . . My only hope is for this case to be resolved, who is the murderer, who is the perpetrator of this murder. I am still waiting for rare justice in Indonesia to be upheld. That's what I am waiting for.

Dan Rather observed in closing, "She may have a long wait."

Suci felt that her visit to Washington was a success. She briefed the Human Rights Caucus of the House of Representatives and met with staff from some of the same congressional offices that As'ad had spoken to a year before. Senator Leahy later added language to a bill requiring the secretary of state to report on the status of the Munir investigation, including "efforts to arrest any individuals who ordered or carried out that crime." And just hours after she met with a senior State Department official, a wire service reported, "The United States will press for a no-holds-barred probe into the murder."

In New York, Usman met with Philip Alston, the United Nations special rapporteur on summary and extrajudicial killings, who sent a formal communication to the Indonesian government. Usman and Suci sent real-time updates on each of these developments to the Indonesian press. Hungry for news about Indonesia from abroad, the papers contained daily reports of her meetings and appearances. Alongside similar efforts in Europe and Asia, these activities built pressure on the Indonesian government to make progress on the case. SBY began facing uncomfortable questions about Munir's death when he went abroad.

For Suci it was a dark time, despite the successful trip to the United States. Polly's release from prison was imminent, and hope of prosecuting the masterminds was dwindling. It was time for a new approach, and Suci returned to Indonesia with an idea.

At that time, hopelessness was widespread among the families of the victims of state violence. With the human rights courts proving to be a failure, the main alternative was a truth and reconciliation commission, or TRC. In the first years of *reformasi*, a few human rights groups had supported the creation of a truth commission, arguing that amnesties for past crimes were needed to protect a fragile democracy. Munir, however, believed the country needed trials more than amnesties.

When the TRC law passed, it contained a provision that victims could get compensation only if they agreed to an amnesty for the perpetrators. Human rights groups challenged that requirement before the new Constitutional Court, arguing that it was unfair to victims, many of whom were destitute.[27] The TRC had not even begun operations when the court annulled not only the amnesty requirement but the entire law. Many observers agreed that the ruling marked the end of any serious effort by the state to address the past.

Soon after she got back from the United States, Suci asked Sumarsih to meet her at KontraS. Sumarsih was the career civil servant who had lobbed eggs at the parliamentary commission that decided the student shootings were not serious human rights violations. Seven years after the death of her son Wawan, the young volunteer medic shot at Semanggi I, Sumarsih was also feeling low.

Suci and Sumarsih found a table in a shady area of the courtyard, joined by a young KontraS staffer. Yati had been in her first semester at the State Islamic University of Jakarta in 1998 when she heard Munir speak on campus about the disappearances. The few students who'd come to his talk decided to march across campus with posters of the disappeared. As often happens, this small public demonstration had the most impact on the protestors themselves. For Yati, it was as if Munir had unlocked a door, allowing her to think critically about her country.

Yati started volunteering at KontraS in 2002. On her first day, she was sent off to court to monitor the trials for crimes against humanity in East Timor. She found the courthouse filled with soldiers, a frightening experience matched only by her return to KontraS at the end of the day. She found the office had been wrecked by a gang of thugs, and her new colleagues assaulted.

Munir taught Yati how to monitor trials in the contested space of the courthouse. In her last meeting with Munir, they had discussed the impact of the soldiers attending the East Timor trials, the fact that the few victims to testify couldn't speak without intimidation, and how the trials had no substance to them. She kept volunteering but turned down job offers at KontraS, right up until Munir was killed. His murder convinced her that the country was still living in the shadow of violence, and she decided to fully commit to human rights work. She was given the job of monitoring the trial of Pollycarpus and became a friend and ally to Suci.[28]

The walled front yard of KontraS was a spacious hub for activists and journalists to discuss politics and cases over glasses of coffee and tea from a stand operated by the mother of a victim of violence. There Suci described to Sumarsih and Yati the awards ceremony in New York. The other recipients that night were Las Damas de Blancas from Cuba. Each week, the Ladies in White walked silently through the streets of Havana to bring attention to their imprisoned husbands and sons. They themselves had been inspired by the Mothers of the Plaza de Mayo, whose children had been disappeared by General Pinochet's regime in Chile.

Suci thought they could try something similar. She suggested that victims' families lead a weekly protest, along with anyone who wanted to join. They settled on Thursdays and debated locations. The attorney general's office? Police headquarters? Suci argued that it had to be the Istana Merdeka, the presidential palace. Without the president's full support, nothing would ever happen. Starting at four p.m. would let people come after school or work, and ensure a rush-hour audience at the busy northwest corner of the Medan Merdeka.

They would wear or carry something black for their suffering, a mark of tragedy and determination. They agreed on black umbrellas. They were calling on the law to protect them, just as umbrellas offered protection from the rain and sun. Should they be silent like the Ladies in White? Sometimes they would be silent, and other times there might be speeches or music. The protests would go on until they secured justice. However, if one day only Suci, Sumarsih, and Yati showed up, that would be the final protest.

They would call it something simple and direct. In Indonesian the suffix *-an* can change an adjective or verb into a noun, or a noun into a set of things. *Duri*, or thorn, becomes *durian*, the spiky fruit. *Kamis*, or Thursday, became *kamisan*, perhaps best translated as *Thursdays*. They scheduled the first *kamisan* in the coming new year.

13

The Singer at the Airport Café

2007

On January 18, 2007, the first *kamisan* protest took place under black umbrellas. Each was labeled in white block letters with a person or location that had become shorthand for a grave and unresolved case: Marsinah, Trisakti and Semanggi, Talangsari. Munir had worked on all of these cases, and now his name was among them. The small protest gave Suci a lift, a way to start the year with action. Suci and Sumarsih had claimed the day for Wawan, Munir, and all the victims of state violence.

That first *kamisan* took place on a very productive day. The attorney general formed a team to request that the Supreme Court review Polly's acquittal, and Suci and Usman went to meet a police investigator at national police headquarters. He had been part of the team that arrested Pollycarpus with enough evidence to get him convicted, and was still part of the investigation.[1]

The police were working on a new line of investigation. The day of Polly's acquittal, the national police chief had quietly requested technical help from the United States Federal Bureau of Investigation to examine five cell phones seized from Pollycarpus. He hoped to learn more about communications with BIN.[2] In early December 2006, police officers hand-delivered the phones to FBI headquarters in Quantico, Virginia. The investigator told Suci and Usman he'd expected the results by now, but there was no news.

They discussed the long-awaited prosecution of the Garuda director. The investigator hoped the charges would go beyond forgery to include his role in a premeditated murder. The problem was that it would be hard to charge an accessory to a crime when the killer had just been acquitted. When the topic turned to BIN, he said he was sure that any written orders to kill Munir had been destroyed, if they ever existed. They needed witness testimony.

Usman agreed, and he was growing impatient. "Let's just arrest the suspects, question them for twenty-four hours, then release them if we have to," he said. "Try some shock therapy." In a country where police torture was widespread, and where arrest orders didn't need a judge's approval, Usman was used to speaking out in defense of the rights of detainees. That he was pushing for such an aggressive approach indicated his impatience for a breakthrough.

The investigator replied, "To arrest someone, you need evidence."

Usman agreed, but argued for using preliminary material to arrest Muchdi and question him about who was supposedly using his phone if not him—his adult children, or his driver—and get them to talk. By fully exercising their authority to question witnesses and conduct searches, the police might get results and encourage other witnesses to cooperate.

Umbrellas at the *kamisan* protest held every Thursday. The banner labels five former generals as suspects, including Hendropriyono and Prabowo. (Matt Easton)

The investigator promised that the police were following up on all leads, including the leaked scenarios memo that described discussions at BIN about killing Munir. The police were looking into all four scenarios, a car crash, black magic, and using poison at home or abroad. They were looking for the source of the arsenic, perhaps a gold dealer rather than a chemical supplier. They were looking into Bambang Irawan, the BIN agent with a medical background once spotted with Pollycarpus in Aceh, and who might have boarded flight 974 under a fake name.

Then he hinted at developments he couldn't fully reveal, such as witnesses who said that Hendropriyono held meetings at BIN about assassinating Munir and other activists. The witnesses were afraid to give statements on the record, but the police were working to confirm the allegations.

The investigator was sure that if BIN cooperated, the police could solve the case in hours. But on top of institutional resistance from the secretive body, it seemed as if Hendropriyono was personally trying to shut down cooperation with the police, and perhaps removing meeting notes from BIN headquarters. But even without BIN's cooperation, he believed he could make arrests that very day if his bosses would let him.[3]

One more significant encounter took place on the day of that first *kamisan*. Suci and Usman met with Ambassador Lynn Pascoe at the American embassy. The ambassador confirmed that the FBI had extracted raw data from Polly's phones and would turn it over to Police Chief Sutanto in Washington. Next week, Sutanto would meet with FBI director Robert Mueller as part of a delegation visiting to discuss cooperation on counterterrorism and narcotics.[4]

After meeting with Suci and Usman, the embassy cabled to Washington that Sutanto's visit would be an opportunity for the United States government to privately stress the importance of the Munir case. The embassy believed the police chief was under pressure from BIN to go through the motions without bringing high-level culprits to justice. The cable concluded with uncertain optimism: "Promising new evidence from the U.S. laboratories on key cell phones in the case should give prosecutors a stronger hand. How Sutanto plays that hand in this high-stakes case will reflect on his commitment to reform."[5]

So many positive developments in a single day—the first *kamisan*, the attorney general's case-review team, the police investigator's hints and promises, and the ambassador's confirmation of the cell phone analysis—gave Suci hope.

The day turned out to be pivotal in one more respect. A few weeks before, the Criminal Investigation Division had come under new leadership. The foot-dragging Suryadharma had handed over the position to Bambang Hendarso Danuri, who had a strong track record combating corruption and illegal logging. On January 18, Hendarso signed an order appointing a team of nine trusted and experienced investigators from the national and Jakarta police, police intelligence, and the elite Detachment 88. The lead investigator, Mathius Salempang, reported directly to Hendarso.[6] The team was empowered to seek witnesses and documents more easily. A smaller team was more efficient, and allowed the investigation to clean house of anyone who might obstruct the work, leak information, or even conspire with targets. Kasum met with the new CID director twice in his first week, and weekly with members of the team, kicking off a period of mutual trust and cooperation.

On February 13, Usman, Indra, and other Kasum members met with police officers from the old and new teams. The police had suggested meeting at a large pyramid-shaped complex of pubs, cafés, and karaoke bars. The somewhat unsavory Café Bengkel lay among the upscale buildings of the Sudirman Central Business District. The group settled into a private karaoke room, and the officers ordered beer from waitresses whom they appeared to know well. Most likely the police just considered it their hangout, but the strange choice of meeting place put Usman on his guard. Activists were occasionally offered women and alcohol in an effort to entrap or discredit them.

Despite the venue and the large group, the discussion felt open and direct from the start. Anton was there, and he expressed frustration with the state of the investigation, saying, "Just as it feels I'm getting close, I'm twice as far away." He blamed the lack of progress on the constant reshuffling of investigators and a climate of suspicion within the police. "Sometimes even I don't know friend from foe," he said. "I'm just being honest. I hope I don't have enemies here, because I wouldn't know, right?

Even in our own organization I'm sometimes called the enemy, so much so that I've been kicked off the Munir team twice. But I just keep going."[7]

The need to transform rumors and shards of information into legally admissible evidence felt overwhelming. Now, after two years of trying to find a gun permit or identity card to prove Polly's connection to BIN, they might have found another way to do it. A police intelligence unit had located a witness to swear the co-pilot was a BIN agent—and that witness was leading to others. These developments were still secret, Anton said, "But testimony that Pollycarpus is a member of BIN maybe—*Insya Allah*—hopefully, is possible."

An investigator cautioned Usman, however, that showing Polly's link to BIN was not enough. They needed evidence of a conspiracy to commit murder, including a motive. He believed the motive might have sprung from major cases Munir worked on that implicated the two generals at BIN personally: the abductions in 1998, and the massacre in Talangsari by soldiers reporting to Hendropriyono in 1989. Usman agreed that these two cases had always stood out, that any sign of progress led to the most frightening forms of intimidation and threat.[8] But Usman believed the motive could be personal *and* institutional. Hendro and Muchdi had ended up at the same unreformed institution, confronted by a tenacious critic who was impervious to bombs, mobs, and threats. Munir had obstructed their careers, but he had also defeated their agency's bid to expand its powers.

The conversation paused now and then as waitresses brought the policemen beer, resuming when they left the room. The question of timing arose. To many Indonesians, these two cases were old news by 2004. Why kill Munir then? Usman thought it had something to do with the presidential elections. The final runoff was held weeks after Munir was killed. Munir and other activists were urging voters to reject all the retired generals—Wiranto, Prabowo, and SBY. For the first time, Munir even endorsed a candidate, the civilian he thought most likely to stop the return of the generals to politics. Polly's other apparent targets, Hendardi and Yeni Rosa (see pages 97 and 110), were also outspoken critics of the military candidates.

Usman wondered if the plan was to make voters think the military killed Munir. That might spur a backlash that would help the leading civilian candidate, the incumbent Megawati. Hendro was a retired general too, but he was a political infighter and a survivor, and his fortunes were closely tied to Mega's success in the polls. According to the leaked scenarios memo, the first discussions within BIN about killing Munir were in March 2004, just before the first round of voting. The grisly package sent to Suci warning her not to blame the army might, in fact, have been meant to *implicate* the military.[9]

The method of murder may support this theory. Causing someone to ingest a fatal quantity of poison is hard, requiring access to their food or drink, and to a poison that is undetectable to a body that has evolved to reject toxic substances. For at least a century, it has been hard to get away with such a crime undetected, due to the state of toxicological analysis. Often, the poison is intended to be discovered in order to sow fear, as in Vladimir Putin's Russia. According to this theory, the murder of Munir was intended to be a public act, either to frighten critics or to sway voters away from the military candidate and toward the civilian, Megawati.[10]

They discussed ways to prove Polly's relationship to Muchdi. Anton displayed his large diagram of phone calls among their suspects. But they still needed a witness to say Polly talked to the general and that they were close. A photo of the two would prove they were lying about not knowing each other. One policeman had heard of such a photo in Surabaya. Suci had heard that a photo had been hidden with Polly's wife's priest before the police searched the house.

Indra shared his own story of looking into Polly's early years in Papua. Like Poengky, he found the co-pilot's old boss at the missionary flight service. Appealing to the man's moral sense as a Christian, Indra got him to open up and learned that Polly started hanging out with soldiers in high school. The man, who'd stood in for Polly's father at his wedding, thought he had a photo from that ceremony of Pollycarpus with a local military commander, possibly Muchdi. Indra spent two days rummaging through the man's old photos and yellowed newspapers in a dusty storage room in the hills above Jayapura, only to come up empty.

A schism emerged within the police investigation. The new team of nine wanted to revisit the assumption that the crime scene was the flight from Jakarta to Singapore. Lead investigator Mathius Salempang felt the theory wasn't based on firm evidence, particularly without knowing the form of arsenic used, and therefore the time of intake. The new team began looking more closely at Munir's brief layover in Singapore's Changi Airport. Investigators who'd worked the case longer, including Anton, worried that a shift in crime scene might be an effort to divert the trail from Polly, and therefore from Muchdi, Hendro, and BIN. Indra and Usman feared the same thing.

Soon there was a scientific basis for reopening the question of the crime scene. The year before, members of the police lab wanted to better pinpoint the time of the poisoning. They asked a toxicologist from Bali named I Made Agus Gelgel Wirasuta to give a quantity of arsenic to a monkey, using the autopsy report as a guide, and record how long it took to die. Gelgel refused to perform a test he considered useless, given the differences between the species. He asked if the police had any samples left from the Dutch autopsy. They did, and he suggested they ask a well-equipped foreign lab to identify the form of arsenic used, so that he could create a timeline. Investigators reached out to contacts in several countries, finally sending samples to a private lab in Tukwila, Washington, outside Seattle. Having been turned down by labs in Japan, Malaysia, and Australia, they did not state that the samples were from the Munir case until the results were in hand.

Usman urged the police to focus on any data the FBI pulled from Polly's cell phones rather than a new toxicology analysis.[11] Layering new findings on top of the Dutch analysis carried some risk. Defense lawyers might use the new results, or a new crime scene, to further muddy the waters of an already confusing case. The risk was real, but new analysis could also open fresh lines of inquiry.

One night in February 2007, Gelgel's phone rang as he was performing his Hindu prayers at home in Bali. He had recently completed a doctorate in Germany on pharmacokinetics, the study of the uptake of drugs in the body and the changes they undergo as a result. Often used to develop pharmaceuticals, this expertise could also help pinpoint the timing of a poisoning.

The call was from the new CID director, Hendarso. He had the results from the lab near Seattle and wanted Gelgel to come to Jakarta to work with them immediately. Gelgel agreed, and when he arrived the next day, police took him to the thirty-fourth floor of the Hotel Shangri-La. Hendarso's team had rented space outside police headquarters to work, safe from intimidation and surveillance. Leading the meeting that night, Hendarso told Gelgel that after global condemnation of Polly's acquittal, the president had ordered the police to reopen the investigation in search of new evidence for a case review. He hoped the lab results from Seattle might answer the question of when, and therefore where, Munir was poisoned.

Gelgel worked through the night to interpret the Seattle findings, alongside two other experts more familiar with the case.[12] In the morning, they presented their findings to Hendarso and several prosecutors. They explained that arsenic is usually found with one of two valences, or capacities to combine with other elements. Each behaves differently and both were found in Munir's body, with trivalent arsenic 83 percent of the total. However, Gelgel concluded that Munir was poisoned with pentavalent arsenic. Once in the body, a chemical reaction known as reduction transforms pentavalent arsenic to its trivalent form. The progress of this transformation can be used to pinpoint the timing of intake.

Hendarso asked Gelgel to calculate a timeline based on this analysis and Munir's symptoms. After again working through the night, Gelgel concluded that Munir had consumed the poison eight or nine hours before his death, and thirty to sixty minutes before he showed symptoms. With that estimate in mind, it was unlikely that Munir was poisoned on the flight from Jakarta. It was much more likely that the crime took place during the layover in Changi Airport.[13]

While Changi had been a subject of interest to both the police and the TPF, their focus had been on the security cameras, Polly's airport hotel stay, and his supposed fuel-dumping investigation. But the new team had quickly begun following up on other leads from Changi that had been dropped or ignored due to the conclusion that Munir was poisoned in the air. Believing that no restaurants or stores were open at that hour, and knowing that the €5,000 in cash that Munir left Jakarta with had been found untouched in his bag, investigators wondered if any of several people seen talking to Munir had given him something to eat or drink.[14]

One lead came from an Indonesian student studying in Germany. Asrini Utami Putri told police in 2005 that she'd seen Munir in transit. Questioned again in 2007, Asrini added that on the flight from Jakarta, she'd chatted in business class with a Garuda employee named Joseph Ririmase. In Changi, he introduced her to a man with long hair who was, like himself, from the Moluccas. He'd referred to the long-haired man as a *preman politik*, or political gangster. Ririmase himself told police the man was a pianist traveling to play at a church in the Netherlands. Without a name, the police called him Si Gondrong, or Long-Hair.

Kasum went looking for Moluccan musicians who might have a connection to Munir.[15] The police had the idea of comparing the flight manifest to passport photos on file, in search of a tall, long-haired man with a mustache. On the fourth day of combing through the files at the East Jakarta Regional Immigration Office, they found him.[16]

J. J. Raymond Latuihamallo turned out to be world famous in the Moluccas, as the joke goes. Known by his nickname, Ongen, he'd never reached national fame, although in 1988 he did appear on *Selekta Pop*, a monthly music video show. Appearing on the single, government-controlled station, Ongen's performance would have had tens of millions of live viewers. Sporting a blow-dried haircut instead of the long hair he adopted later, Ongen strolled through the shimmering set, singing his hit "Sayang Bilang Sayang" ("Darling, Say Darling").

It was the pinnacle of his career. He later named one of his two daughters Sabilsa, a name created from the first syllable of each word in the hit's title. He remained a journeyman musician, singing and playing keyboards at church holiday services in Jakarta and in Moluccan enclaves in the Netherlands. After Indonesian independence, veterans of the colonial army, many of whom were from the Moluccas, had been brought with their families to the Netherlands, and housed at first in the barracks of a recently liberated Nazi concentration camp.[17] Ongen visited Moluccan neighborhoods in the southern city of Breda and other Dutch towns several times each year.[18]

The police called Ongen in on March 30, followed by three days of questioning before a break to allow him to travel to Pasar Malam, the Night Market, a regular celebration of Indonesian music in the Netherlands. With a backdrop of yellow multi-tiered Balinese umbrellas and foam temples, he manned a synthesizer and sang "Maluku, Land That I Love" to sparse applause. Ongen clapped for himself at one point to encourage a better response from the elderly Dutch couples and children of Moluccan exiles in the audience.[19]

It was Ongen's last taste of his life as a man known mostly for his music. On April 20, Ongen flew home with a stopover in Kuala Lumpur, where lead investigator Mathius Salempang took him into protective custody under a new witness-protection law, as arranged through Ongen's family.[20] After stopping in Singapore to have Ongen walk them through the new (and already much altered) crime scene, they touched down in Jakarta. At the airport, dozens more police were waiting, and so were a number of men whom police recognized as BIN agents. One news report described a dramatic encounter. As police officers escorted Ongen to a car waiting near the plane, another vehicle drove up. Two men jumped out and tried to wrest Ongen away from the police, who fought them off and rushed him to headquarters. Police and BIN denied a scuffle took place, as did Ongen. According to an eyewitness, the men just filmed Ongen's arrival in an apparent effort to intimidate him.[21]

Police questioned the singer over the next week, and CID Director Hendarso privately told the American embassy that he was being "very, very cooperative." Police called Ongen a key witness, but it was possible that he was more than that. A magazine interviewed Asrini, the student, and it seemed she could testify to seeing Ongen sitting with both Pollycarpus and Munir. Asrini (identified only by initials) said she sat near Munir on the flight from Jakarta, and recognized him from TV. In Singapore, she disembarked behind him and saw him walk to an escalator near Gate 42. He seemed to be waiting for somebody.

She saw Munir again, before reboarding. He was talking with two people on a sofa at the coffee shop, a branch of the Coffee Bean and Tea Leaf chain. The two men had their backs to her, but she could see that one was tall and had long hair. The other man was wearing glasses. She didn't notice the men eating or drinking and wasn't sure the café was even serving at that hour. The man with glasses resembled Pollycarpus, including his distinctive "bulgy" eyes. She stopped short of stating it *was* Pollycarpus, saying, "I don't want to make accusations."[22]

Journalists found Ongen's house empty and padlocked. Neighbors reported that anonymous phone calls referencing Ongen's two daughters and their schools had scared the family. Soon after Ongen's return from Europe, four policemen had collected Ongen's wife, daughters, a servant, and a dog.[23] Police later confirmed that Ongen and his family had entered protective custody.

More than a month later, on June 6, Ongen reemerged at a press conference. After twice as many journalists showed up than expected, including several TV crews, the event had to relocate from the Hotel Shangri-La to a more accommodating venue, a branch of the American restaurant chain Sizzler.

The singer entered with two plainclothes policemen, Steyr assault rifles slung on their backs. Ongen wore sunglasses perched high like a headband to hold back his long hair. A red floral pattern cascaded down a white shirt unbuttoned at the top to reveal a gold necklace. From the chain, thick as a shoelace, hung a jeweled cross and the same heart pendant he'd worn on a 1983 cassette cover. Ongen sat on a brightly lit banquette between his lawyer and his wife, Hendriette. She was also a Christian singer from the Moluccas. Before they were married, the two appeared on a Christmas album featuring *Jingle Bells* in Ambonese.[24]

For much of the hourlong event, Ongen remained quiet, smiling and holding on to a Bible. His lawyer, Ozhak Sihotang, read a statement and explained that Ongen was a singer, not a lawyer, and so he would do most of the talking for his client. They just wanted to convey the truth, not hide anything.

A reporter asked, "Did you meet or interact with Munir at the Coffee Bean?"

Ozhak answered for him, "No."

"Did you *see* Munir at the Coffee Bean?"

Ozhak and Ongen whispered briefly.

"Let Ongen answer himself!" someone shouted.

Ozhak reminded the crowd that they could not reveal what Ongen told police out of respect for the investigation. The journalists weren't having it. One called out, "Maybe Bang Ongen can answer this question. Give him a chance!"

"Okay, here's a chance."

Ongen said, "It is true that Munir was at the Coffee Bean at that time."

"With who?"

Ongen whispered with Ozhak, before saying into the mike, "With someone."

He didn't know the person and wouldn't describe him or her due to a promise to police. Ozhak said, "I think that's enough Coffee Bean answers." A reporter asked about rumors that Ongen was part of an international ecstasy ring. Ozhak said he'd provided all the information about Ongen there was, but did want to address other rumors in the air: Ongen was not a political gangster or a debt collector, and he'd never met Pollycarpus before September 6, 2004.

Toward the end, a reporter asked directly, "Are you the one who killed Munir?"

Speaking slowly, Ongen said, "To that question I want to say here, 'God have mercy on me.' How unlucky I am if, just because I was in a particular place, I'm accused, or became so easily targeted as a suspect."

His lawyer said, "I think that's enough," and Ongen posed for pictures with his family.

When Ongen was interviewed on TV that night, he offered nothing more. A former TPF member appeared also. Rachland Nashidik, Munir's close friend and colleague, said that looking back, the early stages of the investigation felt like a trail of breadcrumbs in a fairy tale. But they couldn't know who placed the breadcrumbs there. Did they go in the right direction or did they lead to a trap? He urged the police not to make the same mistakes.[25]

In the story of Hansel and Gretel, birds devour the breadcrumbs and the children become lost. One of the most promising trails in the Munir case also seemed to disappear. Early in 2007, the CID director Hendarso met with Usman, Suci, Asmara, Hendardi, and Indra in his office. They were eager to learn if the FBI's forensic analysis of Polly's cell phones had produced any evidence of ties to BIN and his reputed handler, General Muchdi. According to several participants, Hendarso said the FBI had found the content of a communication between Muchdi's and Polly's phones. It was short, either text message or audio, and was something from Muchdi similar to *"Laksanakan,"* or "Do it." And a reply, "Okay." Bolstering this account was the January 19 U.S. embassy cable to Washington referring to "promising new evidence from the U.S. laboratories on key cell phones."[26] There were similarly positive public statements by Hendarso and other Indonesian officials about the FBI cooperation.[27]

But no such evidence ever emerged in court filings or anywhere else. Hendarso denied saying any such thing at his meeting with Kasum, and that section of a recording of the meeting was unintelligible. Senior police and prosecutors denied they had recordings of calls between Muchdi and Pollycarpus. In interviews, police investigators supported the view that the FBI never found anything of value on the phones.[28] Usman and others were confounded by the disappearance of what they hoped was a smoking gun. But with the possibility of the police locating witnesses to the planning or execution of the plot, and to Pollycarpus's links to BIN, the communications might not be as important as they once were.[29]

In early May, Suci enjoyed a small victory in her civil suit against Garuda. Suci and lawyers from Kasum had filed suit the year before, demanding compensation, a full internal investigation, and an apology.[30] They built their case on the daisy chain of irregularities around Munir's death: the letter naming Polly to security, the unauthorized schedule change, the fake assignment in Singapore, the backdated letter, the seat change, the failure to make an emergency landing, and the lack of a comprehensive internal review of the incident. These steps belied the airline manual's broad claim that "passenger safety is everything," as well as more specific rules and procedures.[31]

On May 3, 2007, a panel of judges awarded Suci $73,500. They didn't order the apology or an internal investigation, but the verdict established

Garuda's responsibility. And Suci could surely use the money for the children's education and for advocacy work. But she was horrified at the idea
of appearing to profit from Munir's death. She also remembered a conflict that emerged after Munir was awarded the Right Livelihood Award,
known as the Alternative Nobel Prize, and wondered if she should just
give the money to Kasum. Suci's friend Smita asked an imam for advice,
who said that under Islamic law, the money belongs to Munir's children.
She told Suci, "Don't give it away. It's not yours to give, it's your children's." It stayed in the bank, with Suci using the interest for the family's
expenses and some advocacy efforts. She worried that if she withdrew any
more, people would say she was taking advantage of Munir's death.

The criminal case against Garuda staff was finally picking up speed as
well. On April 10, the police announced two new suspects, using the standard practice of providing only initials to the media. IS clearly referred to
airline director Indra Setiawan, who was arrested April 13 at the house of
a "female friend."[32] RA was assumed to be Ramelgia Anwar, the security
director who backdated the memo. But it turned out to be Rohainil Aini,
the secretary who changed Polly's schedule so he could join Munir's flight.

One night a little more than a month later, CID director Hendarso's
phone rang at two a.m. A member of the Munir team asked him to come
to police headquarters right away. He rushed to the office, assuming the
investigation had run into trouble, but it turned out to be good news.
After two years of giving misleading statements to police, and some forty
days after being detained, Indra Setiawan had finished his evening prayers
and sobbed that he was ready to talk, but only to Hendarso.

His change of heart came very soon after learning that the police knew
his secret, one with no connection to the Munir case. So many rumors of
corruption and affairs had swirled around Setiawan that police wondered
which weakness they might put to good use. Then a more junior member
of the nine-person team heard a strange story about journalists approaching Setiawan. In an apparent effort to intimidate him, they'd shown him
a mock-up of a magazine that revealed his secret. Setiawan had a second
family hidden away in the hills of Puncak near Jakarta.[33]

The investigator had once been posted in East Jakarta and knew where the journalists hung out there. He found an old contact, gave him some money, and told him to find these supposed journalists. The contact brought him three people *and* a copy of the magazine. The investigator brought it up to Puncak, and took a photo of the magazine being held up by Indra's secret second wife. He brought the photo back to show Setiawan in police custody. Looking at the photo, Setiawan must have foreseen the imminent loss of his family, and maybe his freedom. He sobbed, and lowered his head onto his hands, which were resting on the table. "How did you find them?" he asked. "Don't blow it all up. I'll talk."[34]

Ever since Garuda's apparent role in Munir's death had emerged, the question had persisted of who had the power to use a state-owned enterprise to commit murder. Even as it began to look like the answer was BIN, it was still hard to know, and prove, the precise contours of such a relationship. Setiawan provided the missing puzzle piece.

Setiawan often hung out in the restaurant of the Sahid Hotel in the Golden Triangle, Jakarta's financial district. Named for a river in Central Java and a famous song about the waterway, the Bengawan Solo restaurant served high-end, traditional Indonesian food to the sounds of a small gamelan troupe seated cross-legged on the floor, all under the watchful eyes of *wayang* puppets.

Setiawan revealed that one evening in July 2004, he had wrapped up a dinner meeting and crossed the parquet floors to join Pollycarpus at his table as arranged. The co-pilot rattled off weaknesses in Garuda's flight operations. Smugglers on the flight crews. People flying without tickets. The airline had serious problems, and Pollycarpus was ready to help. He handed Setiawan a sealed envelope.

Inside, a one-page letter on BIN stationery noted that the airline played a leading role in counteracting terrorism by cooperating with other institutions. The letter recommended that the director assign Pollycarpus to the airline's security division. It took a long time for Setiawan to tell investigators who the letter was from. At last he revealed that the letter was signed by BIN's deputy director, As'ad Said Ali. As'ad's name had come up in the scenarios memo and the anonymous texts. He'd also been on the lobbying contracts and the trip to remove impediments to military cooperation, one of which was the Munir case.

It was this letter that prompted Setiawan to issue his August 11 recommendation that Polly be assigned to Corporate Security, the only such letter he ever wrote. Polly then used this security assignment to get his schedule changed to board Munir's plane.

The As'ad letter could show BIN's link to Pollycarpus and Garuda, and all three to the plot to kill Munir. It would be a powerful piece of evidence in court. There was only one problem. The letter had been stolen. Setiawan told police that on New Year's Eve, as 2004 came to a close, Setiawan had driven his BMW to the Sahid Hotel. He parked his car in the guarded lot, and went into the hotel's prayer room nearby. During the brief time it took to perform his prayers, someone broke the front left window of the car and stole a black bag with the letter in it.[35] Just outside the restaurant where Polly had handed Setiawan an envelope five months before, the airline director had been released from the burden of its possession.

Setiawan also revealed further evidence of BIN's role. He told the police that when the presence of arsenic was revealed in November 2004, he'd asked to meet Deputy Director As'ad. He wanted to verify that the letter he had acted on was genuine. Any doubts were eased by how quickly Pollycarpus arranged a meeting with As'ad. Polly told him when and where to go, and Setiawan went to BIN and entered the complex without signing the guest book. He was shown to a meeting room and was sitting down when a man entered. Setiawan assumed he was As'ad and exchanged pleasantries until the man announced that As'ad was on his way. When As'ad did join them, Setiawan was afraid to ask about the letter, which had been marked secret, in front of this stranger. When the meeting was over, he got the man's number to put in his phone and used the opportunity to ask, "And whose number is this?"

The man replied, "Muchdi."

Then, when the police began questioning Setiawan about the murder, starting in February 2005, he'd called As'ad, asking, "Why is this happening, Garuda getting pulled in?"

As'ad had replied, "No problem, stay calm. You don't need to worry, it can be resolved."

Setiawan contacted As'ad again to ask if he should tell the police he'd been to BIN headquarters. ("Say you didn't come," advised As'ad after some discussion.) Setiawan called again to ask him if any copies remained of the letter, and As'ad promised to check. Several days later, by chance Setiawan saw As'ad at the Hotel Shangri-La. Hoping to talk to him alone, Setiawan followed him into the bathroom. There was someone in a stall, so he asked vaguely, "What about that letter, Pak?" As'ad replied, "Yes, it's done." Setiawan took that to mean any copies of the letter had been destroyed.

Setiawan had one more meeting of note. On the night of March 3, 2005, Setiawan had testified at the parliamentary hearing on Munir, his answers only deepening public suspicions of Garuda's role in the murder plot. Several hours earlier, he now revealed to police, Setiawan secretly met with the chair of that committee, M. Taufiequrrahman, at the business center of the Hotel Mulia. The men discussed the chronology of events, and Garuda's answers to the questions to be asked that night. A third man was there, whom Setiawan assumed the committee chair had invited. It was Muchdi, and he only listened as the other two spoke. Setiawan told the police, "I wondered if Pak Muchdi wanted to know if I would mention the involvement of three letters." He meant BIN, hesitating to speak it aloud even in the relative safety of police headquarters.

Setiawan told police he had called Muchdi when the police turned their attention to Garuda, when they arrested Pollycarpus, and when prosecutors requested life in prison for the co-pilot. Muchdi always gave the same reply, "No problem. It will be resolved, Pak Indra."[36]

The same police investigators building a case against the former Garuda director were seeking new evidence for the case review of Pollycarpus. As recently as early April, CID director Hendarso had sounded defeatist, saying, "If only a person could be tried twice in the same case, I'd already have arrested Pollycarpus." However, when Hendarso personally delivered new evidence to the attorney general's office on April 13, Usman felt that the police were finally on the right track.[37]

A month later, a new attorney general named Hendarman Supandji was sworn in. Two days into his tenure, he sent the dossier back to the police for more work. He explained that the new evidence had to be even stronger, because the prosecution only had one chance. "If we fail, that's it for us," he said.[38] Prosecutors sent the dossier back to the police several more times before accepting it. Finally, on July 26, prosecutors submitted their case-review request asking the Supreme Court to reconsider Polly's acquittal.

Even after all this back and forth, Suci and Usman worried that prosecutors might have rushed the process, relying on incomplete evidence and flawed arguments.[39] The Saturday before the proceedings began, they met with the attorney general. They learned that the core of the filing would be the new evidence from the Seattle lab and testimony from eyewitnesses, including Ongen and the student Asrini.[40]

Ongen's unusual press conference at Sizzler had hinted at what he'd slowly revealed to police over five interviews. On the first day of questioning, he'd revealed only that he was introduced to Munir in the transit area at Changi. Ongen then asked lead investigator Mathius Salempang to summon a priest, and the three men prayed together.

The next day police asked whom he saw at the Coffee Bean & Tea Leaf. Ongen told them that, from about two yards away in the brightly lit café, he saw Munir talking to a brown-skinned man with glasses and wavy hair. Shown a photo of Pollycarpus, Ongen said it was extremely similar to the man he saw with Munir. He denied sitting with them, as the student Asrini had described. Late the next morning, the police continued their inquiries about the Coffee Bean. Ongen said he ordered tea to drink with some cold medicine, added sugar, and found a seat. Asked what Munir and Pollycarpus had ordered, Ongen replied, "I only know they were drinking and chatting together." He could say, however, that he saw two glasses on their table.

Questioning halted when Ongen left to perform at the Night Market in the Netherlands. It was on his way home that the police took Ongen into protective custody, and questioning resumed.[41] The police asked who'd bought the two drinks on the table. Ongen answered that when he entered the café, he saw Pollycarpus leaving the counter. When Ongen carried his own drink to a seat, he spotted Pollycarpus "sitting with Munir, chatting and drinking."[42]

The final round of questioning on April 25 was apparently brief. Investigators put a single exchange in the record: "Please explain how many drinks Polly brought from the counter to where Munir was."

"Two glasses."

Over five interviews, Ongen had gone from admitting only that he met Munir in the waiting room, to describing him sitting with a man who resembled Pollycarpus at the café, to recalling two glasses on the table. Once in protective custody, he added seeing Pollycarpus move from the counter to the table. In his final interview, he stated, under oath, that he saw Pollycarpus bring two drinks to the table. He'd already noted that next to the cashier was a station where customers could add sugar to their beverages and mix it in.

The new forensic analysis located the poisoning at Changi. Two witnesses, Asrini and Ongen, put Pollycarpus and Munir together at the café, and one of them saw the suspect bring the victim a drink. Prosecutors could finally present a plausible scenario of the poisoning. Judges no longer had to imagine a chain of events that no one witnessed: an accomplice bringing Pollycarpus an inflight meal or beverage to surreptitiously poison before serving it to Munir. The murderer didn't have to gamble that a Dutch passenger would choose champagne, while a Muslim would not only choose orange juice, but just the right glass. Arsenic would also dissolve more easily in hot tea than in cold juice.

If the judges didn't reject the legal basis for a case review—and if the witnesses held to their story—Pollycarpus might well return to prison. His link to BIN was stronger than ever too, thanks to the Garuda director's double life. The police knew about the As'ad letter that paved the way for Polly to board Munir's plane. Usman hoped that even though the letter itself was missing, it could be introduced through testimony or corroborated in Garuda's files.

The attorney general informed Suci and Usman of one more piece of new evidence in the review request. The police had a sworn statement from a BIN agent named Ucok that he had been ordered to kill Munir. This might have been the witness from inside BIN whom the police had hinted at over glasses of beer at the karaoke room. If the witness appeared at the hearings at the Supreme Court, and if he was credible, it would be a pivotal moment in the case.[43] According to the attorney general, even if Polly was not sent back to prison, the new evidence might lead to other prosecutions.[44]

14

Spooks and Spirits

2007

In a case review, lower court judges hear arguments and witnesses before sending the file up to a panel of the Supreme Court for a decision. At the same peeling Central Jakarta courthouse where Polly was first convicted, the legal teams, judges, and spectators assembled on August 9 to hear the prosecution lay out their argument and reveal the new evidence hinted at in newspapers. However, Polly's wife handed the judges a letter to explain that a bout of diarrhea prevented him from coming, and the hearing was postponed.[1]

A week later, prosecutors opened their case with a promise of new expert and eyewitness testimony. The evidence would now locate the crime scene in Singapore and, for the first time, connect the murder to BIN.[2] The prosecution teased testimony not only about the order from BIN to Garuda, but also about an order inside BIN to kill Munir.

After the hearing, Pollycarpus shook hands, posed for pictures, and spoke to the press. Projecting his voice over the chorus of camera shutters and the call to prayer floating in through the open windows, he called the prosecutor's case "a thousand per cent lies." He'd never heard of the Coffee Bean. He'd never visited BIN and didn't even know where it was.

The magazine *Tempo* opened its trial coverage with the question that hovered over the hearings like smog: "Slowly, scrap by scrap, this mystery is being put together. But can this giant puzzle finally be assembled, and the *dalangs* be hauled off to prison?"[3]

Witness testimony was confined to August 22, a make-or-break day for the prosecution. The first of four major witnesses was former Garuda director Indra Setiawan, who made his way to the witness chair through a knot of journalists and past a policeman cradling a long gun, muzzle down. Setiawan's round face, body, and glasses gave the impression of a collection of circles, like a cartoonist's sketch. Light bounced off the sheen of his gray safari suit. The prosecutors announced that, before questioning the witness, they would play a tape:

"Hello?" It was Polly's voice.

"I changed my number," was Setiawan's reply. "How are things? Good?"

"I had the meeting," said Polly. "He said, 'Calm down. It's gone.' That's what he said."

Whoever it was who was urging calm, Setiawan was not convinced.

"I'm afraid," he told Polly. "My brain keeps going round and round since yesterday. My brain has been spinning for days now, thinking about events."

Pollycarpus talks to journalists as his lawyer looks on in August 2007, after prosecutors presented new evidence. (REUTERS/Alamy Stock Photo)

Setiawan seemed afraid something would incriminate him. He was especially worried that someone had seen a letter from someone he called A. He'd once left it lying on his desk, or someone might find a copy of it.

Polly assured him everything was fine but promised to raise the matter with someone he called Mrs. Asmini: "But, Pak, I'll bring this up when, insya Allah, tomorrow I meet with, call on Bu Asmini, okay?"

If it was a code, Setiawan didn't know it.

"Who? Who? Who?" Listening in the courtroom to his own frantic voice, Setiawan brought his hand to his mouth.

"Just Ibu Asmini. Ibu Asmini. I'll meet with Ibu Asmini tomorrow."

The code name, and the unnamed "he" in their conversation, presumably referred to As'ad Said Ali, the deputy director of BIN.[4] It was As'ad who signed the letter recommending Pollycarpus be given a security role, the letter Setiawan was afraid would turn up.

Polly again assured him they'd covered their tracks, saying, "He said, 'Keep calm.' Those things are all gone, including the one at my place. So as long as the one at your place is gone, okay, we're safe."

Setiawan confirmed that the original of the letter had been taken from his car, but he worried that another copy might be in the hands of M, presumably his simple code name for Muchdi. (Later in the call, Polly briefly brought up a Mrs. Avi, who Indra later told police was code for Muchdi, while Joker referred to Hendropriyono. Pramuka, or Boy Scouts, was their code word for the police.)[5]

Polly swore to Setiawan that the whole case was pure politics and would blow over if they just kept calm. And they *should* feel calm, he said, because the chief justice of the Supreme Court, Bagir Manan, was in their pocket: "He still does not want this known, but just so you know, Bagir Manan is one of our people."

A hiss of disapproval filled the courtroom, and a woman's voice emitted a note of pure surprise. Polly's expression never changed behind the hands he pressed together in front of his face as if in prayer or deep reflection. Next to him, a lawyer lay his forehead in his hand. Cameras flashed.

On the recording, Setiawan was having a hard time hearing this good news.

"What, what? Hello? Hello?"

"The head of the Supreme Court and his deputies are our people, Pak."

"What, what? Hello? Hello?"

"The head of the Supreme Court and his deputies are our people, Pak. It may seem like you're being pursued to get new evidence about me. But later, if needed, it will be stopped at the top."

Polly reassured his old boss that after sixty days in detention the police would have to free him. What's more, the police were splintered into factions, all chasing promotions, under mounting stress as time ran out without solid evidence. And if they did complete Setiawan's dossier, prosecutors would reject it, and keep on rejecting it, until he was freed. And Polly was trying to help him from outside. Each night he and his wife hung out at a *warung* behind police headquarters until morning, debating whether to go inside, or chatting up friends on the force.

Setiawan kept coming back to the As'ad letter. Who saw Polly give it to him? Who saw the letter itself? If it goes to trial, will everyone stay quiet? By now lawyers on either side of Polly held their heads in their hands. Only Polly stared straight ahead, his chin buttressed by his thumbs, listening to his voice promise that no one would dare to speak up. With the letter gone, there was no evidence, and in court Polly would deny there was ever a letter. And anyway, 90 percent of officials took their side and would never talk. Polly reminded Setiawan that he himself had spent almost seven hundred days in jail, but they got him out in the end.

"And what about me, Pol? When do I get out?"

Polly tried another tack. "I went to East Java, to the ruins of Raden Wijaya and the Majapahit Empire, and spoke with my ancestor, Gajah Mada. He said the darkness is only for a moment and it won't be long before it is bright."

Polly laughed into his hands, embarrassed about his legal consultations with a conquering hero, dead six hundred years. Two of his lawyers leaned back to consult behind their client's head. The courtroom hummed.

Setiawan's voice said, "I don't know anything about anything. I don't want get caught up in it, all right?"

"That's just it, if you tell investigators, 'I don't know anything,' and the like. These investigators are clever, Pak." He knew what police could do, how they made a flight attendant lie about his actions on board. "They're bandits," he said, "those cheats in there."

He urged Setiawan to just be patient and offered to visit him that weekend. Setiawan didn't respond to the offer, instead asking, "Meanwhile, this As'ad, he doesn't want to be visible, huh?" He'd forgotten to use the code.

"He's underground. He's playing from behind the scenes," Polly explained. "The main thing is, they're all cautioning me, 'We're all working, even at the very top. We're all working, Pol, you don't need to be afraid.' That's how it is, Pak."

Then Polly asked a puzzling question, "Why do you think Petruk was replaced?"

"Who?" Setiawan's confusion was understandable. Petruk is a long-nosed clown, a comic figure in the shadow plays.

"I call him Petruk, okay." At the defense table, Polly threw his face into his hands before emerging with an embarrassed smile. Another bombshell was coming. "What's his name? Abdul Rahman."

At the mention of the former attorney general, the courtroom became restless, and Polly's face dove back into his hands, his body shaking with laughter.

"He was replaced, and the one who took his place is one of our people!" He was referring to Hendarman Supandji, the new attorney general, who had authority over all prosecutions.[6]

Polly made a final plea for Setiawan to be patient just a little longer, and to say nothing to police that they might give to prosecutors. Setiawan said he would to stick to his position that he'd given Polly a security assignment but knew nothing about any plot to kill Munir. Polly closed with one last, "Thank you, Pak. Patience, okay."

"Crazy," a spectator muttered, followed by someone in accented English, "Shocking!"

In May, when Setiawan was in detention, investigators had given him a cell phone. After three days, they took it back and recovered audio.[7] The recording was evidence of coordination between two defendants in the case, and of evidence hidden or destroyed. It also showed consultation with others, including the pseudonymous Bu Asmini. And, in his efforts to keep Setiawan from talking to the police, Polly had claimed as "our people," two men with enormous influence over the justice system: the attorney general and the chief justice of the Supreme Court.[8] The American embassy had a political officer at the hearing, as it often did. His cable to Washington that night observed, "Suciwati shed tears of joy after hearing the wiretapped evidence."[9] It was not just the evidence that moved her, but the fact that it meant that this time the police were serious about solving her husband's murder.

In court, prosecutors had Setiawan confirm that it was his voice on the tape. He also confirmed that he'd recommended Polly for the security role because of the As'ad letter.[10] But he insisted that he never specified that Polly should travel on Munir's flight, and he still had no idea who authorized the trip to Singapore.

The taped call was not the most explosive evidence of the day. After Setiawan was excused, spectators stood on tiptoes, craned their necks, and peered through gaps in the crowd. A small man in his mid-thirties entered and took the witness chair. His beige safari suit, short-sleeved with buttoned epaulettes, sat stiffly over a white turtleneck. His cheekbones jutted from a dark-skinned face, as angular as Setiawan's was round.

A prosecutor read out the name of his witness, trilling the *r* in his title, a claim to minor nobility in the court of the Sultan of Solo: *Rrr*aden Muhammad Patma Anwar. A string of aliases followed, dwindling to a final wisp of a nickname: alias Ucok, alias Empe, alias Aa.

The prosecutor had Ucok (pronounced OO-chock) confirm that his sworn statements to police were correct. Ucok had told police that he was a BIN agent from 2000 until 2005. He shared an office with his boss, Sentot Waluyo, in Building K, Directorate 22, Floor 2. On July 8 or 9, 2004, Sentot relayed to Ucok an order from their boss, the deputy II for domestic investigations, a man named Manunggal Maladi: Munir must die before the presidential elections, by poison or by magic.[11] (Maladi's name, and the use of black magic, were both in the scenarios memo given to the TPF.)

Ucok told police he and Sentot had followed the order by contacting a *dukun*, a practitioner of magic, but didn't trust him with the assignment.[12]

The two then joined another division head, Deputy IV for Counterintelligence Wahyu Saronto, to visit a famous *dukun* named Ki Gendeng Pamungkas, but he wasn't home. Sentot did later meet with the *dukun*, who accepted the job. However, his magic failed, Ucok had said, because Munir was protected by a *keris*, a serpentine dagger imbued with power.

But Ucok also told police about a more scientific approach to murder. One month before Munir's death, Sentot told Ucok over the phone that he'd secured poison. Sentot had laced dried fish with some of the substance. He'd fed it to one of Jakarta's army of nub-tailed street cats, and it had worked. But Ucok swore to police that he knew nothing about the actual poisoning of Munir.

The prosecution was content to let the witness confirm his sworn statements. The defense, however, had questions. They asked about the alleged agent's history. He said that in 1996, as a young journalist, he'd joined discussions with Munir at LBH about the army and the government. Four years later, Ucok was recruited to join BIN's predecessor, BAKIN, by its director. He was given two Colt pistols, a .38 and a .32, and tasked with monitoring NGOs to learn about their activities, networks, and funding.[13]

Under the defense's questioning, Ucok backed off a crucial part of his sworn statement, saying, "I don't know about an assignment to kill Munir." He was only assigned to report on Munir's activities, such as who he met, his favorite foods, and when he ate meals.[14] This interest in Munir's diet may have been suggestive of a poisoning plot, but as evidence it did not compare to a specific order to kill him.

The defense asked about an event in the BIN parking lot. Ucok had told police that in June 2004 he'd been on the back of Sentot's motorcycle. As they slowly moved past a black Volvo about five yards away, they saw a man emerge. Ucok had asked Sentot who it was, and learned it was someone from Garuda who was there to meet with "the bosses." Later, Ucok saw the man in the news and learned his name was Pollycarpus. Asked a series of questions about the incident in court, Ucok swiveled on the office chair between the defense table and the judges panel to answer each question with the single word, *"Lupa."* I forget.

Past and present BIN officials publicly disputed Ucok's account. Before the trial began, the BIN director had denied that Ucok was an agent and suggested he be prosecuted for his false claim to be one. The deputy named in his statement, Manunggal Maladi, confirmed that Ucok's supposed boss Sentot worked for him. He also admitted meeting Ucok but said he was an informant, not an agent, and insisted there were no plans or orders to kill Munir.[15] Hendropriyono dismissed the allegations by saying of BIN, "Magic is not in our culture."[16]

The next witness was Asrini, the student on Munir's flight. Investigators had spent $65,000 escorting Asrini home from Germany under their protection.[17] As she headed to the witness chair, she seemed to see a familiar face in the crowd, and for a moment the worry on her young face gave way to a spark of a smile. Once sworn in, she explained that on the flight from Jakarta she recognized Munir sitting nearby, but didn't talk to him.

In Singapore, on her way to Gate 42 to reboard, she saw Polly at the Coffee Bean. (Suciwati murmured, "Great, great.") Asrini said she saw Polly clearly, from two or three yards away, and she saw Munir with him.

"Anyone else?" Asked the judge.

"I don't know. But there was a person with long hair sitting at the same table."[18]

Even after the bombshell recording, and Setiawan's testimony about the As'ad letter, and Ucok's statements to police about seeing Polly at BIN and being ordered to kill Munir, and Asrini's testimony that she saw the victim and the defendant sitting together at the time the poisoning was thought to have taken place—even after all that, it was still important to show *how* Pollycarpus could have poisoned Munir. The earlier trials had unspooled a jumble of theories of noodles and orange juice, with no eyewitnesses to prove Pollycarpus had access to either. Ongen, over five police interviews about the Coffee Bean, had added a detail at a time about what he saw, until a picture was complete. Would he stick to his story, like Asrini, or claim to have forgotten so much, like Ucok?

Ongen strolled in wearing a white shirt open at the neck to reveal his heart-shaped necklace. He had his usual sunglasses high on his head like a hairband, and a red Bible in hand. A prosecutor began with routine questions, but his tone was not perfunctory. His anger rang like a bell across the packed room, as if he expected trouble.

"Were you asked for information by police investigators in connection with the murder of Munir?"

"I was."

"Was an interrogation report created?"

"It was."

"Did you sign this report?"

"I signed it."

"Before you signed that report, did you read it first?"

"I read it."

"Are the contents of the report you signed true?"

Ongen paused.

With a slight shake of his head, he said quietly, "Not true."

A judge looked up from her papers, surprise on her face. A woman's voice reverberated from the audience, wordless but eloquent in its disappointment.

The prosecutor asked, "What is not true?"

"I mean, I once . . . that I recognized Polly."

The prosecutor read out one of the most important paragraphs in their submission to the court, a synthesis of Ongen's answers to police:

> The witness entered the Coffee Bean. The witness saw Pollycarpus coming from the beverage counter while carrying two drinks. Then the witness ordered a drink and sat down. At the Coffee Bean, the witness saw Munir chatting with Pollycarpus while drinking, then the witness sat at his own table about two yards away.

"True?"

After a long pause, Ongen softly said, "Not true."

Ongen and the judge both looked at the prosecutor expectantly. This time he read directly from Ongen's record of interrogation of April 4, 2007. His answer to Question 49 was:

> I ordered hot tea to take some Decolgen, added sugar, and then
> I looked for a place to sit, toward the left side, and when I sat
> down, I saw in the Coffee Bean there was Munir and a male
> person I did not know. However, after four months or so, I
> learned from the media that the person was Pollycarpus.

Ongen listened, blinking. As the prosecutor finished reading, without being asked, he said one word.

"No."

Why had he signed an interrogation report that wasn't true?

After another long pause, Ongen quietly replied, "I was pressured."

"Pressured how?"

He hesitated. He shifted in his seat. Then, as if quoting a police officer, he said, "I'll make you a suspect. By God, I'll make you a suspect."

The prosecutor said, "Okay, at the next session, I'll present the investigators."

Another prosecutor stepped in to read Ongen's answer to Question 49 a second time, hammering him as to whether he ever saw Pollycarpus.

Ongen maintained his denial, saying, "I never knew it was Pollycarpus."

"Even now, you don't know who he is?"

"I don't know."

The crowd booed and hooted. *"Huuuu."*

The prosecutor read the answer a third time and said, "Look at him now. Did you see him at the Coffee Bean with Munir?"

"No. No."

"What do you mean, no?"

"Not this person."

"Huuuuuu!"

He would only confirm that he saw Munir sitting with another person.

The prosecutors didn't try to resolve a key discrepancy. Asrini had flatly contradicted Ongen's claim that he sat alone at another table. Perhaps

Ongen's statement that he saw Polly carry two glasses was too important to risk hurting his credibility. It was not just a question of accuracy. If Ongen had lied about sitting with the two, it could well mean he was hiding his role as a participant in the plot to kill Munir. While not introduced at trial, a police investigator recalls obtaining receipts from the café for the two hours starting at 11:00 p.m. One order listed two teas and a mineral water.[19] While the three drinks could have been for just two people, Ongen had said he just saw two glasses on the table, never mentioning a bottle of water.

The defense, apparently content with Ongen's recantation, asked no questions. After the long day ended, an American embassy cable concluded, "Given that the case now has implicated the nation's most secretive agency, the evidence presented in these hearings is stunning. Whether or not the case ultimately finds Munir's killers, BIN could be opened up to unprecedented scrutiny."[20]

Usman published an opinion piece a few days later to highlight the "collapse of the tyrannical fortress of silence" imprisoning all Indonesians. Acknowledging that some experts believed an acquittal should be final, Usman defended the case review. He countered, "the law must uncover the truth, so that justice can be upheld. Legal certainty that leaves the truth a mystery means an absence of justice, and this should not be tolerated." Usman wrote that the case was not just about a murder: It was about an abuse of power that caused Indonesia to be forever in pain. He concluded:

> If a body is in agony, the soul will never calm. Munir's killers are the thorns that caused this pain. They are within the flesh of our country's body. These thorns will continue to humiliate us and our national institutions in the eyes of the world and of our children and grandchildren. Therefore, they must be extracted and discarded.[21]

A week later, Ongen returned for a "confrontation" with the investigators he accused of pressuring him to lie. He claimed they had forced him to sleep in a chair, and threatened him in front of his family that they would name him as a suspect. And when the police met him at the airport in Kuala Lumpur, he said, lead investigator Mathius Salempang had threatened, "You're a liar. You're the perpetrator. There were three men, one is dead, one's been punished, and you are a perpetrator."

Ongen told the court, "I fainted then and there. When I came to, I felt my pants and found I had wet myself. I felt terribly, terribly tortured. My liberty had been stolen from me."[22] Even the priest they brought in during his questioning had threatened him: "After praying, he said of Salempang, 'Be careful. That's no two-bit detective.'"

Salempang, a police general, was summoned to the courtroom along with an investigator named Pambudi Pamungkas, who had conducted much of the questioning. They explained that Ongen's lawyer was present for all but one of his five interviews. They showed Ongen's signature on the interrogation record to the court, and swore they'd followed all procedures. As for the protective custody, the police were protecting Ongen at their barracks *after* questioning was complete and at the request of Ongen's lawyer.

After the session, Usman urged police to investigate the circumstances of Ongen's changing testimony. Given the lawyer's request for protection, Usman suspected Ongen *was* under pressure, not by police but "by an even greater threat." But whatever the reason, if Ongen was lying in court, he should be charged with perjury.[23]

The prosecution's last witness was the toxicology expert, Dr. I Made Agus Gelgel Wirasuta, who explained how he had concluded that Munir consumed the poison eight or nine hours before he died, pointing to a Changi crime scene.[24]

On the third anniversary of Munir's death, flowers were delivered, but not to the grave in Batu or to Suci. Reaching through the metal fence of the BIN compound, it was Suci who offered a bouquet of red roses. Their thorns evoked the metaphor from Usman's op-ed: "Munir's killers are the thorns that caused this pain. They are within the flesh of our country." Usman stood beside Suci, both in red shirts featuring Munir's face, with black armbands. Usman wore a formal batik shirt under his red T-shirt and a black *peci* on his head for the occasion, with a large red Munir pin on the front of it. A row of riot police stood inside the fence, pistols strapped into white holsters. Each held a long stave planted firmly between his feet, facing a large and growing crowd of protestors. Cellphone service was switched off within a radius of 200 yards from the BIN gate, hampering both coordination of the demonstration and live reporting by journalists.

It was the only protest ever held at BIN. The night before, the BIN director had called Suci to tell her to call it off. "It's not allowed," he'd said. "Please cancel it." She'd explained that it wasn't in her power to do so, saying of the protestors: "It's not mine, it's theirs." Some held signs that read, REMOVE THE THORNS IN THE FLESH above pictures of a smiling Hendropriyono, Muchdi laughing, Ucok, and other BIN staff implicated so far. The protestors shut down the roadway in front of intelligence headquarters, as passersby joined in to shout, "*Hidup* Munir!" Usman told the crowd he wasn't there to attack BIN; he just wanted those who carried out savage and inhumane acts to be quickly brought to trial. From the back of a pickup truck, Suci echoed the message of the day: "We support cleansing BIN of criminals, not tearing down this institution." The protest moved on to the Presidential Palace.[25] The event was crowded and lively—*ramai*—enough to lift Suci's spirits.

Prosecutors finished with evidence midday on September 12, and the defense presented their counterarguments. They cited experts to say prosecutors had no right to request a case review. They used the argument deployed at Polly's appeal, that changing the time, place, and method of the crime unfairly altered the charges. They submitted a statement from Ongen denying that he saw Pollycarpus at the café and claiming police coerced him into saying he did.[26]

As for the taped call, it was just empty talk and gibberish, Setiawan venting and Polly trying to cheer him up by invoking everyone from the chief justice of the Supreme Court to Gajah Mada's ghost. And because phones are banned in detention and phone taps are illegal outside of terrorism and corruption investigations, it was clear the police were trying to trap Polly. Finally, because the call took place *after* Polly's trial, it wasn't a valid form of new evidence. Nor was the testimony of Ucok and Asrini, since investigators knew of their allegations at the time of the original trial.[27]

There had been few courthouse protests so far, but on this day more than fifty men in black shirts and jackets marched through the gates. Some carried banners and caps reading FORUM BETAWI REMPUG, a mob-for-hire organized around an ethnic identity (the Betawi are the original inhabitants of Jakarta). Their apparent leader, in a leather jacket and sunglasses, showed a business card to a policeman and pointed to the upper floors. Soon they were upstairs, chanting just outside the courtroom. Oddly, they were there to demand a *guilty* verdict, or worse. Back outside again, they all shouted, "Hang!" and a man with a mike responded "Pollycarpus!" It was unclear on whose orders or checkbook they had come.

After a final session on September 19, the case was sent up to the Supreme Court for deliberations. Kasum raised concerns about the neutrality of the chief justice. Since Polly had claimed him as "our people," they urged him to recuse himself and make the proceedings public.[28]

It seemed to Usman that the police were just waiting for the case-review decision, which might come tomorrow or in six months, and could go either way. There was no good reason to delay a thorough investigation of Muchdi, Hendropriyono, and As'ad. The As'ad letter and Ucok's testimony had brought them all within reach, and there were reasons to move quickly. Besides the destruction of evidence and fading memories, Usman worried that the 2009 elections would politicize an already complex case, in an effort to hurt Megawati (who was close to Hendro) or SBY (who had failed to deliver justice).[29]

While the Supreme Court's deliberations were under way, two trials did commence at the Central Jakarta District Court. On October 9, 2007, proceedings began for Indra Setiawan, the former Garuda director, and Rohainil Aini, secretary to the chief of pilots. For both, the charge was facilitating a murder, rather than simple forgery. These trials ensured that the case would continue even if the review request was rejected.[30]

Suci used her testimony in Setiawan's trial to link the case to BIN. She described her meetings with the senior BIN official Bijah Subiakto in late 2004, at which he told her to consider what work Munir had engaged in recently.[31] Pollycarpus took two weeks to honor the summons to testify at Setiawan's trial. When he finally appeared, prosecutors played the tape of the May phone call again, noting references to the As'ad letter that Polly had handed the defendant at the Sahid Hotel. In court Polly denied the existence of the letter (as he said he would on the tape), as well as ever being at BIN headquarters.

The prosecutor raised a new name, asking Pollycarpus, "Do you know Budi Santoso from BIN?"

"No."

"Did the witness ever come to the BIN office with a letter for Budi Santoso to correct?"

When Polly denied doing so, the prosecutor explained to the judges that police had just given him a new record of interrogation for one Budi Santoso. He asked that Budi be brought before the court to challenge Pollycarpus's denials. The gambit worked, and the former BIN agent was called to testify on December 12. Usman was encouraged to see the prosecution pursue every angle.[32]

Budi didn't come. On December 18, he sent a written explanation for his absence: BIN had given him a posting in Pakistan. Usman wanted the judges to issue an order to appear, and the attorney general to tell BIN to make Budi available. After a second and a third summons to Budi, prosecutors read the interrogation record out in court on January 15. In theory, his signed statement had the evidentiary strength of a courtroom witness. In practice, judges might not give it the same value, and prosecutors could not elicit any new details.

However, even the written record was useful. In two interviews held on October 3 and 7, days before the trials began, Budi described helping Polly correct a letter he'd drafted. It was a recommendation that Polly be assigned to the corporate security division of Garuda Indonesia. It was addressed to Setiawan, with a place for As'ad's signature. Budi made a few corrections, moving some formatting from left to right and fixing sentences he thought were awkward or inconsistent with office practices.

Besides the letter, there was the money. Budi told police that around eleven a.m. on June 14, 2004, three months before the murder, his boss Muchdi had him bring 10 million rupiah (just over $1,000 at the time) to his office for a guest. When Budi asked Muchdi's administrative staff who the guest was, he was told, "Polly." He asked who that was. "Pilot," they'd said. He'd brought the cash in and given it to Muchdi. He was not introduced to the man in the guest chair, Pollycarpus.

Using call records as a reference, police had Budi confirm that Polly-carpus called him often around the time of Munir's death to ask if Muchdi was in. Polly had called at ten a.m. and three p.m. on September 7, the day he returned from Singapore. Sometimes Muchdi ordered Budi to find Polly, Budi explained. "I was sometimes the liaison between the two." Budi's final answer in the two-day interview was to say, "Everything I did was on orders from deputy V." That was Muchdi.

Budi's statement detailed the genesis of the missing As'ad letter, a document that linked Pollycarpus, BIN, and Garuda in a conspiracy. He also proved that Polly and Muchdi knew each other. Suci told a press conference, "This statement shows a very close relationship. There's money, transactions. This is the red thread. If the police and the government dare to reveal it, they must immediately investigate and arrest Muchdi."[33]

On January 25, at midday, a five-judge panel of the Supreme Court granted the request for case review of the acquittal of Pollycarpus and reversed the decision.[34] Pollycarpus was once again guilty of premeditated murder, although the judges did not agree on a sentence. Several judges believed they couldn't impose a sentence greater than the original fourteen years.[35] Others, however, including the chief justice, thought that term was too light for a savage, premeditated crime that shamed Indonesia. With no consensus, they voted, and a twenty-year sentence prevailed.

When Polly heard the news from a journalist, he didn't believe it.[36] Nevertheless, a little before eleven o'clock that night, officers from the attorney general's office picked him up and shepherded him through a crush of reporters waiting outside his home. The next morning, his forty-seventh birthday, he woke up in Cipinang Penitentiary.

Suciwati was glad he was back in jail, though she'd hoped for a life sentence, telling the *New York Times*, "It would have been only fair if he were sentenced for life, so that he knows how it feels to lose someone you love." More important, she and Usman wanted police and prosecutors to take action on all the other names in the conspiracy, until the *dalangs* were tried and punished.[37]

15

The Arrest

2008

On February 2, 2008, two weeks after Polly's return to jail, former Garuda director Indra Setiawan made some final comments at his own trial. He described the moment Polly handed him the As'ad letter as "the beginning of my disaster." Three times he repeated, "Murder is indeed cruel, but slander is crueler," a claim once made by Suharto, not long out of power, after Time Magazine devoted an issue to his family's ill-gotten billions. Raising a yellow Quran, Setiawan then issued something between a prayer, an oath, and a denial of taking part in a criminal conspiracy: "Never mind killing, not even planning, not even helping, not even hearing about or helping to plan. If I really did help, give me Your very painful punishment, O Allah."[1] Nine days later, the court convicted Setiawan and sentenced him to a year in prison. With time served, he'd be free in about two months. The chief judge conceded that Setiawan was a victim, but nonetheless he had broken the law. The court acquitted Rohainil Aini the next day, accepting her defense that she was only doing her job when she granted Polly the schedule changes he requested.

Kasum declared the time had come for Muchdi to be arrested. He was implicated in a proven murder and had lied under oath about not knowing Polly. A police investigation was still under way, led by the same team of nine that had reanalyzed the forensics data, found Changi eyewitnesses, and gotten Setiawan, Ongen, and even some BIN personnel to talk, even if the witnesses failed to stand by these statements in court.

And the police weren't done. In February they questioned Muchdi's administrative staff. In May, Chief of Police Sutanto confirmed there was a new suspect, whom he identified only as an *oknum*, an official acting in a rogue or illegal way, from a "certain institution."[2] Indra Setiawan, only six weeks out of prison, received a summons on May 30 to answer questions in the case against Muchdi. In early June, police collected Pollycarpus from Cell 27 of the Upper West Block of Sukamiskin Prison to be questioned again.[3] In one of these interviews, an investigator recalls Polly putting his head down onto his hands on the table before him.

"Don't sleep. We're not done," said the policeman.

"Give me a weapon of some kind, so I can just kill myself. I'm tired."

"Do you know why you're tired? Because you keep lying. Lies on top of lies."[4]

While the police were marshaling their evidence, Usman was going all out to make an arrest politically possible. Knowing that Muchdi was lobbying just as hard to prevent it, Usman felt he was in a war. He spoke to political parties, the president's staff, and foreign embassies. He also went in person to discuss the matter with the leadership of the two largest Muslim organizations, Muhammidiyah and NU. Muhammidiyah's leaders assured him they wouldn't raise any objections if police arrested Muchdi. Muchdi headed an affiliated martial arts organization called Tapak Suci, or the Sacred Footstep. Usman secured a similar pledge from the leadership of NU, if the police were to arrest As'ad, who was a senior member of the organization.

Momentum seemed to be building toward an imminent, high-level arrest. On June 12, CID director Hendarso told a parliamentary commission he would soon name the suspect who ordered the killing.[5]

Usman received word from a police contact that they planned to arrest Muchdi on Wednesday, June 18. Usman wrote an opinion piece to come out in the next day's paper, hoping to build public support before a contentious trial. By that night, journalists were staking out Muchdi's house in South Jakarta. When the morning papers came out, Muchdi had not been arrested. Usman's op-ed looked as baseless as a front-page report of Muchdi's capture that a newspaper had had to retract two months earlier.

In fact, police had only summoned Muchdi to appear for questioning as a suspect at 10:00 a.m. on Thursday, June 19. He did not come at the appointed time. Instead, he was spotted at an event at the headquarters of a new political party, Gerindra. After several years in the political wilderness, Suharto's former son-in-law (and Muchdi's old patron) Prabowo Subianto had returned from Jordan and wanted a springboard for his presidential ambitions. Prabowo counted on old Kopassus comrades like Muchdi, and on his brother's vast wealth, to build this new party.[6]

Later that day, police learned that Muchdi had gone to an apartment he kept on the grounds of the Sahid Hotel. A member of the police team had rented a room several floors below Muchdi for a week to watch him come and go, noting his five bodyguards. Late that afternoon, the team's leader, Mathius Salempang, waited in the parking garage with dozens of police officers armed with rifles. When Muchdi exited the elevator, Salempang walked up to him alone and showed him the arrest warrant. Another officer aimed his gun at Muchdi's bodyguard, anticipating trouble. Muchdi read the letter and began speaking to Salempang, when Muchdi's bodyguard, described in the press as a Kopassus colonel, grabbed Salempang's arm. A police Mobile Brigade officer radioed for orders.

After a tense moment, Muchdi removed his bodyguard's hand from Salempang's arm. He said he would go to be questioned if journalists were not informed. The weapons were lowered, and Muchdi was taken to CID chief Hendarso, waiting nearby with three SUVs.[7]

The convoy arrived at the back of the CID building, and police herded the suspect to a second-floor interrogation room, along with his lawyer. A copy of the detention order was held high in the night air for the reporters to view; they had been staking out police headquarters without waiting to be informed. The order stated that there was evidence to strongly suspect that Muchdi had encouraged someone to carry out a premeditated murder, as well as concern that he'd flee or destroy evidence if not detained. A police spokesperson insisted that the general hadn't actually been arrested but had turned himself in after being named a suspect. Years later, the description still rankled a member of the police team, who knew an arrest when he saw one. The lights outside the building were shut off, but reporters saw a mattress carried inside and speculated it was a courtesy for Muchdi so he wouldn't have to face the press again.[8]

Usman outside the Criminal Investigation
Division building at national police headquarters.

Suci and Usman held a press conference at KontraS that night. With
the bronze bust of Munir behind them, they thanked the police. Looking
more serious and tired than relieved, they reminded the crowd that, as
important as Muchdi's arrest was, the case was still closer to the beginning
than to the end. Had anyone ordered Muchdi to kill Munir? Who else was
in the conspiracy to kill Munir or cover it up? Usman had expected As'ad
to be arrested along with Muchdi. He wondered if the police were unwilling to risk antagonizing both of the largest Muslim groups in Indonesia.

Early the next afternoon, a heavily guarded convoy took Muchdi to the
police Mobile Brigade headquarters a little outside the city. The facility,
which had also housed Ongen during his protective custody, was used for
high-profile detainees. If Muchdi wanted to discuss his legal strategy with
a judge, a prosecutor, member of the Judicial Commission, or a former
national chief of police, he could just talk to the many corruption suspects
he shared the facility with.

Muchdi's lawyers asked religious leaders and other prominent figures to vouch for his release pending trial. They declined, some publicly and vehemently, leaving only Muchdi's relatives and lawyers to serve as guarantors. His request for release was denied.

Muchdi's questioning started the night of his arrest and went on for two weeks. He and four lawyers sat across a table from Mathius Salempang and three investigators, filling a small room. His answers were reportedly a thicket of denials and memory loss.

On July 7, police handed prosecutors his dossier, 171 pages plus hundreds more of attachments. The police had settled on Article 55, participation in a crime, as the primary charge. The deputy attorney general for general crimes explained the next day, "So, Pak Muchdi was what? He ordered it to be done. Proof that it was a murder already exists. Unlike during the Polly trial." Does that mean Muchdi was the *dalang*? "*Dalang* is political language. In the criminal code, it is 'ordering someone to act.'"

The evidence would include a pattern of phone calls, though their content was still not known. Testimony from current and former BIN staff would be important, especially in the absence of a paper trail. And while Indra Setiawan had revealed the existence of the As'ad letter, the document itself was gone. However, prosecutors announced that they had found the next best thing.[9]

A few months earlier, the police chief had informed the head of BIN that they needed to search Muchdi's former office. The BIN chief approved the search, either because he believed BIN wasn't involved, or because the police had a warrant and the president's backing. It was also possible he believed that any incriminating evidence was gone. He would have been wrong. On May 27, police seized a 40-gigabyte hard drive and put it in the hands of an IT consultant. He cloned the drive in order to search for files, including some that been deleted by then.

A search for the name Pollycarpus produced two hits. One recovered document had lost its proper formatting and spacing, but a letter could be re-created:

STATE INTELLIGENCE AGENCY

Jakarta,   July 2004
Number :
Attachments : -
Classification : Secret
Re   : Personnel recommendation   To:
                Internal Security Team   GARUDA INDONESIA Director
                                              J a k a r t a

_____

As an institution of a strategic nature for the interest of the people and the state, Garuda Indonesia plays a leading role in counteracting the threat of terrorism, because it requires cross-sectoral and departmental collaboration, especially in the form of internal security, for State Owned Enterprises, especially Garuda Indonesia.

For the above-mentioned purpose, BIN recommends one of Garuda's pilots.

Name: Pollycarpus BHP
Position: Airbus A330 Pilot
ID: 522659

So that he can be included in the internal security of PT Garuda Indonesia.

Thus submitted for your examination, thank you for your attention and cooperation.

DIRECTOR OF THE STATE INTELLIGENCE AGENCY
                                                         Deputy Director

Drs. As at Said Ali
CC:
Hon. State Minister for State Owned Enterprises

The As'ad letter had been found after four years, in a pagefile.sys document, where data is temporarily stored in Windows computers. The second hit for Pollycarpus was in a spreadsheet of telephone numbers, with the filename Telephone Numbers of Deputy V. On the list were a landline and cell phone number for Pollycarpus.

The search term "Garuda" led to several documents with no relevance and what appeared to be an envelope addressed to the airline's director in the computer's trash bin.[10]

The prosecutors now had the content of the missing As'ad letter. They had evidence that Pollycarpus's numbers were in Muchdi's phone directory. Indra from Kasum had traveled the full length of the country, from a hotel in Aceh to a dusty storeroom in Papua three thousand miles away, searching for evidence of Polly's ties to BIN. They'd never found anything as incriminating as this new evidence. Indra was confident these deleted files would be enough to prove the connection in court.

When Suci heard the trial venue, her heart dropped. *Oh no*, she thought, *South Jakarta*. The South Jakarta District Courthouse was a pleasant new complex with corridors that opened to the sky, allowing colonies of sunlit greenery to flourish among the courtrooms. Water burbled down the tiers of a little fountain. The one-story courthouse had the feel of a well-appointed American elementary school. The problem for Suci was not the building but the judges who worked there. These judges had ruled favorably for both former President Suharto and his son Tommy, who had tried to resolve some legal problems by arranging the contract killing of a judge. The court was also known for a readiness to provide corruption suspects with medical exemptions to avoid detention. Suci tried to stay hopeful that the judges might evolve, especially with all the extra attention on this case from home and abroad.

The trial opened on August 21, and Muchdi was ready. Some three hundred chanting men converged on the courthouse, ripping signs away from Munir's supporters. They filled the courthouse yard, singing the national anthem and making speeches.[11] They roamed the corridors, passing out copies of statements from Europe and the United States with added commentary at the top reading, "Muchdi is a victim of foreign intervention!"

Police in black berets and long guns stood guard throughout the court-house, with five or six officers outside each of the three public entrances to the Garuda Room. The courtroom, like the airline, was named for the national symbol. By the time a hundred or so Munir supporters arrived at eight thirty, Muchdi's people had control of the courtroom.[12] The modest room was further packed with reporters, cameras, ten prosecutors, and fifteen defense lawyers.

A police siren signaled that Muchdi was arriving at the courthouse just before 9:00. In the courtroom, the chief judge delivered three crisp blows of the gavel at 10:00, and the trial was on. Muchdi was led through the crowd in a tan windbreaker over a dress shirt gridded with red squares, like graph paper. With slight variations, a casual jacket and checked shirt served as his courtroom uniform for the rest of the trial.

Lead prosecutor Cyrus Sinaga and a member of his team took turns reading the charging document. They told a story of a murder motivated by revenge. Munir had ended Muchdi's army career, and his efforts to rein in the power of the military and intelligence angered the general further. Once at BIN, Muchdi had tools at his disposal, including a Garuda pilot who was an agent.

The two primary charges both fell under Article 55 (1) of the Criminal Code, which covers two or more people committing a crime.[13] The article has two subclauses, the first covering those who perpetrate, cause others to commit, or take direct part in a crime. Evidence of money transfers and the letter from BIN would show an operational relationship between Muchdi and Polly. They cited a claim from the agent Budi Santoso that Polly told him, "I got an assignment from Pak Muchdi PR to finish off Munir." Prosecutors hedged their bets by offering an alternative charge. If they couldn't prove Muchdi ordered the murder, they would show that he had provoked or instigated the crime though an abuse of power or by providing the means or opportunity. Muchdi watched the prosecutor closely, with only an occasional smile or a rub of his chin.[14] The judge gaveled the session closed, and forty police officers escorted Muchdi past a human fence of hired muscle who had cleared the way of journalists and protestors.

Usman wasn't sure what to think of day one. He worried that the focus on
Muchdi's personal motive would once again hamper investigation of other
intelligence officials, such as Hendropriyono, As'ad, and the two deputies implicated in past testimony.[15] For the most part, however, Usman
felt prosecutors had met their legal burden for the indictment, and he
suspected they were reserving some ammunition for trial. Courtroom
testimony would be crucial, but so would the weight that judges decided
to give the interrogation records of Budi, Ongen, and any other witnesses
who changed their stories or failed to appear.

Each week, Muchdi's forces would enter single file through tight police
security into the court complex, and then through metal detectors into
the building. Once inside, they'd stake out real estate by the courtroom
doors. They drew press attention, with one headline cheerfully noting,
MUCHDI "GROUPIES" ENLIVEN MUNIR TRIAL.[16] The article also noted
how unusual it was that the judges never rebuked their outbursts, many
of which emanated from members of the women's branch of the martial
arts group Tapak Suci Putera Muhammidiyah, or Sacred Footstep of the
Sons of Muhammidiyah. Muhammidiyah was an organization for modernist Muslims, and this group avoided the magical or pre-Islamic elements of other fighting styles native to Indonesia, instead using constant
movement and flow to keep an opponent off guard. Tapak Suci emerged
in Yogyakarta during the 1965 violence by Muslim groups against the
Communists, where Muchdi had come of age. As the group's chief patron,
Tapak Suci was one of his sources of unofficial power, giving him a formal
link to Muhammidiyah and footsoldiers he could mobilize when needed.
He needed them now, and they were among his most reliable supporters,
arriving as much as two hours before each session began.

Another group, the Red and White Brigade wore matching white polo
shirts with red stripes around the short sleeves and collars and RESIST
FOREIGN INTERVENTION! written across their backs. One Brigade member told a trial monitor he was paid about $5 per day, though other groups
got twice as much.[17]

Sahabat Munir, or Friends of Munir, consisted of members of communities that Munir had helped in land disputes or other cases, plus smaller
numbers of family members of those killed and disappeared. Members of

Kasum and staff from KontraS came too, and sometimes foreign observers from embassies or international human rights groups.

Once the courtroom doors opened, the room filled quickly and chaotically. Their advance position allowed Tapak Suci members to claim the front rows most of the time. Often they moved their benches forward, obstructing the work of photojournalists. From there, they could clap for Muchdi and his lawyers, or jeer if a prosecutor stumbled or earned a judge's rebuke. In red shirts, Friends of Munir usually staked out the doors on the left, before filling the back and one side of the room. Suci joined them there when she arrived.

As the jostling pools of blue and red and yellow eddied in, the air became hot and close even before most sessions began. The judges had working air conditioners overhead, but in the rest of the room, the AC units seemed only for decoration. Some days a floor fan was brought in. Journalists clustered near doors to claim a little breeze, or sat out in the corridor on the white tiled floor, watching video of the trial on a small plasma TV mounted high on a wall.

On the day of the defense's response to the indictment, Muchdi's forces were down to about a hundred, outnumbered by those in shirts that read JUSTICE FOR MUNIR, JUSTICE FOR ALL on the back. But greater numbers did not mean control of the courtroom. The Garuda Room was still locked at 9:00, with the largest of Muchdi's thugs standing by the doors. The doors opened, and the two armies surged in, jostling for seats. Someone yelled, "Watch out for pickpockets!"[18]

Not surprisingly, the defense's argument for dismissal told a very different story than the indictment. The most powerful nation on Earth had targeted a decorated war hero. The United States, joined by the European Union and Indonesian activists, had levied the false claims that led to this indictment. Foreign pressure on the legal system had also promoted sloppiness and confusion in this and previous trials. Was the poison hidden in noodles or juice or tea? Was Polly an accomplice or the main perpetrator? Why were the members of the cabin crew, named as accomplices in Polly's verdict, never charged? The judges had crafted their own charges at trial and then again at the case review, instead of relying on the original ones. And Muchdi's fate might hinge on the testimony of Budi Santoso, the BIN agent whose whereabouts were a mystery. And, finally, if the crime took place in Singapore, why try it in South Jakarta?

On September 9, the day the judges would rule whether to proceed to the evidence phase, the Red and White Brigade and the women of Tapak Suci took control of the main door to the courtroom. A group in yellow shirts, with REJECT FOREIGN INTERVENTION on the back, manned the south door, and a group of Papuans claimed the north door for Muchdi. With the arrival of a group of mothers whose children had died in the May 1998 riots (some of the hundred or so Munir supporters), the Papuans yielded their post, only to return soon after. When the doors opened, two Papuans tried to block the way, arms crossed. By the time Friends of Munir made it inside, Muchdi's people had taken most of the seats, and they had to stand in the back and in the aisles.

The judges found that the defense complaints about international pressure, procedural violations, and the absence of Budi Santoso were irrelevant, while the court had jurisdiction due to the location of BIN and Muchdi's residence. All other defense arguments concerned the substance of the case, and would be considered at trial. The trial would proceed.

The hearing over, the defense made a show of great confidence. Muchdi rose from his chair with a broad smile. One of his lawyers embraced him, before the rest shook hands with him over the table. Still grinning, Muchdi turned to shake hands with the supporters pressing forward to greet him. Muchdi's smile faded, and his face tensed. Suci was waiting for him among the crush of well-wishers.

"Just admit it already, Pak. Just admit it," she said. "Then you'll be able to fast."

It was the fasting month of Ramadan, a time for Muslims to behave morally, reflect, and improve themselves spiritually.

Muchdi ignored her, shaking the next hand thrust at him. Then he turned back toward Suci, and paused. His face darkened with anger as he spoke with startling vehemence.

"Shut up, you!"

He used the familiar form of *you*—*Diam kamu!*—as if speaking to a servant or a child. He shook a few more hands, waved, and recovered his smile before exiting the courtroom under police guard.

Muchdi's lawyer complained that Suci had violated his client's right to be considered innocent. He assured the press that Muchdi would not sue her, however, content to let her punishment come in the afterlife. Suci explained she'd only wanted to remind him it was Ramadan, adding, "Let people know what Muchdi really looks like. This shows who he is." She would have a chance to say more as the first witness.[19]

16

The General in His Courtroom

2008

More than two hundred Munir supporters filed into the courthouse grounds on September 16 for the first day of testimony. Muchdi had his people too, but today they were outnumbered. Suci took the witness chair wearing rectangular glasses, small dangling earrings, and a black shirt printed with MUNIR in white block letters, evoking the umbrellas of *kamisan*.

With Muchdi watching from a few yards away, Suci recounted the airport good-bye. She told of retrieving Munir's remains from Amsterdam and burying him in Batu. She described Munir's work on abductions and the threat that sent them on the run one night in the final hours of Suharto's rule, driving through the city until the sun rose. She told how Tuti Koto had come to Munir, too afraid to report her son missing to the police, and how Suci herself, pregnant with Alif, took parents to ask the military police about their missing sons. As a result of their work, she said, a military honor board removed three officers from their commands, and Muchdi was one of them.

Suci described Munir's habit of telling her what had happened each day when he came home after work. One day he'd told her, "The person with the biggest stomachache—he meant like heartache, but that's what he said—was Muchdi, because he only had the job briefly, and it was a prestigious post for a soldier. But then he was suddenly relieved of duty as an administrative punishment. That's something that psychologically would be humiliating. That's what he said."

She'd told Munir they'd have to be very careful. But they knew they were helping people, and whether a person lived or died was in God's hands. Munir had always been out in front at press conferences and in the media about the abductions. When that work led to an honor board, he'd been sharply critical of it. Torture and disappearances were serious crimes, not matters of military discipline to be dealt with in secret.

Ten years later, that secrecy was impeding this very murder trial. The defense pressed Suci on how she knew what happened before an honor board that was closed to the public. She explained that she knew the broad outlines from her husband.

"You never read the decision yourself?"

"Never."

Did she ever see Muchdi's supposed anger herself?

"I was told about it."

"You yourself did, or did not, ever see his anger in connection with this?"

"I did. The other day. When he lashed out at me."

"The other day?" the defense lawyer stammered. "No . . . earlier."

"You asked me about anger, right? Then, yes, I saw it the other day."

The defense pressed Suci about foreign intervention into the case. Who funded KontraS? Who paid for her foreign travel? What had members of U.S. Congress promised her? Suci was ready for this line of attack. She explained that after BIN's deceptive lobbying, she had to learn what they told Congress about Munir and give them true information. She cited a law protecting the right of Indonesians to use international human rights mechanisms.[1]

When Muchdi interrupted to correct his start date as head of Kopassus, the judge promised him the chance to speak after the witness. Suci took the opportunity to note that at the time Munir was warned that Kopassus soldiers were planning to kidnap him, Muchdi was their commander.

A young defense lawyer with a shaved head and rimless glasses was given the floor. He asked if Munir ever solved the mystery of the abductions. Suci said he'd been able to reconstruct much of the crime from talking to those who were released.

"In fact," she said, "he once told me about how *you* were abducted by mistake, and he also conducted advocacy on your behalf."

The lawyer started to answer, but had to pause as Suci's words sank in and laughter and shouts of surprise rang from the gallery. The lawyer nodded a few times and offered a sheepish smile. His name was Desmond Mahesa. In February 1998, Desmond had been forced at gunpoint into a car that sped off, leaving his glasses lying in the gutter. He was freed after two months, but some of those he spoke to quietly in the night in nearby cells, like Tuti Koto's son, the young bus driver Yani Afri, were never seen again.

On the same day as the Trisakti shootings, Desmond had stood a few feet from Munir, risking his life to tell the story of his abduction into a handheld mike, like the one he was holding now to defend the former commander of the soldiers who abducted him. The spectators took it all in stride. Maybe Desmond *was* abducted by mistake, as Munir once told Suci, and was never a real activist. Maybe he'd been turned by his captors in 1998, or won over by Muchdi and Prabowo years later.

Desmond was not only a lawyer doing his job; he was a supporter of the political party Prabowo was forming, with Muchdi's help, as the trial was under way. In fact, Desmond was one of *several* 1998 kidnapping victims to join the party leadership. Pius Lustrilanang, a political activist kidnapped at a bus stop and tortured for two months, also accepted a senior position at Gerindra. He later explained, "In politics there are no eternal friends or foes."[2] Haryanto Taslam, once run off the road and abducted at Taman Mini by Kopassus soldiers, rallied to Prabowo's party as well. Dramatically shifting loyalties were not so uncommon in Indonesian politics. Munir's old boss Buyung, a founder of LBH, represented generals accused of crimes against humanity in East Timor. His decision contributed to a rift with Munir, and throughout LBH, that never fully healed.

Undeterred, Desmond continued to question Suci about the abductions, asking, "Were all the victims abducted by Kopassus?"

"Most victims who spoke to him reconstructed the place they were held as Kopassus."

He pushed back on this allegation, but Suci soon interrupted him to ask, "Where *were* you then?" The crowd hooted.

"But you know where I was," said Desmond. Even so, he continued pressing Suci for proof that Kopassus was responsible, until a judge put a stop to the odd colloquy. The judges asked a few more questions, and Suci left the courtroom, followed by many of her supporters.

The police detail opened the courtroom doors, and the noonday sun backlit former Garuda director Indra Setiawan's entrance. Once sworn in and seated, he recounted Polly's handover of the letter signed by BIN's deputy director, As'ad, at the Hotel Sahid restaurant. He explained that he'd been so busy with travel and creditors the next few weeks that Polly had to prod him to act on the letter, asking, "Is it happening or not, Pak, assigning me to Corporate Security?" Setiawan issued Polly's assignment letter on August 11.

Setiawan never doubted that the As'ad letter was real, because Polly would have been fired for faking such a document. And after the autopsy results came out, when Setiawan asked to meet As'ad, Polly arranged it so quickly that he must have had good access to BIN. Setiawan insisted he didn't know who tasked Polly to go to Singapore, or about anything that took place after he issued his letter on August 11.

The defense pointed out that Setiawan had been convicted as an accomplice to murder. They also noted how he had changed his story, asking, "Do you remember testifying in Polly's trial that you assigned him on your own initiative? But in this trial you say Polly's appointment came from BIN. Which is true?"

Setiawan said that since that early testimony, he'd testified about the BIN letter at his own trial and others.

But why not be honest about it at Polly's trial?

"Uhh, . . . because . . ." he turned to the judges. "Your Honor, am I allowed to not answer?"

"What do you mean?" the judge replied. "If you can answer, then answer. If you can't, than don't."

"I can't answer."

Making Setiawan look unreliable helped the defense. And even if his testimony today was true, it didn't directly implicate Muchdi. The letter from BIN contained only the names Polly and As'ad. The two times Setiawan met Muchdi in person, first at As'ad's office and then at a hotel right before the parliamentary hearing, they had not discussed Munir or the letter.

The defense asked him, "The indictment says Polly is a BIN agent and Muchdi is his handler. Do you know if it's true?"

"I don't know."

"Please note it," the defense said to the judges. "That's all, Your Honor." Muchdi's supporters applauded.

Two of Muchdi's staffers, Zondy Anwar and Arifin Rahman, testified the following week. Prosecutors noted that when police showed Zondy a photo of Pollycarpus, he'd said the co-pilot had visited Muchdi's office. But in court, Zondy disowned this statement. He'd never dealt with the police before, he said, and he felt pressured to sign the record of interrogation.

The police had also shown him the documents recovered from Muchdi's hard drive. Zondy had described in detail how his co-worker Arifin hand-copied the contact list from Muchdi's Nokia, before reading it out for him to type into the computer. Shown the recovered envelope addressed to the director of Garuda, Zondy had recalled Pollycarpus asking him to type it up for him. Now, in court, he no longer remembered creating either document.

A defense lawyer asked Zondy if he was now withdrawing his statements to police. He said he was. Then he clarified that he wasn't *withdrawing* them, because he'd never *said* them. Muchdi's people applauded.

Zondy also confirmed Muchdi's frequent claim that he often left his phones where his subordinates, including the missing Budi Santoso, used them, with or without his knowledge.

Next came Zondy's co-worker Arifin Rahman. His testimony was much like Zondy's, claiming he was under extreme psychological pressure during his questioning because it was his first experience with the police. Arifin loudly denied ever seeing Polly at BIN. He, too, said he wasn't withdrawing his statement, because he never said it. He, too, had seen Budi use Muchdi's phone, about five times.

To Usman, their answers seemed suspiciously similar. But a defense lawyer argued that the real manipulation was by police. According to the written records of questioning by police, some of Zondy and Arifin's answers were identical, right down to the commas. The duplication showed that the investigators had engineered the replies, he said, and they had no value at all.

Testimony continued on September 23 with two of Muchdi's drivers. They told the court that they usually picked Muchdi up from home around eight a.m., but sometimes they came as early as five a.m. for a round of golf before work. Muchdi had many cars, but usually they took the BMW or the Mercedes with police plates. Both said Muchdi sometimes left his phone in the car. They answered some calls to it, but only those from the office, not from Pollycarpus or an unknown number. They too had witnessed Budi Santoso using Muchdi's phones "about five times."[3] When Muchdi had his chance to respond, he attributed some inconsistencies between the two witnesses to their low IQ.

Like Suci, Usman had testified several times over the last three years, but never against Muchdi, and never with the general staring at him from a few yards away. Usman began by describing the TPF's mandate, his role on the team, and their meetings with Garuda and BIN. Then Usman mentioned, almost casually, "We had written information that plans to kill Munir were discussed in BIN meetings."

It was the first time the scenarios memo had been raised in any court. The prosecutor asked to hear more. Usman explained that as the team's mandate was ending, they were leaked a document summarizing a series of meetings in which senior BIN officials, including Muchdi and Hendropriyono, discussed plans to murder Munir before the elections. Usman stuck with the formulation he'd used at the time. While unconfirmed, the document was too important to be ignored. The TPF used it as a reference, seeking to confirm it through other sources, as well as sharing it with police to follow up.[4]

The defense objected that this was all hearsay. When they tried again to shut down discussion of the scenarios memo, the judge rebuked them. "Twice you've tried this," he told them, "but you're mistaken." Munir supporters let out a collective *whoooooooooooo*.

Questioning again went to the abductions, a key factor in the alleged motive for Munir's death. Usman explained how Munir gathered scraps of information from the survivors about how they had been captured and held. That evidence prompted an investigation by the military police, who gave their findings to the armed forces commander. He in turn ordered the court-martial of members of the abduction task force known as Team Mawar, the Rose Team. Military leadership also formed an honor board to examine senior officers. Usman knew from Munir that, as a result, three military officials were removed from their positions, including Prabowo and Muchdi. Usman had also been present at a meeting with the military police that discussed this outcome. No, he'd never seen the honor board's written recommendations. But he *had* seen a summary on the Department of Defense website.

The prosecutor returned to the TPF's findings. Because the team was not a law enforcement body, it had scarcely been mentioned in previous trials. And the TPF's report, of course, had never been released. Usman seized on the chance to bring its findings into the courtroom. He explained that the TPF had concluded that the killing of Munir was linked to his work, including his advocacy on the abductions. The team had recommended to the president and police that they investigate Muchdi and Hendropriyono, among others at BIN and Garuda.

The defense's strongest card was still the lack of eyewitness evidence implicating Muchdi. Did Munir ever say the defendant threatened him? Had Usman ever seen Muchdi talk to Munir or Polly? Usman had to answer no.

Two days later, the senior human rights lawyer Hendardi was sworn in. He was testifying as a former member of the TPF, but he had also been a subject of Polly's odd attentions. He recounted the story of the co-pilot's visit to his office, his offers of free tickets to Papua, and even a suggestion to travel there together.

Like Usman and Suci, Hendardi steered the conversation back to Hendro and Muchdi whenever a question allowed. Hendardi recounted how the two generals refused to allow the TPF to question them or to obtain a single document. Nevertheless, other interviews and documents led the team to urge police to investigate officials at BIN and Garuda for conspiratorial murder. There was no way one man could have pulled off this crime.

Hendardi raised the scenarios memo too. A prosecutor asked, "Are you in this hearing, able to show some of these documents? Do you still have them?"

Hendardi nodded. He had them there, ready to show the court. But the chief judge reminded prosecutors it wasn't the job of a witness to prove the case. They would only look at evidence from the police. "We can't just have witnesses bringing in documents."

Muchdi's people hooted and yelled, "Hurray for the judge!"

The prosecutor asked Hendardi what he knew about the memo. He didn't remember the details, but knew it said who was involved in the murder, and when and where the planning meetings were. He knew magic had been proposed, and that poison was tested on animals.

When the defense asked about the timeline of Muchdi's transfer and the honor board's recommendation, tempers began to flare. Muchdi's lawyer became more combative, drawing an objection from prosecutors and a call from the judge to calm down. The heated exchanges continued over Muchdi's alleged hatred of Munir and the source of threats against him. Then the defense returned to the honor board:

"Did you ever read the order to create it?"

"No, but I read *about* it."

"Did you ever meet with the honor board?"

"No."

"Do you know who its chair was?"

"I might have known at the time, but now I forget."

From the crowd, "He's lying!"

"And where did you learn about the dismissal of the accused?"

"From the media and also, what was it? The official Defense Department website."

Muchdi used his opportunity to respond to complain that Hendardi didn't know when the honor board was formed, but still claimed it had cost him his position.

Someone yelled, "It's false testimony!"

Hendardi said, "I stand by my statement."

The judge wrapped it up. "Complaint noted," he told Muchdi. "Thank you, Pak Hendardi."[5]

On October 9, Poengky was the first of two witnesses to appear. Asked if she knew Munir, she replied, "I knew him extremely well." This was true, as she'd worked with Munir off and on since he hired her for her first job in Surabaya in 1992.

Poengky explained how Munir had determined that the abductions in 1998 were all carried out by the same people, concluding that the perpetrators were from Kopassus. She knew Munir felt the honor board was a means to shield those behind the abductions rather than punish them.

When did she first hear the name Pollycarpus? She first heard of "Polly from Garuda" from Suci in Amsterdam, when they collected Munir's body. Later, in 2005, she'd traveled to Papua and learned Pollycarpus was so unreliable that colleagues were surprised Garuda hired him. She'd also heard he was close to local army officers, even joining target practice with the head of the Jayapura District Military Command.

"Who was that?"

"Bapak Muchdi."

When she said she wouldn't name her sources for fear of putting them in danger, Muchdi laughed, idly rubbing his thumb on the green felt of the judges' dais as he slouched rightward.

During an exchange on the quality of military justice after the abductions, both lawyer and witness raised their voices, until the judge warned them to stay with facts, not opinions. When Poengky tried to add something, the lawyer shut her down to ask, "Have you ever been to Kopassus headquarters?"

"I said that . . .

"My question is, have you ever gone to Kopassus headquarters!"

"Never."

"Yes, that's the answer I was asking for. So there is no point in fantasizing about something that can't be, right? You've never been to the Kopassus headquarters?"

"Because I've never been abducted, Pak."

The defense lawyer was silent for a moment. Then his eyes flashed, and he snapped, "I didn't ask that!" As Muchdi's people booed loudly, the lawyer swiveled to face the judges, demanding they reprimand Poengky. They did, and he smiled with satisfaction, saying, "Just answer what is asked. Don't you act up in the courtroom." He pressed her on the timing of Muchdi's removal from Kopassus before the honor board was formed. Like Hendardi, Poengky didn't see a problem, explaining, "I don't see a conflict. They were removed first, then came an honor board and the decisions, and Prabowo was retired." In Muchdi's case, the board might have affirmed a provisional decision to take away his command.

In his response to Poengky's testimony, Muchdi denied that he was the local commander in Jayapura in 1988. He was stationed in Papua then, but was not assigned to Jayapura until the following year. By then Polly had already left for Garuda training in Jakarta.[6]

Next up that day was the alleged former BIN agent Ucok, who had by now started a horticulture business in the hills near Bogor. Ucok had once told police under oath that his BIN supervisors ordered him to kill Munir with magic or poison. He had backed away from these sworn statements at Polly's case review. Now he'd appeared at Muchdi's trial when summoned, but it was unclear what he would say.

Ucok's turn on the stand did not begin auspiciously. Asked if he knew the defendant, Ucok laughed, and Muchdi's people joined in. But shown his signed interrogation record and asked if he had signed and initialed them under pressure, he said, "Acknowledged. No pressure."

Lead prosecutor Cyrus Sinaga asked Ucok if he ever worked at BIN. He answered, "I forget, Pak." The reply sparked more laughter from the crowd.

Sinaga repeated Ucok's words, "You forget. You forget where you worked." The laughter continued.

"Because it's been a few years."

Sinaga tried again, "Did you ever work for BIN?"

"*Saya lupa*," he said. I forgot. The laughter was particularly raucous from the women of Tapak Suci in the front.

"In that case, I'll read it out loud, that you used to work at the BIN office."

"I've really forgotten, Pak. I'm not well anymore, that's the problem."
Laughter.

Ucok did confirm the accuracy of answers from a recent police interview, ending with one of considerable interest: "I knew of the plan for
murder because I'd been ordered to carry out the murder of Munir."

"Correct."

Sinaga read a question and answer from the interview:

> Who ordered you to carry out the killing of Munir, and what
> do you know about the plan to kill Munir?

> The plan to kill Munir had four steps planned by Pak Sentot
> Waluyo, namely observation and monitoring, *teror*, magic, and
> poison.

Ucok confirmed it was correct.

When it came to confirming his answers about who Sentot was (a junior
BIN agent) and how Ucok knew this (he had an ID and a .38 handgun, and
Ucok often brought people to his office at BIN), Ucok now said he had
forgotten. But then, asked to confirm that he'd known Sentot since 2003
and that they often worked as a pair, he hesitated.

"True?" the prosecutor prodded.

A pause. "True."

The prosecution asked about the time Ucok, riding pillion on Sentot's
motorcycle, asked about a man they saw in the BIN parking lot, where
guests were rare. Sentot had said the man was from Garuda, there to see
"the bosses." Police had shown him a photo, and Ucok identified the man
from the parking lot as Pollycarpus.

He no longer remembered that incident at all.

A prosecutor asked if any of the measures against Munir were ever
implemented, reminding him, "Your answer at that time was, 'I tried to
do the four steps to kill Munir in Indonesia, namely at Imparsial and at
his house. It wasn't carried out because, to my surprise, Munir died on the
plane from Jakarta to the Netherlands.'"

Ucok tentatively unfurled a word: "*Beetuuul.*" True.

"Yes?"

"True."

"What do the four steps mean? Can you explain?"

"I forget," he laughed. "What I remember is just *teror* by phone. I forget the rest." He'd called Imparsial from a pay phone one morning to say something like, "Let Munir know he's a traitor to the state." The call was brief, but the response he got from a member of Munir's staff was memorable: "*Sialan luuhh!*" Many Indonesian profanities have innocuous translations but still carry weight in the original. *Sialan* comes from the word meaning unlucky, but in effect it approaches "You bastard!" or worse. The word sparked laughter in the courtroom.

The defense began their questioning with the observation, "You forget a lot." Given his statements to police, Ucok's sudden forgetfulness helped Muchdi. But the defense seemed to want him to do more than muddy the waters. They wanted him to clearly retract the earlier statements as lies told under pressure.

"Did you forget before, or did you just forget now?"

"Since before, Pak. I just wasn't focused on this issue, Pak."

"If you forgot, why did you answer that way when police questioned you?"

"Yes, I maybe forgot. I'm not making this up. I forgot."

"So the words about you being given guns, those were whose words?"

"Wait a moment," cautioned the judge.

But there was little reason to fear the defense would lead the witness to an accusation against police. Ucok was already interjecting his two favorite words, "*Saya lupa.*"

The court's patience began to wear thin. One judge erupted: "*What* do you forget? You forget the question, you forget the answer, or you forget the whole lot?!" Ucok tried a joke, "The only answer I still remember is just that I was told '*Sialan luuuh.*'" He laughed.

Unamused, the judge continued. "You once said you were given two weapons. Did you or did you not say this to police?" The reference was to the Colt pistols Ucok said he was given when he joined the intelligence agency.

"I forgot, Pak. I don't remember."

The defense lawyer seized the moment to ask, "In other words, you deny this information?"

A prosecutor interrupted, "Earlier he said it was true!"

A defense lawyer tried a different tack, asking, "Permit me to ask if something happened to you. Have you had a serious illness?"

"No."

"No. Have you ever been treated in a hospital for a long time?"

"No."

Later, a judge reminded Ucok that while forgetting is human, "If you do really remember, after swearing an oath, you're in violation of your religion, and that's a sin. And it is between you and God, and the great Provider will grant you forgetfulness forever!" (Laughter, and a cheer for the judge.) The judge did not mention any worldly punishment for perjury.

Ucok replied, "I'm sorry, Pak. My condition is beginning to improve."

The judge asked, "I want a firm answer from you. You worked at BIN since when?"

"I forget, Pak, I truly forget."

"Are you with BIN now?'

"I don't know."

"Why do you say you don't know?"

"I really don't know, Pak." He laughed. "It's really true, by God. I don't know."[7]

Ucok had told police that Pollycarpus had been at BIN, and that he himself was ordered to kill Munir, though someone else succeeded first. He didn't confirm these statements in court, but neither did he clearly withdraw them. But he was clearly unwilling to stand by them in court, due either to a current medical condition or to the fear of a future one.

Five days later, Pollycarpus was brought up from prison in Bandung. After the usual recitation of no-show witnesses, Budi Santoso and As'ad the most important among them, Polly entered the courtroom in aviator sunglasses, a white shirt, and a gray tie. A few white hairs stuck up from his thick head of hair.

Polly's answers were cagey, even prickly. Asked if he remembered meeting someone, meaning Munir, at the Jakarta airport on September 6, 2004, he retorted, "It's an airport, there are lots of people." But mostly, Polly denied things. He never had contact with Munir before that flight, never called Munir or BIN, never discussed being assigned to a security role with Indra Setiawan, and never met Munir or Ongen in the Singapore airport.[8]

The prosecution spent significant time on the schedule changes, the switched seats, and the fuel dumping investigation. Polly's description of switching seats with Munir was still a work in progress. First he struggled to remember if it ever happened, rubbing his forehead with a concerned look before saying, "If I'm not mistaken, the one he sat in was my seat." But it was no longer a big misunderstanding, as he'd claimed in his case review. He really had offered the seat to Munir, but "it was small talk. To be of service." It was a strange use of their limited time by the prosecution. Some of these elements had already been declared "legal facts" in Polly's guilty verdict, and they were somewhat removed from the question of Muchdi's guilt.[9]

Asked if anyone had encouraged him to confess, Polly claimed several people tried to persuade or bribe him. Among them he said, was Marsudhi, head of the TPF and then the police investigation. He'd supposedly said, "Enough already. Just tell me, what kind of motorcycle do you want?" The investigator offered him a Harley Davidson, but Polly turned it down.[10]

The sun reached its zenith, and a distant call to prayer filled the restless room. A judge waited for the muezzin to conclude before asking Polly if he knew Hendardi. He hesitated, before saying he only knew the lawyer from the media. Reminded that Hendardi testified that Polly had offered him free flights to Papua, Polly gave one of his convoluted answers about a friend named Joni, a Portuguese houseguest, and a project to help children in Timor-Leste. He went on for so long that the judge interrupted him.

"No, no. My question is simple. Do you know someone named Hendardi?" Polly said they'd met *before* 2004 and discussed going to Timor-Leste together, not Papua.

As the questioning continued, the judges showed they were keeping the details of a complex case straight, such as correcting the defense as to the

year Polly left Papua. They provided illustrative examples of contradictory testimony: Polly said he never called Munir's phone, while Suci said
he did. Polly claimed he never brought a letter from BIN to the Hotel
Sahid, but Setiawan said he did. Despite a record of phone calls with Budi
Santoso, Polly denied knowing him. On these matters the judges would
assess the truth themselves.[11]

Polly said he asks himself, "What did I do wrong? What did my ances-
tors do wrong? That's how I think sometimes." Toward the end of the day,
as Polly started to proclaim his innocence again, the judge cut him off,
reminding him that he was there as a witness in a case against Muchdi.
They were not all there for him.

Polly might be forgiven for forgetting it was about Muchdi, with so
few questions about the defendant. Polly's denials and refusal to implicate
Muchdi earned him applause and cheers as he left the courtroom: "*Hidup*
Polly! *Hidup* Polly!"

Usman thought lead prosecutor Cyrus Sinaga's courtroom demeanor had
changed during the trial. At first, he had seemed confident and occasionally brave, vigorously defending Suci when Muchdi's lawyers tried to
bully her on the stand. He'd used a neutral or even commanding term of
address for Muchdi, such as *saudara terdakwa*, "you the accused." During
the trial, however, it had become the more respectful Pak Muchdi. He
let defense lawyers try to push witnesses around or lead them, without
objecting.

Sinaga appeared to be a man under a great deal of pressure, even though
the security forces had made efforts to protect him from violence and
intimidation. Sinaga been given a police escort, some of the forty Mobile
Brigade officers assigned to protect judges and prosecutors during the trial, on top of the elite squads assigned to the courthouse. Sinaga told Indra
from Kasum that when a new fruit vendor appeared outside his house for
a few days running, he reported it to the police, only to learn the man was
an undercover cop. Sinaga was also reportedly given a small case containing a gun to carry with his briefcase.

Sinaga would have been aware that the ex-president's son Tommy
Suharto had been convicted of the contract killing of a judge in his cor-

ruption trial. He would have known that, among the three officials who had died mysteriously, one was a prosecutor and one was an attorney general, and both men had been effective and incorruptible. Muchdi had retired from the military and, quite recently, from BIN. But he still had the hired *preman* and the martial arts groups who showed up at his trials. Some saw his reliance on these hired thugs as a sign that Muchdi lacked support from intelligence agents or soldiers, but this could not be known for sure. And anyway, he would know how to locate current and former members of the police or military prepared to break the law for him.

One day Sinaga, a few weeks after he read out the indictment, was pulling into his driveway when another car slammed into his. He was uninjured, but Usman thought that was about the time Sinaga started to avoid looking directly at Muchdi, who slouched in his chair directly across the courtroom, grinding his teeth, ripping the paper from a pack of cigarettes into ever smaller pieces.

A week after Polly testified, a man in a green safari suit entered to give testimony. Kawan was a Kopassus soldier seconded to BIN since 2004. He worked under the missing agent Budi Santoso, splitting his time between logistics support in Jakarta and monitoring former members of the pro-Indonesian militias along the border with the new nation of Timor-Leste.

Budi Santoso had told police that Kawan had been in his office when Polly said, "I got an assignment from Pak Muchdi to finish off Munir." His ability to confirm Budi's statements to police was most likely the reason Kawan had been called in.

Kawan had not been summoned directly by the police. In a rare sign of BIN support for the investigation, Kawan's superiors at BIN had called him at his post on the border to tell him to come to Bali for a police interview. He left before dawn to travel across West Timor to Kupang, where he boarded a short flight to Bali. Police picked him up at the airport that evening, among the surfboards, backpacks, and tourists, and drove him a few minutes to the sprawling Hotel Kartika Plaza. At this midrange resort at one end of Kuta Beach, three investigators questioned him through the night.

He'd been cooperative, but in the courtroom there were immediate

signs of trouble. Asked the routine question of whether he'd read his interrogation record before signing it, Kawan said he hadn't, because he'd been
very tired and trusted the investigators. A prosecutor then slowly read
from Kawan's sworn statement. Police had shown him Polly's photo, and
Kawan had confirmed seeing him one morning in Budi's office.

Now Kawan denied ever seeing Polly. Raising his voice, he said, "I knew
of him only through the media, *only through the media!*"

Kawan had also told police that Budi assigned him to monitor, mobilize,
and "create conditions" with regard to the security situation in Jakarta.
This work included attention to people considered too vocal. He'd monitored KontraS senior staff at work and home, taking note of people and
vehicles going in and out. In court he denied ever doing this kind of work
in Jakarta, rather than the Timorese border.

More broadly, he denied that the words in the interrogation record were
his. When a defense lawyer asked if the police pressured him, he described
the questioning as insistent and repetitive.

"There was pressure," he said, "but I could handle it."

The defense later pressed him: "You say you never saw Polly in the
office of Budi Santoso. So your interrogation record, do you let it stand or
do you withdraw it?"

After further back and forth, Kawan said he wanted to withdraw the
record, "because there is a lot that differs from the words that came out
of my mouth."

The defense lawyer pressed him again, "So are you saying 'I withdraw
it'? Your statement is what you are saying at this trial? Is that what you
are saying?"

He paused. "Yes, I withdraw it."

A trial observer noted a nod from Muchdi.

Kawan claimed that by the end of his questioning he'd gone twenty-
four hours without sleep. The police used strong language, asking the
same questions over and over. They never coerced him, but there was
pressure, and he signed the record without reviewing it.

"The police offered to read it out but I told them I trusted them," he
said, adding, "I didn't have my glasses, so I couldn't read it."

"Why say you trusted them, but now you withdraw?"

"Because I was truly tired then. I was tired then." He spoke slowly. "And I wanted it to be over with as quickly as possible."

The Polly trial had shown that if prosecutors did not have experts validate documentary evidence, the defense would claim it was invalid or falsified. After Kawan, the prosecution called a young IT consultant to explain how he cloned Muchdi's hard drive and recovered deleted files. As Jhoni Torino tried to explain sectors and clusters, the defense perforated his testimony with repeated objections about his qualifications, with little pushback from prosecutor or judges. In their own questioning, the defense probed whether he was really an expert in digital forensics. Had he taught or written books on the subject? They asked judges to note that the prosecution had called an unqualified witness. They also claimed that data could be added during cloning, but Torino countered that such deception would be easily detected.

Another technology consultant, Ruby Z. Alamsyah, testified about the call data record, or CDR. In early June, police had at last obtained the records for three cell-phone numbers: Muchdi's, one of Polly's, and Munir's. For some reason, they had requested records only for September, leaving out August, when a plot might have been hatched, and November, when the autopsy results sparked a flurry of calls.[12]

Prosecutors had the witness walk them through the record of several calls in September 2004, including those between Muchdi's phone and Polly's. On September 7 at 10:40 a.m., Muchdi's cell, located within Surabaya's airport, had called Polly's home phone. Soon after, there was a return call lasting ninety-four seconds. Polly would have just returned from Singapore.

The defense again objected to the witness's qualifications, and again explored whether the data could be falsified. Could a CDR be altered? The expert replied that security is tight around this important record, which is used for billing. Changes would require high-level intervention at the phone company.

Muchdi's lawyers also suggested that you could clone a SIM card, making it look as though a particular number had made a call. The expert said the nine-hour cloning operation would require some expertise in IT and electronics, but no specialized training. Asked about ways to record calls, the expert said it was possible, but only by prior request of a court or other responsible parties.

After the session, Muchdi's lawyer reminded the media that the attorney general's office had never produced a recording they had once promised of Muchdi and Polly. The prior court order that the expert had said was necessary was very unlikely in this case. The lawyer also claimed to have easily cloned his own SIM card in six hours, and that in the "world of intelligence, anything can become possible."[13]

Prosecutors called police investigators to rebut claims that they'd pressured witnesses to sign false statements. The investigator Daniel Tifaona described his interview with Kawan at the resort in Bali:

"Before we started, he said his glasses got left behind in Kupang. We provided some that we bought for him, reading glasses." He had the glasses throughout the interview and when he initialed each page of the typed record. He even took them when he left. He'd been weak and tired in the overnight interview, but had been given snacks and drinks.

What was the atmosphere like after you finished?

"One sentence after signing, one sentence that he conveyed, and it can be cross-checked, was 'Pak Daniel, I still have a wife and child.' That sentence was heard by the whole team."

To Kawan's fears for his family, Daniel had responded, "Just leave it to God."

As for Muchdi's admin staff, Zondy and Arifin, who also claimed the police had pressured them, Daniel said they were accompanied by BIN lawyers and given snacks, drinks, and prayer breaks. He'd also placed a video camera on the table and explained to them that they were taping the interview in case there were ever claims of pressure. The police were ready to provide the tapes if judges so ordered.

Hearing this, the Friends of Munir clapped and yelled, as the judge called for order. He urged the prosecutors to focus on the discrepancies between courtroom testimony and the statements, rather than the process, but the prosecutor continued asking about claims of pressure. The judge asked a few questions about content, including one about Zondy's and Arifin's responses to being shown Polly's photo. Daniel confirmed that both told him they'd seen Polly in Muchdi's offices.

The lead defense lawyer was not in court, and his team asked no questions, perhaps as a protest against calling the investigators over their objection. When other investigators testified similarly, the defense again asked no questions, calling it a waste of time.[14]

Two people on the prosecution's witness list hadn't appeared in court when called. They were Budi Santoso and As'ad Said Ali, both still employed at BIN. In late September, the defense had announced that they had a letter from Budi in Islamabad. On embassy letterhead and addressed to the court, the letter withdrew all four statements to police without explanation.[15]

A similar letter had surfaced during Indra Setiawan's trial the year before, when Budi had also failed to appear. Despite the letterhead, the Ministry of Foreign Affairs had said they knew of no such letter. Usman assumed the new letter was another BIN effort to block testimony and discredit sworn statements to the police.

Budi was an important witness, a confirmed BIN employee who had worked directly under Muchdi. His number appeared in the call records, linked to both Polly and Muchdi. Previous trials had revealed that he'd given police incriminating information about both men.

On November 6, the dwindling ranks of the journalists swelled again to hear Budi's interrogation records read out. The trial routine was upset slightly when police stopped a Tapak Suci martial arts group member from bringing in a stash of gunpowder, apparently for its magical properties. After Muchdi's yellow-shirts outmuscled a group of elderly women, survivors of the mass killings and arrests of 1965, to control the front of the room, the Friends of Munir took their usual space at the back and near one entrance.

Making their case for the read-out of Budi's interrogation record, prosecutors explained that they'd sent sixteen summonses, to all of Budi's known home and work addresses. BIN had replied that Budi was on assignment. The Foreign Affairs Ministry had informed them he wasn't in Pakistan, after being sent to Afghanistan in September. (His whereabouts were a mystery. The Indonesian ambassador in Kabul later told journalists that Budi never turned up there. A journalist who had staked out his residence in Islamabad in 2007 never saw him.[16] His house in Yogyakarta was peeling and overgrown, and another family was living in his assigned BIN housing in Jakarta.)

The judges agreed to the readout: summonses had been sent, the questioning had been under oath, and the procedures allowed it. Prosecutors began with Budi's two interviews from October 2007, already cited in Polly's case review. In them, Budi described helping Polly edit the As'ad letter and bringing 10 million rupiah to Polly in Muchdi's office, three months before the murder. This transaction was also documented in Budi's cash book, seized by police and now submitted as evidence. It documented the amount and the recipient, described as "Poli/Pilot?" because Budi had never met him and had to ask Muchdi's staff who the man in the boss's office was. Budi had also described himself as the liaison between Polly and Muchdi, and he stated, "Everything I did was on orders from deputy V."

It turned out that police had questioned Budi twice more as they built the case against Muchdi in 2008. In March, Mathius Salempang and his investigators secretly traveled to Kuala Lumpur to interview Budi, followed by a second interview in May. In a secure room at the residence of the Indonesian ambassador to Malaysia, Budi again described the As'ad letter and the cash payment. This time investigators could show him the cloned letter, which he confirmed was the one he'd helped edit. Budi also revealed that Pollycarpus later told him, "I was given the task by Pak Muchdi to finish off Munir." He described another payment to Polly in a supermarket parking lot, when the co-pilot was first being questioned by police. Budi also made two payments of 2 million rupiah via the agent Kawan, for him and Pollycarpus to use for "hunting Munir."

Budi had told police that he personally had never attended a meeting about killing Munir. He was willing to say that, based on the facts—the As'ad letter, the money transfers, and Polly's presence in Muchdi's offices—"this was an intelligence activity."[18]

In the first round of questioning in October 2007, Budi had described the many calls he received from Polly looking for Muchdi. Questioned in 2008, he added some content. At 6:25 p.m. three hours before boarding,

Polly called to announce his trip to Singapore that night, saying, "On the plane, I'll be with Munir." The next morning at 10:47 he called to say, "I caught a big fish in Singapore." Budi asked if he had already reported this to Muchdi, and he said he had. A few days later, Polly came to the office and said, "I have finished off Munir with poison."[19]

Given As'ad Said Ali's continued absence, on November 6 prosecutors read out the record of his one interrogation, in March 2008. After questions about As'ad's usual role in signing letters, an investigator had asked whether BIN might place an agent in a government agency.[20] As'ad said it would require high-level discussion and a request from the other agency. While vague, his answer implied that having a BIN agent inside Garuda was possible, but might require sign-off by Muchdi, As'ad himself, and perhaps Hendropriyono.[21]

The police asked about the meeting that the Garuda director, Indra Setiawan, claimed Polly arranged for him with As'ad in late 2004. As'ad confirmed the meeting, as well as his own action summoning Muchdi to join them but said they only discussed general issues about Garuda and the political situation. He also confirmed running into the Garuda director at the Hotel Shangri-La bathroom. Setiawan had told police that he'd asked As'ad about copies of the letter, and the curt reply was, "It's done." As'ad told police, "What I remember was just small talk."

The police asked As'ad if he ever signed a letter addressed to Setiawan.

He didn't remember. However, since the matter involved a strategic state-owned enterprise, and Muchdi's staff had helped draft and correct the document, "if there was such a letter, then it would be within my authority to sign it." He said that after hearing of the letter at Setiawan's trial, he checked the records, asked Muchdi, and ordered staff to look for the computer used to type the letter, but found nothing. As'ad denied ordering anyone to write the letter, and directed the attention of the police toward Muchdi, saying, "The person who made this letter I think is deputy V, and responsibility for implementing this task falls to deputy V."

Investigators listed all the facts supporting the claim that Polly was a BIN agent: phone records, the taped call with Setiawan, the letter As'ad signed, and the payments. As'ad had responded that Polly was not an

organic agent, but based on these facts, "There is a big possibility that
Pollycarpus is a nonorganic agent. However, the person who can confirm
this is his handler." Nonorganic agents were the responsibility of deputies,
like Muchdi, and the directors they supervised.

In his response, Muchdi didn't dispute As'ad's statements, but he added
that top BIN leadership, including As'ad, know everything deputies do.
So did the agency's main clients, the coordinating minister for politics
and security, and the president.

The prosecution rested.

The defense's focus in calling witnesses appeared to be dismantling the
revenge motive. They would first sever Muchdi's link to the 1998 abductions, then argue that without motive there was no case. They could draw
upon the opacity of Indonesian military justice. It was widely understood
that after the abductions, Muchdi, Prabowo, and Colonel Chairawan
faced an honor board, that all three officers lost their commands, and that
Prabowo was forced to retire. It had been reported at the time in newspapers at home and abroad.[22] In his 2003 memoir, former commander of the
armed forces Wiranto wrote that Prabowo had admitted Kopassus was
involved in the kidnappings, and that Team Mawar had been acting on his
orders to monitor threats to stability in the run up to the March assembly.
Wiranto wrote that the honor board had recommended dismissal of both
Prabowo and Muchdi, and that he had acted on that recommendation.[23]
However, there was no official record of the board's proceedings or its
recommendations. It was widely understood that Munir's efforts had cost
Muchdi his command, effectively ending his military career. But it was
hard to prove it.

Usman and Hendardi both mentioned the only known written record
of the honor board's recommendation. The Indonesian Defense Department had once created a brief web page describing the abductions. It
explained that Team Mawar was formed to monitor activists but over-
stepped its authority, without orders, by detaining nine of them, who
were later released. The page also stated that after the honor board made
its recommendations to the head of the armed forces, General Wiranto
then "handed down a punishment . . . in the form of ending military ser-

vice (retirement)" for Prabowo. For both Muchdi and Chairawan, punishment "was in the form of relieving them of their posts."[24] The web page had since been deleted, but a copy had been saved offline. Judges are reluctant to accept evidence not in the police dossier, however, and outdated trial procedures also make many forms of electronic evidence inadmissible.[25]

Given all the ambiguity about the honor board, the defense had the wind at their backs as they called their first witness. Muchtar Zein, head of the army's legal division, occupied the top legal post at Kopassus when Muchdi assumed command in March 1998. He testified that neither the military police nor the honor board questioned Muchdi about the abductions. Prosecutors pointed out that he was Muchdi's junior and had never attended the honor board hearings or seen the relevant documents.

As for the Team Mawar abduction squad, Zein said he'd *heard* of the unit but had forgotten what it was. Asked about his own work on the abductions case, Zein said, "I'm just a witness to talk about Muchdi's career. Why are these questions so broad?"

A prosecutor asked, "Were you ever an advocate for Team Mawar?"

The crowd hooted at the pointed question.

"I was." He may not be sure what Team Mawar was, but apparently he'd represented members of the kidnapping squad at their court martial.

He forgot a lot. A judge commented, "The more questions I have, the more you forget." Zein remembered nothing about the creation of the honor board or his work representing soldiers accused of abductions. One frustrated judge finally said, "In that case, I won't continue my questions to you."

"Fine," Zein said. Muchdi's people and some journalists laughed, as Zein made his way to the exit.

The next defense witness was Djasri Marin, deputy commander of the military police in the relevant months of July to November 1998.

A defense lawyer asked, "Did you ever investigate within Kopassus?"

Yes, he'd investigated the eleven soldiers in Team Mawar, leading to their court martial for exceeding authority. They were just supposed to monitor people, but they took away their freedom. An honor board can ask the military police to conduct an investigation, but it only did so for

Prabowo. He never got an order to investigate Muchdi. Marin, a one-star general at the time, couldn't say for sure whether the honor board examined Muchdi at all, as he did not have sufficient rank to take part in the process.

Marin's testimony allowed the defense to maintain that there was no evidence Muchdi was even investigated for the abductions, let alone punished. At the same time, of course, if the witness didn't know what took place before the honor board, he could not testify with certainty on the subject.

The final defense witness was a legal expert who testified on a range of issues. Most important to the defense, he stated that a motive must be proven once cited in the charging document.[26] Over the course of the day, the defense attacked the broad thrust of the case, rather than the particulars. The witnesses had been forgetful and evasive, or had limited access to the relevant information. However, if the defense team's goal was to give judges enough of a legal basis to justify a not-guilty verdict, it might be enough.

17

The Verdict

November 2008–January 2009

On the morning of November 18, Muchdi took his seat in the witness chair. The crowds of his supporters were smaller than usual. Nevertheless, they still dominated the room with their outbursts, which drew no response from the judge. The chief judge first asked Muchdi about BIN procedures for visitors, expenditures, and letters.[1]

"Let's return to the time you were Kopassus commander," the judge said next. "Were members of Kopassus tried at a military tribunal?"

Muchdi said his command was very short, and "in that short time, never—*never*—was a member of Kopassus prosecuted." The judge persisted, and Muchdi eventually conceded that he'd heard two or three soldiers were tried later. He didn't know exactly when the abductions took place, but had "heard they took place before I took over, up until March 1998." (In fact, at least nine abductions occurred under his command).

Muchdi confirmed that Budi Santoso headed a directorate in his division, and they would meet each Monday to discuss Budi's activities. Muchdi explained that he had three or four phone lines in the office, and about five mobile numbers. He sometimes left his cell phones with a driver or secretary. He had never ordered staff to type up a list of his contacts. Shown the recovered contact list, he said he'd never seen it outside these hearings.

A judge asked whether a BIN deputy like himself could take action or set policy related to "activities that disturb the stability or security of the state."[2]

"That, uh . . . really, I think they can't."

A judge later rephrased the question with much more specificity, asking if BIN ever targeted Munir for monitoring or operations.

Muchdi replied, "I'm sorry, Your Honor, I learned of Munir only after he died. This Munir became a big deal after he was dead. Before that I never heard of him and never knew who Munir was."

His answer was improbable. Munir was known throughout Indonesia and around the world not only for his work on the disappearances, which Muchdi had surely followed closely, but on every major human rights incident, law, and policy since. What's more, Muchdi had told police in 2005 that he'd once asked Munir's old boss Buyung to warn Munir not to be too vocal. He'd even testified about that conversation at Polly's first trial.

Muchdi claimed he never recruited Polly or *any* nonorganic agent, as that was the job of directors under him. Deputies had the authority to do so, but he never used it. Then, turning to motive, prosecutors asked if Muchdi had followed the proceedings of the court martial. He replied "Yeah, I don't know. Not my business. I only heard the results." Actually, on further reflection, he didn't even know what decision the body had come to.

Cyrus Sinaga, for the prosecution, asked why Muchdi left his command of Kopassus after only two months, citing the Department of Defense website, which he wanted to show the court. The judge told him to finish the questioning first. The prosecutor did so, asking more pointedly, "Were you relieved of your position as Kopassus commander to become deputy inspector general because of the kidnapping of activists in 1997–98?"

"There was no connection. I was transferred from that command because the political situation at that time was changing from President Suharto to President Habibie."

Sinaga again tried to introduce the statement from the website, saying "I'd like to show the court that he was relieved from duty due to a recommendation from the honor board."

Muchdi and both lawyers talked over each other at growing volume until the judge stepped in. Muchdi's people clapped and called out, as the judge asked the prosecutors to explain what this information from the website was and how they got it. Had police secured it as evidence? To more applause, he criticized the prosecutors for introducing new information months into the trial and without following procedure. The prosecutors pleaded to introduce several sentences from a government web page to back up a widely known set of facts. The defense objected, and the judge ordered the prosecutors to move on to another topic. The prosecutors asked Muchdi a few more questions about his command responsibility for Team Mawar. They also asked about his two meetings with Indra Setiawan, which he confirmed, and then they yielded the floor to the defense.[3]

The defense began by asking about Muchdi's honors and awards. "I don't want to sound arrogant," the general said, before rattling off his leadership and benefactor roles for a dozen religious, educational, political, and veterans' bodies. It was a roster of his sources of prestige, influence, income, courtroom protestors, and, perhaps, his genuine support for martial arts, Harley Davidsons, and Islamic education in remote regions.

The defense turned to what they considered the "fatal flaw" in the prosecution's case, the lack of a motive. They asked about Muchdi's transfer from Kopassus commander to deputy inspector general. Muchdi explained that there were many paths to promotion and that as a two-star general he was a good fit for the deputy inspector general position. (While technically a lateral move, not a demotion in rank, as an administrative position with no troops under his command, his new post had been far less prestigious.)

Returning to his time at BIN, he denied ever ordering Budi Santoso to give Polly money. What about that letter in evidence, the one signed by As'ad? Muchdi said it did not look like a normal BIN letter, because the addressee and the sender were on the left, instead of the right.[4] The lawyers and the judge all examined a copy of the letter and the envelope, and then Budi Santoso's cash book.[5]

After a brief break for the call to prayer, which some lawyers used to have a smoke outside the room, a defense lawyer asked him to explain his job as deputy V for *penggalangan*, variously translated as mobilization, consolidation, support, or covert operations. Earlier, he'd fended off a similar question from a judge, saying the answer was too technical, but he'd explain it to him in private. This time, when Muchdi said it would take too long to explain, his lawyer asked for an example of *penggalan-gan*. He cited the division of the provinces of Papua and Riau into several smaller provinces. These actions were criticized at the time as an intelligence operation to divide and rule. Muchdi seemed to confirm that view, stating that BIN's efforts were necessary, "in the context of defending the integrity of the unitary state."[6]

"And in the context of defending the unity of the Republic of Indonesia, did certain activities from an NGO draw attention from your department?"

"Never."

"Never? Whether it was named KontraS or something else, in the context of protecting, like you said?"

"Never. Since we have various deputies, perhaps that was the job of other deputies."

"And in your department, were there duties related to the taking of people's lives?"

"Well, I don't think it got to that. I think that is not the job of BIN, that."

His lawyer asked if he had been at Surabaya airport on September 7, 2004. Phone records showed calls between Muchdi's cell phone at that location and Polly's landline that day. He couldn't have been in Surabaya, Muchdi said, because, "apparently I was in Malaysia."

His lawyer added, "This can be shown." The legal teams and the defendant gathered as the judges were shown the stamps in a green passport showing his travel to Malaysia from September 6 until September 12. Muchdi's people applauded.

The hearing, and so the evidence stage of the trial, concluded soon after. To the laughter of his colleagues, a defense lawyer taunted the prosecution about the recorded evidence they had touted in the press, yelling, "Where's the recording? Where's the phone conversation?" Muchdi smiled as he shook his lawyers' hands. Usman shook Sinaga's hand and chatted with him, under the watchful eyes of five bodyguards. Courthouse staff gathered up mikes and turned off the lights, one by one. The defense lawyer, outside the room now, between drags on a cigarette, yelled out, "Where's that conversation?"

Inside the courtroom, a defense lawyer made the case to the press that the motive was unproven. What's more, prosecutors had promised tapes of Muchdi's phone calls and videos of witnesses being questioned, but it was all *omong kosong*, empty talk. And as for the calls between Polly and Muchdi on September 7, the day of Munir's death? Well, you could either believe Muchdi's passport, an official government document showing he was in Malaysia, or a phone company printout with no stamp or signature.

A volley of closing arguments unfolded over four hearings. On December 2, prosecutors rose in turns to read the *surat tuntutan*, recapping the case and requesting a sentence. Sinaga read out first the facts they believed proven in court: Munir said Muchdi hated him more than anyone after the loss of his command. Muchdi was assigned to BIN, with Budi Santoso under him. Muchdi had been in contact with Pollycarpus since he was stationed in Papua. The agent Ucok knew of a plan to kill Munir using monitoring, *teror*, magic, and poison. Polly gave a letter signed by As'ad to Garuda's director. Polly called Muchdi and Budi Santoso (who reported directly to Muchdi) before and after the murder. Budi Santoso brought 10 million rupiah to Polly on Muchdi's orders, and 2 million rupiah to Kawan "to support the hunt" for Munir.

Moving on to their legal analysis, prosecutors explained that because Polly had already been found guilty, they didn't need to prove the underlying crime of premeditated murder. Hearing that they would not try to prove the murder charge, the lead defense lawyer laughed and wrote something on a slip of paper. His colleagues chatted and smiled, barely paying attention. The judges remained focused.

The prosecutors sought to show that Muchdi participated in the crime, by proving either of the two alternative charges under Article 55 (1) of the Criminal Code, which concerns two or more people committing a crime. One charge covered those who *provoke* or *instigate* a crime, by an abuse of authority or by providing means or opportunity. The alternative charge covered those who carry out, cause others to perpetrate, or take direct part in the criminal act. Sinaga called on the judges to find Muchdi guilty on either charge and sentence him to fifteen years in prison. He noted that although Muchdi never acknowledged wrongdoing and was disrespectful

Muchdi Purwopranjono listens as prosecutors request a sentence of fifteen years for his role in the murder of Munir. (REUTERS/Alamy Stock Photo)

in court, this short sentence was appropriate due to his long service to the nation.

The session ended just past noon. As the courtroom emptied, journalists chased after Muchdi. He angrily began a statement, finger pointed directly into the cameras. The lead defense lawyer whispered something to him, and Muchdi began to speak more calmly: "You all already know this is the culmination of conspiracy and tyranny and slander against me," he said, "and you need to know that slander is more cruel than murder. I leave the rest to counsel."[7]

"True!" his supporters gathered around him yelled out. "*Hidup* Muchdi!"

The prosecutors' request for a short sentence angered and disappointed Suci and Usman. For the field operative, Pollycarpus, prosecutors had asked for life and secured twenty years. It made no sense to seek a lower sentence for the man who ordered the murder. A life sentence seemed more appropriate.[8]

Suci and her supporters decided to boycott the next session to protest the sentence request. Muchdi's supporters from the martial arts group Tapak Suci scrambled to claim the front seats anyway, to the amusement of the defense lawyers. Muchdi's other groups settled into the room in their matching shirts, like a color-coded diagram of how to influence a trial using nationalism, religion, and *premanism*.

The defense began their closing arguments by quoting Martin Luther King Jr.: "Injustice anywhere is a threat to justice everywhere." They reminded the judges that the perpetrators of a crime are often those you least suspect. In this case, BIN was *most* suspected, but only because the real killer had outwitted the police and the prosecutors. The trail of evidence that implicated the spy agency was actually proof of innocence: "It makes no sense for BIN to be so careless in leaving traces of killing Munir, so undoubtedly the real murderer is now laughing." The call records were part of this sleight of hand, so that no one would suspect that the real murderers were those closest to Munir.

After these rhetorical flights, the defense returned to the more grounded argument that the evidence simply did not support the charges. They questioned the use of secondhand testimony of Munir's "hunch" about Muchdi's anger at him to prove the motive. Prosecutors had phone records, but no witnesses who heard the calls and could say they concerned a murder.

One more round of filings broke no new ground, a *replik*[9] from prosecutors, and a *duplik*[10] from defense that was a cocktail of legal arguments, insults, and nationalist appeals.

Muchdi's state of mind at this moment, or at least his public presentation of it, can be seen in an interview he gave a few days before the verdict was due. (The interview was published a week later in the magazine *Mahkamah*).[11] In his view, the attacks on him were attacks on Indonesia, nothing less than an effort to break the country into pieces like Yugoslavia. Asked who would benefit from a guilty verdict, Muchdi laughed and asked, "What are you doing? Pretending you don't know? Yes, who else, of course. Those who became lackeys of foreign imperialism within the country, or foreign parties who tried to destabilize Indonesia's national security." He invoked this potent strain of nationalism to question even the forensics report from "the same Netherlands that colonized our people for about 350 years."

Muchdi asked, "If I wanted to kill Munir, why would I have to order someone else to do it?" He didn't want to brag, but he was a great fighter in several martial arts traditions. And as a Special Forces soldier, he was trained in individual combat, "So if I wanted someone dead, I'd just kill them myself."

But he had no reason to kill Munir, he said. He claimed to be the one who ordered Team Mawar's victims freed in 1998, so why would he nurse bitterness toward Munir? And Munir was "just average," not especially brave, and no different from many other activists who "exploited Indonesia's ugliness abroad to make a living."

No, the killer was more likely one of Munir's friends or colleagues, since premeditated murder always involves the people closest to the victim. He speculated that the motive was making Indonesians fight each other, or perhaps to seek a profit: "Make proposals here and there, so people sympathize, then disburse funds. Because Munir died, many could travel abroad, right?"

On the morning of the verdict, on the third day of 2009, the Tapak Suci contingent disembarked at the courthouse bus stop at 6:35 in the morning, only to find Munir's supporters already lined up to enter. They had come in numbers large enough to overflow into the roadway in front of the courthouse, blocking half the lanes. They kept on coming, in buses spangled with paper signs with the imperative ARREST above photos of Muchdi and Hendropriyono. In all, over a thousand Munir supporters came from greater Jakarta and the surrounding villages and cities of West Java. Farmers, workers, victims' families, and Munir's friends and colleagues from nearly every human rights organization dominated the front of the courthouse, chanting "Munir! Munir! Open the doors!" A smaller number of Muchdi supporters, unusually quiet, gathered in the parking lot.

At 7:25, police began to admit visitors to the courthouse grounds. They took photos of entrants and inspected their clothes and bags, men on the left and women on the right. Today it was mostly men, though the women of Tapak Suci pushed and elbowed through the crowd too. Outside, a police officer urged everyone to accept any decision in an orderly way or risk the mockery of other countries. An elite police squad lined up in helmets and shields. The crowd chanted, "*Hidup* Munir! *Hidup* Police! *Hidup* Indonesia!"

Once inside the building, Munir's supporters assembled at the doors on the right side of the courtroom, with Muchdi's groups on the left side. One group lined up shoulder to shoulder dressed all in black and wearing dark sunglasses. A pro-Muchdi group in white arrived from the political party he was forming with Prabowo. Calling themselves Satuan Relawan Gerindra, or Gerindra Volunteer Unit, its acronym SATRIA referenced the old warrior caste of Javanese knights. Yelling "Free Pak Muchdi!" they joined the Red and White Brigade to the left of the doors. Seeing Munir supporters dominate the lobby, a Brigade member yelled out "Just kill 'em!" The atmosphere heated up further, each side yelling "Muchdi!" or "Munir!" The Tapak Suci members began to sing the national anthem: "Indonesia, my homeland, land where my blood is spilled." The police officer from the parking lot stood in the space between the two mobs assembled in front of the locked courtroom doors.

It was barely past eight o'clock. Munir's supporters sang out, "Who does Cak Munir belong to? He belongs to us all!" A man in a shirt featuring Indonesia's first president, Soekarno, tried to reclaim the mantle of nationalism from Muchdi's supporters , saying, "The person on my shirt would weep to see a murderer protected, no matter if he's a warrior. If he's guilty, he must be punished." He urged the crowd to stay calm in the face of provocateurs. Munir's supporters yelled out the 1928 Sumpah Pemuda, or Youth Pledge, and sang patriotic songs at full volume.

Two defense lawyers arrived with more SATRIA members. The lead defense lawyer smiled to see the crowds. The police officer called on everyone to respect the court, and threatened to move the hearing. He demanded an end to speeches on courthouse grounds and urged that there be no new victims.

Suci arrived to applause at eight thirty in a white shirt with a picture of her husband on it. The victims of the 1965 purges welcomed her, and one elderly survivor sang an old song called "Di Timur Matahari," as others joined in:

In the east the sun began to glow.
Wake up and stand up, all my friends.
Let's arrange our ranks.

The police officer requested yet more backup from the local police station.

Just before nine, a siren signaled the arrival of a convoy of three black Nissans. Journalists surged alongside, kept at bay by a tight guard, which formed around Muchdi as he stepped down. When the courtroom doors finally opened a half hour later, Munir supporters quickly filled the room. Photographers stood on folding ladders. A black-clad security team stood behind a small, tense team of prosecutors.

The judges were seated by 9:45, and Muchdi was brought in, an Indonesian flag pin on the lapel of his tan windbreaker. A judge read out the prosecutor's sentence request, and the defense call for acquittal. He stated the judges' findings of fact, based on witness statements they found credible and consistent with other testimony and evidence.

To prove guilt, the judge continued, these facts must be connected to either of the two charges. For the first, the prosecutors had to prove that, motivated by feelings of revenge and bitterness, Muchdi had misused his authority to provide Pollycarpus with the means or opportunity to kill Munir, in the form of operational funds or the As'ad letter.

The judges recalled Suci's testimony that Munir worried about the threat from Muchdi, and pointed to Suci's response that "you have to be prepared to be in danger." This comment signaled worry and a need to be careful, but "did not yet depict the presence of revenge or bitterness from the Defendant."

The judges also considered whether the As'ad letter showed Muchdi misused his authority. They noted Muchdi's claim that the letter was fake because BIN letters are signed on the right, not the left. They considered that a strict reading of the law doesn't allow electronic evidence in a criminal trial. However, courts must accommodate advances in technology to ensure a fair process, and so they accepted the cloning results alongside other evidence.

But did the recovered document prove Muchdi's guilt? The letter doesn't mention Muchdi, and only asks that Pollycarpus be given a security role, which is not a crime. Statements from Budi Santoso and As'ad pointed to Muchdi's likely role in creating the letter, but that did not prove Muchdi instigated Pollycarpus's crime of killing Munir.

The judges accepted as fact that there were many calls between numbers owned by Muchdi and Polly. But no evidence showed it was Muchdi using the phone or what was discussed in those calls. Furthermore, judges accepted the evidence that Muchdi was in Malaysia in September 2004, buttressing the argument that someone else had used Muchdi's phone or SIM card.[12]

The final element in this charge was that Muchdi had misused his authority by supporting Polly's crime with BIN funds. Budi Santoso's statement and cash book supported this proposition. However, Polly and Muchdi denied it, and no evidence corroborated who issued the money, who received it, and for what purpose.

The judges found that prosecutors did not prove Muchdi misused his authority, whether to secure a security assignment for Pollycarpus or by providing funds to kill Munir. Therefore, they had not proved the first charge.

The judges moved on to the alternative charge. The question here was whether Muchdi perpetrated, ordered others to perpetrate, or directly participated in the act.[13] Muchdi did not execute the murder himself. After reviewing all the evidence and arguments of the trial, the judges echoed their reasoning in the first charge to find it not proven that Muchdi instigated or ordered Pollycarpus to kill Munir. That left only "those who participate" which would require prosecutors to prove that Muchdi gave out assignments, roles, and money. As the judges had already rejected the letter and the money as evidence of a crime, these elements too were not fulfilled.

The judges declared Muchdi free of all charges against him. The court formally restored his rights and standing, his honor and his dignity, returned all evidence to the rightful owners, and ordered Muchdi freed immediately.

Outside, jubilant Muchdi supporters shouted out the national anthem. They were trying to drown out a thousand Munir supporters chanting, "*Pembunuh!*"

Murderer! Murderer! Murderer!

Suci was devastated. "I have already lost my husband, and now I lost justice," she told a journalist at the courthouse, her voice quavering. "This is very painful. Something I feared has now come to pass."[14]

She strove for greater control in an interview back at KontraS. "It hurts, but I must remain rational. I cannot be emotional," she said. "There is still a long way to go."[15] She continued,

> I feel I'm not alone. I'm still going to fight until the truth of this case comes out. Many people support what I am doing, and their support is real: they came to the hearings, heated things up in front of the presidential palace, and said they will continue their support no matter what. That energy keeps me from giving up. . . . I have to keep a flicker of hope alive. If that flame is extinguished, I won't know what to do. Right now, I am protecting that flame.

After the interview, she had to go home to tell Alif and Diva, now aged nine and five, that their father's murderer had been freed.

Suci believed Muchdi had intimidated the judges through his supporters in the courtroom. While both sides had vocal supporters, it was Muchdi's people who yelled at witnesses, laughed at prosecutors, and applauded the defendant with no response from the judges.

Usman blamed Muchdi's acquittal on the poor performance by the prosecution, and he attributed that failure to fear: everyone could see how scared the prosecutors were during the trials. However, the problem was not just their evident fear of Muchdi in the courtroom. Usman thought they had undermined their own case to protect forces even more powerful than Muchdi. As in the disappearances, the Pollycarpus trial, and other cases, the prosecutors had framed the crime as a personal vendetta. This strategy had protected Muchdi's superiors, As'ad and Hendropriyono, as well as BIN as an institution. It also undermined the case against Muchdi due to a vague and unproven motive. Usman told the *New York Times*, "This has been a devastating result. The whole justice system here is so weak. That said, this is far from over."[16]

The weak performance of the witnesses had also been crucial to the acquittal. An aggressive, effective team of investigators had identified, questioned, and coaxed into cooperating an array of BIN witnesses, including Budi Santoso, Ucok, Kawan, Zondy, and Arifin. Every one of these witnesses had then failed to appear, retracted sworn statements, or had "forgotten" not just earlier answers, but even basic facts about their lives. They alleged they were questioned while sick, scared, or unable to see without glasses, all denied by investigators ready to show the interrogation videotapes, if the judges had let them. In many countries, the number of witnesses who withdrew their statements in part or in whole would have prompted immediate measures to protect them and an investigation into their intimidation.

The chair of the National Human Rights Commission found it strange that the judges didn't consider these unusual retractions, which appeared to be "a game played by BIN agents." The police had accomplished a great deal, he said, "but the moves made by those BIN agents rendered all that hard work meaningless. The Supreme Court must see what's behind this when examining the verdict."[17] The Commission pledged to review the verdict and share findings with the Supreme Court.

Munir's friends second-guessed their own decisions. "We were overconfident on the testimony we had," Indra from Kasum recalled. He had been sure that, step by step, the prosecutors would get convictions for Pollycarpus, then Muchdi, and finally Hendropriyono. "If only there had been orders from above, and real witness protection for their families . . ."[18]

Usman had been convinced by allies that it was enough to use top-level advocacy to secure support from the president and Muslim leaders. Now he thought the low-key strategy had been a mistake. A consistent, massive show of support, of the type organized on the day of the verdict, might have encouraged more bravery by prosecutors, witnesses, and judges.

Usman called on the president to restore his own credibility by using his full authority to instruct the police to collect more evidence.[19] President Yudhoyono did summon the attorney general and the national chief of police for an explanation of the collapse of the case. But soon after, as he and his top aides faced criticism from Muchdi's allies, the president emphasized that he couldn't interfere with the judiciary.

Immediately after the verdict, Muchdi collected his belongings at the Mobile Brigade detention center. He went home for a ceremony of thanks with his family and dozens of children from a nearby orphans' home. Standing outside his house to receive a stream of well-wishers, Muchdi joked with journalists and answered a few questions. Had he always been sure he would be acquitted? "I was positive. Yes of course, there was no evidence whatsoever or any witnesses to implicate me." He described the ruling as "a present for Indonesia."[20] With elections three months away, he planned to travel the country campaigning for Prabowo's Gerindra Party.[21]

Muchdi's defense team pledged to sue Suciwati, Usman, Hendardi, Poengky, and other activists for defaming him in court and in the press. Muchdi did file a complaint against Usman with police on January 8, citing the humiliation of being called a killer during the trial.[22] Usman refused to back down, calling the accusation an attempt to silence him and to shift attention from the Munir case. He'd faced down the same tactic from Hendropriyono and was happy to repeat his statements, telling the press, "I am wholly convinced that Muchdi was involved in Munir's death." The police dutifully named Usman a suspect, but didn't summon him for questioning. He was adamant that if they did call him in, he would not appear. This was a law to be resisted.

A few days later, Usman left to study at a short human rights program in England, sure he'd be arrested at the airport. He wasn't stopped, however, and on a cold day in January he arrived in Nottingham, legendary home to a generous fighter and unjust law enforcement. Usman felt empty inside and yet weighed down, heavy with the knowledge that they had failed.

18

The Aftermath

2009–2021

A few weeks after the Muchdi verdict, the Supreme Court overturned the acquittal of Garuda secretary Rohainil Aini. She would return to a month or two of prison, considering time served.[1] Kasum portrayed this conviction as an act of unfairness, with Rohainil imprisoned for a minor role in the plot just as the mastermind was set free. They also hoped this verdict would create momentum for an appeal of Muchdi's acquittal.[2]

However, the Supreme Court upheld Muchdi's acquittal six months later. The court did not consider the substance of the prosecution's appeal due to an apparent act of negligence.[3] Prosecutors are formally barred from appealing an acquittal, but they surmount this obstacle by arguing that a verdict wasn't a "pure acquittal" (*bebas murni*), because judges made mistakes or exceeded their authority. In Muchdi's case, the prosecutors failed to make this argument correctly, and so the Supreme Court found no legal standing to appeal.

A few legal avenues remained open. Experts convened by the National Human Rights Commission found so many irregularities in Muchdi's trial and appeal that they recommended not only a retrial, but also an inquiry into whether the prosecutors' "fatal negligence" was intentional.[4] A second option was to refile the appeal with the missing argument.

A third more promising option was to use new evidence to request a case review, the mechanism that had returned Pollycarpus to prison. However, it seemed to Usman that police and prosecutors had stopped looking for new evidence. He was most likely correct. One police investigator remembered a clear message from the top to halt the investigation after the Muchdi verdict. "Word came down from SBY, through my bosses, that jailing the operator was enough," he recalled. "We were done."[5]

A few weeks after the failed appeal, Suci and Usman crossed the length of Java in a small caravan of cars. The idea for a trip to East Java emerged during an alarming presidential campaign season. In a first round of voting in July, President Yudhoyono's reelection would be challenged by the president he'd unseated, Megawati, and by his own vice-president, a tycoon named Jusuf Kalla. To Suci and Usman' s dismay, all three tickets looked to Suharto-era military men to boost their electoral prospects.

The incumbent was a retired general, of course. Megawati was not only still close to Hendropriyono, but had selected as her running mate none other than Prabowo Subianto, onetime Kopassus commander and Suharto's former son-in-law.[6] On the third ticket, Jusuf Kalla had chosen the retired four-star general Wiranto. The last head of the armed forces under Suharto, Wiranto still occupied that position at the time of the scorched-earth campaign in East Timor in 1999, a crime against humanity for which he was indicted by a UN-backed court in that country. None of the tickets would be good for the Munir case or any other unresolved human rights violations. In a debate, all three candidates agreed that it was time to move on from the past, focusing on forgiveness and reconciliation over accountability.

In Giuseppe di Lampedusa's novel *The Leopard*, a member of the Sicilian nobility in a unified Italy realizes, "If we want things to stay the same, everything must change." The Indonesian elite made the same calculation. They accepted the procedural democracy of free elections and peaceful transitions, as long as everything else could stay the same: criminality, corruption and impunity. Efforts to secure the rule of law stalled or moved backwards. The retired generals—Wiranto, Prabowo, Yudhoyono—formed or joined parties as vehicles for their political ambitions. The menace of communism, the need for stability, and other Suharto-era justifications for repression lost some of their power, but were supplanted by the imperative to protect the nation from those within and abroad who sought to break it apart.

Suci and Usman saw the despair of the mothers of young men disappeared at the hands Prabowo's soldiers or shot dead at protests while Wiranto commanded the military. As an alternative to sitting home and watching these men in sunny, slick campaign commercials, they headed east. The group included Tuti Koto, whose son disappeared one day in 1997, as well as Sumarsih, the *kamisan* founder whose son Wawan was killed at Semanggi I. The daughter of a man who disappeared during the 1984 Tanjung Priok massacre at Jakarta's harbor joined, too, among others.

They set off across Java to speak out about their cases and meet with other victims. The group drove up the slopes of Mount Arjuno and wended their way through the twisted trees to Munir's grave. Sitting on the dry soil, Tuti Koto embraced the simple headstone and keened for the man she had inspired to found KontraS, and who gave her hope in return. Hearing the old woman's cries, Suci had a sense of falling. She felt a hole deep in her heart.

They descended to Malang to visit the father of Bimo Petrus. The underground courier had disappeared just weeks before Suharto fell, when the Kopassus kidnapping squad was already under Muchdi's command. In the young man's old room, much as he'd left it more than a decade before, his father showed off cartoons his son had drawn and read from his last letters home.

They drove north to Porong on the outskirts of Surabaya. There they ascended a levee holding back a vast sea of mud, its gray surface broken here and there by a few rusted zinc rooftops and dead trees. Three years before, natural gas drilling was believed to have caused an unrelenting geyser of mud. By 2009, levees protected the railway and nearby towns, but the "mud volcano" was not expected to exhaust itself for another twenty years. The lake might remain a geological feature of the land for centuries.

To avoid liability, the gas company reincorporated offshore and blamed the disaster on an earthquake in a neighboring province. Displaced villagers scraped together a livelihood by offering tourists motorbike tours, DVDs with mudflow footage, and salt made from the sudden inland sea that had submerged their fields, homes, and cemeteries. Suci and her traveling companions shared their encounters with impunity with the displaced villagers in their makeshift homes of plywood and thatch.

Not far from the levee, Suci, Sumarsih, and a few others stopped at an unofficial tourist site known as Tugu Marsinah. A *tugu* is a monument, but in this case it was simply a cement entrance marker outside a complex of worker housing. In 1993, the young factory worker Marsinah was last seen alive at this spot, saying goodnight to her friends under a mango tree. Marsinah had been killed for winning a twenty-five cent per day raise at her watch factory, which now lay submerged beneath the mud.

Suci and the others posed for a photo next to the *tugu*. They opened their black *kamisan* umbrellas against the bright sun, revealing the white block letters reading TRISAKTI, SEMANGGI, MARSINAH, MUNIR.

Next, the convoy crossed a multi-colored suspension bridge, opened weeks before, to the island of Madura in search of beef satay. By the roadside they spotted an old man in a white dress shirt and a plaid sarong tending to the coconut shell charcoal grill on his cart. He cooked up their large order, and the group ate the skewers of meat, laughing in the bright sunshine.

A few days later, on election day, Suci and Usman published an opinion piece in the *Jakarta Post*, datelined Porong, the muddy new lakeshore that Marsinah once called home. For the families on their tour, they explained, "The past is something we live with every day. And so it is for the rest of Indonesia." Suci and Usman never endorsed candidates, but they could not ignore the fact that two men linked to grave human rights abuses, Wiranto and Prabowo, were contenders for vice-president. They wrote, "It is unlikely that such figures would be credible candidates for a national office in a country that had made full and accurate accounting of the past."[7]

President Yudhoyono won a resounding victory that day. Usman and Suci had little faith left in this president to address the past, but were relieved that Prabowo and Wiranto failed to return to the apex of power. And there was always the chance that Yudhoyono would use the freedom of a second term to seek progress in the Munir case.

The president did not advance the case in his second term, however. In 2011 his attorney general stated that the courts had already resolved the case against Muchdi with permanent legal force.[8] Kasum demanded a meeting to argue that new evidence justified a case review. They cited facts contradicting Muchdi's alibi that he was in Malaysia when Munir died.[9] They also asserted that police had a recording of a call between Muchdi and Pollycarpus but never shared it at trial.[10] The attorney general was not swayed.

By 2013 the only active criminal case was Polly's. This time it was the defendant who requested a case review in a bid to overturn his conviction for a second time.[11] The Supreme Court did not do so, but did reduce his sentence back from twenty years in prison to the original fourteen. With sentence reductions for good behavior, Pollycarpus would be free soon.

A television show phoned Suci live for her reaction to the decision, and she began with a sad and tired air. Her words slowly picked up speed and vehemence as she described her loss of faith in the police, the prosecutors, and the courts. The unsolved murder was not just a blow to those who had lost Munir as husband, father, or brother, she said. It was a source of shame for the nation.

Suci with Alif and Diva on a visit to Bali in 2011. (Matt Easton)

Not long before Munir died, the couple had bought a house in his home-town with some of the prize money from the Right Livelihood Award. They had planned to move to Batu once Munir's work seemed less urgent. There would be time to read and write. Maybe he'd try farming the vol-canic soil, the small-scale trading of his youth, or opening a modest legal aid office.

In early 2011 Suci and the kids moved into the Batu house. She still took part in advocacy and legal actions from there and joined *kamisan* protests on her frequent visits to Jakarta, but the move gave her and the kids some space and normalcy. They lived in Batu for a couple of years, before mov-ing down to Malang, closer to Suci's extended family.

On December 8, 2013, Munir's birthday, Suci invited seventy-five peo-ple to Batu and five hundred came, crowding into the little house to cel-ebrate the opening of a small museum and human rights center. Omah Munir, Javanese for Munir House, had exhibits on the issues and cases Munir worked on. Some of his belongings were on display too, such as the desk he slept on at LBH Surabaya, his leather jacket for riding his motor-bike home, the bulletproof vest he'd urged Usman to wear, and his library of books on history, sociology, Gandhi, and Martin Luther King Jr. The museum hosted discussions, concerts, and art exhibitions, and welcomed a small but steady stream of visitors between events.

Yudhoyono's second and final term would end in 2014. Prabowo had spent the last few years deploying his family's wealth, along with appeals to nationalist and authoritarian strains in the electorate, to build his party enough to give him a shot at the presidency. Prabowo's leading rival was Joko Widodo, the popular mayor of Jakarta. Known as Jokowi, he was a former furniture maker from Solo in Central Java. A civilian from a younger generation, Jokowi was compared to Barack Obama, a man of the same age and modest background. They even bore a slight resemblance to each other.

Jokowi pledged to address past human rights violations, with a commit-ment that seemed genuine. In one interview, he spoke about the poet Wiji Thukul, who numbered among the disappeared activists from 1998. Wiji Thukul had worked in a furniture factory near the sultan's palace in Solo, and Jokowi said he knew his wife and children, and his poetry too. "He must be found," the candidate said. "He can be found, whether alive or dead. It's impossible thirteen people can't be found, with no explanation."

In contrast, Prabowo defended the abductions in a debate. "When we come across groups of people who build bombs, riot, and threaten the safety of the country, threaten the country, because of that it is the duty of officers to prevent these threats from spilling blood," he said. "My conscience is clean."

Muchdi's lawyers had argued there was no evidence the secretive honor board ever investigated or punished him in 1998, and thus no revenge motive could be proven. But in June 2014, a few days before a presidential debate, someone leaked the four-page recommendation on Prabowo that the body made to the head of the armed forces.[12] The board had indeed recommended his dismissal from military service.[13] That document didn't mention Muchdi, but did confirm reporting about the honor board's decision, making it likely Muchdi had been similarly punished as reported at the time.

Jokowi won with a narrow majority, and human rights activists breathed a sigh of relief. Suci had once found reason to hope in Jokowi's campaign promises, but her concerns quickly grew. Jokowi had called her during the campaign, presumably seeking support. She'd asked him why she saw him at a televised event sitting next to Hendropriyono. Sounding uncomfortable, Jokowi explained he'd been invited and seated next to Hendropriyono. What was the problem?

Once elected, Jokowi announced his transition team, Indonesia's first. Presumably with encouragement from Megawati as head of his party, Jokowi named Hendropriyono as a top advisor.[14] When he took office in October, Jokowi also made it clear that his almost singular focus would be infrastructure and the economy. Several weeks later, Pollycarpus was released from prison after serving eight years of his fourteen-year term. He'd received regular sentence remissions to mark holidays and for his work with Boy Scouts while in prison.

To spur Jokowi to act on past crimes, in November 2014 the National Human Rights Commission took the unusual step of releasing their findings on seven major human rights cases. Most were inscribed on the *kamisan* umbrellas: massacres of 1965, the mysterious Petrus killings of alleged habitual criminals in the 1980s, the Tanjung Priok incident of 1984, the 1989 Talangsari massacre by Hendropriyono's troops, the disappearances of 1997–98 by soldiers under the command of Prabowo and Muchdi, the student shootings at Trisakti and Semanggi under Wiranto's command, and two incidents in Papua known as Wasior and Wamena.[15] For most of these cases, Jokowi could create a human rights court with a decree and some pressure on his coalition in parliament. But Jokowi would say only that the government was still looking for the wisest path to address these cases, stressing the importance of reconciliation.

Over seven years, *kamisan* protests had never missed a week. Attendance never dropped to just the three founders, their threshold to end the protests, though some Thursdays in the first few years came close. Over time, however, *kamisan* began to attract a larger, young crowd with concerts, art, and speeches. Each speaker ended with a ringing call-and-response:

Long live
Victims!
Don't be silent
Resist!
Jokowi!
Wipe out impunity!

The word "resist," or *lawan*, evokes a famous line from a poem by Wiji Thukul: "There is only one word: resist!" The appeal to Jokowi was the idea of Sumarsih, who still hoped he would act on these past cases. Suci no longer thought there was any point in appealing to him. She refused to meet with Jokowi, and turned down a presidential visit to Omah Munir.

Despite Suci's lack of faith in Indonesia's leadership, she never stopped seeking levers to spur state action on the case. In 2011 Suci had appealed to a new body called the Central Information Commission (Komisi Informasi Pusat, or KIP) in search of the As'ad letter. The letter, requesting the head of Garuda assign Polly to a security role, had only ever been found on Muchdi's hard drive. Suci also asked for Muchdi's alleged orders to travel to Malaysia in September 2004, the alibi that judges had cited in their verdict. In both cases, the commissioners accepted BIN's claim that there was no such document on file. In the latter case, the absence of the document served to undermine Muchdi's alibi.[16]

In 2016 Suci and KontraS decided to seek another document. Eleven years after the TPF disbanded, the government had never released its final report. Copies had surfaced online, but the public had never seen a complete, official copy of the findings and recommendations, including the call to investigate Hendropriyono, As'ad, and others.

KontraS first asked the State Secretariat, the agency responsible for handling state documents, to release the report. The agency replied that it didn't have the document and didn't know where it was. The six bound copies that Usman, Asmara, Marsudhi and the rest of the team had painstakingly produced, in the face of threats, secrecy, lies, and deadlines, had disappeared.

Shocked by this claim, lawyers from KontraS went back to the information commission. Usman and Hendardi testified about the handover of the report to the president, and submitted news coverage of the event. KontraS argued that the Secretariat was responsible for preserving the report, and its loss was an act of negligence. The Secretariat argued that it had nothing to do with human rights investigations. What's more, their logbook showed that the president never gave them the report, and they had no authority to release it even if he had.

When the commission announced its decision, the room rang with cheers from Munir's friends and colleagues holding up paper masks of his face. The body sided with KontraS and Suci, ordering the State Secretariat to release the report within two weeks.[17] Jokowi directed the attorney general to investigate the loss of the report *and* to track down new evidence in order to act on the case.[18] It was the strongest high-level statement in years. A prosecutor told Usman he was preparing new evidence and waiting for a direct order to move ahead.[19]

But the attorney general's office never followed up on the president's directive. They said they would just ask former TPF members for unofficial copies of the report, with no mention of investigating its disappearance, let alone seeking new evidence.[20] Investigation was the job of the police, they said, and only if the police submitted new information would prosecutors act on it.[21]

Although the information commission had said its decision was not open to appeal, the Secretariat nonetheless brought the matter to an administrative court known as the PTUN.[22] This body ruled quickly in February 2017, taking Suci by surprise. Without hearings or witnesses, the court ruled that the TPF report was not a public document and the Secretariat had no obligation to release it. A legal expert affiliated with KontraS described the ruling as an absurd and terrible precedent, made on a very narrow procedural basis.[23] Many observers didn't even understand why the court had jurisdiction.[24]

The Supreme Court later agreed that the State Secretariat didn't have to disclose the report because it never received it. Suci felt this decision legalized the hiding or even destruction of the TPF report.[25]

September 7, 2017, the thirteenth anniversary of Munir's death, fell on a Thursday that marked the 505th weekly *kamisan*.[26] A large audience listened to poetry, music, and drama, wearing shirts that read, MUNIR IS STILL HERE, AND MULTIPLYING. In the palace, across the busy road, a top presidential staffer parried questions about the cases from the past. He announced that President Jokowi had asked the coordinating minister for political, legal and security affairs to take the lead on addressing six major human rights cases, including the murder of Munir.[27] That minister was General Wiranto, a man credibly linked to numerous human rights violations before and after Suharto's fall. For many observers, the moment Wiranto was given this human rights portfolio, it became unmistakably clear that Jokowi would never try to uncover crimes of the past.[28]

Jokowi's reluctance to address the past posed a major obstacle to resolving the Munir case. A police investigator told Indra, "We're ready to act, but not without an order from Jokowi." A prosecutor made similar comments to Usman. According to Marsudhi, former head of both the TPF and the police investigation, the murder of Munir was never a strictly criminal matter. "This is a political case," he explained, "about the abuse of power."[29]

Alongside the political dimension of the case was the influence and corruption that plagues the judicial system in Indonesia. "You have to see the courts as part of the system of criminal activity," Munir once said. "Those who free the perpetrators are part of the system of power."[30] Judicial independence has improved since the Suharto years, but corruption and incompetence remains systemic. The courts remain so plagued by influence-peddling and other corruption that a commission was formed to map out the problem of the "judicial mafia," a network of graft that includes police, prosecutors, lawyers, appeals court clerks, judges, and prison officials. For a fee, court officials can modify charges, arrange for favorable judges, falsify verdicts, terminate cases, secure health waivers, or deliver sentences that can never be carried out.[31] Considering the number of trials and appeals and the pervasive corruption in the courts, it would be unusual if bribes had not been offered, solicited, or paid in the Munir case.

One more point of pressure could have been used to avoid accountability. Many of those who worked the hardest on the Munir case found their careers stalled, or worse. Marsudhi was never promoted again beyond his one star, and he eventually retired. Other police investigators have been stuck in a mid-level rank when they might have risen to police general. The prosecutor Cyrus Sinaga was jailed in a corruption scandal that also implicated the former number-two investigator on the Munir police team. The accusations were not necessarily manufactured, but Usman and others think the two were treated more harshly or were more closely monitored for an opportunity to punish them.

Not everyone has seen their careers suffer. TPF member Retno Marsudi became minister of foreign affairs under Jokowi, and Bambang Hendarso Danuri, despite his energetic investigation as head of the Criminal Investigation Division, became national chief of police. One of his former top investigators, Arief Sulistyanto, by 2018 had risen to become head of the CID. According to Sulistyanto, the Munir case didn't need to be reopened, because it was never closed. The investigation could proceed anytime new evidence came to light.[32]

A decade after Muchdi's acquittal, what evidence might still emerge? Usman and Suci still believed that a thorough investigation might answer questions that went beyond the matter of Muchdi's guilt. How many people were involved in the field operation to kill Munir? Despite his denials, an eyewitness swore she saw the singer Ongen sitting with Pollycarpus and Munir in the Coffee Bean. Some in the Kasum team found it suspicious that Dr. Tarmizi administered a sedative and an antiemetic, which stopped Munir from vomiting up the poison, and did not suggest an emergency landing.

The role of the BIN agent Bambang Irawan has never been confirmed. A medical doctor, there were early reports that he was on Munir's flight under a fake name, returning from Singapore a few days later. There was also the Dutch-Indonesian couple, the husband, a chemical engineer, sitting next to Munir and the wife sitting next to Pollycarpus. The husband was seen helping the doctor give Munir medicine, while a news report said the wife passed a bottle of water to her husband to give to Munir to drink after he felt sick.[33] The police cleared the couple after an interview, but suspicions lingered.

Usman believed the operation might have been carefully planned to ensure full control of the environment. Munir was a big fish, Polly had supposedly said. They would want a big net, planting people around Munir in business and economy classes and in the airport. The massive amount of arsenic in Munir's system could be explained by multiple poisonings, in case any one of them failed.

Marsudhi once compared his job to assembling a mosaic from pieces of evidence. One missing piece was the rumored recording of a conversation between Muchdi and Pollycarpus, perhaps even an order to carry out the crime. Such a command was first rumored to have been recovered from Polly's phones by the FBI. A U.S. Embassy cable seemed to indicate something of value *was* recovered by the FBI: "Promising new evidence from the U.S. laboratories on key cell phones in the case should give prosecutors a stronger hand." Several participants at a meeting with the CID director Hendarso clearly remember him saying a terse order was recovered, something like "Do it." But Hendarso later denied making such a claim.[34]

However, in recent interviews, two Indonesian police investigators affirmed that the FBI never found anything of value.[35] In response to a series of Freedom of Information Act requests, the FBI located relevant documents, but withheld all but three of the forty-eight pages to protect privacy or investigation methods. The remaining three pages, redacted of all useful content, indicated evidence was collected from five sources, presumably cell phones belonging to Pollycarpus. The withheld forty-five pages might resolve the mystery of the missing order, reveal other text messages or calls of interest, or hold nothing not already known from the phone records presented at trial.

In 2011, a deputy attorney general confirmed that there *was* a recording of Muchdi and Polly, but that it was not enough to trigger a case review.[36] However, even if this recording did not discuss the murder, such a recording might be proof of perjury to conceal a criminal plot, as the two denied ever speaking to each other.[37]

Witness tampering is another area to investigate. The BIN agents who changed their accounts to police or simply failed to appear in court— Ucok, Kawan, Sentot, and Budi Santoso—could be questioned again, as could prosecutors who were reportedly threatened to the point of requiring armed guards and personal firearms. The witness protection board, still new at the time of the Muchdi trial, is now well-established. Offered protection, former witnesses, police, and prosecutors might talk about the intimidation they faced.

The missing agent Budi Santoso supposedly sent two letters withdrawing his statements to police. Six years after the trial, *Tempo* reported that at least the first was fake.[38] The magazine reported that when the letter surfaced, Budi panicked and contacted the police. Reporters viewed video of Budi telling investigators during the questioning that followed, "That letter was an effort to force me to return to Indonesia. . . . I'll be killed when I come home, so that the Munir case is pinned on me."[39] One of his interrogators confirmed that Santoso was afraid of being killed and blamed for the crime. After thirty years at BIN, the agent had many friends at the agency warning him that he was in danger. The whereabouts of Budi Santoso remain unknown. In 2019, a former BIN agent said it would be dangerous for him to even ask around about Santoso.[40]

Santoso's fear might be amplified by a number of suspicious incidents since the Muchdi trial concluded. In April 2012, the long-haired singer Ongen spoke at a church service in Jakarta about his experience as a witness in the Munir case. He did not admit any role in the plot, but congregants were still surprised to hear him speak publicly about the matter after his long silence. He told a member of the congregation that he was considering writing a book.[41]

A few weeks later, on May 3, 2012, Ongen was driving home after shopping with his wife and a daughter. After getting into an argument with another driver at a red light in South Jakarta, Ongen and the other man got out of their cars and confronted each other, until Ongen's wife and daughter pulled him away. During the confrontation, the other driver, who claimed to be in the military, splashed him with a water bottle.[42] Moments after Ongen resumed his drive home, he became short of breath and pulled the handbrake. The family was on their way to a hospital when Ongen died.[43] The death was ruled a heart attack. Ongen had no history of heart disease, and no autopsy was performed.

Four others with looser ties to the case are said to have died under mysterious circumstances: a flight attendant, the priest present at Ongen's questioning, a court clerk, and the BIN deputy who met with Suci in late 2004.[44] In the absence of credible investigations and trials, such questions, rumors, and accusations hang in the air like smoke from a distant fire.

Above all, amid this speculation, remains the question of the *dalangs*, the masterminds of the murder plot. Marsudhi, former head of the TPF, told a radio interviewer in 2017 there were leads from the TPF investigation that could still be followed up. Prosecutors have the authority to continue the legal process, and he could not understand why they didn't use it. Asked who had caught the TPF's attention besides Muchdi and As'ad, Marsudhi seemed to think for a moment:

> Who else? I've forgotten. At that time we wanted to summon
> Hendropriyono because he was the leader. However as a leader
> he must know, or he might know, the actions of his subordi-
> nates. Because I thought it would be impossible for them to act

on their own. Of course they act under orders. That's why we called Hendropriyono several times, but he refused to appear.[45]

Marsudhi's assessment is supported by the leaked documents that implicate Hendropriyono in the planning of Munir's murder, along with Muchdi and two other BIN deputies. It seems likely that the agency's director would be aware of a politically sensitive plot seemingly involving the heads of three different divisions. And while never cited in court, a journalist who viewed a tape of the agent Budi Santoso's interrogation reported his description of a meeting in which Hendropriyono claimed Munir intended to "sell" Indonesia abroad and had to be stopped.

Hendropriyono has, in a way, acknowledged his responsibility as head of BIN at the time of Munir's murder. One night in October 2014, an American journalist named Allan Nairn interviewed Hendropriyono in the general's mansion. Part of the interview was about the 1989 attack by Hendropriyono's soldiers on a Muslim community in Talangsari. The general told Nairn that the hundred or more victims had set their own huts on fire as an act of suicide. Nairn asked if he would be willing to make that case in a court. After some hedging, Hendropriyono at last replied, "And you know, I feel, I have children, I have family, and I can feel how they feel. So to me, I'm responsible for everything that I did and there is nothing that I will refuse. I understand what you mean. If there is a court for me for human rights violations, I will accept."

When families of the dead in Talangsari filed a defamation complaint against Hendropriyono for the allegation of suicide, Nairn spoke to police as a witness and released some audio. He also told the press Hendropriyono was willing to appear in court for Talangsari, the murder of Munir, and the violence in East Timor in 1999.[46] It should be noted that Hendropriyono made that offer with the knowledge that being called before a court was extremely unlikely. And asked by *Tempo* magazine about his willingness to accept responsibility for Munir's murder, he said, "If the person who killed Munir was a BIN person, I have moral responsibility, not command responsibility. Command responsibility lies only in a war situation: if my men kill, I will be directly responsible. In a peacetime situation, if my men kill people while I am sleeping, should I be responsible?"[47]

Hendro seemed concerned about Munir's family's view of him. "Regarding Munir, what I am very concerned about before I die is that I wanted his family to understand that if Munir was killed, it wasn't me who killed him. The one who ordered it was also not me," he said in a 2016 interview. "Honestly, I am personally very sad, and I really want to help, to approach Munir's family, because I sympathize."

Interestingly, a kind of middleman known as a *makelar kasus*, or case broker, once contacted one of Munir's relatives to say that someone wanted to pay *islah*, compensation for Munir's death. He agreed, but only if the payment was in person and accompanied by an admission of guilt. The offer was withdrawn, and Munir's brother never learned who the offer was from. Hendropriyono, using wealth from his successful law and consulting practice, is believed to have made substantial *islah* payments to families of the victims of the Talangsari massacre to encourage them to drop demands for accountability. He had also offered a cash gift to a furious Asmara Nababan when the National Human Rights Commission was considering the Talangsari case.

Hendropriyono continued to be an advisor to Jokowi. Just as important to his power and prestige, his son-in-law was a rising star in the military, with a series of rapid promotions to four-star general. In November 2021, his son-in-law became Indonesia's military commander.

As for Muchdi, after his acquittal he became active again in Prabowo's Gerindra Party, as well as his philanthropic, martial arts, and religious organizations. He was in the news again in March 2011. *Al Jazeera* reported that retired generals were supporting hardline Muslim groups to incite religious violence and undermine President Yudhoyono. Muchdi, one of those named in the report, acknowledged only being in touch with all kinds of Muslim groups, including more radical ones. One security sector reform expert, a former member of Munir's staff at KontraS, explained, "The aim is to topple Yudhoyono through de-legitimization of his rule, to show that civilian-controlled government is failing and that we should go back to military rule."[48]

Muchdi left Prabowo's party in 2011 to join the older Muslim party, PPP, quickly announcing a run for a leadership position. The plan ended in lawsuits and accusations, and Muchdi moved to Berkarya, the party of

President Suharto's son Tommy.[49] When the party threw its weight behind Prabowo for the 2019 elections, Muchdi made a surprising announcement of support for Jokowi over his former patron and comrade-in-arms. Muchdi then tried to wrest control of the party from Tommy Suharto, with both men claiming their faction was the true party.[50]

As Jokowi faced off against Prabowo in 2019, the matter of the disappearances again returned to the fore. During campaign season five years earlier, someone had leaked the honor board's recommendation to dismiss Prabowo. This time, an online video showed a former honor board member speaking at a recent private event. Agum Gumelar, a retired senior general, Jokowi supporter, and former Kopassus commander, said he'd had "heart-to-heart" talks with the members of the abduction team when they were facing court martial in 1999. "And from this," he said, "I know of the death of those people, and where they were disposed of. I know the truth."[51] There had been rumors over the years of bodies buried under a toll road, and unidentified remains had turned up in the Pulau Seribu Islands near Jakarta, but the fate of the missing thirteen activists remained a mystery. But Gumelar's comments, perhaps meant to undermine Prabowo by reminding voters of his past, once again led nowhere.[52]

Jokowi won another narrow majority, requiring no further rounds of voting, but Prabowo did not concede, alleging fraud. His supporters set fire to a police dormitory and vehicles, leaving six dead and hundreds injured. Some of those linked to the violence were old members of Team Mawar, the abduction squad Prabowo commanded two decades before.[53] Prabowo also challenged the results in court, but lost quickly.

Just a few months later, Jokowi appointed Prabowo as his minister of defense.[54] Prabowo then chose as his special assistant the onetime colonel, Chairawan, the third officer to go before the honor board. Two more Team Mawar alumni were later named to strategic posts in the Defense Ministry. Both had been convicted at the court martial, one dishonorably discharged. However, they had appealed their sentences, a process not made public, and over time both men had been promoted to brigadier general.[55] With Wiranto as chief security minister, Prabowo at Defense, and Hendropriyono as a presidential advisor, Usman joked that it made him feel young again to see all the same faces from when he was a student in 1998.

By 2019, the *kamisan* protest had been under way for a dozen years without missing a week. Famous musicians and actors drew a young crowd of students and activists. *Kamisan* protests began in Bandung and Malang, before sprouting up in twenty cities. What started as a tactic to put pressure on the president had become a way to remember the victims in photos, music, theater, and art, and to produce a modicum of accountability by naming perpetrators still comfortably enjoying public life. One *kamisan* regular, the father of a victim of the shootings at Semanggi, always rode in on a souped-up motorbike bedecked with a hand-carved wooden sign reading, WIRANTO, YOU HAVE RUINED MY LIFE. White words painted onto his cherry red helmet read, I SEEK JUSTICE.

The six hundredth *kamisan* took place on September 5, 2019, two days before the anniversary of Munir's death. An empty lectern sporting the national seal mocked Jokowi for his absence from the struggle for human rights. Glass and metal boxes, which normally held the *krupuk* shrimp crackers found at every food stall, were artfully redeployed as stackable frames, forming walls of photos from past protests and cases. Billowing black banners hung high in the air like spinnakers, displaying quotes from figures in the Munir case. Stickers were handed out bearing cartoon portraits of Marsinah, the poet Wiji Thukul, Munir, and even *kamisan* cofounder Sumarsih, standing nearby.

There was a stage for speeches and one for music. At the first, Bivitri Susanti, a lawyer and activist of Usman's generation, spoke to the growing crowd. "Justice must be fought for. Nothing is given freely by this country," she said. "Six hundred times we were here, six hundred Thursdays we shouted about justice, but what do we see?"

At the music stage, Cholil Mahmud, the lead singer of the band Efek Rumah Kaca, spoke about *teror*'s persistent, changing forms, from Munir's murder to the 2017 acid attack that blinded a corruption investigator named Novel Baswedan in one eye.[56] The performer's words were backed by a rhythmic beat of both percussion and voice. On his shirt, a caricature of Munir was all mustache and broad smile, reminiscent of the snapshots of the airport goodbye thirteen years before. Cholil led a chant of "We will never stop!" before stepping back to join twenty singers in black to perform a haunting a cappella version of Cholil's hit song about Munir, "Di Udara," or "In the Air." The lyrics include:

> *I could drown in the ocean.*
> *I could be poisoned in the air.*
> *I could be killed on the pavement.*
> *But I will never die.*
> *I will never stop.*[57]

While setting up, Bivitri had noticed counterprotestors without concern, assuming they were paid by the day. Later, she saw a man near his parked car, handing out materials and giving instructions. It occurred to Bivitri that he wanted to be seen and, looking closer, she recognized Pollycarpus.

Each person or place on the black umbrellas of *kamisan* comes with an anniversary, ignored by the state but marked by families. The night before the twenty-first anniversary of the Semanggi I shootings, Usman went to a new art and music venue in a gently restored Art Deco factory compound that once proudly printed currency for a new nation. The "creative complex," was so new that the marquee still announced the opening night show by Glenn Fredly. The pop star happened to be a supporter of the *kamisan* protests, and his late uncle Ongen had once seemed likely to be a star witness in the Munir case.

The walls of a small gallery in the complex were covered in large comic book–style illustrations of the bloody events of Semanggi I, when security forces fired on protestors in September 1999. In the display cases lay handwritten poetry, childhood photos, and other belongings of Wawan, Sumarsih's son. A mannequin displayed the shirt Wawan was wearing when he was killed. A single bullet hole in the fabric was framed by a faint red halo. Wawan's father explained that the ring of blood was clearer before a maid mistakenly washed the shirt. He took a long bullet from his pocket to demonstrate the angle at which a similar one had pierced the shirt, and then Wawan's heart and lungs, as he came to the aid of an injured protestor exactly twenty-one years before.

Next to the gallery was a small room with speakers set up. The original plan had been for Usman, now the founding director of Amnesty International's Indonesia office, to speak before a musician played. When the performer had canceled, Usman offered to play something himself. He thought people were tired of hearing him talk. His first idea was to craft a song from a letter Sumarsih wrote to her son after his death. But the letter worked best as a letter, to be read out simply and without music. One of Wawan's poems would make a better song.

In advance of the event, Usman recorded ideas for a song on his phone, picking out chords on a guitar if there was one nearby, as there usually was, or humming it if not. Usman lived in an apartment with his wife and two small children. His son was named in part for Wisanggeni, a fearless and blunt-spoken hero from the *wayang* stories who is cast into Candradimuka crater, only to be strengthened by its flames. In a tiny room in the apartment, Usman kept some guitars and drums next to stacks of CDs and books about John Lennon and the Rolling Stones. It wasn't as spacious as the studio he'd had at his mother's house as a teenager, but he could play around with song ideas there. As he worked with a friend to pull the ideas together into a song, it felt strangely easy, the quickest composition they'd ever done together.

Usman rehearsed a little with two singers he knew right before the event. The lead singer was used to playing in clubs and cafés, but this might have been his first song with a social message. The female vocalist was a late addition to the plan. Usman told them how the phrasing should go, and they made some last-minute changes together. They told Usman he should sing it himself, but he didn't want to hit a wrong note. He wanted the song to be just right for Wawan, and for Wawan's parents, seated with others on the floor in the crowded little room.

The song started with gentle melody, an effort to capture something of Wawan's disappointment:

> *For months I was gripped by fear, afraid of being tortured.*
> *For months I ran from a normal life,*

But the struggle, almost over, was destroyed.
Now reformasi *is just a mask for rulers.*

I still want to fight, but that cannot be.
Chasms on my left and right, stone walls before me and behind me.
I'm alone. Should I run out like the others?
Not yet, I still have my life, and that's my final sacrifice.
I want to be free . . .

Starting from the plucked melody and gentle vocals, Usman and the two singers slowly built to a furious wail of guitar and voice. Wawan's anger came out, and then a sense of the violence that killed him. From inside the parliament building, Usman had heard the gunfire as it went on and on, and would never forget how long and brutal it was. Usman strummed, fast and percussive, evoking the extended volley of bullets like the one that had pierced Wawan's T-shirt, hanging nearby.

Afterward, Usman sat outside on a curbstone in the dark with the two singers and friends. An air conditioner's steady drip formed a rill that ran toward them, glinting in the lights of the cafés and boutiques that occupied the old printing plant. Usman was quiet. He'd wanted to do something different for Wawan's parents, more symbolic and emotional than what he could put into a speech. He wasn't sure he could do that, but now he thought he might have succeeded. He'd felt Wawan with him in some supernatural way as the composition emerged so easily. During the performance, he nearly felt as if he *was* Wawan for that brief moment. At the very least, he had captured Wawan's anger. He felt almost transformed, something beyond his twenty years of the experience in human rights. Munir had always urged him not to be too much of a lawyer, or to allow himself to be caught up in the details of a case that might never be resolved in a courtroom. More importantly, Munir had also taught Usman that there are many ways to comfort and support survivors of grave crimes.

The intensity of these feelings began fading in the days that followed, as Usman returned to meetings in Jakarta and conference calls with London. His children had heard Usman play the song over and over before the show, and even made some suggestions. They kept singing it for a while afterwards. One morning Usman's daughter was sleeping so deeply that her mother couldn't wake her up, even with a shake. Usman got his guitar and played the opening melody. His daughter's eyes fluttered open.

A few days after Usman's performance, Suci picked her way around the motorbikes parked in a narrow alley in Bandung, West Java. She walked past a little *warung* with a sign offering *intel* for sale. The menu item was named for the first syllables of *indomie telor*, or instant noodles with egg (though more often the joke went in reverse, using the name of the dish to refer to an informer). Inside the glass display case there was also a portrait of Munir. This impromptu shadow box held some of Indonesia's favorite things: instant noodles, a play on words, a hero, a ghost.

The alley opened into a rubble-strewn clearing, the remnants of a half-demolished *kampung*. Most of the households had been forced out to make way for a planned project, their homes smashed to bits. A few had refused to move, and student activists who supported their right to remain in place or receive fair compensation had created an open-air headquarters among the ruins. The remaining walls were spangled with graffiti lit by colored tube lights affixed at all angles.

Munir's old friend and driver, Sugiarto, had driven Suci to Bandung along with Yati, the KontraS staffer and third founder of *kamisan* with Suci and Sumarsih. Seventeen years after Yati's first day as a volunteer, when she'd returned from monitoring the East Timor trials to find hired thugs had smashed the office to pieces, Yati had followed in the footsteps of Munir, and Usman after him, to become head of KontraS.

Amid the rubble in Bandung, the 2005 Australian documentary on the Munir case, *Garuda's Deadly Upgrade*, was playing on a screen. A driving soundtrack accompanied images of Pollycarpus and Muchdi, intercut with Usman explaining the suspicious Garuda documents. A small canteen sold tea and coffee in thin plastic cups to a crowd of students and young activists who waited expectantly. Floor tiles, perhaps a kitchen once, peered from a sea of broken bricks and roof tiles, all spattered with red mud after an earlier downpour. A shiny zinc roof covered the sound system for tonight's unusual event.

Eight students began to read. Potent monologues have been written and performed in the voices of Suci, Munir's killer, Marsinah, and others.

These performers were reading material that lacked the same artistry but had no less drama.

They took turns reading out the TPF report. For months now, young activists, many born after the fall of Suharto, had been reading out the report at public events around the country. Their goal was to reveal the truth and shame the government. If these young people could make the report public, why did the state lack all courage to do so?[58]

The detailed report had the full attention of more than a hundred people standing and sitting in the ruins. After the reading, Suci and Yati took the stage. Nearby rested several opened black umbrellas from Bandung's own *kamisan* protests. "Fifteen years," said Suci. "It's been hard. I'll be honest." Then she described a new initiative, an ambitious human rights museum named for Munir. Yati took care to explain what the TPF report was, and the reasons behind its mysterious disappearance: the suspects named in the report remained at the pinnacle of power, with money, status, and political influence.

More than an hour of questions from the audience followed. Suci appreciated the many questions that came from a place of knowledge of the case. She was tired of explaining, and felt refreshed by the energy of this young generation of activists. Soon came the call and response they all knew from the *kamisan* protests.

"Don't be silent!" Suci yelled, raising her fist in the air.

"Resist!" roared the crowd.

The word bounced off the jagged walls and into the night sky above.

Postscript

Kamisan has continued without a break, although the coronavirus pandemic forced it to move online. September 2021 marked the seventeenth anniversary of Munir's death, leaving one more year before the statute of limitations would run out on a capital crime. Kasum, revived a year earlier after a period of dormancy, pushed for the National Human Rights Commission to declare the Munir case a serious human rights violation rather than an ordinary crime, allowing an investigation by the commission and prosecution without any time limit. The commission was divided on whether the murder met the definition, although it might still make the determination at a later date, even after eighteen years had passed.[1] More than one hundred organizations and figures called on President Jokowi to ensure the case was resolved.

Pollycarpus never admitted to being a BIN agent or part of the plot to kill Munir.[2] At an interview at a café in 2018, a journalist asked if he would ever be willing to provide information to solve the case. Dressed in black with a red tie and sunglasses, he answered, "Reveal what? How? Go ahead and find new evidence, but don't ask me anymore." When the reporter persisted, he snapped, "Remember that I will curse you for seven generations if you accuse me. Do you dare? Many have died after I cursed them." He looked at the reporter and added, "Come on, respectfully, order a drink. It's safe. If you get an upset stomach, don't accuse me, okay?"[3] Pollycarpus contracted Covid-19 and died in October 2020.

In early 2021, construction finished on the Munir Museum of Human Rights in Batu. The city provided the land, building costs, and an annual budget, and the Omah Munir Foundation will manage the museum. Three floors of interactive exhibits will encompass the human rights movement in Indonesia. The contents of Omah Munir will move there, including Munir's old desk, his books, his bulletproof vest. But Suci has made it clear that it will not be a history museum.[4] There will be spaces for workshops and discussions, a library, and a theater. Even before it opened, the museum put many of Munir's papers in an online digital archive and created one of the most listened-to podcasts in the country.[5]

The museum is an expansion of Suci's efforts through Omah Munir to take some positive inspiration from Munir's life, not just sadness about how it ended. It is also a way to pursue progress in Indonesian society and culture outside the justice system that has failed her so far.[6] Pervasive impunity in Indonesia has forced survivors and advocates to turn to more local and unofficial ways to memorialize victims of state violence.[7] These survivors are taking control of transitional justice by necessity, while also realizing Munir's vision of putting them at the center of human rights work.

Munir's face still appears frequently on walls and highway pillars, in the form of posters and brightly painted graffiti. Alongside his face can be found calls to RESIST FORGETTING! or one of Munir's famous quotes, such as WE HAVE TIRED OF VIOLENCE. In 2020 an anthropologist wrote:

> Munir's face haunts the urban landscape, a silent reminder of the ideals of the Reformasi movement, of which he is the most visible hero. He appears on city walls as a kind of public conscience, a witness mutely reminding passersby that they move through a space of violence, injustice and forgetting.[8]

For Suci and for Usman, for Munir's friends and all of those he helped to search for justice, there is no forgetting. In 2019 an interviewer asked Suci if she was optimistic about finding the *dalangs* of Munir's murder. She replied, "If I wasn't optimistic, I would have given up already. I continue to kindle hope within myself." For how long? "Maybe until I die. This is a commitment. This is a choice."

Acknowledgments

Sam Gibson first suggested collaborating on a book and then encouraged me to take the concept forward myself. The committed agents Peter and Amy Bernstein were willing to take a chance on a topic unfamiliar to many readers, and patiently helped me rework the proposal and find the perfect home for it at The New Press.

Carl Bromley and Ben Woodward acquired the book and Ben has provided essential guidance on structure, content, and other decisions at every stage of the process. I also want to thank Emily Albarillo for her patient, rigorous management of the final editing process, and Gary Stimeling for his superb copy editing.

Many sources in Indonesia are named in the text or endnotes, including some of those most generous with their time and insights: Bivitri Susanti, Deddy Prihambudi, Hendardi, Indra Listiantara, Mugiyanto Sipin, Maria Sumarsih, Nezar Patria, Poengky Indiarti, Smita Notosusanto, Rachland Nashidik, Sugiarto, Yati Andriyani, and Munir's sister Annisa and his brother Rasyid. Others who provided me with essential context, and who are integral to the full story of Munir's work and the search for justice after his death, include Andreas Harsono, Chairul Anam, Indria Fernida, Haris Azhar, Mufti Makarim Al-Akhlaq, Edwin Partogi, Ifdhal Kasim, Alif Iman Nurlambang, Marsudhi Hanafi, Robertus Robet, Romo Sandyawan Sumardi, Aboeprijadi Santoso, Binny Buchori, Stanley Harsha, and many, many others. Gufron Mabruri and other friends at Imparsial and KontraS helped me locate dusty files and obsolete video cassettes. Lexy Rambadeta provided access to his video archive as well.

I also benefited greatly from insight and information from those who prefer to remain anonymous, including a small but helpful number of former members of the police investigation, BIN, and the prosecution teams. I hope that more members of these and related institutions will have the courage to speak about this case and its troubled course through the Indonesian justice system.

Sidney Jones, who first introduced me to human rights work and is a model for how to write about the subject with clarity and style, was beyond generous with her time and expertise as I finalized the manuscript. Other experts on Indonesia who answered questions and guided me to helpful sources include Jeffrey Winters, Ariel Heryanto, Robert Hefner, James Fox, and Margaret Scott.

Essential readers of the manuscript, and true friends, include Neil Carlson, Brendan Lorber, Galuh Wandita, Fred Rawski, Lila Cecil, and Kieran Dwyer. I'm also grateful for earlier feedback and advice from George Anderson, Keith Romer, Lesley Duval, Xujun Eberlein, Frank Kramer, Ann Marie Baldonado, and Patricia Materka. Ypie Boersma was a valuable source and a reader, as well as a great help in securing the release of official Dutch records.

A number of writers offered encouragement and advice by email or at workshops and conferences, including Peter Maass, Sebastian Junger, John Sedgwick, Evan Ratliff, Albert Samaha, and Taylor Plimpton. Jason Leopold and J. Patrick Brown gave me essential advice on FOIA requests, and Eugene Casey explained FBI terms and procedures. Robert Templer shared his insight on the political use of poisons, and Christian Brueckner helped me to understand the biochemistry.

I am grateful to Marto for use of the cover image. Thank you to Iwan Fals for permission to use lyrics from *Pulanglah* and to Cholil Mahmud for permission to quote from *Di Udara*. I encourage readers to find and listen to these two powerful songs about Munir. Thank you also to the families of Wiji Thukul and Norma Irmawan (Wawan) for allowing use of their poems.

One of the protagonists in this book is Indonesia itself, a country that has challenged, mystified, and delighted me over many years. While this book focuses on the violence and injustice found there, I hope that the warmth, spirit, and humor of Indonesia and its people come through as well. I feel a need to acknowledge Indonesia here as I would an old friend, and to thank those who helped me understand it and feel at home there from my earliest stays, including John MacDougall, Sabastian Saragih, Job Purba, and other friends in Malang, Jakarta, and Medan, as well as Timor-Leste.

On the home front, Madelon Gauthier has been the best partner a writer could hope for, every step of the way. She has offered advice from broad strategy to word choice, and the gift of time, to travel or to write, despite the extra burdens on her. This book might not have been started, and would surely never have been finished, without her.

Holly Gauthier and Stuart Deutsch also offered support and suggestions along the way and helped out with the even more important project of keeping first one and then two small children happy and safe in a difficult time. George and Anne Gauthier's interest and encouragement have been a constant as well.

My mother Paula was a helpful reader with an eye for clarity, suspense, and design. Together with my father, Bob, she brought me up in a household filled with a love of words and reading. I once told my daughter that her grandmother never forgot being told as a child that books were like friends. My daughter corrected me: books *are* friends.

A book must be written somewhere, and much of this one was researched, written, and edited at the Brooklyn Creative League, as well as at the Center for Fiction, the C-Scape Dune Shack, and the bars and coffee shops of Fort Greene, which allowed me to sit at their outside tables for long periods and in all kinds of weather.

Usman Hamid has been a good friend and a vital source for understanding human rights, music, and history in Indonesia. I met Suci a few months after Munir died. She has become a close friend and a source of inspiration as a parent and an activist. Both Usman and Suci were always willing to answer my questions and take me to locations freighted with memories. I would not have attempted this book without knowing I had their support to write about Munir's life, work, and death as fully and accurately as I know how. I came to this story as a human rights advocate rather than as a journalist, and cannot claim full objectivity. I have tried my best to ensure that these relationships and imperatives have not made the telling of this story any less accurate or reliable.

Notes

Prologue: A Red and Clouded Sky (2004)

1. This exchange and some details in chapter 6 about Schiphol Airport come from interviews with Poengky Indarti, Usman Hamid, and Suciwati, and from a September 5, 2014, KBR radio interview with Sri Rusminingtyas, at https://kbr .id/berita/09-2014/sri_rusminingtyas__/68750.html.

2. A KontraS staff member heard the news from a friend at Garuda and texted Usman: "*Mnr died on the journey to Amsterdam. His body is in police custody.*" Refusing to believe it, Usman asked a friend who had worked for the Dutch government to confirm the rumor. Poengky also received a call from an unidentified Garuda employee.

3. Suciwati, "Ceritaku: Aku dan Anak-anak Munir Tak Henti Menuntut," *Beritasatu*, March 27, 2012.

1: Suciwati (1990s)

1. See, for example, Geoffrey B. Robinson, *The Killing Season: A History of the Indonesian Massacres, 1965–66* (Princeton, NJ: Princeton University Press: 2018).

2. Eyewitness accounts of the army's role, as well as consistent patterns across locations, undermined the government line that the killings were the spontaneous response of outraged civilians. However, the lack of documented orders, investigations, or trials have long obscured the extent of the military role in the violence. Then, in 2015, researcher Jess Melvin walked out of an archive building in Aceh with a box of photocopies. Instead of the usual copies of already-public reports and propaganda, these papers meticulously documented the role of the military in initiating and carrying out the killings. Jess Melvin, "Documenting Genocide," *Inside Indonesia* 122: October–December 2015.

3. The killings were often carried out, as the *New York Times* reported, "with ritual forms of extreme cruelty." Seymour Topping, "Slaughter of Reds Gives Indonesia a Grim Legacy," *New York Times*, August 24, 1966. At the same time, Western press accounts often focused on the supposedly irrational savagery of the killers, rather than the political purpose, military planning, or American support behind the violence.

4. Robert Cribb, "Genocide in Indonesia, 1965–1966," *Journal of Genocide Research* 3, no. 2: 232.

5. Even before 1965, an alliance of Muslims, nationalists, and the military challenged communist land-reform campaigns, and the army began training Muslim youth in the countryside and the cities of Malang and Surabaya. Robert Hefner, *Civil Islam: Muslims and Democratization in Indonesia* (Princeton, NJ: Princeton University Press, 2000), 65–80.

6. One high school student in hiding along the Brantas saw his principal beheaded, followed by an old, one-eyed bicycle repairman from his village. Their heads were put in a sack, and their bodies floated past the boy as he lay hiding in the rushes. The student wandered around East Java. Once, a member of a killing squad asked him to help murder a man whose beautiful wife he wanted for himself. The husband was killed, but by then the wife had fled. Anonymous, "By the Banks of the Brantas," republished in Robert Cribb, "The Indonesian Massacres in Eyewitness Accounts" in Samuel Totten et al., *Century of Genocide: Eyewitness Accounts and Critical Views* (New York: Garland Publishing, 1990).

7. Although this document, known by the acronym *Supersemar*, was presumably written by the right-wing Suharto, the times required that even the destruction of the Communist Party have a revolutionary purpose: "For the sake of the security of the course of the anti-feudal, anti-capitalist and anti-Nekolim [neocolonial imperialist] revolution heading towards a just and prosperous society based on Pancasila, and on a Socialist Society for Indonesia, it is necessary to take swift, firm and determined action against the PKI." The original document has never been seen and is supposedly lost.

8. Heryanto, Ariel, "Where Communism Never Dies," *International Journal of Cultural Studies* 2 (1999): 147–177.

9. See James T. Siegel, *A New Criminal Type in Jakarta* (Durham: Duke University Press, 1998), 103–116; and David Bourchier, "Crime, Law, and State Authority in Indonesia," in Arief Budiman (ed.), *State and Civil Society in Indonesia* (Clayton, Victoria: Centre of Southeast Asian Studies, Monash University, 1990), 177–212.

10. Indonesians were encouraged to practice family planning by billboards and statues of small loving families. The policy was also enforced through exclusion from government jobs and aid programs for those with a third child. The government family-planning program was target-driven, even mobilizing the army to implant IUDs and other birth control devices. It was criticized for coercing women to accept contraception without informing them of its risks and effects.

11. The Madurese had been part of a massive project to shift people from the dense islands of Java, Bali, and Madura to the so-called Outer Islands, places like Borneo, Sumatra, and Irian Jaya, which shared an island with Papua New Guinea. There was more land there, though much of it was ecologically fragile or used by indigenous people. Every five or ten years, deadly conflict broke out on the island of Borneo between Madurese transmigrants and indigenous Dayaks. After each spate of burned villages, sporadic beheadings, and other violence, migrant families fled. With nothing to show for years of effort, and no land on Madura to return to, they settled in the poor fringes of small cities, places like Mergosono.

12. Ministry of Manpower Decree No. 342 of 1986 was revoked in January 1994, but the military could still intervene through its internal security body Bakorstanas or through its role in local government. See "The Limits of Openness: Human Rights in Indonesia and East Timor," Human Rights Watch/Asia, 1995. Restrictions on labor unions were intended to tamp down workers' demands, but they also reflected the government's association of unions with communism. All the same, as Munir observed in a 1994 paper, intervention in strikes long predates

the New Order. Examples include suppression of an 1881 strike of sugar workers in the Dutch East Indies, as well as Emergency Law No. 15 of 1951 on Resolving Labor Disputes, which states, "The development of the Indonesian state and society requires guarantees of security and order."

13. In 1980, fifty prominent figures raised their concern that the government was using Pancasila as a cudgel against opponents. Suharto only intensified his weaponization of the concept, while his fifty critics found themselves suddenly unable to travel, get a bank loan, or see their words in print.

14. The New Order's Trilogy of Development was stability, growth, and equity. In the factories, it turned out that the long sides of the triangle were rapid growth and political stability at any cost. An equitable share in the economy was often in conflict with a strategy that hinged on a large labor supply with no bargaining power for fair wages or working conditions.

15. Suci had organized just one protest before. In grade school, a boy in her class was graded unfairly on a test. She usually fought with the boy, but she rallied the whole class behind him, telling them, "This is a friend of yours, and it isn't right!" The class marched to the principal's office, shouting and banging on whatever they could find to make noise. The teacher was forced to fix the low grade.

16. A 1969 Manpower Law guaranteed the right to organize, but other laws, such as one on subversion, allowed the military and other officials to fire or jail labor activists. Since 1985, all unions had to be part of SPSI, both ensuring state control and creating yet another vehicle for Golkar's dominance. In the 1990s someone tried to create a truly independent union. A client of Munir's named Muchtar Pakpahan was prosecuted in a legal case that later served as a precedent for Munir's own murder case.

17. She prepped co-workers to negotiate, urging them to insist on a signed agreement. Waiting outside the factory, her heart sank to see their representatives emerge empty-handed. They'd secured a few small concessions, but nothing was in writing. Suci was trying to keep a low profile, but the workers crowded around her. "You go ahead, Icus," someone said. "You represent us." Her nickname was Suci backward, playful Malang slang. She went inside, got a written agreement, and revealed herself as the source of agitation. The next day, the manager invited her for a meal at a new eight-story business hotel projecting up from the Malang skyline. He offered her training, followed by promotion off the floor. When she turned it down, he fired her as a warning to the others.

18. LBH used the term "structural legal aid" to describe efforts to address the political and economic forces that keep people poor and their rights unprotected.

19. Suharto created the National Commission for Human Rights in 1993 in response to criticism of his human rights record. Despite its limited powers, the body's investigative and documentation role played an important role in uncovering and publicizing human rights violations.

2: Munir (1990s)

1. The research project was the first time Suci, twenty-five, had lived away from home. On her first visit home, after just a week or so, her father was shocked

to see she'd lost ten pounds. She decided to commute, leaving early each morning and returning on the last train to the turn-of-the-century Old City Station.

2. Law No. 5 of 1963, known as the Subversion Law, made it illegal to "distort, undermine or deviate from the ideology of Pancasila" or "disseminate feelings of hostility or arouse hostility, disturbances or anxiety among the population." The "hate-spreading laws" (Criminal Code Articles 154–156) criminalized "public expression of hate or insult to the government." The "lèse-majesté" laws (Criminal Code Articles, 134, 137(1), 207, 208) criminalized disrespect toward the president, vice-president, and other government officials. See "Academic Freedom in Indonesia: Dismantling Soeharto-Era Barriers," Human Rights Watch, 1998.

3. Meicky Shoreamanis Panggabean, *Keberanian Bernama Munir* (Bandung: Mizan, 2008), 108.

4. His younger brother recalled, "Munir couldn't stand to see something that was not right to him. He would face it, whatever the risk, even if he was outmatched." Ratrikala Bhre Aditya, dir., *Bunga di Bakar* (Institut Studi Arus Informasi et al, 2005).

5. The schism in HMI was due to Law No. 5 of 1985, which required every organization to make the state philosophy of Pancasila its basis, part of a strategy to bring all aspects of society into line with the state. In 1986, the HMI congress made this change, except for one faction that opposed any basis other than Islam and included many critics of the regime.

6. "Munir: Agama Harus Menjadi Maslahat bagi Manusia," interview reposted at islamlib.com/gagasan/pergulataniman/munir-agama-harus-menjadi-maslahat -bagi-manusia.

7. Personal communication.

8. For a comprehensive history of the 1965 killings as a blueprint for anticommunist mass violence and anti-communist killings around the world, see Vincent Bevins, *The Jakarta Method: Washington's Anticommunist Crusade and the Mass Murder Program That Shaped Our World* (New York: PublicAffairs, 2020).

9. Arief Budiman, "The Democratic Path to Socialism: Chile's Experience under Allende," PhD diss., Harvard University, 1980, published in Indonesian as *Jalan Demokratis ke Sosialisme: Pengalaman Chile di Bawah Allende* (Jakarta: Pustaka Sinar Harapan, 1987). The English version, and possibly the Indonesian, was published with the financial support of LBH founder Adnan Buyung Nasution. The volume was among the "dangerous materials" a court ordered to be destroyed in the 1990 conviction of a student activist named Bonar Tigor Naipospos for subversion, although it was available in bookstores.

10. Meicky Shoreamanis Panggabean, *Keberanian Bernama Munir* (Bandung: Mizan, 2008), 51–52.

11. Graha Budaya Indonesia, "Interview with Munir Said Thalib, June 25, 1999," YouTube video, https://www.youtube.com/watch?v=sZIQ2cKocBM.

12. "Mantan Pedagang Melawan Kekerasan," *Forum Keadilan*, August 24, 1998.

13. For a while, Munir both headed the Malang post and served as Surabaya's labor coordinator.

14. "Mantan Pedagang Melawan Kekerasan," *Forum Keadilan*, August 24, 1998.

15. David O'Shea, dir., *Garuda's Deadly Upgrade* (Thames Ditton, UK: Journeyman Pictures, 2005).

16. The episode showed Munir how thoroughly fear silenced victims, and how essential it was for someone to take a stand. Munir interview with Wimar Witoelar, *Perspektif Baru* 126, July 26, 1998. Munir was arrested as well around that time. When a plastics factory fired workers after they protested wages and conditions, Munir helped them sue the company. In April 1994, the Supreme Court handed these workers the first legal victory of its kind in Indonesia. The company appealed, and Munir went to discuss the case with his clients one night in August. He was arrested at about eleven p.m., taken to a local police station, questioned for two hours and released. "Urgent Action 316/94," Amnesty International, August 26, 1994, https://www.amnesty.org/download/Documents/184000/asa210391994en.pdf.

17. The raise would comply with a recent law setting a minimum wage of $1.08 in East Java.

18. The military was also embedded in the civilian bureaucracy. Active duty soldiers held thousands of powerful positions, at one point making up a majority of all governors and district heads.

19. Michelle Ford, "Beyond the Femina Fantasy: Female Industrial and Overseas Domestic Labour in Indonesian Discourses of Women's Work," *Review of Indonesian and Malaysian Affairs* 37, no. 2 (2003): 93.

20. Munir interview with Wimar Witoelar, *Perspektif Baru* 126, July 26, 1998.

21. Kekerasan Penyidikan Dalam Kasus Marsinah, YLBHI (Indonesian Legal Aid Foundation), December 1995.

22. Deddy Prihambudi, in Dandhy Laksono, dir., *Kiri Hijau Kanan Merah* (Watchdoc et al., 2009).

23. Once when they were *pacaran*, Munir asked her to wear a headscarf. *Jilbab* were less common than today, though most women in Munir's family wore headscarves. She asked him if it was important, and he replied, "No, but I'm Arab; I assumed my girlfriend, my wife, would wear one." She told Munir that she had chosen Islam herself, and if she ever wore a *jilbab* it would be her choice too. She told him about her concerns about people who made overt signs of piety but whose actions were not consistent. Religion was supposed to make things better, but she had heard from her father about 1965, and seen the Madurese flee to her neighborhood after violence along the coast of Borneo. Munir never mentioned the subject again. Interview with Suciwati and Sonya Ayu Kumala, "Pengungkapan Karakter Dalam Proposisi Analisis Wacana Naratif Seorang Aktivis" (Thesis, Universitas Indonesia, 2012).

24. Michael Shari, "A Smoke and Mirrors Act from Tutut? Suharto's Daughter Steps Back from Business—Sort Of," Bloomberg.com, November 3, 1997. A 1999 *Time Asia* story on the family's empire estimated her wealth at $700 million, part of a total of $15 billion Suharto and his six children still held on to even a year after the crash and his fall. John Colmen and David Liebhold, "The Family Firm," *Time Asia*, May 24, 1999.

25. Takeshi Kohno, "Emergence of Human Rights Activities in Authoritarian Indonesia: The Rise of Civil Society" (PhD Diss., Ohio State University, 2003).

26. A 2003 inquiry by the National Commission for Human Rights identified 5 deaths, 149 injuries and 23 enforced disappearances. National Human Rights Commission, "Komnas HAM dan Penyelesaian Kasus 27 Juli 1996," August 12, 2016.

27. The PRD did seek to end the regime, though it was a small organization that was largely in hiding. The PRD's 1996 manifesto states, "After 30 years, eight months and 22 days of the New Order government, the Indonesian people can no longer accept and tolerate this government, economically, politically or socially."

3: But Don't You Wait (1998)

1. Restrictions were intended to preserve a depoliticized "floating mass" (*massa mengambang*) of citizens who didn't identify too closely with any party or group, with the purported goal of reducing social conflict.

2. Munir remembered the incident as one that showed him who was truly loyal, not just to him, but to the cause they were working for. Meicky Shoreamanis Panggabean, *Keberanian Bernama Munir* (Bandung: Mizan, 2008), 56–58.

3. In a 1999 magazine article, General Prabowo defended himself by saying, "I am not the only commander who received the list."

4. Testimony of Suyat's brother Slamet in the report of the National Human Rights Commission Inquiry Team, as reported in Muammar Fikrie, "PRD: Ode Pemberontakan dan Horor Penghilangan Aktivis," Tirto.id, February 17, 2020, and in the *Jawa Pos*, April 16, 1998, quoted in "Indonesia: More Pressure Needed on Disappearances," Human Rights Watch, June 22, 1998.

5. The National Committee for Democratic Struggle (Komite Nasional untuk Perjuangan Demokrasi, or KNPD) held a press conference to reject the election results. KNPD was an above-ground anti-Suharto organization that served as a link between the underground PRD and Megawati's PDI.

6. The group was Indonesian Student Solidarity for Democracy, known by the Indonesian acronym SMID.

7. The 1992 United Nations Declaration on the Protection of All Persons from Enforced Disappearance state that those subject to enforced disappearances "are arrested, detained or abducted against their will or otherwise deprived of their liberty by officials of different branches or levels of Government, or by organized groups or private individuals acting on behalf of, or with the support, direct or indirect, consent or acquiescence of the Government, followed by a refusal to disclose the fate or whereabouts of the persons concerned or a refusal to acknowledge the deprivation of their liberty, which places such persons outside the protection of the law." The practice is often traced back to Adolf Hitler's 1941 *Nacht und Nebel* (Night and Fog) directive targeting political activists and resistance figures in occupied areas. As Heinrich Himmler instructed his Gestapo in implementing the directive, "An effective and lasting deterrent can be achieved only

by the death penalty or by taking measures which will leave the family and the population uncertain as to the fate of the offender." The practice was then widely adopted in the Latin American dictatorships of the 1970s.

8. KontraS in part grew out of a network created in 1996, the Independent Monitoring Commission for Human Rights Violations, or KIP-HAM.

9. "Ihwal Pembentukan KontraS," *detikNews*, July 14–20, 1998; "Munir SH, Koordinator Pokja KontraS: 'Tidur pun Saya Pernah Mimpi Diculik Orang,'" *Suara Merdeka*, July 17, 1998.

10. Jiwon Suh, "The Politics of Transitional Justice in Post-Suharto Indonesia" (PhD Diss., Ohio State University, 2012), 120–21.

11. Jiwon Suh, "The Politics of Transitional Justice," 117.

12. "Pius: Saya Diculik, Diborgol Dan Disiksa," *Suara Pembaruan*, April 27, 1998.

13. Tim Weiner, "A Tale of Torture from an Indonesian Dissident," *New York Times*, May 8, 1998.

14. Mawa Kresna, "Kisah Tim Mawar Menculik Para Aktivis 1998," Tirto.id, February 4, 2020. This detailed article is based on the National Human Rights Commission's 2006 report on disappearances, the investigation report of the Jakarta police, the records of interrogation of soldiers by military police, and the April 6, 1999, decision of the Jakarta High Military Court.

15. Pius Lustrilanang, "Critical Mass," *Washington Post*, May 17, 1998. In addition to this hearing, Senator Paul Wellstone raised Pius's case on the floor of the Senate. "Human Rights Abuses in Indonesia," May 11, 1998, U.S. Senate, *Congressional Record* 144, no. 58.

16. "Kilas Balik 1998: Cerita Penculikan Desmond, Mata Ditutup Kain Hitam hingga Jatah Selimut dan Celana Pendek," *Kompas*, May 21, 2018; "Desmon Mahesa Bertemu Para Aktivis Yang Diculik," *SiaR*, May 12, 1998.

17. *Winds of Change*, documentary (Alley Kat Productions, South Fremantle, Western Australia, 1999).

18. From Wiji Thukul, "Catatan '97," January 15, 1997. Included with permission from the poet's family.

4: Usman (May 1998)

1. Usman's great-grandfather had helped to spread religious teachings by performing traditional Islamic music on the *gambus*, an Arabian lute.

2. *Jagos*, skilled in martial arts and magic, traditionally enforced the ruler's will while offering protection to villagers in rural Java. After Java became a Dutch colony the term took on illegal connotations. David Bourchier, "Law, Crime and State Authority in Indonesia," in Arief Budiman (ed.), *State and Civil Society in Indonesia* (Clayton, Victoria: Monash University, 1990), 181.

3. Keith B. Richburg, "6 Dead as Riots Rock Indonesia for 3rd Day," *Washington Post* Foreign Service, May 7, 1998.

4. Edward Aspinall, "Indonesian Protests Point to Old Patterns," *New Mandala*, October 12, 2020.

5. Stefan Eklöf, *Indonesian Politics in Crisis: The Long Fall of Suharto 1996–98* (Copenhagen: Nordic Institute of Asian Studies, 1999).

6. David Liebhold, *Time Asia*, May 15, 1998, in Eklöf, *Indonesian Politics in Crisis.*

7. Report of the Joint Fact-Finding Team on the Events of May 13–15, 1998.

8. Suharto privately said the students didn't understand that if he was dismissed, the army would take over. Robert E. Elson, *Suharto: A Political Biography* (Cambridge: Cambridge University Press, 2001), 292.

9. Bonardo Maulana Wahono, "Nezar Patria dan Reformasi Rasa Kecewa," Lokadata, May 21, 2018.

10. Also in the car were Dadang Trisasongko and Bambang Budhiwidjardjo. Interviews with Suciwati and Sugiarto; testimony by Usman Hamid and Poengky Indiarti at Muchdi trial; "Mantan Pedagang Melawan Kekerasan," *Forum Keadilan*, August 24, 1998.

11. Prima Gumilang, "Kisah Mencekam Mugiyanto Korban Penculikan 1998 Dekati Maut," CNN Indonesia, May 23, 2016.

12. Hariwi, dir., *Cerita Tentang Cak Munir* (AlienS Films, 2014).

13. "Penculikan Sebagai Proyek Otoriterianisme," Munir and Robertus Robet.

5: Reformasi! (1998–2001)

1. The Joint Fact-Finding Team appointed by Habibie in July 1998 found the May violence was linked to officials at the "highest levels." The team called for investigation of a Jakarta commander, Major General Syafrie Syamsoeddin, and of Prabowo as commander of the Strategic Reserves. It also recommended a military trial of Prabowo for the disappearances.

2. If the name KontraS denoted being Contra Suharto, his political demise didn't mean the work was done. In one interview, Munir gave an alternative explanation of the name, stating "Yes, people say the S in KontraS is Suharto, and if Suharto is out, we are done. But that S is 'security approach,' and you can have that without Suharto." *Perspektif Baru*, 1998.

3. Max Lane, *Unfinished Nation: Indonesia Before and After Suharto* (London: Verso, 2008), 177.

4. The mix of prosecution, truth-seeking, reparations, reform, and reconciliation measures is known as transitional justice.

5. The twenty-fourth and final activist to disappear had been a street musician named Leonardus Nugroho Iskandar, known to friends as Gilang. He was last seen the day before Suharto's resignation, and three days later villagers found his body in a forest in East Java, tied to a tree, with a large chest wound. The usual total of twenty-four abduction victims (nine released, one found dead, and thirteen missing) is a somewhat arbitrary figure. It includes all victims who were

PRD members, semi-opposition party activists, or who were probably abducted or held by Kopassus in 1997–98. Other Indonesians went missing before, during, and after this time, particularly in conflict areas, but did not fit this profile.

6. U.S. Embassy, Jakarta, "Kidnap Victim Believes More Than Special Forces Involved," July 22, 1998 (declassified).

7. See "Interview," *Indonesia* 67, April 1999. General Theo Syafei notes that an officer who committed a crime while following orders might be subject to court martial, but not sanction by an honor board. The converse might be more common, a violation of honor that was not an illegal act. The honor board was not a common procedure, the previous one having followed the Santa Cruz massacre in East Timor in 1991.

8. For an alternative theory, see Kevin O'Rourke, who does not believe Prabowo had the motive or capability to foment the riots. He contrasts the abductions, meant to prop up the president, with the May riots and student shootings, which could be foreseen to hurt Suharto's standing. Kevin O'Rourke, *Reformasi: The Struggle for Power in Post-Soeharto Indonesia* (Sydney: Allen & Unwin, 2002), 108–11.

9. Bacharuddin Jusuf Habibie, *Detik-detik yang Menentukan* (Jakarta: THC Mandiri, 2006), in "Prabowo Dipecat atau Diberhentikan? Ini Cerita BJ Habibie," *detikNews*, July 31, 2017.

10. Stefan Eklöf, *Indonesian Politics in Crisis: The Long Fall of Suharto 1996–98* (Copenhagen: Nordic Institute of Asian Studies, 1999).

11. Prabowo claimed to have reported his actions to the army commander, General Feisal Tanjung. Tanjung claimed he never ordered the kidnappings, but another general, Theo Syafei told an interviewer while the honor board was under way, "That won't wash. If a subordinate reports to his commander, and it turns out that the commander does nothing to stop him, it means that he permits his subordinate to carry out that mission. All the more so in cases like this, where the sequestering of the people who were kidnapped lasted for months, yet the commander, after receiving the subordinate's report, did nothing. This is clearly a sign: what was done was permitted." "Interview," *Indonesia* 67, April 1999.

12. "Laporan Rekonstruksi Kasus Penculikan Pengantar untuk Menilai Persidangan 11 Anggota Kopassus," KontraS, December 22, 1998, in the digital archive of the Munir Human Rights Museum in Batu.

13. Although the honor board preceded the court martials, Munir viewed it as an attempt to fill the gaps in logic created by assigning blame to mid-ranking soldiers. It defied logic that Kopassus soldiers on their own kidnapped activists in multiple provinces, and even islands, before holding them up to a year and half, without the agreement and facilities of the state. It was beyond their capacity to ensure that the regional military commanders of each area would not interfere and that the national police chief would claim that the victims had been detained by the police.

14. Achmad Nasrudin Yahya, "Yun Hap's Last Days, UI Students Victims of Semanggi II Tragedy," *Kompas*, January 20, 2020.

15. Munir observed that Suharto's agents often arrested people before they could protest. After his fall, anyone could speak freely and protest openly, but with no guarantee they wouldn't be shot. And unless the military was reformed, and Suharto and his men were prosecuted for their crimes, that situation was unlikely to change. "Interview with Munir Said Thalib, June 25, 1999," video file, YouTube, posted by Graha Budaya Indonesia, Tokyo, Japan, https://www.youtube .com/watch?v=sZIQ2cKocBM.

16. A police investigator collected new samples from the crime scenes and carried them to an Australian lab, without identifying the source. He was told there was a match to other samples from Marsinah. But after learning that the tests concerned the Marsinah case, the lab reclassified the results as inconclusive. Supporting this account is a report that in December 2000 the East Java police chief said Australian lab tests had confirmed Marsinah's blood was in the home of the factory owner and in a vehicle. (Department of State, *Country Reports on Human Rights Practices for 2001*.) But three years later, police described the new evidence as inconclusive and the investigation as final. "Hasil Uji DNA Marsinah di Australia Masih Kabur," *Tempo*, August 7, 2003.

17. On May 6, 1998, newspapers had quoted Wiranto as saying, "The moment the students leave their campuses their protests become uncontrollable." This was interpreted by some as a signal that the anti-government protests *would* be tolerated, but only on campus. Keith B. Richburg, "6 Dead as Riots Rock Indonesia for 3rd Day," *Washington Post* Foreign Service, May 7, 1998.

18. Wiranto characterized them as soldiers who had "exceeded their authority." See "Indonesia Country Report on Human Rights Practices for 1998," U.S. Department of State, February 26, 1999.

19. "Tim Mawar Akui Culik 9 Korban," *Kompas*, February 17, 1999; "Hakim Harus Panggil Kolonel (Inf) Chairawan," *Kompas*, February 25, 1999.

20. Munir, "Tentara Di Anjang Pelanggaran HAM," 1999.

21. Munir interview with Wimar Witoelar, *Perspektif Baru* 126, July 26, 1998; see also *Batas Panggang* (video), at www.youtube.com/watch?v=eriMPuKg7Dw. Munir later wrote, "This half-hearted court proceeded like a flash of political camouflage to cover up what had happened around the 'politics of disappearing people' throughout the New Order." Munir, "Wiji Thukul," preface to Wiji Thukul, *Aku Ingin Jadi Peluru* (Jakarta: Indonesia Tera, 2000).

22. In 1978 Prabowo led a Kopassus unit that killed the guerilla commander Nicolau Lobato. He had also been linked to a retaliatory massacre of about 80 men, women and children in 1983 after guerrillas killed 12 Indonesian combat engineers. Kraras is still known as the "village of widows."

23. *Chega!: the Final Report of the Timor-Leste Commission for Reception, Truth and Reconciliation (CAVR)*, Part 4: Regime of Occupation.

24. "Hasil Investigasi Tim KontraS Timor-Timur Paska Jajak Pendapat Tahun 1999," available in the digital archive of the Munir Human Rights Museum in Batu.

25. James J. Fox, "Ceremonies of Reconciliation as Prelude to Violence in Suai,

East Timor," in *Violent Conflicts in Indonesia*, Charles A. Coppel, ed. (Abingdon, UK: Routledge, 2006).

26. "Indonesia/East Timor: Forced Expulsions to West Timor and the Refugee Crisis," Human Rights Watch 11, no. 7; Geoffrey Robinson, *East Timor 1999: Crimes Against Humanity* (Geneva: UN Office of the High Commissioner for Human Rights, January 2005), 86.

27. Father Francisco, hands raised, had called out, "Enough. Don't shoot anymore. All of us are Timorese." According to witness testimony given to East Timor's truth commission, a militia member approached Father Francisco, seemed to hug him, and then walked him down to the grotto of the Virgin Mary and shot him. When he didn't die, the man unsheathed a sword and stabbed him.

28. Fox, "Ceremonies of Reconciliation," 176.

29. This account draws heavily on Robinson, *East Timor 1999*, 184–88, which describes the events in Suai based on the KPP-HAM report, UN reports, court documents, witness statements, and media accounts.

30. Hamish MacDonald, "Australia's Bloody East Timor Secret: Spy Intercepts Confirm Government Knew of Jakarta's Hand in Massacres," *Sydney Morning Herald*, March 14, 2002; "Silence over a Crime Against Humanity," *Sydney Morning Herald* and *The Age*, March 14, 2002; and *Masters of Terror: Indonesia's Military and Violence in East Timor in 1999* (Canberra: Strategic and Defence Studies Centre, Australian National University, 2002).

31. The divided island was an artifact of Dutch and Portuguese colonialism, which created a boundary separating members of the same linguistic and cultural groups and even extended families.

32. "Investigation Team Finds 25 Bodies in Mass Graves," *Jakarta Post*, November 26, 1999. Reports on the grave excavation and autopsies by the Forensic Department of the Faculty of Medicine of the University of Indonesia were cited in the Damiri Judgment at https://www.asser.nl/upload/documents/DomCLIC/Docs/NLP/Indonesia/Damiri_Judgement_31-7-2003.pdf.

33. The team identified three types of perpetrators: those who committed crimes directly; those who ran the field operations; and those responsible for national security policy, including senior military officials. The team's findings were consistent with, among others, Robinson, *East Timor 1999*, which found that the evidence "points conclusively to a powerful [Indonesian military] role in the recruitment, training, and operations of the militia forces, and to direct [Indonesian military] complicity in the grave violations they committed."

34. Two senior generals were named: Major General Adam Damiri, the regional military commander and Major General Zacky Makarim, an adviser to the Indonesian task force on the referendum.

35. The title Gus, from the old Hindu-Buddhist honorific Bagus, is used in East Java for the sons of respected Islamic teachers, while Dur was short for the President's given name.

36. On November 23, 2000, the parliament passed the Human Rights Court Act No. 26 of 2000, replacing a decree known as PERPU No.1/1999.

37. "Winds of Change," (Alley Kat Productions, 1999).

6: Reformasi Stalls (2001–2004)

1. A 2000 U.S. Embassy cable describes the Muslim leader and politician Amien Rais telling embassy staff that Munir knew of the involvement of Jakarta elites, Wiranto among them, in the conflict in the Moluccas and other spots, and planned to give his sensitive analysis directly to the president. Munir had previously observed that Indonesia's diversity allowed elites to cultivate violence between ethnic and religious groups, thus distracting or pressuring reformers and other critics without ever directly targeting them.

2. A day before, Wahid had tried to preserve his presidency by dissolving parliament. In response, a special session of the People's Consultative Assembly session planned for August was moved up to the next day. Wahid was officially impeached for naming a police chief without parliamentary consent, although two corruption allegations were also under investigation.

3. The relationship between Megawati and Hendropriyono transcended politics. One New Year's Eve, Megawati invited more than a hundred people to her father's old mansion in the hills to celebrate her husband's birthday. A guest remembers Megawati sitting crossly in front of a huge window, when suddenly her whole face lit up. The guests turned to see who had arrived and saw Hendropriyono. Later he took a microphone and sang "Help Me Make It Through the Night" as Megawati looked on, beaming. Interview, 2019.

4. Megawati also endorsed General Sutiyoso, running for reelection as governor of Jakarta, despite his role in the deadly attack on her followers in 1996.

5. Article 43 (2) of Law 26 of 2000 states that an ad hoc human rights court "shall be formed on the recommendation of the lower house of parliament of the Republic of Indonesia for particular incidents upon the issue of a presidential decree." The International Center for Transitional Justice and KontraS has noted that the National Human Rights Commission and some members of parliament believe the attorney general's office "has misread the act. They believe that it is illogical for the lower house of Parliament, which does not have investigators or technical experts, to investigate whether gross violations have occurred or to make a determination without evidence from law enforcement officials." Only prosecutors can legally undertake such an investigation, and in fact have a legal duty to do so if the National Human Rights Commission finds that gross human rights violations have taken place. Indeed, prosecutors did launch investigations into the Tanjung Priok and East Timor cases *before* ad hoc courts were created. The International Center for Transitional Justice and KontraS, *Derailed: Transitional Justice in Indonesia Since the Fall of Soeharto*, 2011, 42.

6. "DPR Tak Bakal Rekomendasikan Pengadilan HAM 'Ad Hoc,'" *Kompas*, June 28, 2001.

7. "Indonesia: Attacks Against Two Well-Known Human Rights Organisations," OMCT, March 22, 2002; U.S. Embassy, Jakarta, "Human Rights Organizations Beaten, but Limping Along," April 12, 2002 (declassified cable).

8. Meicky Shoreamanis Panggabean, *Keberanian Bernama Munir* (Bandung:

Mizan, 2008), 61.

9. "Mantan Pedagang Melawan Kekerasan," *Forum Keadilan*, August 24, 1998.

10. See Damiri Judgment and also useful summary and context for the case at www.internationalcrimesdatabase.org/Case/1007/Damiri.

11. U.S. Embassy, Jakarta, "Human Rights Organizations Beaten but Limping Along," April 12, 2002 (declassified cable).

12. David Cohen, "Intended to Fail: The Trials Before the Ad Hoc Human Rights Court in Jakarta," International Center for Transitional Justice, August 2003, vi. The Human Rights Courts law adopted the language of the International Criminal Court. However several mistranslations and omission of "other inhumane acts of a similar character" served to exclude many serious violations from the scope of the law.

13. Willy Pramudya, ed., *Cak Munir: Engkau Tidak Pernah Pergi* (Jakarta: Gagasmedia, 2004), 13.

14. "Munir, Menanti Kebijakan Anti-Terorisme," in *Terorisme: Definisi, Aksi dan Regulasi* (Jakarta: Imparsial, 2003), xiii, in Imparsial, "Tembok Tebal, Pengusutan Pembunuhan Munir," September 2006.

15. Once, when Munir was quite small, he'd run his hand longingly along the smooth finish of an expensive car, not realizing his father was watching from across the street. His father took it as disrespect and berated him for desiring material objects, and Munir never forgot it. Panggabean, *Keberanian Bernama Munir*, 53.

16. Tim Lindsey, "Muddling Through," *Inside Indonesia* 87: July–September 2006.

17. Sri Lestari Wahyuningroem, "Towards Post-Transitional Justice: The Failures of Transitional Justice and the Roles of Civil Society in Indonesia," *Journal of Southeast Asian Human Rights* 3, no. 1 (June 2019), at 133.

18. Munir, "Indonesian Civil Society Strategy for Ending Impunity," Prepared for the 13th INFID Conference, Yogyakarta, September 2002.

19. Poengky Indarti, "Munir: Perjuangan Awalnya dalam Mendukung Kebangkitan Gerakan Buruh di Jawa Timur dan Perjuangan Akhirnyadalam Melawan Impunity di Indonesia," *Jurnal Perburuhan Sedane* 3, no. 2 (2005).

20. Personal communication, Marcus Mietzner, 2021. An expert on Indonesian military reform, Meizner wrote a strong letter to the American embassy, arguing that it was Munir's independence and critical thought that made him an appropriate scholarship recipient.

21. Interview, Jeffrey Winters, December 2019; Munir, "Pelanggaran HAM Sebagai Pilihan Politik Rezim Militer dan Tantangan Perubahan Politik serta Implikasinya: Studi atas praktek penghilangan orang dan peran politik militer di Indonesia," draft proposal for a dissertation, February 11, 2004.

7: The Red Thread (2004)

1. Sri Rusminingtyas, the friend who'd been asked to meet Munir at the airport, was there as well. Two days earlier, she'd been the one to tell Dutch investigators

that Munir was a prominent human rights activist with many enemies, and she had identified the body. Sri returned with a photo from her recent Jakarta wedding, featuring Munir, Suci and the kids, Poengky, and Usman, to help the investigators recognize the group.

2. Interviews with Usman Hamid and Suciwati, personal communication from Poengky Indarti, and Suciwati, "Munir, Cahaya Yang Tak Pernah Padam," in *Saatnya Korban Bicara: Menata Derap Merajut Langkah* (Jakarta: Jaringan Relawan Solidaritas, Jaringan Solidaritas Korban untuk Keadilan, and Yayasan TIFA, 2009).

3. "Suciwati: Solidaritas Mereka Memberikan Saya Semangat," *Perspektif Baru*, at www.perspektifbaru.com/wawancara/458.

4. Office records later confirmed the date of Pollycarpus's visit to PBHI as March 16, 2004.

5. Two of Munir's brothers, both doctors, accompanied Suci to meet Dr. Hakim Tarmizi, the passenger who treated Munir on board. He shared the facts of Munir's last hours, which Suci found helpful, though she never understood why he administered an anti-emetic that made it harder for Munir to rid his body of the poison.

6. Poengky handed out her card at the Garuda meeting. Soon after, Pollycarpus called Imparsial, but she was out for a medical procedure. He reached her the next day, claiming he'd just called to check if the number on her card was really hers. Knowing she'd been in the hospital, he wanted her to know he was very good at concocting traditional medicines. Feeling this man was acting extremely suspiciously, Poengky used the opportunity to ask Polly again about meeting Munir. This time he said he'd also once come to Imparsial bringing two Timorese people to meet Munir, and again after Munir died to express his condolences. Poengky did not find a record of either visit, but it was possible. Transcript of Testimony by Poengky Indiarti, Trial of Muchdi Purwopranjono, October 9, 2008.

8: King of Poisons (2004)

1. The article also notes, "The new attorney-general, Abdul Rahman Saleh, is considered incorruptible and vigorous. This will improve the chances for a criminal investigation." Dirk Vlasblom, "Indonesische activist vergiftigd (Indonesian activist poisoned)," *NRC Handelsblad*, November 11, 2004, translation by INFID European Liaison Office.

2. David O'Shea, dir., *Garuda's Deadly Upgrade* (Thames Ditton, UK: Journeyman Pictures, 2005).

3. "Indonesian Team Hampered by Netherlands' Requirements," *Indopos*, November 21, 2004.

4. Munir's stomach contents, heart blood, and urine were examined by inductively coupled plasma mass spectrometry, and the stomach contents were also examined by X-ray fluorescence spectrometry. Report of the NFI, October 1, 2004.

5. "Indonesië: Overlijden Mensenrechtenactivist Munir," Memorandum from the Director of Asia and Oceania to the Minister of Foreign Affairs, October 13, 2004.

6. See record of Dutch parliamentary debate, "Tweede Kamerdebat over Dood Indonesische activist Munir," November 30, 2004, at https://zoek. officielebekendmakingen.nl/h-tk-20042005-1942-1949.pdf.

7. A source in Dutch intelligence later told Rachland Nashidik that the delay was partly due to the issue of the death penalty, but also because officials did not want the report politicized. They felt that the goal of the poisoning was to have the Dutch announce that an anti-military campaigner was killed, just days before the vote, so they delayed release of information. See "Kesaksian Intel Belanda dalam Kematian Munir," *Tempo*, September 7, 2016.

8. "KontraS Interviews Garuda Employee on Munir's Death," *Jakarta Post*, November 19, 2004.

9. Djoko Tjiptono, "Pollycarpus, Yeni, dan Wiranto," *detikNews*, March 24, 2005.

10. "Dokter Sepesawat dengan Munir Diperiksa," Liputan6.com, November 25, 2004.

11. "Pollycarpus: Saya Difitnah, Ada yang Ingin Mengorbankan Saya," *detikNews*, December 3, 2004; "Imparsial Demands that the SBY Government Investigate Munir's Murder," Radio Netherlands Worldwide, November 13, 2004.

12. O'Shea, *Garuda's Deadly Upgrade*.

13. Munir had also spoken of his concern that someone outside their circle knew about his departure, due to a phone call Suci had received from "Polly from Garuda."

14. Record of Interrogation, Suciwati, in Muchdi dossier; testimony by Choirul Anam in first Pollycarpus trial, November 11, 2005.

9: Getting Garuda (2005)

1. "Aktifis HAM Dunia Desak Pengusutan Kasus Kematian Munir," *Suara Pembaruan*, November 24, 2004; "Aktifis HAM Tuntut Presiden Realisasikan Tim Independen Penyelidikan Munir," *Kompas*, December 3, 2004; "Pejuang HAM," *Kompas*, December 9, 2004.

2. Andrew Burrell, "Man of the Moment," *Australian Financial Review*, October 29, 2004. The story was published after Munir's death and Yudhoyono's win. SBY's relationship to past violations was also complicated by the significant role of his father-in-law, General Sarwo Edhie Wibowo, in the killings of 1965–6.

3. Domu P. Sihite, Tini Hadad, and Amiruddin Al Rahab replaced I Putu Kusa, Smita Notosusanto, and Bambang Widjojanto.

4. The high-water mark was about a hundred feet uphill and over a mile inland in some areas. Beyond that point lay a jarring sense of normalcy, with ATMs and Kentucky Fried Chicken outlets in the capital, and the slow rhythms of growing rice or coffee in rural areas. On Simeulue Island, oral traditions of a wave that came on the heels of a 1907 earthquake allowed residents to recognize the telltale sign of water withdrawing from the beaches. They headed for high ground and avoided mass casualties despite proximity to the epicenter.

5. "TPF-Polri Rapat Paparkan Kemajuan Kasus Kematian Munir," *detikNews*, January 13, 2004, in Imparsial, "Tembok Tebal." Three other documents provided information of limited value: a trip report from Pollycarpus, the death-on-board report, and a diagram of a 747-400 interior.

6. "Ajuan Pokok-Pokok Pertemuan TPF dan Tim Penyidik Kasus Munir," January 26, 2005.

7. "Beredar SMS Pollycarpus Direkrut BIN Sebagai Agen Utama Intelijen," *detikNews*, February 1, 2005.

8. Pollycarpus denied receiving a gun or firearms training, but Kasum eventually found a witness to undermine that claim. Someone who had been in Polly's house reported seeing him with a gun more than once.

9. Joseph H. Daves, *The Indonesian Army from* Revolusi *to* Reformasi, vol. 3, *Soeharto's Fall and the* Reformasi *Era* (self-published, 2014), 298.

10. The operators also took requests to record the actions of VVIPS, or very very important persons. Marsudhi noted the potential for an inverse privilege, noting, "I think there's a significant possibility that there may also be requests to *not* record certain activities."

11. While working for Timor-Leste's truth commission, known as the CAVR, I reviewed hundreds of files of Timorese charged with supporting the guerrillas. Nearly every dusty cardboard folder contained a photograph of the suspect forced to recreate their supposed crime of handing over a pack of cigarettes, a few coconuts, or a bit of crumpled currency to an actor playing a brother or father who had joined the guerrillas or the clandestine movement.

12. "Polri Meyakini Munir Diracun oleh Orang di Pesawat," *detikNews*, February 15, 2005.

13. See Article 43 of Law No. 15 of 1992 and Article 17 of the Warsaw Convention.

14. The normal chain of communication would be through the operational director, the vice-president for flight operation, and the chief of pilots.

15. "Laporan Pertemuan TPF Munir Dengan Manajemen Garuda," Jakarta, February 4, 2005.

16. Interview, Marsudhi Hanafi, November 24, 2019.

17. The team also shared their concern for the airport's badly outdated technology, as well as the fact that police investigators first claimed the recordings had been erased, when in fact they'd never existed. Summary, *Laporan Tim Pencari Fakta*, March 3, 2005.

18. Usman revealed this promise to the press the next day, explaining that the president had raised BIN at their meeting and promised that no one would get special protection. A spokesman for the president confirmed that he had welcomed the questioning of BIN officials if needed. "SBY Persilakan TPF Munir Minta Keterangan ke BIN," *detikNews*, March 3, 2005.

19. David O'Shea, dir., *Garuda's Deadly Upgrade* (Thames Ditton, UK: Journeyman Pictures, 2005).

20. O'Shea, *Garuda's Deadly Upgrade*; "Pollycarpus Banyak Berbohong," *Suara*

Pembaruan, March 8, 2005; "Polly Dianggap Berbelit-belit, DPR Tidak Puas," *detikNews*, March 8, 2005.

21. "DPR Kecewa dengan Jawaban Pollycarpus," *Indopos*, March 8, 2005.

22. O'Shea, *Garuda's Deadly Upgrade*.

23. There were a few exceptions to the growing group unity. Some members viewed the forensics expert, Dr. Abdul Mun'im Idris, with some skepticism from the start, wondering why one of the experts on the police delegation to Amsterdam wasn't appointed. Dr. Mun'im sparked more concern by pushing for a second autopsy, which Usman and Suciwati thought was a pointless and risky exercise. Usman also remembered that after the Trisakti shootings, Dr. Mun'im played a helpful role at first. But soon he seemed to say whatever the police wanted, even suggesting that the four students had died from drug overdoses before the protest began. Dr. Mun'im had also provided technical assistance to Munir in investigations in Aceh and into the *Petrus* shootings of suspected habitual criminals from the 1980s. Usman knew Munir thought Dr. Mun'im might have manipulated the forensic results. But once the president named him to the TPF, getting rid of him would be hard. Asmara's solution was to just stop inviting him to meetings.

24. Interview, Usman Hamid, June 2018.

25. "TPF KM Akan Selidiki BIN," *Media Indonesia*, March 5, 2005. Polly's lawyer was pushing back on demands for his arrest by calling for Indonesian coroners to redo the autopsy and threatening to file a complaint over the release of the August 11 assignment letter. He argued that Munir could have been poisoned by other Garuda staff, KontraS employees, Indonesian or foreign intelligence, or even a retired general with a grudge. *Indopos*, March 3, 2005. Indonesia's Code of Criminal Procedure divides a police investigation into two phases, although in practice they often overlap. The preliminary investigation, or *penyelidikan*, into a possible offense is carried out by a junior investigator to determine whether a full investigation should take place. If there is sufficient evidence for a second phase, *penyidikan*, a more senior investigator seeks evidence to clarify whether an offense has occurred and to locate the suspect. When both phases are complete, police hand the dossier to prosecutors, who can send it back within fourteen days if they find it incomplete. The Munir investigation seemed stuck in the first phase. See *Pedoman Pelaksanaan KUHAP*.

26. "Cops Quiz Garuda Staff Again over Munir Case," *Jakarta Post*, March 9, 2005; "Pollycarpus Diperiksa dengan Lie Detector," *Indopos*, March 9, 2005.

27. "Sakit, Polly Diperiksa Lie Detector," *Indopos*, March 15, 2005.

28. "Pollycarpus Diperiksa 13 Jam lebih," *Media Indonesia*, March 15, 2005.

29. "Mabes Polri Lanjutkan Pemeriksaan Polycarpus," *Suara Pembaruan*, March 15, 2005.

30. See Warrant No. Pol: SP Han/05/III/2005/DIT-I. Polly's lawyer continued his public defense after the arrest, asserting that Pollycarpus was not Rambo, a one-man army, but part of a well-regulated bureaucracy at the airline. He said, "There's no way Polly had a personal desire and just went to Singapore."

31. "PC Jadi Tersangka Pertama," *Indopos*, March 19, 2005.

32. "Polly: Saya Hanya Terima Tugas Atasan," *Indopos*, March 23, 2005.

33. "Munir Case a Domestic Matter: Minister," *Jakarta Post*, March 28, 2005.

34. Usman tried to stay optimistic. A resolution to the case would be a huge step forward for Indonesia, but the reverse was true as well. At an event marking the seventh anniversary of KontraS, Usman warned, "If this case is never resolved, then, I'm sure, we will not have the strength to resolve other human rights cases in the future." "Kontras Yakin Kasus Munir Terungkap," *Suara Pembaruan*, March 22, 2005.

35. The Dutch government seemed to have made a distinction between general evidence that a crime had occurred, like the toxicology results they shared, and documents like the police interviews at Schiphol that might point to an individual suspect and expose that person to capital punishment.

36. "Dutch to Share Evidence in Munir Case," *Jakarta Post*, March 20, 2005. Indonesian investigators had no plans to repeat toxicology tests, despite urging by Pollycarpus's lawyer, but samples were needed in case anyone challenged the tests. They later provided an essential breakthrough in the case. "KontraS Yakin Kasus Munir Terungkap," *Suara Pembaruan*, March 22, 2005. The Dutch handed some documents to the Indonesian embassy on March 21. "Belum Temukan Motif Polly," March 24, 2005; "Dicari Pemberi Perintah Polly," *Indopos*, March 25, 2005.

37. "Arman Janji Tak Hukum Mati," *Indopos*, March 29, 2005.

38. "KontraS Yakin Kasus Munir Terungkap," *Suara Pembaruan*, March 22, 2005; "Belanda Segera Kirim Barang Bukti Kasus Munir," March 23, 2005.

39. "Polisi: Polly Bukan Eksekutor," *Indopos*, March 22, 2005.

40. "Polisi Dalami Keterangan Tiga Karyawan Garuda," *Kompas*, March 29, 2005; "Penyidik Periksa Lagi Mantan Dirut Garuda," *Kompas*, March 30, 2005.

41. Polly had also told police that he canceled a planned flight to Beijing on September 5 because the car did not show up to bring him to the airport. Now he admitted the flight schedule was changed at his request—but only to attend an all-pilots meeting in Jakarta on September 7.

42. *Final Report of the Tim Pencari Fakta Kasus Meninggalnya Munir (TPF)*, Jakarta, 2005, 29.

43. Police dossier for Pollycarpus Budihari Priyanto trial.

44. Djoko Tjiptono, "Pollycarpus, Yeni, dan Wiranto," *detikNews*, March 24, 2005.

45. Saint Polycarp, bishop of Smyrna, was one of the principal Church Fathers. In about 155 CE, at the age of either eighty-five or one hundred, he was burned at the stake for refusing to burn incense to the health of the emperor, a standard way of acknowledging the authority of the government. The fire failed to consume Polycarp, so he was speared, and his blood put out the fire.

10: Chasing BIN (2005)

1. Step Vaessens, in David O'Shea, dir., *Garuda's Deadly Upgrade* (Thames Ditton, UK: Journeyman Pictures, 2005).

2. "Garuda Diperalat untuk Bunuh Munir," *Media Indonesia*, March 8, 2005.

3. "TPF Kasus Munir Akan Selidiki BIN," *Media Indonesia*, March 5, 2005; "TPF Akan Selidiki Intelijen," *Kompas*, March 18, 2005; "TPF Munir Diminta Mengecek Info Keterlibatan Anggota BIN," *detikNews*, March 17, 2005.

4. *Kompas*, March 19, 2005.

5. "Arman Janji Tak Hukum Mati," *Indopos*, March 29, 2005.

6. "Protokol Pencari Fakta di Lingkungan Badan Intelijen Negara (BIN) Oleh Tim Pencari Fakta Kasus Meninggalnya Munir," May 2, 2005.

7. "TPF Munir Yakin BIN Terlibat Pembunuhan," *detikNews*, May 9, 2005.

8. See *Final Report of the Tim Pencari Fakta Kasus Meninggalnya Munir (TPF)*, Jakarta, 2005, 36.

9. "Kepala BIN Larang Buka Akses untuk TPF Munir," *detikNews*, June 15, 2005; "Melindungi BIN dari Kematian Munir," Merdeka.com, October 31, 2016.

10. "Nomor Siluman Beranak-pinak," *Tempo*, December 14, 2014.

11. Record of interrogation of Muchdi Purwopranjono, May 18, 2005.

12. "Ditelepon TPF Munir, Muchdi Bilang Salah Sambung," *Kompas*, September 23, 2008; interview on blog, https://rusdimathari.wordpress.com/2008/06/20/usman-hamid-tentang-muchdi-pr.

13. "Pernyataan Kepala BIN Dinilai Hidupkan Kembali Mesin Represi," *Kompas*, May 31, 2004.

14. "Munir Tidak Masuk Radar Kami," interview with A. M. Hendropriyono, *Tempo*, June 7, 2005.

15. The TPF sent another invitation for June 7. When he didn't show, they requested his presence the next day. Again he didn't appear, with no reason given. A fourth request on June 15 was never acknowledged. "Melindungi BIN dari Kematian Munir," Merdeka.com, October 31, 2016.

16. "Melindungi BIN dari Kematian Munir," Merdeka.com, October 31, 2016.

17. Police questioned Nurhadi on May 11 and Muchdi on May 18.

18. The police had only revealed the Hendro interview at a closed-door meeting with legislators and the TPF. The TPF's *Final Report* states that CID director Makbul Padmanegara, on June 17, 2005, said the police would not share Hendropriyono's record of interrogation, or even an oral summary, for reasons that were unclear.

19. Muchdi's record of May 18 was summarized in Polly's trial dossier, and Irawan's was leaked, but Hendropriyono's has never surfaced.

20. "Muchdi PR Tak Penuhi Panggilan TPF Munir," *detikNews*, June 2, 2005; "Hendro Belum Nongol, Pengacaranya Tiba di Kantor TPF," *detikNews*, June 6, 2005.

21. "Empat Skenario Pembunuhan Munir," *Kompas*, June 15, 2005; "Plot Alleged in Death of Indonesian Activist," Alan Sipress, *Washington Post*, June 25, 2005; "Usman Hamid: Kontras Tak Terlibat Skenario Pembunuhan Munir," *detikNews*, June 14, 2005. The BIN director told the press he had no idea what document the TPF was referring to, and denied there was evidence of his agency's involvement

or even proof Munir was poisoned. "Bin Tidak Tahu Soal 4 Skenario Pembunuhan Munir," *detikNews*, June 15, 2005.

22. Tiarma Siboro, "TSO/SBY Told to Empower Munir Probe Team," *Jakarta Post*, June 13, 2005. A flight attendant told police she saw a sixty-year-old man sitting in 3J help the doctor find medicine in the kit. This was almost certainly Lie Khie Ngian. According to reports, Lie had also changed his itinerary at the last minute to be on the flight. He told police his departure was moved up from September 13 to September 6 because his visa expired that day.

23. Minutes of Reconstruction, June 23, 2005, in police dossier for Pollycarpus trial (English translation).

24. "After One Year," a Human Rights First white paper, footnotes 24, 25, and 27. A member of the TPF told me in 2005, "We failed to find documents to prove Polly's formal status [as a BIN agent]. This is not our fault, but BIN's and President Yudhoyono's failure to ensure full cooperation. The key point is the president. If he wants to crack open the case, he has to do something to pressure the chief of BIN and open up access to investigators."

25. The proposed audit would cover five weaknesses. First, police questioning showed poor technical capacity on topics like aviation security and forensics. Second, police bureaucracy slowed decision making. Third, there was poor coordination with other agencies, as seen in the delay to secure a mutual legal-assistance agreement with the Dutch. Fourth was the failure to share information with the TPF. Finally, the police failed to fully investigate Garuda and Pollycarpus's time in Singapore.

26. Top state officials at the meeting included Coordinating Minister for Political, Legal and Security Affairs Widodo Adi Sutjipto, Minister of Law and Human Rights Hamid Awaludin, State Secretary Yusril Ihza Mahendra, Cabinet Secretary Sudi Silalahi, Attorney General Marzuki Darusman, National Police Chief General Dai Bachtiar, BIN Director Syamsir Siregar, and Presidential Spokesperson Andi Mallarangeng.

27. President Yudhoyono had been Megawati's coordinating minister for politics and security while Hendropriyono was BIN director, a cabinet post. Besides the normal turf wars over national security and intelligence issues, they disagreed on whether Muslim-Christian violence in Central Sulawesi had an Al Qaeda connection. Hendropriyono said it did, and was later proved partly right when an Al Qaeda–linked training camp was discovered.

11: The Pilot's Choice of Poison (2005)

1. Under the New Order, the military justified its role in politics and internal security by pointing to the state ideology Pancasila and the Dual Function doctrine. During *reformasi*, the military began warning of Indonesia's break-up due to excessive democratization and foreign conspiracies. By the end of 2001, the term NKRI was used not just by the military, but by politicians, journalists, and even NGOs. Marcus Mietzner, "The Politics of Military Reform in Post-Suharto

Indonesia: Elite Conflict, Nationalism, and Institutional Resistance," East-West Center, 2006.

2. Interview, member of the prosecution team, November 2019.

3. The defense also complained that the TPF's findings had shaped opinion about the involvement of intelligence agents. This first mention of BIN was surely noted by the agency's deputy director from his seat in the courtroom. Human Rights First, "After One Year," footnote 45.

4. The metaphors flowed: Pollycarpus was an offering to ward off misfortune, and a "test rabbit" for legal theories.

5. As for the second charge, the defense argued that signing a letter without authority isn't forgery, and that Pollycarpus's role in creating the documents was unclear. Other defense arguments concerned an unfair modification in the charges (from *assisting* to *carrying out* a murder) and the legal distinction between undertaking, ordering the undertaking, or involvement in a crime.

6. The robes were Napoleonic in origin, due to the French occupation of the Netherlands in 1795 and subsequent legal reforms.

7. Letter No. GARUDA/DZ-2270/04 dated August 11, 2004, signed by Indra Setiawan. The letter specified that the assignment was "especially in matters connected to Aviation and Internal Security." Throughout the case, confusion sprang from lax and inconsistent use of three terms: corporate security, aviation security, and internal security. Aviation Security, or Avsec, is a formal set of safety practices; all flight and cabin crew receive some general training in them. Some are given extra training in skills like handling incidents on board, and Pollycarpus had received two days of training in dangerous goods in November 1998. Corporate Security is a formal department within Garuda that covers procedures on the ground and in the offices. Some documents also refer to "internal security," which has a separate cost center, or billable department, within the airline.

8. Another discrepancy arose around the August 11 appointment letter. According to Setiawan, when the police requested an official copy of the letter in February 2005, his staff couldn't find it in the files. They typed up another copy, misspelling Polly's full name, and Setiawan then signed it. The next discrepancy was Polly's corporate security ID card, dated May–June 16, 2004, or *before* the assignment letter. Setiawan blamed employees who forgot to change the date on an older card they used as a template.

9. Prosecutors had requested that Setiawan be available to respond to Ramel's testimony, and he sat in the front row. The chief judge called on Setiawan to respond to Ramel's assertion that he never asked for more security assistance. Neither man wanted to revise his testimony, so the judge said the panel would assess who was telling the truth.

10. Ramel told the court that his memo wasn't a formal task or assignment letter (*surat tugas*) for the trip, and he didn't know if one existed.

11. This memo was mistakenly handed to Pollycarpus instead of being filed, so a *third* version was generated for the file on September 20.

12. Record of Interrogation for Rohainil Aini, December 8, 2004. Aini also testified that Pollycarpus had a trip scheduled to Beijing on September 5, but it had been canceled on August 31 so he could attend a pilots' meeting in Jakarta on September 7. At one point, Pollycarpus had claimed that the Beijing trip was canceled simply because a Garuda car never came to pick him up. Captain Karmel was adamant that Pollycarpus had requested the cancelation of the Beijing trip in person on August 30. The prosecution's implication was that he canceled the Beijing trip to allow him to travel with Munir.

13. A magazine called *Ekspos* had forty straight pages on the case, a mix of real news, interviews with Muchdi and Polly, cartoon-like diagrams of Munir vomiting or lying dead in his seat, with x's for eyes, and speculation by an "observer of intelligence" that Munir might have been killed due to conflict within KontraS because he didn't share prize money or other funds from abroad.

14. Brahmanie said that at a crew meeting after Munir's death the captain told her that Polly had said, "There's a man named Munir downstairs. Can he be allowed to see the cockpit?" The answer was no. Another participant at that meeting did not hear this request, and the pilot did not even remember Polly's visit.

15. "Surat Keterangan Dalam Penerbangan/Preliminary Certificate of Death," September 7, 2004. The document was signed by Dr. Tarmizi and the purser Majib Nasution and witnessed by the pilot and two others. At the bottom the doctor wrote the list of medications he had administered. The document notes the location as over Romania, although the exact coordinates recorded by the Dutch investigator indicate a location fifty miles north of the border with Ukraine. The pilot's telex read, "MR. MUNIR WHO SERIOUSLY ILL. HE WAS PASS AWAY AT 0405 UTC. PLS INFO TO AMS. THNKS . . . CAPT W. KIRONO."

16. Records later obtained from one of Polly's cell phones show six text messages and a call to Yetty on one day, November 18, 2004, a few days after the autopsy results became public. Before and after that set of messages, Polly's phone was in contact with a BIN agent, the BIN landline, and Muchdi's cell phone.

17. The defense asked only why there was no autopsy in Indonesia. The witnesses explained they had discussed doing one, but the blood and stomach fluids were already drained, the body had been embalmed and buried for two months, and the family didn't approve.

18. Hian Tian told police that from 1999 Pollycarpus often brought her to the headquarters of BIN's predecessor, Bakin, to meet intelligence agents he knew from working with them to preserve the Unitary State of the Republic of Indonesia, or NKRI. She also knew him to be friends with the pro-Indonesian militia leader Eurico Guterres. Record of Interrogation, Hian Tian, June 10, 2005.

19. The expert testified that forgery can include an otherwise valid document that violates procedure, such as one signed by someone without the proper authority. He also explained that, while the statute requires only the *possibility* of a loss for the forged document to be considered a crime, Garuda sustained an actual loss. Pollycarpus had secured pay, transportation, and lodging using documents that violated procedure, based on lies. "Saksi Ahli: Surat Tugas Polly Palsu," *detikNews*, November 16, 2005.

20. Some activists prefer the term *survivor* to *victim*, but *korban* is used widely in the movement for justice that Munir helped create. It comes from the Arabic term *qurban*, meaning a sacrifice or offering to God, like the livestock slaughtered on the holiday of Eid-al-Adha to commemorate the prophet Ibrahim's willingness to sacrifice his son, until God sends a ram to take his place.

21. Steve Pillar Setiabudi, dir., *His Story* (Journeyman, 2006).

22. The verb *mengingatkan* could be charitably translated as the milder "remind." However, in this context "warn" seems more apt.

23. Interview, Suciwati; see also Sonya Ayu Kumala, "Pengungkapan Karakter Dalam Proposisi Analisis Wacana Naratif Seorang Aktivis" (Thesis, Universitas Indonesia, 2012), 144.

24. "Pollycarpus Changes His Tune on Munir Case," *Jakarta Post*, November 9, 2005.

25. Asked how often he'd changed seats with someone, Polly recalled three other times. There was a foreigner named Brian, the former presidential candidate Amien Rais, and a sick woman from New Zealand.

26. He had previously claimed he got up from his seat due to a form of PTSD from an incident when a drunk passenger once attacked him.

27. See Pledoi Pollycarpus and KontraS, "Monitoring Persidangan Pembunuhan Munir, Persidangan XXIII," December 12, 2005.

28. At first only the mysteriously pro-Pollycarpus Eastern Indonesia Students Committee was protesting in the alley. Twenty members stood silently holding a banner that called on the judges to SAY WHAT IS WRONG IS WRONG, AND WHAT IS TRUE IS TRUE. At ten a.m., some five hundred Munir supporters arrived, demanding that the masterminds be held accountable.

29. Under civil law, judgments are often short. Where an important case demands a longer decision, it is due to a summary of evidence more than to legal reasoning and precedent for a decision, as in the common law system. The verdict included some findings of fact, ranging from smaller details (such as that no one at Garuda had assigned Pollycarpus to go to Singapore, and that he called Munir's phone on September 2) to broadly significant ones, including the fact that there "were parties who did not like Munir due to his criticism, such that there was a motive to take Munir's life."

30. "Penyelidikan Kasus Munir Kembali ke Titik Nol," *Kompas*, December 20, 2005; "JPU Kasus Munir Ajukan Banding," *detikNews*, December 21, 2005.

31. "Suciwati Tidak Peduli Pollycarpus Cuma Divonis 14 Tahun," *detikNews*, December 20, 2005.

12: I Will Not Only Hope (2006)

1. "Polly Merasa Jadi Kambing Hitam," *Indopos*, December 13, 2006; "Tim Penyidik Kasus Munir Bubar," *Koran Tempo*, December 14, 2005; "Penyelidikan Kasus Munir Kembali ke Titik Nol," *Kompas*, December 20, 2005.

2. Suci met with police on January 13 and with the attorney general January 26.

She urged the attorney general to undertake the essential investigatory step of obtaining the details of the calls to and from Muchdi from the phone company.

3. "4 Orang Sebut Muchdi Terlibat Kasus Munir Akan Digugat," *detikNews*, February 21, 2006.

4. U.S. Embassy, Jakarta, "Munir Case: Justice Still Elusive," July 18, 2006.

5. In a private letter to the president, Suci noted that Munir was killed for his dream of justice, but it was still possible to "show all Indonesian people that it is still worth hoping for the *Ratu Adil* (Just Ruler) they long for, that the law will be enforced and will punish the guilty, no matter their position and power."

6. The Indonesian system has few obstacles to appeal right up to the Supreme Court, and unlike their American counterparts, Indonesian prosecutors can submit an appeal as well as defendants. Tim Lindsey, "Muddling Through," *Inside Indonesia* 87: July–September 2006.

7. Jakarta High Court Decision No. 16/Pid/2006/PT.DKI of March 27, 2006, confirming the verdict of Central Jakarta District Court No. 1361/Pid.B/2005/PN. Jkt.Pst of December 20, 2005. Indonesian judges very rarely dissent, but the chief judge and one member found that the change to facts of the murder invalidated the guilty verdict, even comparing the decision to an act of rape. They believed the evidence didn't prove that a premeditated murder took place, that Pollycarpus carried it out, or that it happened on the first leg of Munir's journey. Pollycarpus would remain in prison, but the dissent hinted at possible problems when the case went before the Supreme Court.

8. Supreme Court Verdict No. 1185 K/Pid/200, October 3, 2006. The Supreme Court has fifty-one judges, with cases being heard by smaller panels of three to five. These judges examine decisions of the lower courts as a court of cassation (annulment), or *kasasi* in Indonesian. This top appellate court, typically acting as judges of law (*judex juris*) rather than judges of fact (*judex facti*), is another Napoleonic legacy. As the mechanism passed through the Dutch, colonial, Guided Democracy, and New Order judicial systems, the distinction between law and fact weakened, and the court become more like a full appeals court in the common-law system.

9. At issue was the use of *petunjuk*, or indications: a pattern of circumstantial evidence to determine guilt in the absence of witnesses, under Article 188(1) of the Code of Criminal Procedure. One judge dissented, finding that Pollycarpus was correctly convicted and should be serving a life sentence. Artidjo Alkostar, a former LBH lawyer, found the trial judges' reasoning proper and their theory consistent with the prosecution's main thrust: a series of actions by the defendant intentionally caused the death of the victim.

10. See "Putusan Eksaminasi Publik atas Proses Hukum Kasus Pembunuhan Munir (Public Examination of the Legal Process in the Munir Murder Case)," March 14, 2007. Article 253 (3) of the Code of Criminal Procedure allows the Supreme Court to hear additional testimony, or to direct another court to do so. In a collection of rulings published by the Supreme Court in 2014, a former deputy chief justice similarly commented that the Court should have sent the case back to a lower court to hear additional evidence. In particular, it made little sense

to throw out the murder conviction while leaving in place the verdict on forg-ery, an act with no clear purpose by itself. Taufiq, "Analisa dan Anotasi terhadap Putusan Mahkamah Agung Tanggal 3 Oktober 2006 Nomor 1185 K/Pid/2006," in *Himpunan Putusan Yang Telah Berkekuatan Hukum Tetap Dalam Bidang Pidana Dan Pidana Khusus Mahkamah Agung Republik Indonesia*, Jilid 3, Perpustakaan Dan Layanan Informasi Biro Hukum Dan Humas Badan Urusan Administrasi Mahkamah Agung Republik Indonesia 2014, at perpustakaan.mahkamahagung .go.id/assets/resource/ebook/27.pdf.

11. "Munir Minum Racun Sendiri?" *Republika*, October 5, 2006.

12. The editorial disparaged SBY's recent nomination for the Nobel Peace Prize for his role in ending the conflict in Aceh. "Forget the Nobel, Remember Munir," *Jakarta Post*, October 6, 2006.

13. "Munir Probe Chief Failed Before: Activists," *Jakarta Post*, October 8, 2006; U.S. Embassy, Jakarta, "Ambassador Reaffirms Support for Justice in Munir Slay-ing," October 11, 2006.

14. Article 263 of the Code of Criminal Procedures specifies that convicted per-sons or their heirs may submit a request to the Supreme Court for reconsideration of a final and binding judgment on the basis of new circumstances, contradictory statements forming the basis of the judgment, or a manifest error by the judge.

15. "Kejagung: Putusan Pollycarpus Sudah Final," *Kompas*, October 5, 2006; "AGO May Seek Pollycarpus Review," *Jakarta Post*, October 7, 2006.

16. U.S. Embassy, Jakarta, "Ambassador Reaffirms Support for Justice in Munir Slaying," October 11, 2006.

17. I was on the Human Rights First staff at the time and played a role in invit-ing Usman and Suci to New York and arranging meetings.

18. Andreas Harsono and Nathaniel Heller, "Jakarta's Intelligence Service Hires Washington Lobbyists," Center for Public Integrity, September 7, 2006 (updated May 19, 2014).

19. The lobbyists contacted the offices of National Security Advisor Condoleez-za Rice, Deputy Secretary of State Richard Armitage, and the State Department's counterterrorism coordinator Cofer Black, among other State Department offi-cials.

20. Alston Bird, Exhibit A to FARA Registration statement, December 11, 2003. FARA stands for Foreign Agents Registration Act of 1938. Individual generals have also hired lobbyists to burnish their image after human rights abuses. In 2001, General Wiranto signed a contract to pay a quarter of a million dollars to lobbyists to "correct the record and restore the General's reputation in the United States as an Indonesian patriot whose first concern is for the stability, integrity, and economic prosperity of his country." Letter of Engagement, signed by Gen-eral Wiranto and Trans Pacific Partners, LLC, June 26, 2001. In 2015 former Kopassus commander Prabowo Subianto hired American lobbyists as well.

21. The FARA filing states, "Collins & Company intends to educate key officials on the importance of Indonesia's cooperation in combating international terror-ism, Indonesia's strides in strengthening democratic institutions and Indonesia's

efforts in asserting civilian control over the military. Additionally, Collins and Company will aid Indonesia in seeking to demonstrate to the U.S. Congress that it is time to remove legislative and policy restrictions on military-to-military cooperation with Indonesia."

22. They met with the staff of representatives Dan Burton, Robert Wexler, and Gregory Meeks.

23. Interview, As'ad Said Ali, November 2019. A top Leahy staffer told the investigative journalists that the senator agreed to the fifteen-minute meeting to state his opposition to resuming full military ties without reforms.

24. Meeting between Christine Rosendahl and congressional staffer Sean Hughes, Office of Representative Jim McDermott, October 13, 2005. BIN officials also met with key committee staff and several senators and representatives, including Senator Chuck Hagel (later secretary of defense) and Senator Lisa Murkowski. The next day they met with Keith Luse, of the Senate Foreign Relations Committee, and Mark Lipper, a foreign policy advisor to Senator Barack Obama. The lobbyists drafted a floor statement lauding Indonesia's successful elections for Representative Joe Wilson to deliver and place into the *Congressional Record*. "Democratization in Indonesia: A New Era," *Congressional Record*, November 3, 2005.

25. The foundation's secretary asked the journalists, "How could we have this much money? How could we pay $30,000 per month?"

26. Dan Rather Reports, "The Best Congress Money Can Buy," November 21, 2006 (video), www.youtube.com/watch?v=NowpCswP40c.

27. The NGOs asked the Constitutional Court to review Article 27, which said compensation may be awarded when a request for amnesty is granted; Article 44, which states that gross violations of human rights resolved by the commission cannot be brought before a human rights court; and Article 1(9) on amnesty. *Tim Advokasi Kebenaran dan Keadilan*, LBH Jakarta, 2006.

28. "Pertemuan Pertama, Munir Membuka Mata Hati Yati Andriyani soal Pelanggaran HAM," *Kompas*, September 11, 2019; "Koordinator KontraS Mengenang Inspirasi dan Pertemuan Terakhir dengan Munir," *Kompas*, September 9, 2019; "Meninggalnya Munir Membuat Yati Andriyani Bertekad Perjuangkan HAM," *Kompas*, September 9, 2019.

13: The Singer at the Airport Café (2007)

1. Meeting transcript, January 18, 2007, Kasum files.

2. The embassy felt the request was a very positive development that should be kept secret, as Indonesia was "very sensitive about foreign assistance in this sensitive investigation." The next month, however, Police Chief Sutanto made public that the FBI would be involved in the case. U.S. Embassy Jakarta, "Indonesian Police Ask for U.S. Help in Munir Case," November 3, 2006; "FBI dan Kasus Munir," *Media Indonesia*, November 25, 2006.

3. U.S. Embassy Jakarta, "New Munir Case Evidence Gives Widow Hope," January 19, 2007.

4. U.S. Embassy Jakarta, "New Munir Case Evidence Gives Widow Hope," January 19, 2007.

5. U.S. Embassy Jakarta, "Visit of Indonesian Police Chief Sutanto to Washington," January 19, 2007. It is unclear if description of the evidence as "promising" is speculative or if it is based on knowledge that something useful was found on the phones.

6. Besides its larger size, the previous team had had an additional layer of bureaucracy, the director for transnational crime, between the investigation team leader and the director of the Criminal Investigation Division.

7. "Transkrip & Pointer Pertemuan dengan Tim Munir Mabes Polri," February 13, 2007, Kasum document.

8. Usman reminded the group that in 2004, local police arrested KontraS investigators gathering data about the deaths at Talangsari. The police had said it was on orders from Jakarta, due to terrorists entering the area. Hendropriyono also once made the mistake of trying to bribe Asmara when he headed the National Human Rights Commission and Talangsari was under consideration. Outraged, Asmara demanded an apology. Hendro apologized for the "misunderstanding" and promised it would never happen again. Asmara wasn't even part of the Talangsari inquiry team, so it was likely that bribes were offered to his colleagues, too. Whatever the means, the National Human Rights Commission's efforts were shut down quickly. After victims' families occupied the commission's offices to demand action, the body had launched inquiries focusing on the student shootings and the massacre at Talangsari. Some action followed on the shootings, but investigators never even went to Sumatra. A second team formed in 2003 also went nowhere. An inquiry was eventually completed in 2006.

9. The TPF had noted that the threats to Suci and Munir's mother were meant to silence Munir's family, but also that "the message intended to be conveyed through this terror was to discredit the armed forces and cause conflict between NGOs and the armed forces." *Final Report of the Tim Pencari Fakta Kasus Meninggalnya Munir (TPF)*, Jakarta, 2005, 45.

10. A related question was why Munir was killed outside the country. It would have been easier to accomplish the task in Indonesia, with far less international scrutiny and an autopsy more open to manipulation or suppression. An airplane or an airport are both strange choices, given the presence of witnesses and cameras, and the ease of identifying nearly anyone with access to the victim. But if Usman's suspicions were correct, an airplane would also provide a controlled environment.

11. "Kontras Desak Polri Fokus Selidiki Hubungan Telepon Pollycarpus," *detikNews*, February 7, 2007.

12. They were the flashy Mun'im Idris, formerly of the TPF, and a toxicologist from the University of North Sumatra named Amar Singh, who had worked on the case since the police delegation to Amsterdam in 2004.

13. The account of Gelgel's work comes from his trial testimony and the article "Uji Laboratorium Pengubah Skenario," *Tempo*, December 8, 2014. Hendarso and Salempang also told the U.S. Embassy on April 26 that the American lab

had identified a form of arsenic that would take effect between thirty and sixty minutes after ingestion, leading to a new timeline for the murder. U.S. Embassy, Jakarta, "Progress in the Munir Case," May 1, 2007.

14. Meeting notes, February 1, 2007, Kasum files.

15. "Perjamuan Terakhir di Coffee Bean," *Tempo*, April 16, 2007.

16. Police source cited in "Misteri Si Gondrong di Kedai Kopi," *Tempo*, December 8, 2014. One investigator remembered unraveling this mystery differently. He thought they got the nickname Ongen from a witness, perhaps Ririmase. By asking people from the Moluccas, they soon learned his identity. Interview, November 2019.

17. Many of the stateless refugees dreamed of returning to an independent Moluccan republic. In the 1970s, frustrated younger members of the diaspora carried out sporadic terrorism in the Netherlands. The Moluccan community has since largely abandoned the idea of a return and has adopted Dutch citizenship. While much smaller than such movements in Aceh and Papua, Moluccan separatism was among the challenges to Jakarta cited to justify an opposing fervor to defend the Unitary State of the Republic of Indonesia or NKRI.

18. In 1677, European powers gathered in Breda to sign a treaty that, among other things, gave the Dutch control of the remote and tiny Banda Islands in the Moluccas, then the only source of immensely valuable nutmeg. (The British fared well in the treaty, acquiring sovereignty of the New Netherlands, including New Amsterdam, which they renamed New York.)

19. "Pasar Malam Zwolle, 07-04-2007," YouTube video, youtube.com/watch?v=UVUgwR9HTAc.

20. Interview, police investigator, November 2019. See also U.S. Embassy, Jakarta, "Progress in the Munir Case," May 1, 2007.

21. "Fighting Over Ongen," *Tempo*, May 8–14, 2007; "Kasus Munir: Polri-BIN Bantah Rebutan Ongen," *detikNews*, May 10, 2007; interview, police investigator, November 2019.

22. "Five Views, One Incident," *Tempo*, April 24–30, 2007. According to one investigator, however, Asrini did identify the man as Pollycarpus through a photo lineup. When boarding in Jakarta, she'd squeezed by him in the aisle, seen his face very close-up, and remembered the dark bags under his eyes. Interview, police investigator, November 2019.

23. "Fighting Over Ongen," *Tempo*, No. 36/VII, May 8–14, 2007.

24. Transcript of Ongen Latuihamallo Press Conference, June 6, 2006, Kasum files and "Ongen Setelah Dua Purnama," *Tempo*, June 11, 2007. See also "Ongen Bantah Bunuh Munir," Deutsche Welle, June 6, 2007.

25. "Kasus Munir: Wawancara Eksklusif dengan Ongen," Liputan6.com, June 7, 2007.

26. U.S. Embassy Jakarta, "Visit of Indonesian Police Chief Sutanto to Washington," January 19, 2007.

27. In one of Hendarso's first public statement as CID director, he observed that FBI cooperation had already borne fruit, though he gave no details.

28. A Freedom of Information Act request to the FBI produced a 302 form created by the FBI dated January 10, 2007, that shows five items analyzed, but the results were redacted, and forty-five other pages were withheld altogether on grounds of either privacy or confidentiality of technique of analysis.

29. Indra and Usman developed a theory about what happened to the data from Quantico. A senior police general named Gories Mere was on the team that went to Washington in January 2007. A former head of police intelligence, Mere was credited with counterterrorism successes and had strong ties to BIN, Hendropriyono, and others in Megawati's circle. (Mere later joined Hendropriyono's lucrative consulting firm.) He also seemed to be at police headquarters every time Kasum met with investigators, even though he had nothing to do with the case. They wondered if this senior police official had been tasked with shutting down the investigation or destroying evidence. Mere's car was reportedly broken into at the airport soon after his trip to the United States, around the time the police began denying anything was found on the phones. Indra was afraid crucial evidence had been stolen or destroyed, the break-in being a cover story, because a police three-star general's car is not often robbed.

30. Article 1370 of the Civil Code provides legal ground for a beneficiary to file a claim for unlawful or negligent death. See also Article 3 of Ministry of Transportation Regulation No. 77 of 2011 on the Liability of Air Carriers and Article 166 of the Indonesian Aviation Law.

31. Garuda Indonesia Basic Operational Manual 5.2.1. The manual also states that even if a doctor is present, the Garuda crew is responsible for making decisions. See also Choirul Anam, "Penerbangan Cak Munir di Intip Pembunuhan," berpolitik.com, April 25, 2007.

32. "Ungkap 'Surat Sakti' BIN, Kini Indra Setiawan Plong," *detikNews*, August 11, 2007. A police source told a journalist that Setiawan repeatedly asked to speak to senior BIN officials from the moment he was arrested.

33. In Indonesia, polygamy is rare but legal with permission from the first wife. Lacking that, and the recognition of the state, marrying a second wife is illegal even if there is a religious ceremony.

34. Interview, police investigator, November 2019.

35. While it is possible the burglary was staged or prearranged, it does not appear to have been made up altogether. Hotel security staff confirmed to *Tempo* that the break-in took place, and it was reported to local police and to Garuda security at the time. "Pertaruhan Terakhir, Munir," *Tempo*, August 20–26, 2007; "Saksi Kunci Pembuka Surat Rahasia," *Tempo*, December 8, 2014.

36. Police dossier in Muchdi trial. See also testimony of Indra Setiawan at September 16 session of Muchdi trial, including a partial readout of his Record of Interrogation. When *Tempo* reported on Setiawan's account to police of the meetings, the member of parliament Taufiequrrahman confirmed the meeting but claimed they only ran into Muchdi at the hotel by chance. He knew Muchdi from when the general was chief of staff at the regional military command in East Java a decade earlier. "Roger, Roger, Intel Sudah Terkepung," *Tempo*, August 20–26, 2007; "Tiga Tahun Terantuk Tiga Huruf," *Tempo*, September 10, 2007.

37. U.S. Embassy, Jakarta, "Progress in the Munir Case," May 1, 2007.

38. Like a building, the case needed a strong foundation, "so that we don't get hit by a typhoon." "Takut 'Angin Ribut,' Hendarman Minta Tambahan Bukti Kasus Munir," *detikNews*, May 11, 2007.

39. "KontraS: Peninjauan Kembali Terlalu Dipaksakan," *Suara Pembaruan*, July 21, 2007.

40. The father of one of the prosecutors who drafted the case-review request had drafted the last such request from prosecutors, to review the acquittal of the labor activist Muchtar Pakpahan in the 1990s.

41. They also asked about the reasons for his travel in September 2004, the café menu, and the process of ordering. A senior police official told the press that Ongen had canceled his departure for the Netherlands a few times, before securing a seat on a very full plane. "Ongen Setelah Dua Purnama," *Tempo*, June 11, 2007.

42. "Inilah Bocoran BAP yang Ditolak Ongen Latuihamallo," *detikNews*, August 29, 2007.

43. U.S. Embassy, Jakarta, "Munir Case: Attorney General Files Appeal Based on New Evidence," August 6, 2007.

44. Speaking to the press after the meeting, Usman never mentioned Ucok or As'ad. The conversation had been confidential and it would be better not to tip anyone off before the case-review hearings had begun. Polly's lawyer, Assegaf, was a lawyer for Garuda and so was also representing Indra Setiawan. He had seen the prosecution's filing too, and he announced to the press that the director had only taken the actions he was charged with after a senior BIN official sent him a *surat sakti*, a "magic letter." His client couldn't refuse a request from BIN, one that cc'd his boss, the minister of state-owned enterprises. Assegaf also argued that the letter showed that Munir's death was not a BIN assassination, because *intel* usually does a "silent operation." "Pollycarpus Bertugas Atas Permintaan BIN," *Koran Tempo*, August 12, 2007. Assegaf also revealed that the letter was missing, and he wrote to BIN to ask them to confirm whether As'ad sent a letter to Setiawan, and whether an agent named Ucok was ordered to kill Munir. Assegaf's letter provoked two immediate responses. BIN's director said there was no such letter from As'ad, and the agency would never issue orders to a state-owned enterprise. He also urged the arrest of anyone lying about being a BIN agent, such as this Ucok. The second reaction was from Usman and Suci, who reported Assegaf to the lawyers' association. They were furious at what they saw as an effort to warn BIN of crucial evidence, giving its agents the opportunity to intimidate witnesses on the eve of the case review. "Pengacara Polly Minta BIN Jelaskan 4 Hal Tentang Indra & Ucok," *detikNews*, August 13, 2007.

14. Spooks and Spirits (2007)

1. The same day, Keith Luse, a senior staffer on the U.S. Senate committee that oversees military aid, visited Jakarta. The CID director Hendarso told Luse, "This will not be finished until we get whoever is behind the case." Hendarso

assured him that his team of nine had worked full-time for a year to carry out the president's orders to resolve the Munir case. U.S. Embassy, Jakarta, "Munir Case: Senate Staffer Gets Upbeat Appraisal," August 13, 2007.

2. They would also argue for their legal standing to invoke a mechanism some believed was intended for defendants. To do so, they cited favorable interpretations of the law, the few and controversial precedents, and the emerging concept of victims' rights. Prosecutors also argued that even with the crime scene now in Singapore, the case fell under Indonesian jurisdiction because the *effect* of the crime, Munir's death, took place on an Indonesian airline.

3. "Roger, Roger, Intel Sudah Terkepung," *Tempo*, August 20–26, 2007.

4. Setiawan later confirmed these code names to police, but it was fairly clear at the time. Besides the similarity of the names Asmini and As'ad, and the references to a letter, Polly said he previously contacted "Mrs. Asmini" through her adjutant a "Navy two-star." There was a retired admiral at BIN and, while not an adjutant, he had worked directly under As'ad as deputy VII. His name was Bijah Subiakto; he'd invited Munir to meet shortly before his death, and later he held several cryptic meetings with Suci before getting spooked and removed from his job. If Polly was referring to Subiakto, it might mean he really did have information about the plot to share with Suciwati. Polly later claimed to police that Bu Asmini was a woman from Ambon who stayed at his house for three years until she died in 2006. He did not provide proof or explain why she had an admiral for an adjutant. See "Misteri Joker, Avi, dan Asmini," *Tempo*, August 27, 2007.

5. Polly also had an explanation for Bu Avi. She was the wife of a Garuda pilot and had helped him a lot. Discovering such a person existed, investigators called her in and asked her to confirm Polly's explanations. She had cried and denied his claims. "Misteri Joker, Avi, dan Asmini," *Tempo*, August 27, 2007.

6. When Hendarman Supandji took over as attorney general in May 2007, just weeks before the taped phone call, his departing predecessor had emphasized the need to resolve the Munir case. Supandji did send Polly's case-review file back to police within days of taking over, as Polly promised, but that may have been a coincidence.

7. A police investigator says Setiawan did not know about the recording device (interview, November 2019). However, the timing and his behavior on the call make it possible that after finally revealing the As'ad letter, he was trying to get Polly to discuss it on tape.

8. After the hearing, Pollycarpus described his recorded comments as "just a joke to have some fun" in order to cheer up his old boss. Everyone named on the tape denied being *orang kita*—Polly's people. "Rekaman Telepon Polly-Indra Bukti Baru Kasus Munir," Liputan6.com, August 22, 2007.

9. U.S. Embassy, Jakarta, "Munir Case: Stunning Revelations at Hearing," August 23, 2007.

10. "PK Munir's Testimony, Pointed to Polly," BBC, August 22, 2007.

11. "Kasus Munir: Pertaruhan Terakhir Munir," *Tempo*, August 20–26, 2007.

12. While a *dukun santet* specializes in black magic, people might also turn to a

dukun for help with relationships, work, and health. They might want to obtain invulnerability, a youthful appearance, the ability to sweet-talk people, a frightening appearance (popular with police), business success, an improved appearance by the insertion of a silver or gold splinter into their skin, advice or assistance, divination about past or future, or treatment for illness. See Nicholas Herriman, "A Din of Whispers: Community, State Control, and Violence in Indonesia," PhD Diss., University of Western Australia, 2007.

13. Lieutenant General Arie Kumaat had served as head of military intelligence and then the nominally civilian BAKIN from 1999 until 2001. He died in 2002.

14. U.S. Embassy, Jakarta, "Munir Case: Stunning Revelations at Hearing," August 23, 2007.

15. Maladi also claimed that it was Ucok who wanted to harass Munir, in 2003, but Sentot ordered him not to. "Beber Semua Kartu Truf," *Jawa Pos*, August 27, 2007; "Kasus Munir: Pertaruhan Terakhir," *Tempo*, August 20–26, 2007.

16. "Roger, Roger, Intel Sudah Terkepung," *Tempo*, August 20–26, 2007. Some at Kasum agreed that a magical approach did not seem typical of BIN. However, a former BIN agent told me the strength of mystical beliefs in Indonesia made Ucok's claims entirely possible.

17. U.S. Embassy, Jakarta, "Munir Case: Senate Staffer Gets Upbeat Appraisal," August 13, 2007.

18. "Saksi: Munir, Polly, Si Gondrong Duduk Semeja di Coffee Bean," *detikNews*, August 22, 2007.

19. Interview, November 2019.

20. U.S. Embassy, Jakarta, "Munir Case: Stunning Revelations at Hearing," August 23, 2007.

21. "Opini: Membuang Duri dalam Daging," *Kompas*, August 27, 2007.

22. Ongen also said that when he asked his escort who would be waiting at the Jakarta airport besides the police, he was told, "Three letters." He did not explain, but the reference was to BIN. "Kasus Munir: Ongen dan Penyidik Saling Bantah," DW.com, August 29, 2007.

23. "Kontras: Selidiki Lagi Kesaksian Ongen," *Tempo*, August 30, 2007. Suci went further, telling the press it was clear that Ongen was the one lying in court that day. "Suciwati: Ongenlah yang Bohong," *detikNews*, August 29, 2007.

24. Gelgel explained how he was tasked to review the results from Seattle, which found a combination of trivalent arsenic at 83 percent and pentavalent arsenic at 17 percent. He estimated the timeline based on these figures and a pharmacokinetic simulation of how the poison would behave inside the body. "Ahli Toksikologi Temukan Arsen Campuran di Tubuh Munir," *detikNews*, August 29, 2007. See also Central Jakarta State Prosecutor, "Permohonan Peninjauan Kembali Putusan Mahkamah Agung (Request for Case Review of the Supreme Court Decision)," July 26, 2007.

25. "Suciwati Desak BIN Cabut Duri Dalam Daging," *Jawa Pos*, September 8, 2007; "Tiga Tahun Terantuk Tiga Huruf," *Tempo*, September 10, 2007; "Mawar Munir Ditolak Petugas BIN," *detikNews*, September 7, 2007.

26. "Bantah Novum, Polly Ajukan 5 Pakar," Seputar-Indonesia.com, September 9, 2007.

27. "Kuasa Hukum Polly: Sidang PK adalah Pelanggaran HAM," *detikNews*, September 12, 2007; "Pengacara: Rekaman Polly-Indra Bualan, Tak Bisa Jadi Novum," *detikNews*, September 12, 2007; "Pollycarpus Ajukan Kontra Memori PK," HukumOnline.com, September 12, 2007.

28. "Kasum Ragukan Netralitas Bagir Dalam Sidang PK Munir," *detikNews*, November 1, 2007.

29. "Kasus Munir Jadi Komoditas Politik," *Kompas*, October 27, 2007; "Pelanggaran HAM: Pengungkapan Kasus Munir Ditawarkan Saat Pemilu," *Kompas*, October 17, 2007.

30. Setiawan's lawyer argued that, although he signed the August 11 recommendation letter, he knew nothing of any murder plot. If Polly later broke the rules to fly on Munir's plane, that was his fault alone. Aini was still represented by Assegaf, who claimed his client was a mere scapegoat for police under pressure to make progress after Pollycarpus's acquittal.

31. "Suciwati Pernah Diminta Anggota BIN Kejar SK Polly," *detikNews*, November 7, 2007.

32. "To Prove Polly's Assignment, Prosecutor Presents BIN Witness," Antara news agency, November 27, 2007.

33. "KASUM Minta Polisi Jadikan Muchdi PR Tersangka," *detikNews*, January 17, 2008.

34. Decision No. 109 PK/Pid/2007, January 25, 2008.

35. They cited article 266 (3) of the Code of Criminal Procedure, which says, "The penalty imposed in the decision for a review shall not exceed the penalty decided in the original verdict."

36. Pollycarpus testimony at Muchdi trial.

37. Seth Mydans, "Conviction in Poisoning of Indonesian Rights Activist," *New York Times*, February 6, 2008. The article notes that the U.S. Congress had recently voted to hold back $2.7 million in military aid unless Jakarta set a deadline for completing the criminal investigation. See also "Suciwati: Mantan Jenderal dan Petinggi BIN Harus Diusut," *detikNews*, January 26, 2008.

15: The Arrest (2008)

1. "Indra Setiawan Reads Defense While Bringing Al Quran," *detikNews*, February 1, 2008.

2. On April 16 police sent prosecutors a notification of commencement of investigation (*surat pemberitahuan dimulainya penyidikan*, or SPDP), no. 17/IV/2008/ Dit I Bareskrim.

3. "Pollycarpus Siap Dikonfrontasi dengan Muchdi," *Kompas*, June 28, 2008.

4. Interview, police investigator, November 2019.

5. On June 16, prosecutors met with police to go over the dossier, an effort to avoid sending it back repeatedly to fix gaps in evidence. "Kapolri Tutup Rapat Calon Tersangka Kasus Munir," *Kompas*, June 17, 2008.

6. Prabowo invited Muchdi to take part in early discussions about the name and symbol for the party. Chairawan Nusyirwan, the third officer to go before the honor board in 1998, joined the party as well. Chairawan had moved to the military intelligence body BAIS and retired as a major general.

7. "Jejak Arsen dari Pejaten," *Tempo*, December 14, 2014, 51.

8. Surat Perintah Penahanan No. Pol: SP. Han/28/VI/2008/Dit-I; "Muchdi Detained over Munir Murder," *Jakarta Post*, June 20, 2008; Interview, police investigator, November 2019; see also "Muchdi PR Diperiksa Intensif," *Kompas*, June 19, 2008; "Kronologi Muchdi PR Jadi Tersangka Pembunuhan Munir," *detikNews*, June 20, 2008.

9. "Muchdi Terbukti Menyuruh Bunuh Munir," *Kompas*, July 8, 2008.

10. There was a document number on the envelope, R-451/VII/2004, the R standing for *rahasia*, or secret. The date of the file was July 24, 2004, around the time Setiawan says Polly gave him the letter. "Saksi Ahli Bongkar Isi Komputer BIN," VIVAnews, October 21, 2008. The spelling of As'ad's name as "As at" is either an alternate spelling or, more likely, a typo by staff.

11. "The First Session, Muchdi PR," DW.com, August 21, 2008.

12. KontraS, "Monitoring Persidangan I Kasus Pembunuhan Munir Dengan Terdakwa Muchdi Purwopranjono," August 21, 2008; "Muchdi Tebar Senyum Tiba di Pengadilan," *detikNews*, August 21, 2008.

13. The crime of participation is known as *penyertaan* in Indonesian and *deelneming* in Dutch.

14. "JPU: Muchdi Pr Sakit Hati pada Munir," *Kompas*, August 21, 2008.

15. U.S. Embassy, Jakarta, "Subject: Former Intelligence Official Stands Trial in Munir Case," August 22, 2018.

16. The article described them as "dozens of stocky men who call themselves Solidarity for Muchdi's Freedom," though they admitted being from the ethnic *preman* group Forum Betawi Rempug and the Muslim martial arts group Tapak Suci. "'Groupies' Muchdi Pr Meriahkan Sidang Munir," *detikNews*, December 11, 2008.

17. The reliance on civilian mobs may have been a sign of lack of support from the military. One analyst theorized that the absence of overt support from other soldiers was because the president, ex-military himself, had "personally given the nod for the prosecution to go ahead." Gerry Van Klinken, "Indonesian Politics in 2008: The Ambiguities of Democratic Change," *Bulletin of Indonesian Economic Studies* 44 no. 3 (December 2008): 365–81.

18. KontraS, "Monitoring Persidangan II Kasus Pembunuhan Munir Dengan Terdakwa Muchdi Purwopranjono," September 2, 2008.

19. KontraS, "Monitoring Persidangan IV Kasus Pembunuhan Munir Dengan Terdakwa Muchdi Purwopranjono," September 9, 2008; "Muchdi PR Ben-

tak Suciwati," Liputan6.com, September 9, 2008; "Muchdi Pr Bentak Suciwati," *detikNews*, September 9, 2008.

16. The General in His Courtroom (2008)

1. Law No. 39 of 1999 on Human Rights, article 7. Suci held in her lap a large envelope with documents to undermine the defense's claims of foreign intervention. They included a report on BIN lobbying in the United States, to justify her own efforts there, and letters from the Indonesian parliament to Myanmar's government on human rights, to show that such communications were normal and proper. She submitted them to the judges after her testimony.

2. "Mengenal Pius Lustrilanang, Pernah Dipecat dari PDI-P hingga Menjadi Pimpinan BPK," *Kompas*, September 26, 2019.

3. "Saksi Melihat Budi Santoso Pakai HP Muchdi," HukumOnline.com, September 24, 2008.

4. "Dokumen Rahasia Ungkap Keterlibatan Hendro Priyono," *Kompas*, September 23, 2008; "Pembunuhan Munir: TPF Terima Informasi Tertulis dari BIN," *Kompas*, September 24, 2008.

5. After Hendardi vacated the witness chair, Secretary to the Chief of Pilots Rohainil Aini was brought in. She confirmed that her change notice, which allowed Polly onto Munir's flight, had referenced the August 11 assignment letter from Indra Setiawan, a copy of which she said had somehow appeared on her desk. Presumably the prosecution was trying to trace a chain back from the death of Munir to Polly's placement on flight 974, to the August 11 assignment letter, to the As'ad letter, and so to Muchdi. But when not done effectively, the questioning seemed less relevant to Muchdi's guilt than to Polly's. The defense expressed irritation about questions with no connection to the defendant.

6. Several online bios contradict Muchdi's claim of a start date of 1988. But even if true, he likely spent time in Jayapura before becoming district military commander.

7. The judges again prodded him to remember if BIN paid him a salary, but he said "his condition" got in the way. When a defense lawyer asked if he grew marijuana as part of his horticultural business, the nod to his memory lapses drew laughs, and the reply, "No, no, just ornamental plantings."

8. Polly said he forgot what his cell numbers were in 2004, both the Nokia and the red Sony Ericsson that he'd been told were taken to America.

9. Now that both Polly and Setiawan had been convicted, it was unclear how much it mattered whether Karmel or Ramel was his supervisor. And after four years, prosecutors still confused the company-wide practice of aviation security with the departments of Corporate Security and Internal Security. They once even referred to corporate aviation, showing a sloppiness that risked confusing an already complex conspiracy.

10. Polly claimed other investigators told him he'd go free if he just said he'd been to the BIN offices. Someone else offered him four billion *rupiah* to help

support his family if he confessed. Once in prison, he said he was approached several more times with such offers.

11. Muchdi skipped his opportunity to respond, speaking only once during the testimony. When his lawyer complained about a camera flash, Muchdi joined in to point at the perpetrator across the room, yelling, "The one with the blue shirt!"

12. Some of these records had been otherwise obtained, including one of Polly's phones showing dozens of calls and messages in November 2004 to and from phones owned by Muchdi, Indra Setiawan, the Garuda security chief, and the BIN agent Budi Santoso. One theory of why the police and prosecutors used only September's calls at trial was that other months might have implicated Hendropriyono or senior politicians in the crime or coverup.

13. The final expert appeared a week later, a Telkom staffer who again explained calls on September 6 and 7. He confirmed that call records cannot be falsified, and also that the *content* of a conversation cannot be retrieved after the fact.

14. For the next witness, police investigator Pambudi Pamungkas, questioning improved slightly, but still focused on process. Pambudi denied Kawan's claim to have signed the interrogation record without reading it: "Not true, and that's impossible." His account varied from Daniel's only in that he remembered giving Kawan his own reading glasses, rather than sending someone to buy a pair. Prosecutors read out Zondy's admission to police that he typed the contact list and envelope.

15. The judges had also received a copy by DHL but wouldn't address it unless submitted through proper channels. "Kasus Munir Menanti Pengakuan Budi Santoso," *Tempo*, January 12, 2009.

16. Dandhy Dwi Laksono, *Jurnalisme Investigasi* (Bandung: Kaifa, 2010).

17. A journalist who later viewed a videotape of the interrogation reported that Budi described a meeting at which Hendropriyono claimed Munir was planning to "sell" Indonesia abroad and had to be stopped. "Jejak Arsen dari Pejaten," *Tempo*, December 14, 2014, 49. Hendropriyono famously made similar comments to parliament in May 2004, accusing twenty NGOs of selling out the country.

18. Given the chance to respond, Muchdi first rejected the statements in totality because they were not made in person. Then he denied specific statements, large and small. He claimed that as director of planning and operations, Budi knew everything that happened in Muchdi's section, so any answers of "I don't know" were not credible. Regarding Budi's alleged conversations with Polly, he found it impossible that after four years he could remember precisely what someone said to him. And even if Polly *was* a BIN agent, Muchdi would have dealt with him only through the directors under him, such as Budi.

19. See Muchdi dossier and trial monitoring reports. The 2014 report in the magazine *Tempo*, based on videos of the interrogation, included the observation that Budi teared up, saying, "I wonder how someone could kill another so easily."

20. As'ad said for letters in support of operations he receives a letter from high-level "conceptors" such as deputies, the principal secretary, and expert or special staff. If the document meets administrative requirements, he signs it, often with-

out knowing the substance in any detail.

21. An investigator had asked if BIN leadership had to know of every nonorganic agent. As'ad replied that, "Leadership, including me, does not have to know about the recruiting and assignment process of this agent." (The term *jejaring* translates as network or web, but can refer to an individual within it as well, and so is translated here as "agent")

22. For example, the *Washington Post* reported, "Lt. Gen. Prabowo Subianto, who was once a rising star in the armed forces and had close ties with the U.S. military, has been discharged following an investigation by a special military board, the defense minister, Gen. Wiranto, told reporters today in Jakarta, the capital. Two other army officers, Maj. Gen. Muchdi Purwopranjono and Col. Chairawan, were removed from their posts but not from the army." Cindy Shiner, "Indonesian Military Fires Suharto In-Law," *Washington Post*, August 25, 1998.

23. Using the Indonesian acronym for the honor board, Wiranto wrote, "The DPK also recommended the dismissal of the then Commander of Kopassus, Major General Muchdi PR. I approved the decisions taken by the DPK. . . ." *Witness in the Storm* (Jakarta: Delta Pustaka Express, 2004).

24. "Peristiwa Penculikan," at web.archive.org/web/20020416140336/http://www.dephan.go.id/fakta/p_penculikan.htm.

25. Tim Lindsey and Jemma Parsons, "The One That Got Away?" *Inside Indonesia*, December 21, 2008.

26. A discussion about whether proving intent required showing motive hinged, as many Indonesian legal matters do, on the interpretation of Dutch legal terms such as *uitlokking* (instigation) and *medepleger* (accomplice). The defense also used the expert to argue that it was not enough to show that money was given without linking the funds to a criminal act. As for the phone calls, he explained that it was rare to make a case without the content of the calls, but possible with intensive communication.

17: The Verdict (November 2008–January 2009)

1. Muchdi explained that deputies cannot send letters over their own names but can propose a draft concept to the BIN director or deputy director for their signature. That policy would be consistent with a letter to Garuda from Muchdi's office but signed by As'ad.

2. Earlier, when a judge asked for BIN's remit, Muchdi had said it was "consistent with threats to the state that arise, first concerning the problem of terrorism, then problems of separatism and also threats to the unity of the nation."

3. Muchdi had already confirmed meeting Indra Setiawan in As'ad's office. When the prosecution asked about other meetings with the airline director, Muchdi replied, "Once, by chance at a hotel, as Indra said the other day . . . Hotel Mulia or whatever . . . it's called saying hello." There was no follow up to ask about Setiawan's claim that the meeting was *not* by chance, but to discuss his imminent appearance before the parliamentary commission.

4. The irregular layout was a frequent defense argument, but it was possible that the original formatting had not survived being deleted, cloned, and recovered, or that Polly hadn't correctly formatted it even with the help of BIN staff.

5. Muchdi said he knew of no funding for Polly, and it would be normal for him not to. He pointed to the crowd and said he had an example here today. The chair of the West Papuan legislature was there, and BIN once gave him money for a meeting: "If it's just 50 million rupiah or below, it's never through me." His example didn't address the fact that nothing prevented him from ordering his staff to provide a payment of any size. (It also raised questions about why the intelligence agency was giving money to a legislator from a region marked by conflict and political intrigue.)

6. The International Crisis Group noted at the time that the decision to divide the province "has done more to create tension and turmoil there than any government action in years." International Crisis Group, "Dividing Papua: How Not to Do It," April 9, 2003.

7. Like the Garuda director before him, with this dramatic comparison Muchdi was echoing Suharto's comments from 1999, after a magazine reported on how much of Indonesia's wealth his family had looted over the years.

8. "Kontras Nilai Tuntutan Muchdi Perlemah Kasus Munir," Liputan6.com, December 5, 2008.

9. The *replik* is the prosecutor's response to the *pledoi*. Munir supporters returned in force as prosecutors rebutted the notion they had been deceived by the "real killer." They cited evidence of communication, motive, and Polly's recruitment to BIN. It was a strong argument, read in a flat, halting tone. Journalists tuned out, Muchdi's men dozed in the back, and the defense lawyers fell asleep or looked at their phones. Usman listened intently near the front of the room.

10. The defense divided the document into eleven sections. The first section concerned undue international pressure in the case. They noted that sixteen of the supposed phone contacts were between September 6 and September 12, when they claimed Muchdi was in Malaysia. They also addressed Polly's alleged recruitment as an agent, motive, the funds from Budi, the As'ad letter, and so on.

11. "Wawancara dengan Muchdi Pr," *Majalah MAHKAMAH*, January 4, 2009.

12. The judges also took into account Ucok's claim that he was ordered to kill Munir, but noted this order did not come from Muchdi himself.

13. The Indonesian term *menyuruh melakukan*, or *to order to do*, correlates to a Dutch legal term *doenpleger*. The *doenpleger* orders someone to do something criminal, without that other person bearing liability, such as unknowingly distributing counterfeit money. The term *uitloker*, or instigator, is used when the crime is committed jointly. Many Indonesian legal arguments hinge on the precise meaning of Dutch legal terms, even though younger lawyers have not studied Dutch and the terms may no longer be in use in Dutch courts. An internet search for *doenpleger* leads mostly to Indonesian websites.

14. "Muchdi's Acquittal, 'Worst New Year Gift,'" *Jakarta Post*, January 2, 2009.

15. "Suciwati: Many of the Facts Came from Their Side," *Tempo*, January 6–12, 2009.

16. Peter Gelling, "Indonesian Resolve to Improve Courts Questioned After Acquittal in Activist's Killing," *New York Times*, January 1, 2009.

17. "Rights Body to Examine Muchdi Verdict," *Jakarta Post*, January 3, 2009.

18. Interview, Indra Listiantara, November, 2019. Indra felt that his faith in the police had been badly misplaced. Others thought he had become too close to the police, and later pulled him from Kasum.

19. "Susilo Bambang Yudhoyono Under Fire Over Spy's Acquittal," *The Australian*, January 3, 2009.

20. "Muchdi Purwoprandjono: I Always Knew I Would Be Acquitted," *Tempo*, January 6–12, 2009.

21. Prabowo assigned him the important job of organizing party observers at polling sites throughout the country for legislative elections in April. A source told a political newsletter they suspected he was profiteering: "In the April legislative election, Prabowo assigned his ex-military friend, Muchdi Purwoprandjono, to coordinate party witnesses. However, as the money was disbursed, no witnesses for Gerindra Party were in the field." *Van Zorge Report on Indonesia*, July 15, 2009, 9.

22. "Former BIN Deputy Chief Seeks to 'Shut Down' Munir Defenders," *Jakarta Post*, January 17, 2009.

18: The Aftermath (2009–2021)

1. "MA Hukum Rohainil Aini 1 Tahun Penjara," HukumOnline.com, January 21, 2009.

2. Markus Junianto Sihaloho and Heru Andriyanto, "Suciwati Gets United Nations Support to Challenge Muchdi's Court Acquittal," *Jakarta Globe*, January 23, 2009.

3. "Muchdi Pr Bebas Diduga Akibat Jaksa Lalai dalam Pengajuan Kasasi," *detikNews*, February 9, 2010; "Jelang Vonis Antasari: Jaksa Cirus, Spesialis Kasus Besar & Kontroversial," *detikNews*, February 11, 2010.

4. Irregularities included possible witness intimidation, the absence of key witnesses, and the failure to follow standard procedure in the appeal. Team member Frans Hendra Winarta, a prominent human rights lawyer, stated that the "prosecutor was not independent and the judges were incompetent." "Presiden Didesak Bantu Investigasi Ulang Kasus Munir," *detikNews*, March 2, 2010; "Rekomendasi Kasus Munir Diulang," BBC Indonesia, February 9, 2010.

5. Interview, November 2019.

6. Despite spending an estimated $100 million, much of it from his wealthy brother, Prabowo's Gerindra Party never got enough votes to put him at the top of a ticket, forcing him to settle for being Megawati's vice-presidential candidate.

7. Usman Hamid and Suciwati, "The Past Is Not Forgotten and Will Never Be Forgotten," *Jakarta Post*, July 7, 2009. (I worked closely with Suci and Usman on this piece of writing.)

8. Taking sides in the still unresolved debate, he believed case review was the sole right of the defendant. "Kejagung Masih Pertimbangkan PK Muchdi," HukumOnline.com, September 8, 2011.

9. Following a 2011 mediation with Kasum, BIN stated that a search for an assignment letter for Muchdi to travel to Malaysia in September 2004 found there was no such document. "Kesepakatan Perdamaian," Komisi Informasi Publik, August 12, 2011. The decision of the Information Commission stated definitively, "BIN never officially ordered Muchdi to travel to Malaysia." Central Information Commission Decision No. 120/IV/KIP-PS-M-A/2011. See also "Komisi Informasi Buka Data Baru Soal Kasus Munir," *Tempo*, January 4, 2012. Furthermore, the passport Muchdi produced in court was green, while official travel is done using a blue passport.

10. "KASUM Sodorkan Novum untuk PK Muchdi," HukumOnline.com, November 5, 2011.

11. The defense presented fifteen arguments why the previous case review was improper. Most relitigated whether the prosecution even had the right to request a case review. Another familiar argument was that by shifting the time and place of the murder, the judges had invalidated the verdict. They also argued that Polly had new evidence in the form of Muchdi's acquittal and Ongen's recantation of seeing Polly with Munir at the Coffee Bean. Finally, they claimed to have found flight logs showing that the Singapore flight was over nine hours, and so Munir must have been poisoned *after* boarding that flight. "Pollycarpus Ajukan PK ke MA," DW.com, June 7, 2011.

12. The board had found that by ordering the abduction of activists, Prabowo had committed an act of insubordination, as well as the criminal acts of depriving the victims of their freedom. Two generals who served on the board confirmed the details of the dismissal. "Menyunting Dokumen Rahasia 'Pemecatan' Prabowo," *Kompas*, June 11, 2014; "Karena Menantu Soeharto, Prabowo 'Tak Dipecat' dari ABRI," Medcom.id, June 10, 2014. For a translation of the honor board recommendation and useful context, see "The Verdict on Prabowo Subianto—a Translation," *Indonotes*, at indonotes.wordpress.com/2014/06/15/the-verdict-on-prabowo-subianto-a-translation.

13. The term used was *diberhentikan*, or dismissed. A member of the honor board explained on TV that they had softened the original term, "fired" or *pemecatan*, out of respect for Prabowo's status as Suharto's son-in law, though the meaning was the same. "Kesaksian Agum Gumelar dan Fachrul Razi Soal Pemecatan Prabowo," Merdeka.com, June 11, 2014.

14. "Hendropriyono's Appointment Raises Eyebrows," *Jakarta Post*, August 10, 2014.

15. "Komnas HAM Publishes Reviews of 7 Major Human Rights Abuses," *Jakarta Post*, November 15, 2014.

16. "Komisi Informasi Buka Data Baru Soal Kasus Munir," *Tempo*, January 4, 2012; "KIP: Surat Penugasan BIN untuk Pollycarpus Tidak Ada," *Tempo*, January 4, 2012; "Denied Letter, Activists to Push to Reopen Munir Case," *Jakarta Post*, January 5, 2012.

17. Arbi Sumandoyo, "Kejanggalan Raibnya Laporan TPF Pembunuhan Munir," Tirto.id, October 17, 2016.

18. Website of the State Secretary, "Kemensetneg Tak Diperintah KIP Umum-kan Hasil TPF Kasus Meninggalnya Munir." A few weeks before the ruling, Jokowi had noted the need to act on old human rights violations, including the Munir case. "Jokowi: 'PR' Kita Pelanggaran HAM Masa Lalu, Termasuk Kasus Mas Munir," *Kompas*, September 22, 2016.

19. Out of office for two years, former president Yudhoyono found himself blamed for the missing report and the failure to secure justice for Munir. He summoned his old cabinet to his residence in Bogor to consult notes and memories. They presented a statement on Yudhoyono's response to the TPF's recommendations, stressing it would have exceeded the president's authority to declare someone a defendant or a guilty party. Furthermore, it became inappropriate to release the TPF report once his government decided to treat it as a legal document for use by law enforcement. The statement also noted that Yudhoyono's efforts to act on the TPF's findings didn't mean "the door to seek pure truth and justice for Munir's death was closed to anyone, if there really was still truth that had not been revealed." The former cabinet members promised to search for the six official copies of the report, while former TPF head Marsudhi would send Jokowi his unofficial copy, though it lacked the hundreds of pages of attachments that held much of the evidence. Yudhoyono acknowledged that maintaining secrecy due to an investigation was no longer necessary, and supported its prompt release. Marsudhi's unofficial copy was sent to the palace that same day.

20. "Jaksa Agung Telusuri Keberadaan Dokumen TPF Munir," Tirto.id, October 14, 2016. The former head of the State Secretariat, Yusril Ihza Mahendra, said the report had been given directly to the president in 2005, and SBY never ordered him to put in the Secretariat's files. "Yusril: Laporan TPF Kasus Munir Diserahkan Langsung ke SBY," *Kompas*, October 13, 2016.

21. "Kejagung Sebut Penyelidikan Kasus Munir Wewenang Kepolisian," Tirto.id, October 28, 2016.

22. KIP decision 025/IV/KIP-PS-A/2016, at komisiinformasi.go.id/uploads/documents/fcf668c6cb94534c91714b23da1485553351abff.pdf.

23. KontraS called the verdict a purely political decision, and reported the failure to call witnesses or hold hearings to the Judicial Commission. "Kontras: Putusan PTUN Tak Gugurkan Kewajiban Buka Dokumen TPF Munir," *Kompas*, February 20, 2017; "Menurut Kontras, Ada Upaya Lemahkan Putusan KIP Soal Dokumen TPF Munir," *Kompas*, February 21, 2017. See also Dr. Herlambang P. Wiratraman, "Senyum Pembunuh Di Balik Istana? Eksaminasi Putusan Pengadilan Tata Usaha Negara Nomor 3/G/KI/2016/PTUN.JKT," February 16, 2017, at herlambangperdana.files.wordpress.com/2019/10/eksaminasi-putusan-ptun-soal-ki-5-may-2017.pdf.

24. "I feel really stupid. I don't think it makes sense, in my mind, that a KIP decision can be overturned by the administrative court," a member of parliament said. "This is proof that there is no justice in this country. The country should reveal information to members of the public who ask for justice, instead of suing

them back." These forthright comments came from Desmond Mahesa, abducted by Kopassus in 1998. A decade later, he'd cross-examined Suci as a defense lawyer for Muchdi. A decade after that, he was a member of parliament from Gerindra, Prabowo's party.

25. "Aktivis HAM Kecam Putusan MA Soal Dokumen Kasus Munir," Tirto.id, August 16, 2017. KontraS held to their view that even a Supreme Court decision did not remove the government's responsibility to find and release the document under the decree that created the TPF.

26. Each week focused on a different case or issue, and this day marked the anniversary of Munir death's. A large audience listened to poetry, music, and drama, wearing shirts that read, MUNIR IS STILL HERE, AND MULTIPLYING. It seemed true, with his face on so many masks, shirts, and banners. A young student performed a monologue entitled "I Am Munir's Killer," by the writer Seno Gumira Ajidarma. It began, "I am a mangy dog, that's why I killed Munir. Of course, of course I didn't kill him with my own hands. What for? I can kill through other people's hands, as I usually do, when I need to."

27. The official, Teten Masduki, was a former human rights activist and friend of Munir. "Istana Minta Wiranto Beri Penjelasan Soal Kasus Munir," *Kompas*, September 8, 2017.

28. Asked about the Munir case the same day, Wiranto complained, "That's all you talk about . . . don't ask me." He admonished the questioner for not asking about development or national security, then went to pray. "Wiranto Soal Munir: Mbok Bicara Pembangunan Kita Bagaimana?," Tirto.id, September 8, 2017; "Wiranto Sebut Tidak Mudah Ungkap Dalang Pembunuhan Munir," *Kompas*, September 11, 2017. In August 2018, the National Human Rights Commission refused to join Wiranto's proposed integrated team to resolve cases outside legal channels. They said the case files the Commission had submitted to the attorney general will remain open legal files, whatever reconciliation efforts happen in parallel. Only a judicial route could determine what happened and who the perpetrators are, and ensure clear compensation, which are all the rights of victims. Kustin Ayuwuragil, "Tolak Kompromi Wiranto, Komnas HAM Minta Kasus Diproses Hukum," CNN Indonesia, August 7, 2018.

29. Interview, November 2019.

30. Ratrikala Bhre Aditya, dir. *Bunga Dibakar: Kisah Munir* (Institut Studi Arus Informasi et al., 2005), https://www.youtube.com/watch?v=zfdogyZj_nM.

31. "History and Reality of the Judicial Mafia," inanews.co.od, May 17, 2020. In June 2020, a team from the Corruption Commission that included Novel Baswedan, an investigator who had recently been partially blinded by an acid attack, arrested the clerk of the Supreme Court, who had the power to advance or halt appeals and case reviews. Accused of accepting over $3 million dollars in cash from just one company, he was roughly the thirty-fifth court official arrested since 2010.

32. "Kabareskrim: Jika Ada Fakta Baru, Polri Pasti Lanjutkan Kasus Munir," *Kompas*, September 7, 2018; "Haris Azhar Minta AM Hendropriyono Diperiksa di Kasus Munir," CNN Indonesia, September 13, 2018.

33. Cited to "a source" in "SBY Told to Empower Munir Probe Team," *Jakarta Post*, June 13, 2005. Prosecutors asked a witness about this report in the Muchdi trial.

34. Interview, Indra Listiantara, November 2019.

35. It is also unclear why Singapore was never able to produce any security footage from the night of the murder. In 2007 a policeman told Usman the problem was technical. The footage was possible to retrieve, but it would be expensive and difficult. In an interview, a police investigator reported he went to check out the security camera system in Singapore and found them not working, which he thought was strange. Marsudhi became frustrated with the police for failing to produce any written requests for the footage or any replies. While judges did accept the eyewitness testimony that Pollycarpus sat with Munir at the Coffee Bean, footage might have answered the question about the role of Ongen and anyone else, not to mention saving several years of misdirected attention and debate about the crime scene.

36. "Kasus Munir Masih Bergulir, Bukti Rekaman Muchdi dan Polly," *Kontan*, June 26, 2011.

37. Other leads that were never fully confirmed include whether Muchdi spent the night of September 6 in Surabaya, at a command center for the operation. Police told Usman about these rumors in 2007 and it was also noted in at least one news report. If true, it would explain why Muchdi's cell phone was in touch with Pollycarpus from the Surabaya airport on September 7. "Satu Kasus, Beragam Polisi," *Tempo*, April 16, 2007.

38. "Kasus Munir, Muchdi Bebas Karena Surat Palsu?," *Tempo*, December 6, 2014.

39. "Jejak Arsen dari Pejaten," *Tempo*, December 14, 2014, 48–49.

40. Interview, police investigator, November 2019; interview, former BIN agent, Jakarta, November 2019.

41. Personal communication, July 2021.

42. Questions linger about this incident too. No police report was filed, and the source of this story appears to be a friend of the family on the night of Ongen's death. The friend was a member of parliament named Yorrys Raweyai, a senior *preman* with long-standing ties to the Jakarta underworld and the military. Ongen's family has reiterated the account since then.

43. "Key Witness in Munir Case Dies," *Tempo*, May 3, 2012.

44. Several people who follow the Munir case pointed to a flight attendant who flew as extra crew on Flight 974 flight and returned home immediately. Her seat on the manifest was one row behind Munir's ticketed seat, but she was reportedly upgraded as well to maintain a proximity of one row away from the victim. According to a police investigator, she told her daughter that her job was to keep watch that day. In 2005 or 2006, a man who was not her usual Garuda driver picked her up at home. On the way to the airport she died in a crash that left the driver unhurt. The police investigator visited the scene and found it suspicious, but couldn't prove anything. Interview, police investigator,

November 2019; "Tewas di Lingkaran Pembunuhan," *Tempo*, December 8, 2014.

45. "Interview: Marsudi Hanafi: Salinan TPF Cukup untuk Penyidikan Awal Kasus Munir," KBR, September 12, 2017.

46. "Allan Nairn: Hendro Siap Diadili Kenapa Jokowi Nggak Mulai Itu," Suara .com, February 10, 2015.

47. Hendro added that the murder seemed too sloppy to be a BIN operation: "If it really was intelligence, that is extremely embarrassing to kill someone that way. That is the dumbest way. The body of a victim of poisoning will surely be opened up, and the arsenic discovered." "Saya Bukan Intel Kemarin Sore," *Tempo*, December 8, 2014.

48. Observers had pointed to similar patterns under President's Habibie and Wahid, as well as earlier in the Yudhoyono administration: Christian-Muslim violence in the eastern islands, bombings, and the widespread murder of *dukun santet*, practitioners of black magic, in East Java just after Suharto's fall. By 2011, the interreligious violence in the eastern islands had faded, and a new flashpoint was whether to ban the Ahmadiyah sect of Islam. Stirring up violence against Ahmadiyah villages would be an effective way to generate religious conflict close to the capital.

49. "Killer of Rights Activist Munir Joins Tommy Suharto's Berkarya Party," *Jakarta Globe*, March 8, 2018.

50. "Muchdi PR Dukung Jokowi, Timses Tak Urusan dengan Kasus Munir," CNN Indonesia, February 11, 2019; "Muchdi PR Sebut Prabowo Tak Bisa Membangun Seperti Jokowi," CNN Indonesia, February 10, 2019.

51. MetroTV broadcast the video with Indonesian subtitles, posted at www .youtube.com/watch?v=2vILGgNh0bY, March 14, 2019.

52. Gumelar also claimed that Prabowo once told him the kidnappings had been carried out on Suharto's orders. Jonas Fredryc Tobing, "Kesaksian Agum Gumelar dan Fachrul Razi soal Pemecatan Prabowo," Merdeka.com, June 11, 2014. The video is at https://www.merdeka.com/politik/kesaksian-agum-gumelar-dan -fachrul-razi-soal-pemecatan-prabowo.html.

53. "Bau Mawar di Jalan Thamrin," *Tempo*, June 8, 2019.

54. The *New York Times* called the move "indicative of the president's willingness to curtail civil liberties" to secure support in parliament for his economic agenda. "Indonesian General Accused of Kidnapping Is Named Defense Minister," *New York Times*, October 23, 2019. Prabowo's appointment caused some awkwardness at the Pentagon, as he had been barred from entering the United States for years due to his human rights record. Prabowo visited his American counterparts in October 2020 after the Trump Administration lifted the ban.

55. "Former Tim Mawar Commander Among Five Appointed to Prabowo's Expert Staff," *Jakarta Post*, January 1, 2020. By 2007, KontraS had flagged the fact that members of the Tim Mawar abduction squad, supposedly imprisoned and discharged, were moving up the ranks of the army. It turned out that after appeals, the five ordered dismissed were allowed to remain in the army, and four of the eleven team members had been promoted to strategic positions.

56. After the government's six months of ineffective investigation and its usual use of low-level scapegoats, the *Jakarta Post* wrote that the effort "is more than just disenchanting. It is harrowing, for now we know that the state has, again, failed to resolve a high-profile case, putting its credibility at stake. We shall not forget. Before Novel, there was Munir." "Justice for Novel, Justice for All," *Jakarta Post*, July 22, 2019.

57. "Di Udara (Live at Aksi Kamisan 600)," YouTube Video, September 5, 2019, www.youtube.com/watch?v=3cuA85Sl6m4.

58. Muhammad Aminudin, "Tujuh Anak Muda di Malang Bacakan Dokumen TPF Munir," *detikNews*, October 16, 2019.

Postscript

1. "It's now or never to bring masterminds in Munir case to justice: Activists," *Jakarta Post*, September 7, 2021; "Amnesty: Kasus Pembunuhan Munir Harus Digolongkan Sebagai Kejahatan Luar Biasa," *Tempo*, September 7, 2021. Kasum argued that the murder of Munir met the definition of a gross human rights violation because it was an extrajudicial killing by actors from multiple government agencies, that was intended to threaten the human rights community and civil society more broadly.

2. The closest he came was in 2014, when *Tempo* asked him if he was a BIN agent. He'd replied, "Just ask BIN. There's no point in my answering; later they'll answer if I'm a member of BIN agent or not. If I say no, later it's said to be yes. I say yes, later it's said to be no. Right?" "Polly si Peluluk," *Tempo*, December 8, 2014, 55.

3. "Pollycarpus: Banyak Yang Mati Setelah Saya Sumpahin," Lokadata.id, September 10, 2018, and linked video.

4. Eko Widianto, "Museum HAM Munir untuk Hak Asasi Manusia," December 10, 2019.

5. In the series, celebrities read remembrances and obituaries published a hundred days after Munir died.

6. Vanessa Hearman, "Remembering Munir," *Inside Indonesia*, March 29, 2014.

7. Post-transitional justice tends to focus on the quality of democracy, question initial compromises, and consist of mostly non-state initiatives, among other features. Sri Lestari Wahyuningroem, "Towards Post-Transitional Justice: The Failures of Transitional Justice and the Roles of Civil Society in Indonesia," *Journal of Southeast Asian Human Rights* 3, no. 1 (June 2019): 124–54.

8. Karen Strassler, *Demanding Images: Democracy, Mediation, and the Image-Event in Indonesia* (Duke University Press Books, 2020), 7.

About the Author

Matt Easton has carried out research, advocacy, and other duties as a staff member or consultant at Human Rights First, Human Rights Watch, Physicians for Human Rights, the Ford Foundation, the United Nations, and other organizations. He has lived and worked in Indonesia, Timor-Leste, India, and Zimbabwe and now resides in New York.

Publishing in the Public Interest

Thank you for reading this book published by The New Press. The New Press is a nonprofit, public interest publisher. New Press books and authors play a crucial role in sparking conversations about the key political and social issues of our day.

We hope you enjoyed this book and that you will stay in touch with The New Press. Here are a few ways to stay up to date with our books, events, and the issues we cover:

- Sign up at www.thenewpress.com/subscribe to receive updates on New Press authors and issues and to be notified about local events
- www.facebook.com/newpressbooks
- www.twitter.com/thenewpress
- www.instagram.com/thenewpress

Please consider buying New Press books for yourself; for friends and family; or to donate to schools, libraries, community centers, prison libraries, and other organizations involved with the issues our authors write about.

The New Press is a 501(c)(3) nonprofit organization. You can also support our work with a tax-deductible gift by visiting www .thenewpress.com/donate.